TRUE STORY
SWEAR TO GOD

TOM BELAND

SAN FRANCISCO

TRUE STORY SWEAR TO GOD
BY TOM BELAND

PUBLISHED BY
AIT/PLANET LAR
2034 47TH AVENUE
SAN FRANCISCO, CA 94116

FIRST EDITION: JANUARY 2003
SECOND EDITION, DECEMBER 2005

10 9 8 7 6 5 4 3 2 1

COVER ILLUSTRATION BY TOM BELAND

ISBN: 1-932051-09-0

PRINTED AND BOUND IN CANADA BY QUEBECOR PRINTING INC.

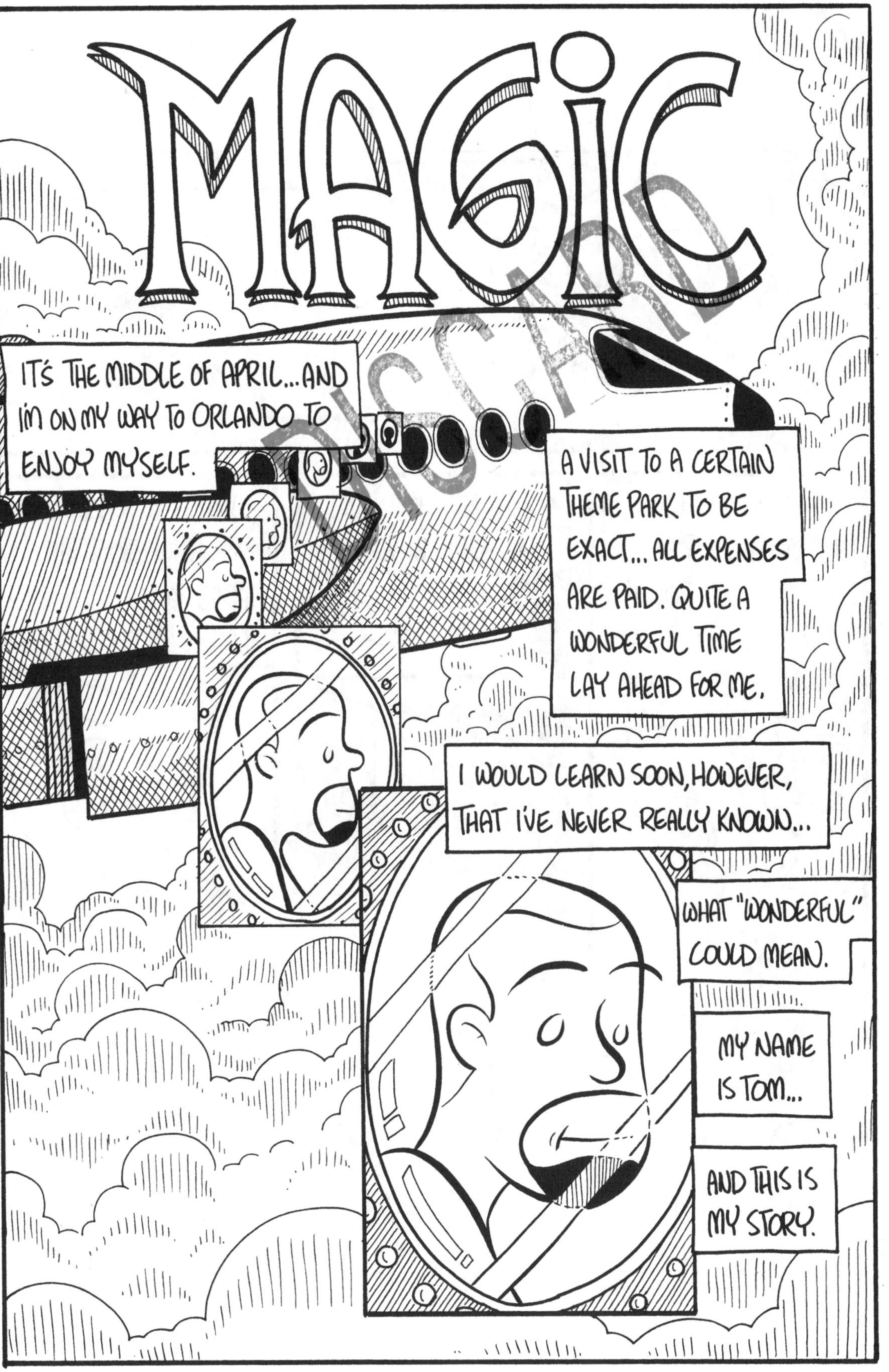
MAGIC
IT'S THE MIDDLE OF APRIL...AND I'M ON MY WAY TO ORLANDO TO ENJOY MYSELF.
A VISIT TO A CERTAIN THEME PARK TO BE EXACT... ALL EXPENSES ARE PAID. QUITE A WONDERFUL TIME LAY AHEAD FOR ME.
I WOULD LEARN SOON, HOWEVER, THAT I'VE NEVER REALLY KNOWN...
WHAT "WONDERFUL" COULD MEAN.
MY NAME IS TOM...
AND THIS IS MY STORY.

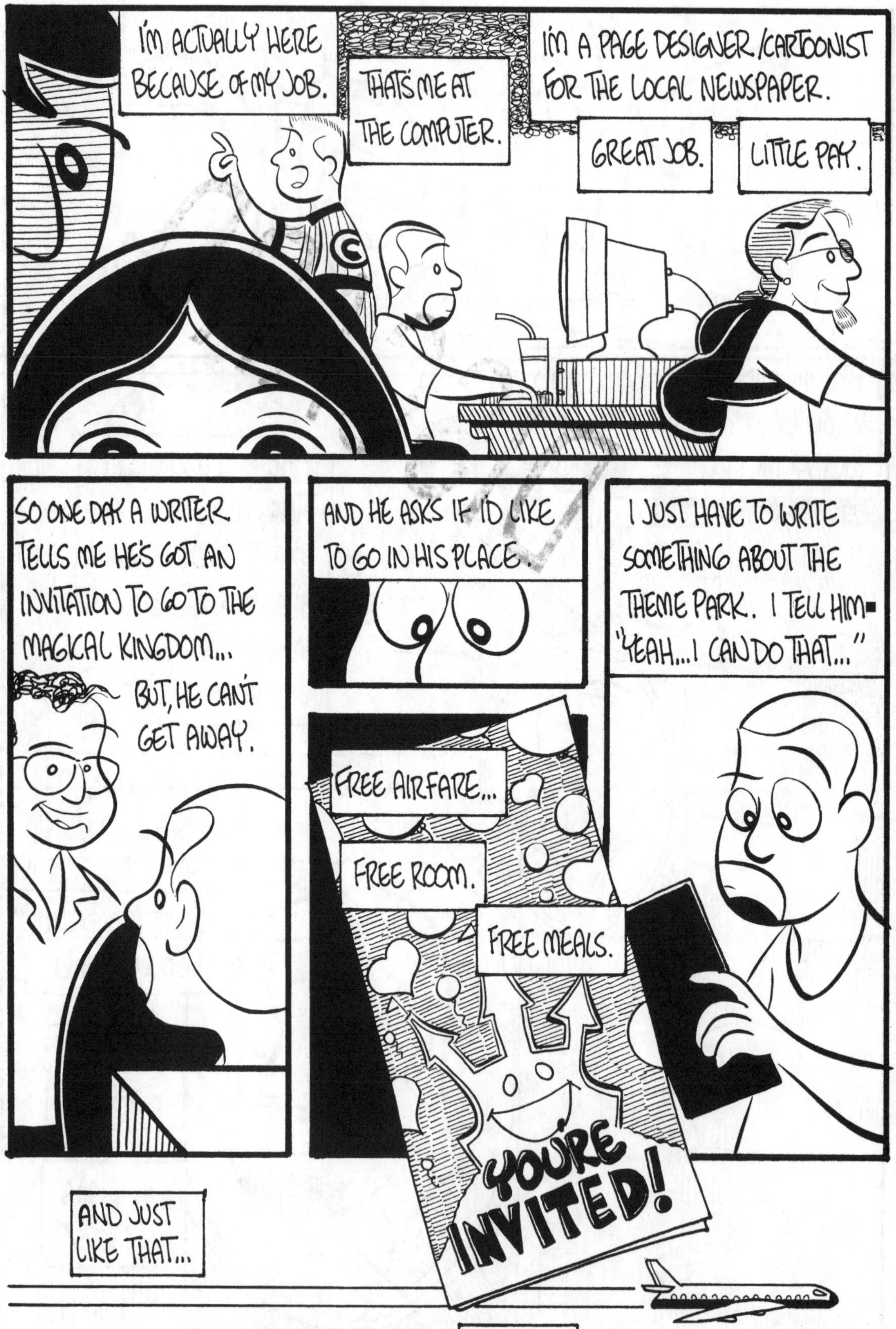
I'M ACTUALLY HERE BECAUSE OF MY JOB.
THAT'S ME AT THE COMPUTER.
I'M A PAGE DESIGNER /CARTOONIST FOR THE LOCAL NEWSPAPER.
GREAT JOB.
LITTLE PAY.
SO ONE DAY A WRITER TELLS ME HE'S GOT AN INVITATION TO GO TO THE MAGICAL KINGDOM...
BUT, HE CAN'T GET AWAY.
AND HE ASKS IF I'D LIKE TO GO IN HIS PLACE.
FREE AIRFARE...
FREE ROOM.
FREE MEALS.
YOU'RE INVITED!
I JUST HAVE TO WRITE SOMETHING ABOUT THE THEME PARK. I TELL HIM- "YEAH...I CAN DO THAT..."
AND JUST LIKE THAT...
I'M GONE.

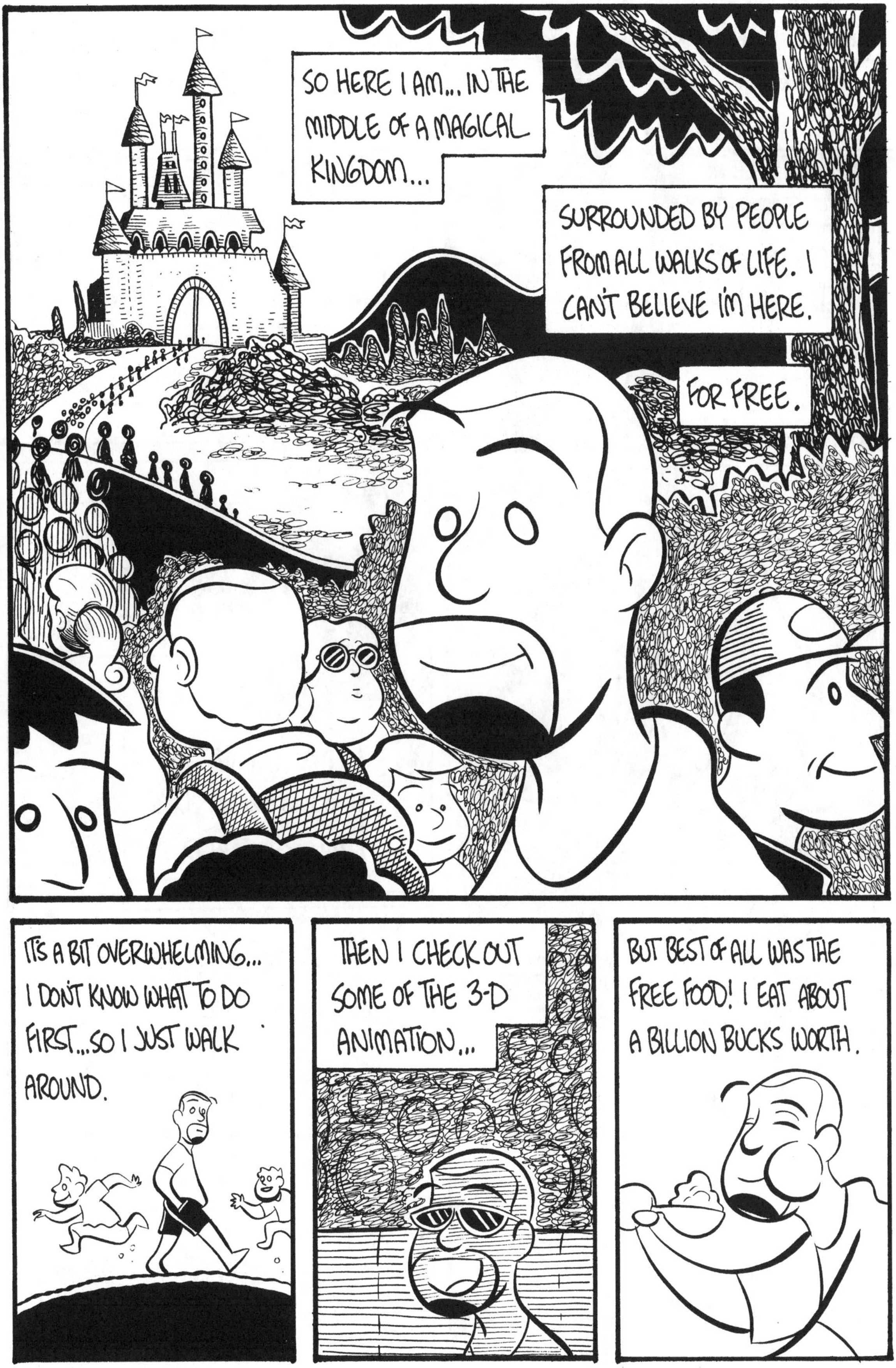
SO HERE I AM... IN THE MIDDLE OF A MAGICAL KINGDOM...
SURROUNDED BY PEOPLE FROM ALL WALKS OF LIFE. I CAN'T BELIEVE I'M HERE.
FOR FREE.
IT'S A BIT OVERWHELMING... I DON'T KNOW WHAT TO DO FIRST... SO I JUST WALK AROUND.
THEN I CHECK OUT SOME OF THE 3-D ANIMATION...
BUT BEST OF ALL WAS THE FREE FOOD! I EAT ABOUT A BILLION BUCKS WORTH.

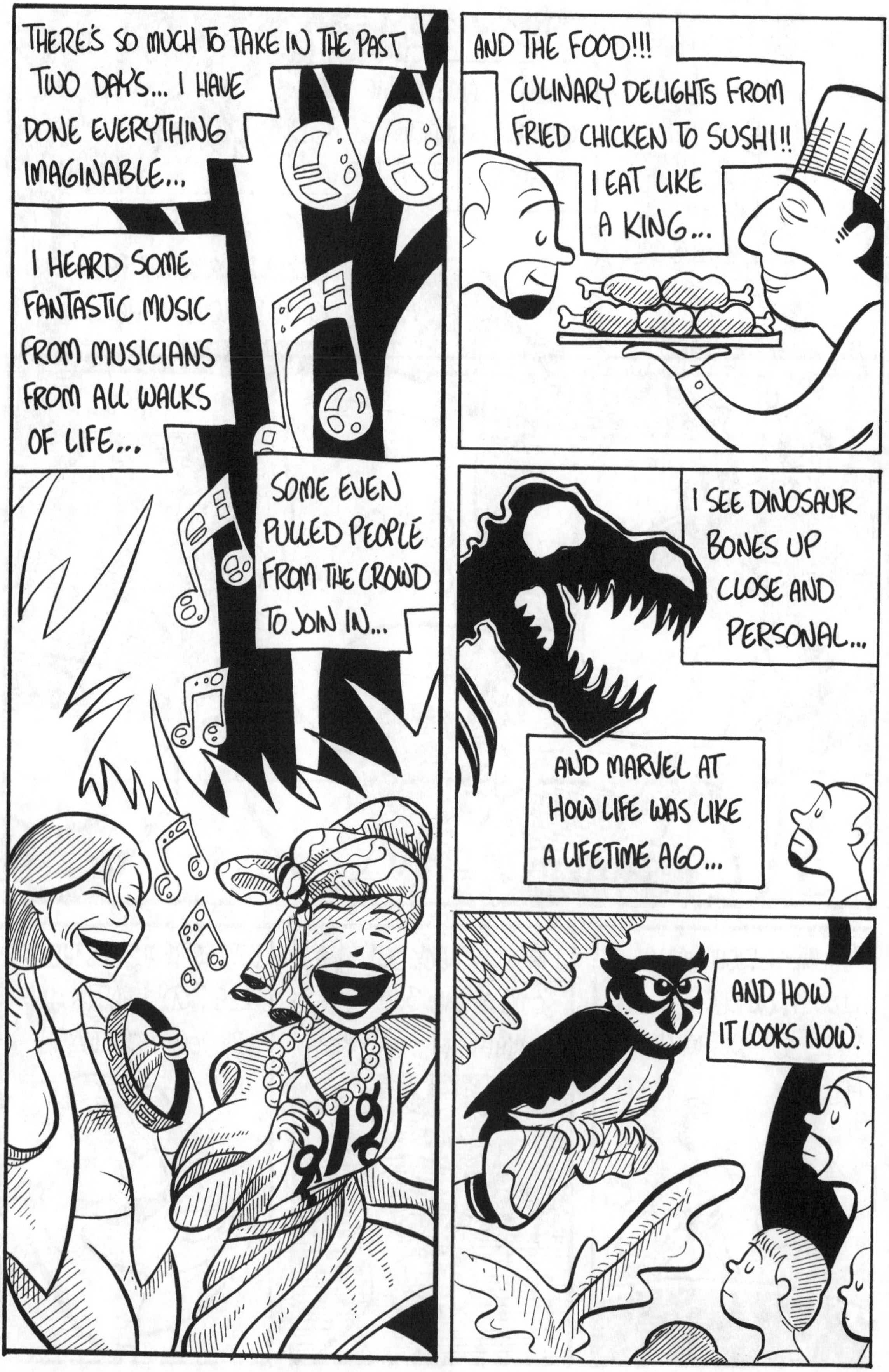
THERE'S SO MUCH TO TAKE IN THE PAST TWO DAYS... I HAVE DONE EVERYTHING IMAGINABLE...
I HEARD SOME FANTASTIC MUSIC FROM MUSICIANS FROM ALL WALKS OF LIFE...
SOME EVEN PULLED PEOPLE FROM THE CROWD TO JOIN IN...
AND THE FOOD!!!
CULINARY DELIGHTS FROM FRIED CHICKEN TO SUSHI!!
I EAT LIKE A KING...
I SEE DINOSAUR BONES UP CLOSE AND PERSONAL...
AND MARVEL AT HOW LIFE WAS LIKE A LIFETIME AGO...
AND HOW IT LOOKS NOW.

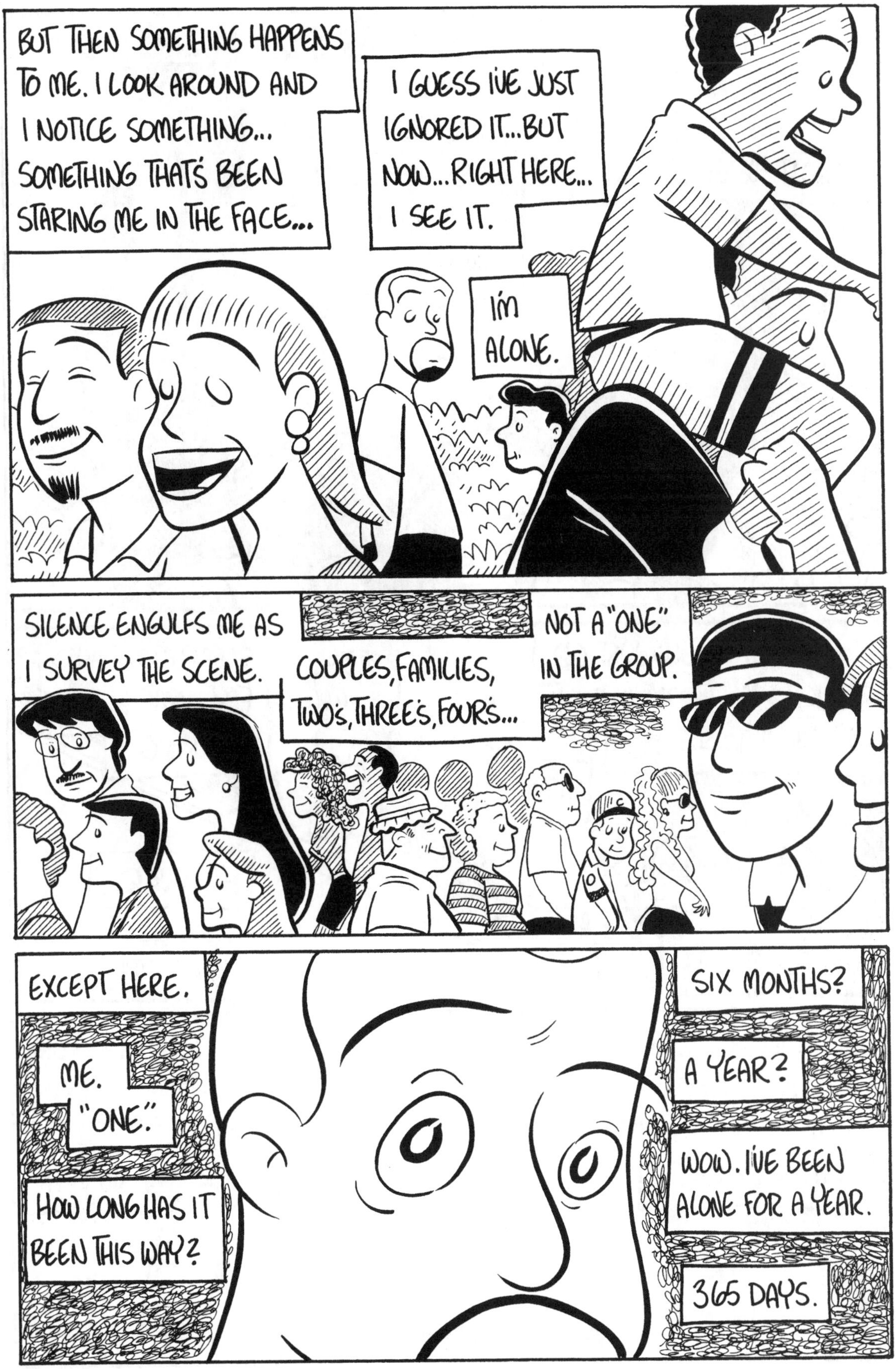
BUT THEN SOMETHING HAPPENS TO ME. I LOOK AROUND AND I NOTICE SOMETHING... SOMETHING THAT'S BEEN STARING ME IN THE FACE...
I GUESS I'VE JUST IGNORED IT...BUT NOW...RIGHT HERE... I SEE IT.
I'M ALONE.
SILENCE ENGULFS ME AS I SURVEY THE SCENE.
COUPLES, FAMILIES, TWO'S, THREE'S, FOUR'S...
NOT A "ONE" IN THE GROUP.
EXCEPT HERE.
ME. "ONE."
HOW LONG HAS IT BEEN THIS WAY?
SIX MONTHS?
A YEAR?
WOW. I'VE BEEN ALONE FOR A YEAR.
365 DAYS.

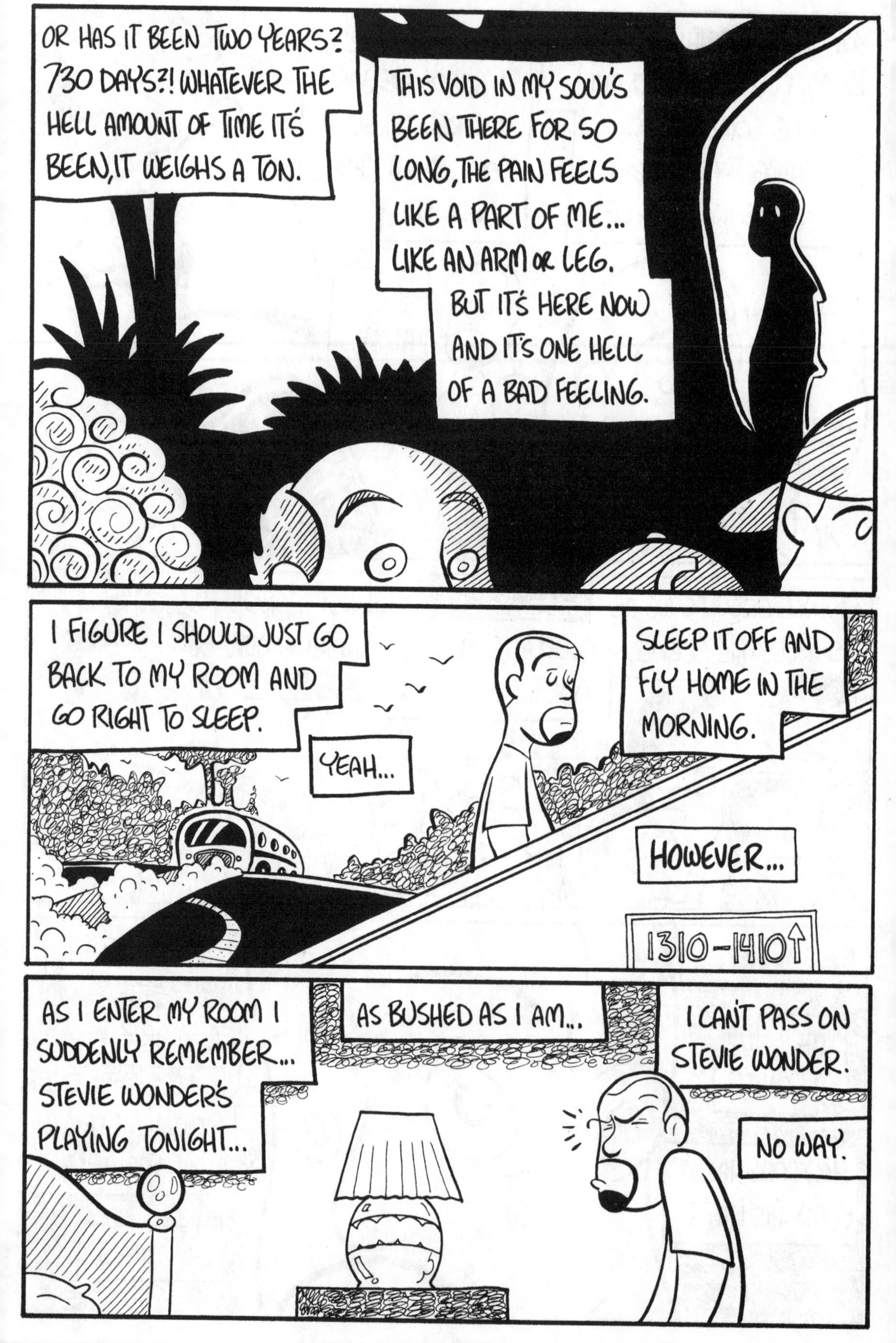
OR HAS IT BEEN TWO YEARS? 730 DAYS?! WHATEVER THE HELL AMOUNT OF TIME IT'S BEEN, IT WEIGHS A TON.
THIS VOID IN MY SOUL'S BEEN THERE FOR SO LONG, THE PAIN FEELS LIKE A PART OF ME... LIKE AN ARM OR LEG.
BUT IT'S HERE NOW AND IT'S ONE HELL OF A BAD FEELING.
I FIGURE I SHOULD JUST GO BACK TO MY ROOM AND GO RIGHT TO SLEEP.
YEAH...
SLEEP IT OFF AND FLY HOME IN THE MORNING.
HOWEVER...
1310-1410
AS I ENTER MY ROOM I SUDDENLY REMEMBER... STEVIE WONDER'S PLAYING TONIGHT...
AS BUSHED AS I AM...
I CAN'T PASS ON STEVIE WONDER.
NO WAY.

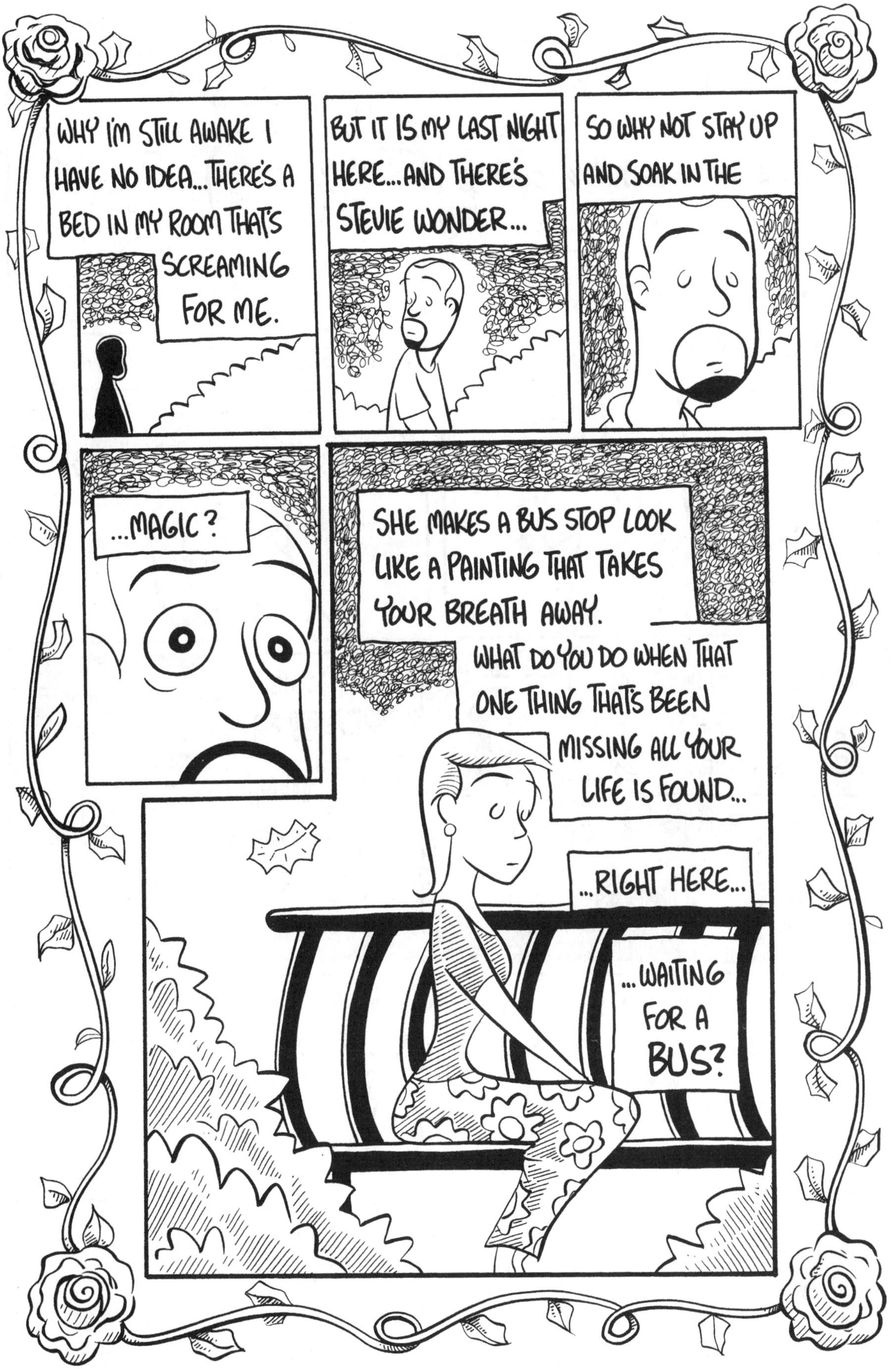
WHY I'M STILL AWAKE I HAVE NO IDEA... THERE'S A BED IN MY ROOM THAT'S
SCREAMING FOR ME.
BUT IT IS MY LAST NIGHT HERE... AND THERE'S STEVIE WONDER...
SO WHY NOT STAY UP AND SOAK IN THE
...MAGIC?
SHE MAKES A BUS STOP LOOK LIKE A PAINTING THAT TAKES YOUR BREATH AWAY.
WHAT DO YOU DO WHEN THAT ONE THING THAT'S BEEN
MISSING ALL YOUR LIFE IS FOUND...
...RIGHT HERE...
...WAITING FOR A BUS?

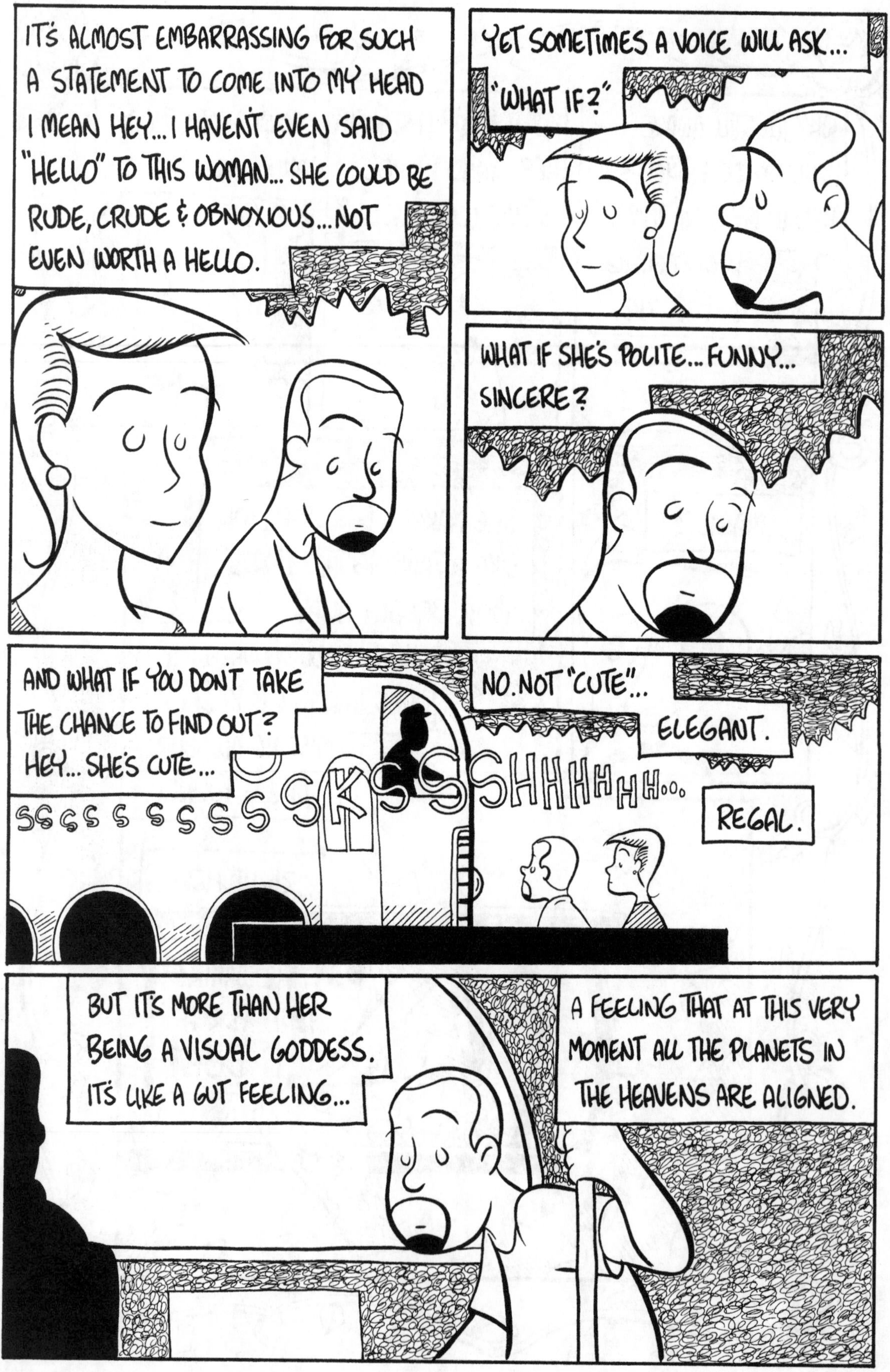

IT'S ALMOST EMBARRASSING FOR SUCH A STATEMENT TO COME INTO MY HEAD I MEAN HEY... I HAVEN'T EVEN SAID "HELLO" TO THIS WOMAN... SHE COULD BE RUDE, CRUDE & OBNOXIOUS... NOT EVEN WORTH A HELLO.
YET SOMETIMES A VOICE WILL ASK...
"WHAT IF?"
WHAT IF SHE'S POLITE... FUNNY... SINCERE?
AND WHAT IF YOU DON'T TAKE THE CHANCE TO FIND OUT? HEY... SHE'S CUTE...
SSSSSSSSSSKSSSHHHHHH...
NO. NOT "CUTE"...
ELEGANT.
REGAL.
BUT IT'S MORE THAN HER BEING A VISUAL GODDESS. IT'S LIKE A GUT FEELING...
A FEELING THAT AT THIS VERY MOMENT ALL THE PLANETS IN THE HEAVENS ARE ALIGNED.

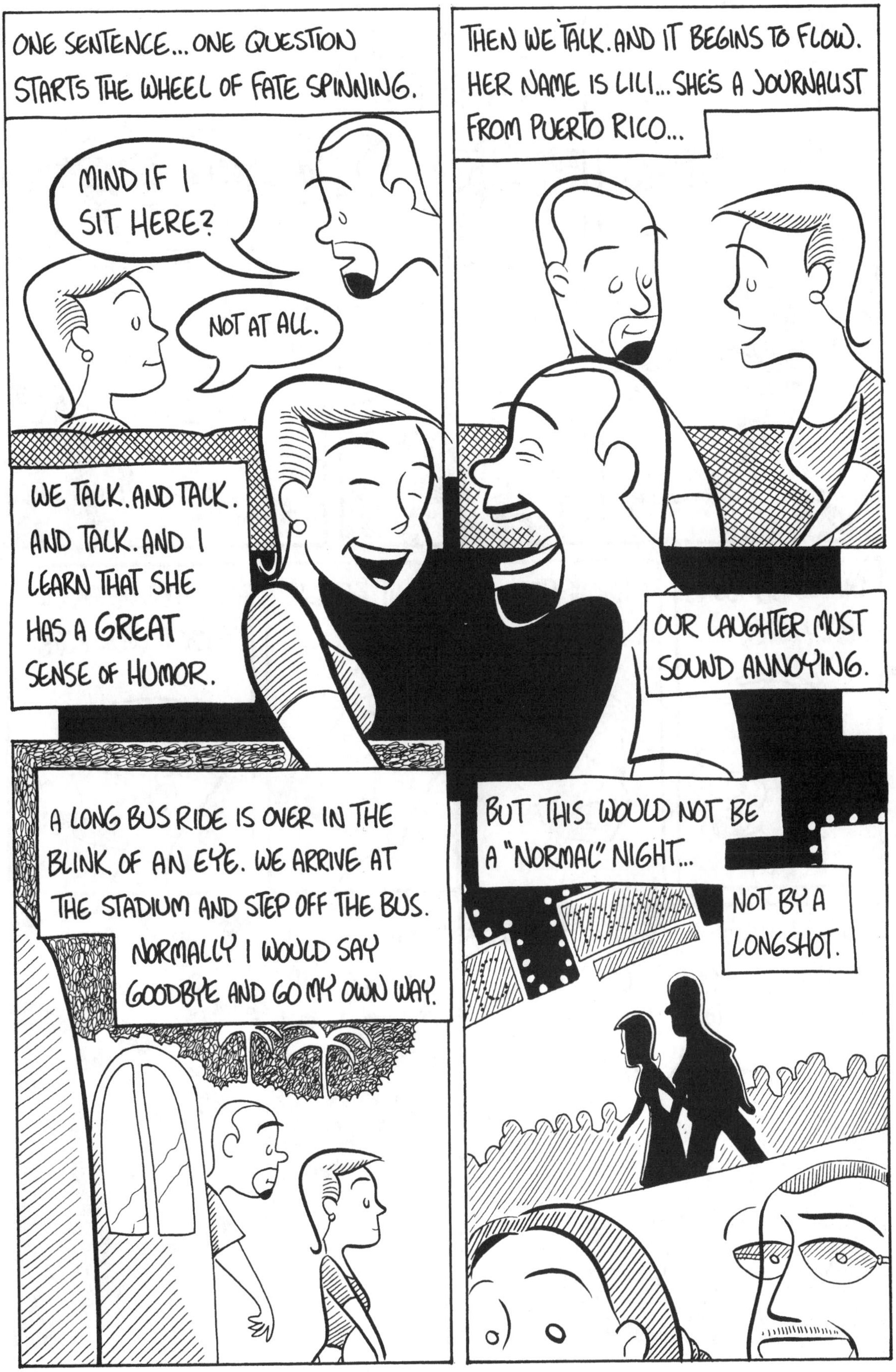
ONE SENTENCE... ONE QUESTION STARTS THE WHEEL OF FATE SPINNING.
MIND IF I SIT HERE?
NOT AT ALL.
THEN WE TALK. AND IT BEGINS TO FLOW. HER NAME IS LILI... SHE'S A JOURNALIST FROM PUERTO RICO...
WE TALK. AND TALK. AND TALK. AND I LEARN THAT SHE HAS A GREAT SENSE OF HUMOR.
OUR LAUGHTER MUST SOUND ANNOYING.
A LONG BUS RIDE IS OVER IN THE BLINK OF AN EYE. WE ARRIVE AT THE STADIUM AND STEP OFF THE BUS.
NORMALLY I WOULD SAY GOODBYE AND GO MY OWN WAY.
BUT THIS WOULD NOT BE A "NORMAL" NIGHT...
NOT BY A LONGSHOT.

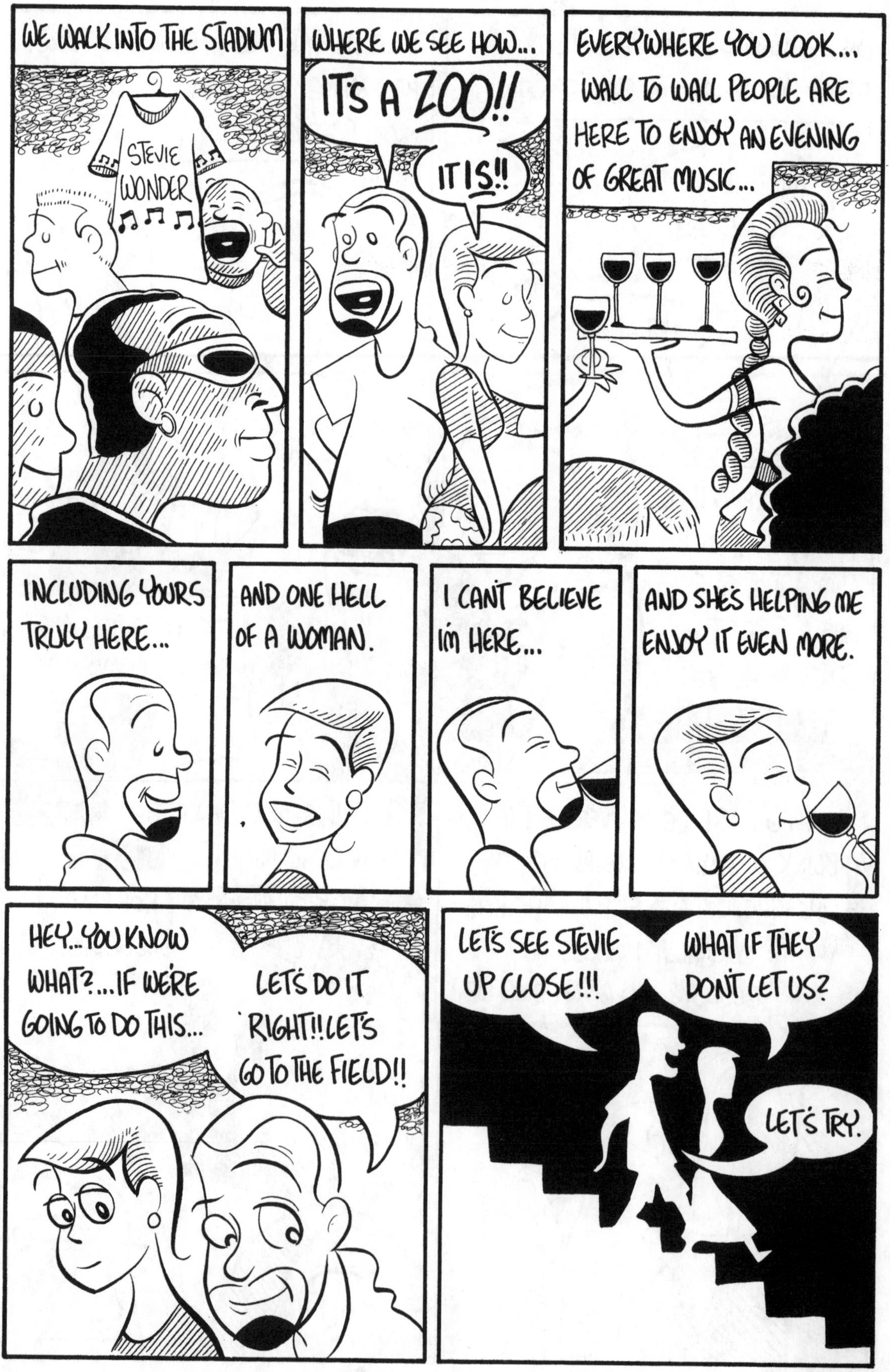
WE WALK INTO THE STADIUM
STEVIE WONDER
WHERE WE SEE HOW...
IT'S A ZOO!!
IT IS!!
EVERYWHERE YOU LOOK... WALL TO WALL PEOPLE ARE HERE TO ENJOY AN EVENING OF GREAT MUSIC...
INCLUDING YOURS TRULY HERE...
AND ONE HELL OF A WOMAN.
I CAN'T BELIEVE I'M HERE...
AND SHE'S HELPING ME ENJOY IT EVEN MORE.
HEY...YOU KNOW WHAT?...IF WE'RE GOING TO DO THIS...
LET'S DO IT RIGHT!! LET'S GO TO THE FIELD!!
LET'S SEE STEVIE UP CLOSE!!!
WHAT IF THEY DON'T LET US?
LET'S TRY.

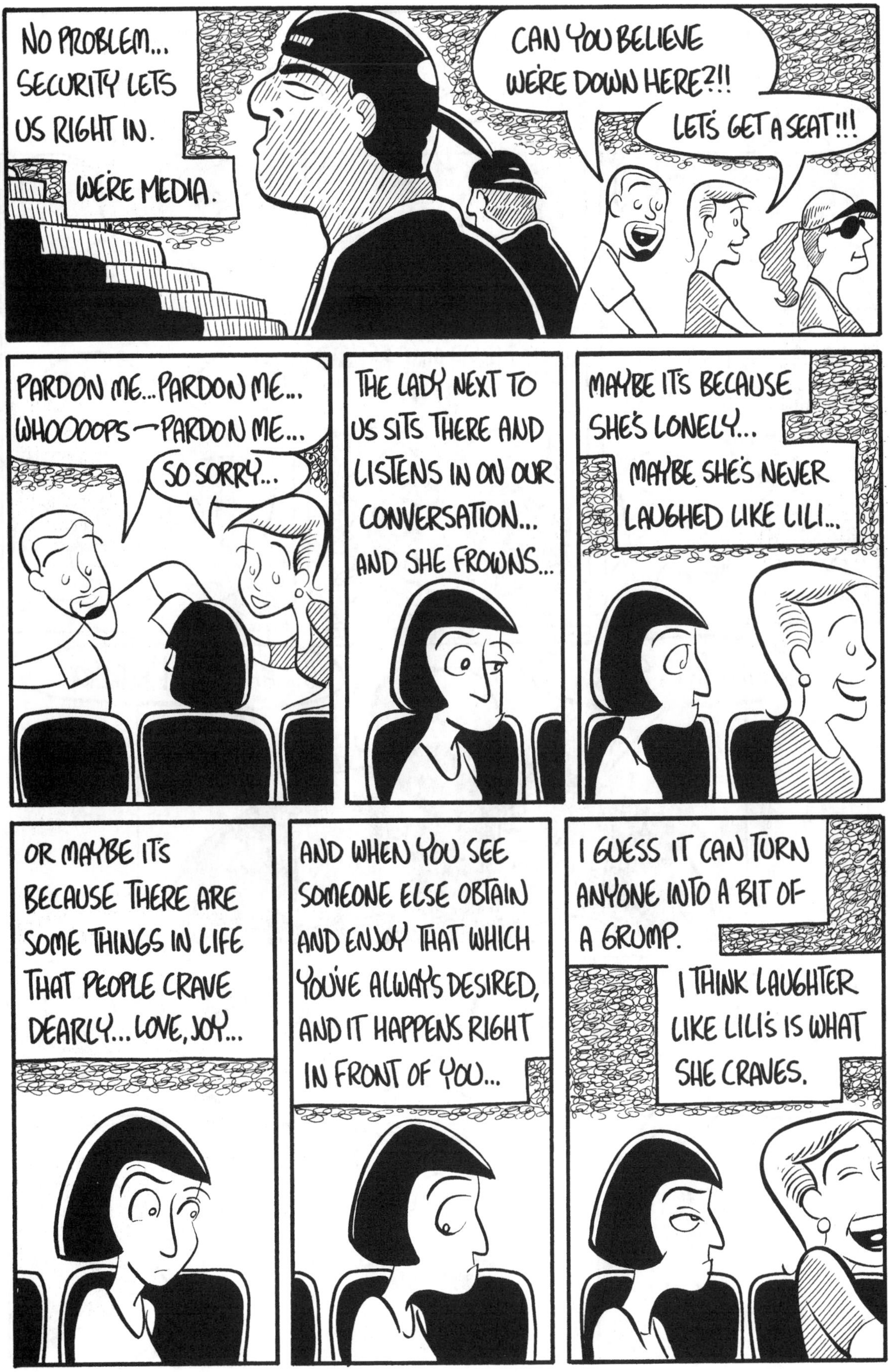
NO PROBLEM... SECURITY LETS US RIGHT IN.
WE'RE MEDIA.
CAN YOU BELIEVE WE'RE DOWN HERE?!!
LET'S GET A SEAT!!!
PARDON ME...PARDON ME... WHOOOOPS—PARDON ME...
SO SORRY...
THE LADY NEXT TO US SITS THERE AND LISTENS IN ON OUR CONVERSATION... AND SHE FROWNS...
MAYBE IT'S BECAUSE SHE'S LONELY...
MAYBE SHE'S NEVER LAUGHED LIKE LILI...
OR MAYBE IT'S BECAUSE THERE ARE SOME THINGS IN LIFE THAT PEOPLE CRAVE DEARLY... LOVE, JOY...
AND WHEN YOU SEE SOMEONE ELSE OBTAIN AND ENJOY THAT WHICH YOU'VE ALWAYS DESIRED, AND IT HAPPENS RIGHT IN FRONT OF YOU...
I GUESS IT CAN TURN ANYONE INTO A BIT OF A GRUMP.
I THINK LAUGHTER LIKE LILI'S IS WHAT SHE CRAVES.

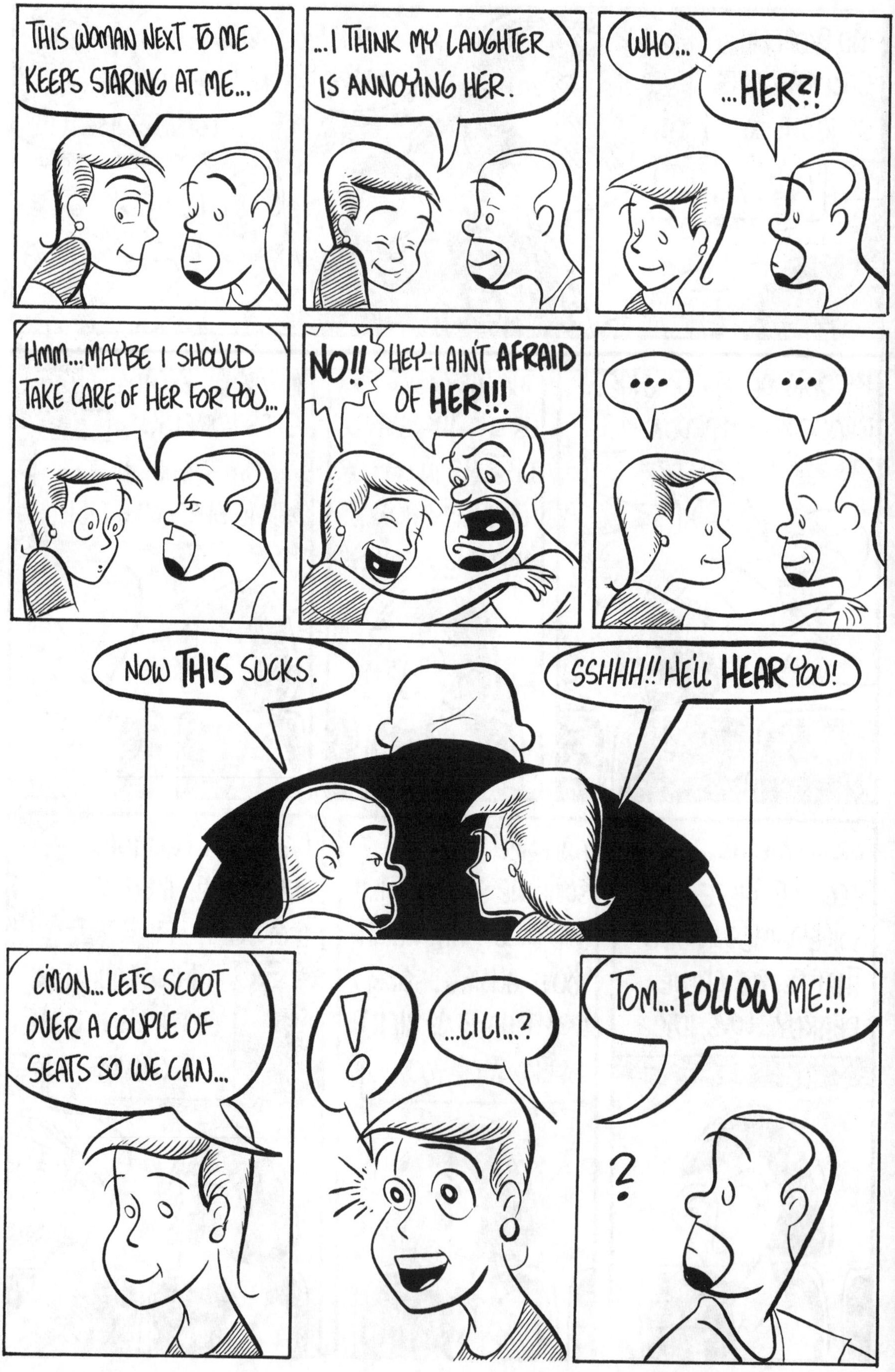
THIS WOMAN NEXT TO ME KEEPS STARING AT ME...
...I THINK MY LAUGHTER IS ANNOYING HER.
WHO...
...HER?!
HMM...MAYBE I SHOULD TAKE CARE OF HER FOR YOU...
NO!!
HEY-I AIN'T AFRAID OF HER!!!
...
...
NOW THIS SUCKS.
SSHHH!! HE'LL HEAR YOU!
C'MON...LET'S SCOOT OVER A COUPLE OF SEATS SO WE CAN...
!
...LILI...?
TOM...FOLLOW ME!!!
?

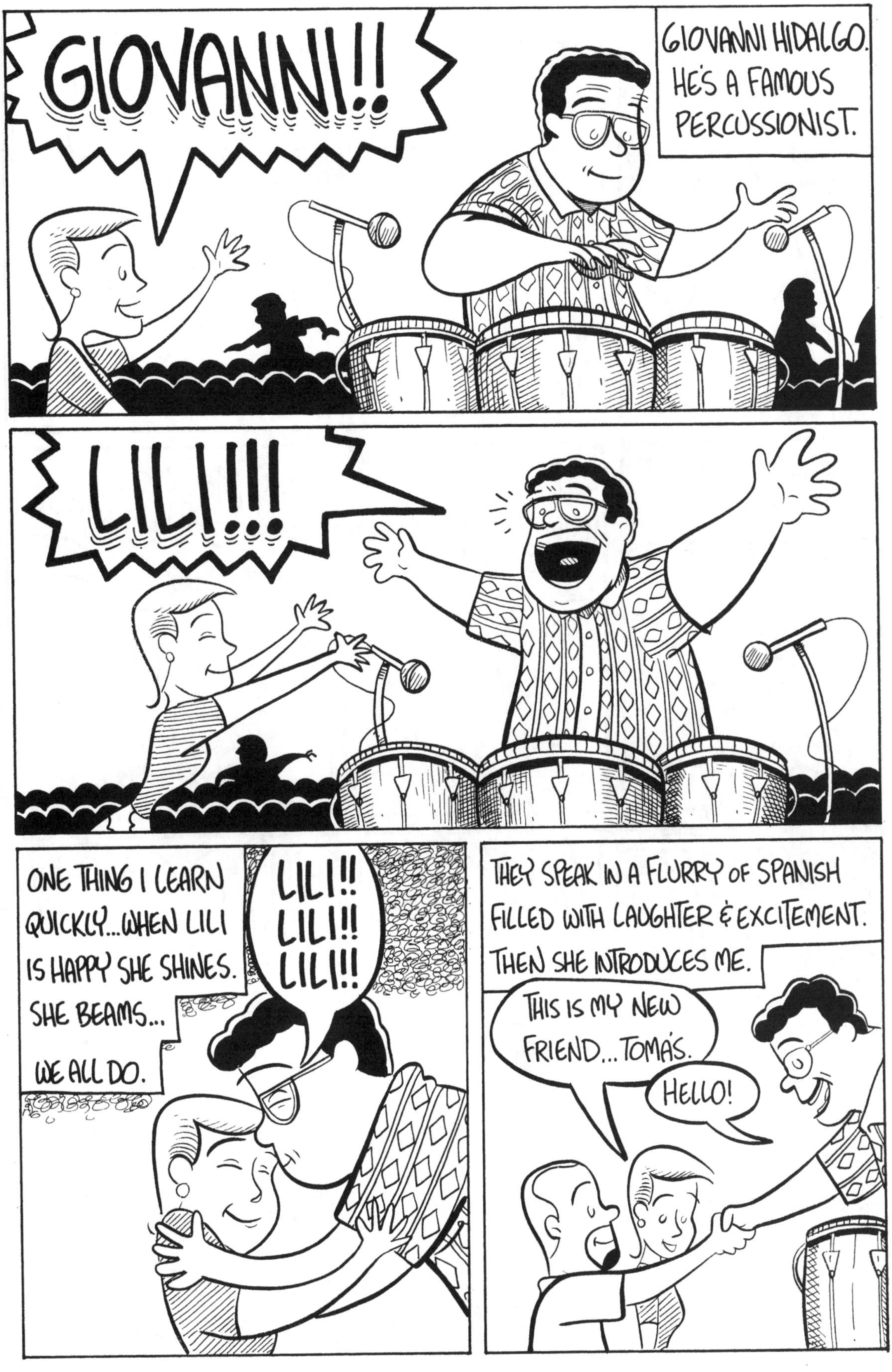
GIOVANNI!!
GIOVANNI HIDALGO. HE'S A FAMOUS PERCUSSIONIST.
LILI!!!
ONE THING I LEARN QUICKLY...WHEN LILI IS HAPPY SHE SHINES.
SHE BEAMS...
WE ALL DO.
LILI!! LILI!! LILI!!
THEY SPEAK IN A FLURRY OF SPANISH FILLED WITH LAUGHTER & EXCITEMENT. THEN SHE INTRODUCES ME.
THIS IS MY NEW FRIEND... TOMÁS.
HELLO!

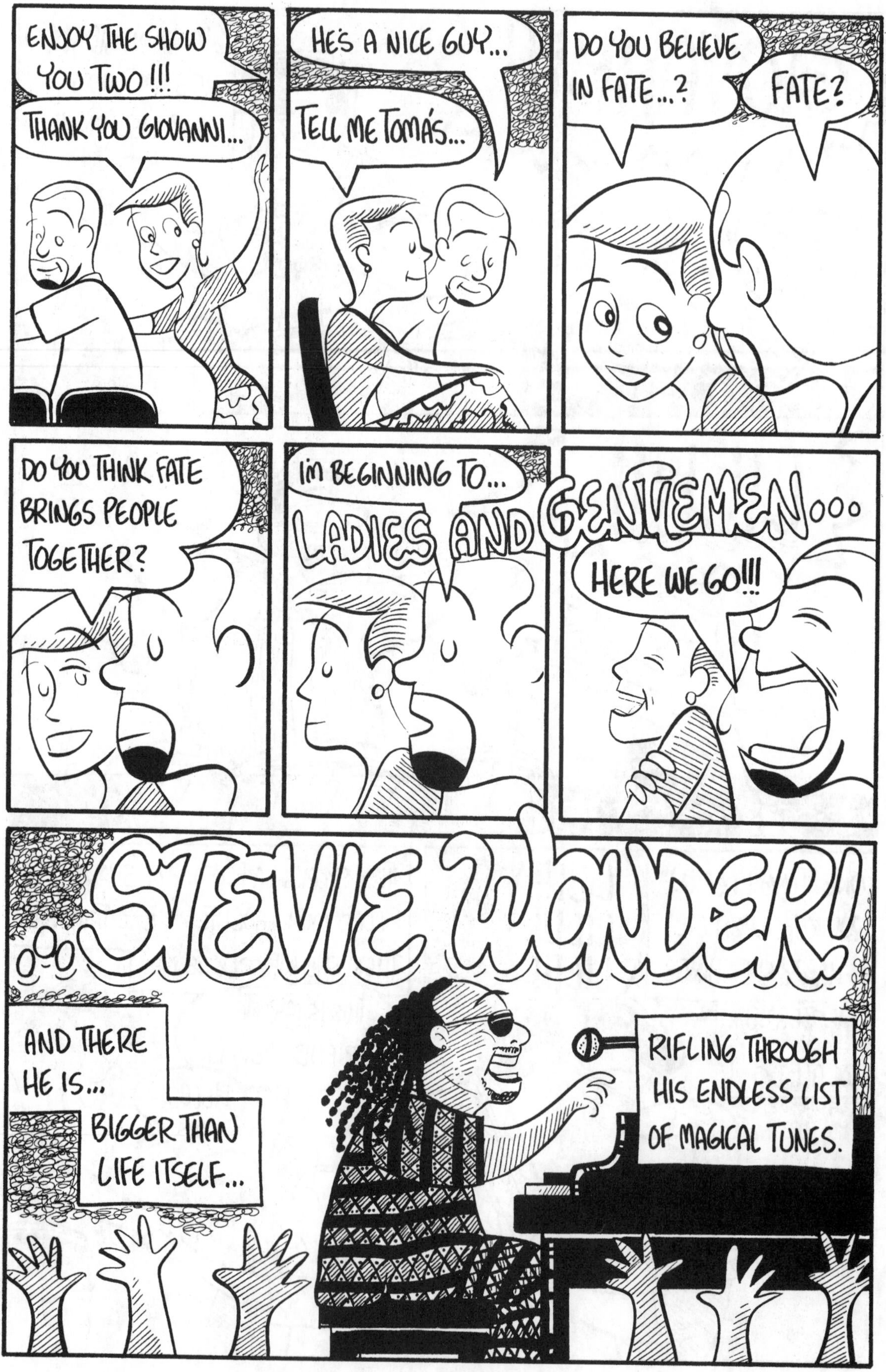

ENJOY THE SHOW YOU TWO!!!
THANK YOU GIOVANNI...
HE'S A NICE GUY...
TELL ME TOMÁS...
DO YOU BELIEVE IN FATE...?
FATE?
DO YOU THINK FATE BRINGS PEOPLE TOGETHER?
I'M BEGINNING TO...
LADIES AND GENTLEMEN...
HERE WE GO!!!
...STEVIE WONDER!
AND THERE HE IS...
BIGGER THAN LIFE ITSELF...
RIFLING THROUGH HIS ENDLESS LIST OF MAGICAL TUNES.

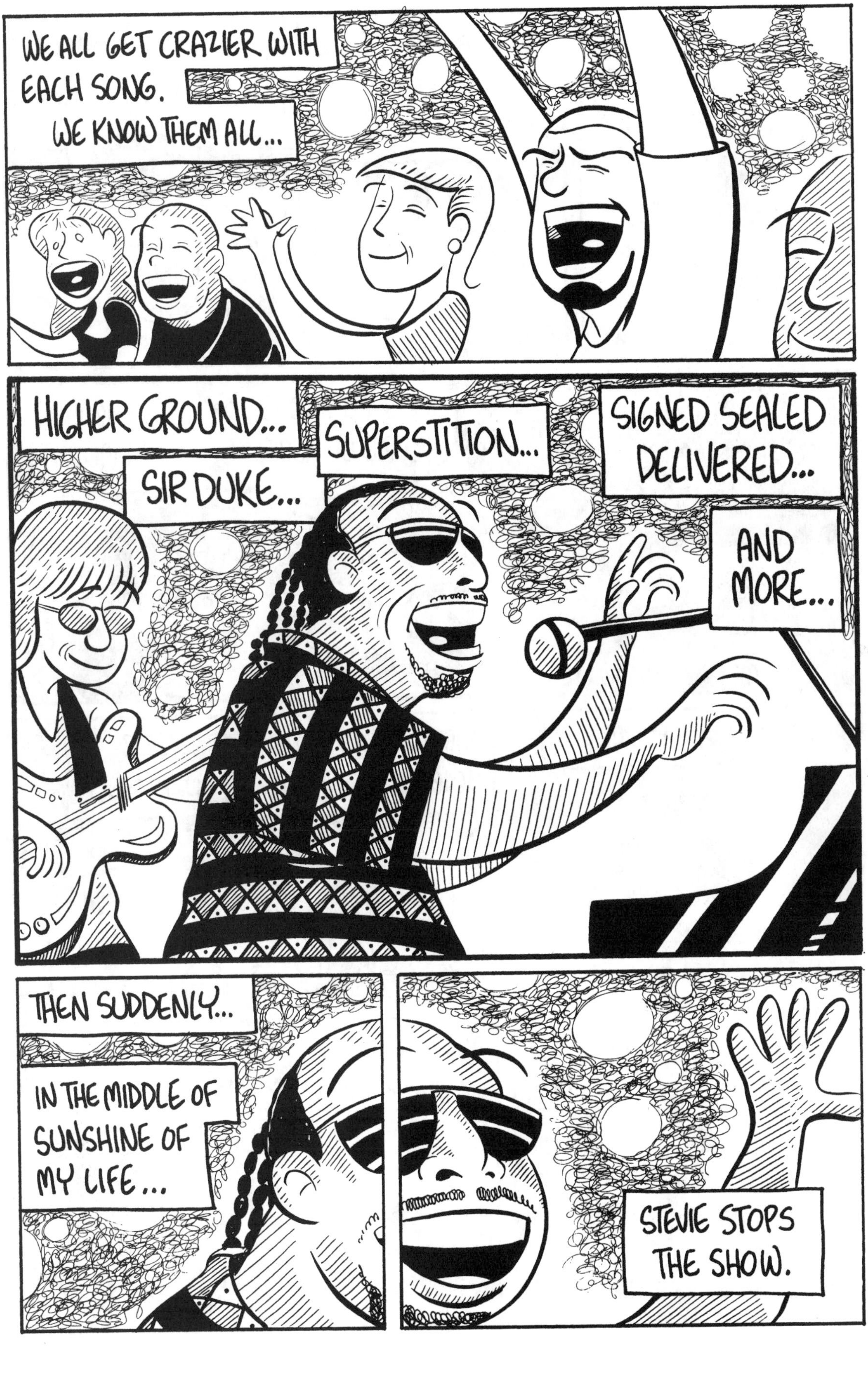
WE ALL GET CRAZIER WITH EACH SONG.
WE KNOW THEM ALL...
HIGHER GROUND...
SIR DUKE...
SUPERSTITION...
SIGNED SEALED DELIVERED...
AND MORE...
THEN SUDDENLY...
IN THE MIDDLE OF SUNSHINE OF MY LIFE...
STEVIE STOPS THE SHOW.

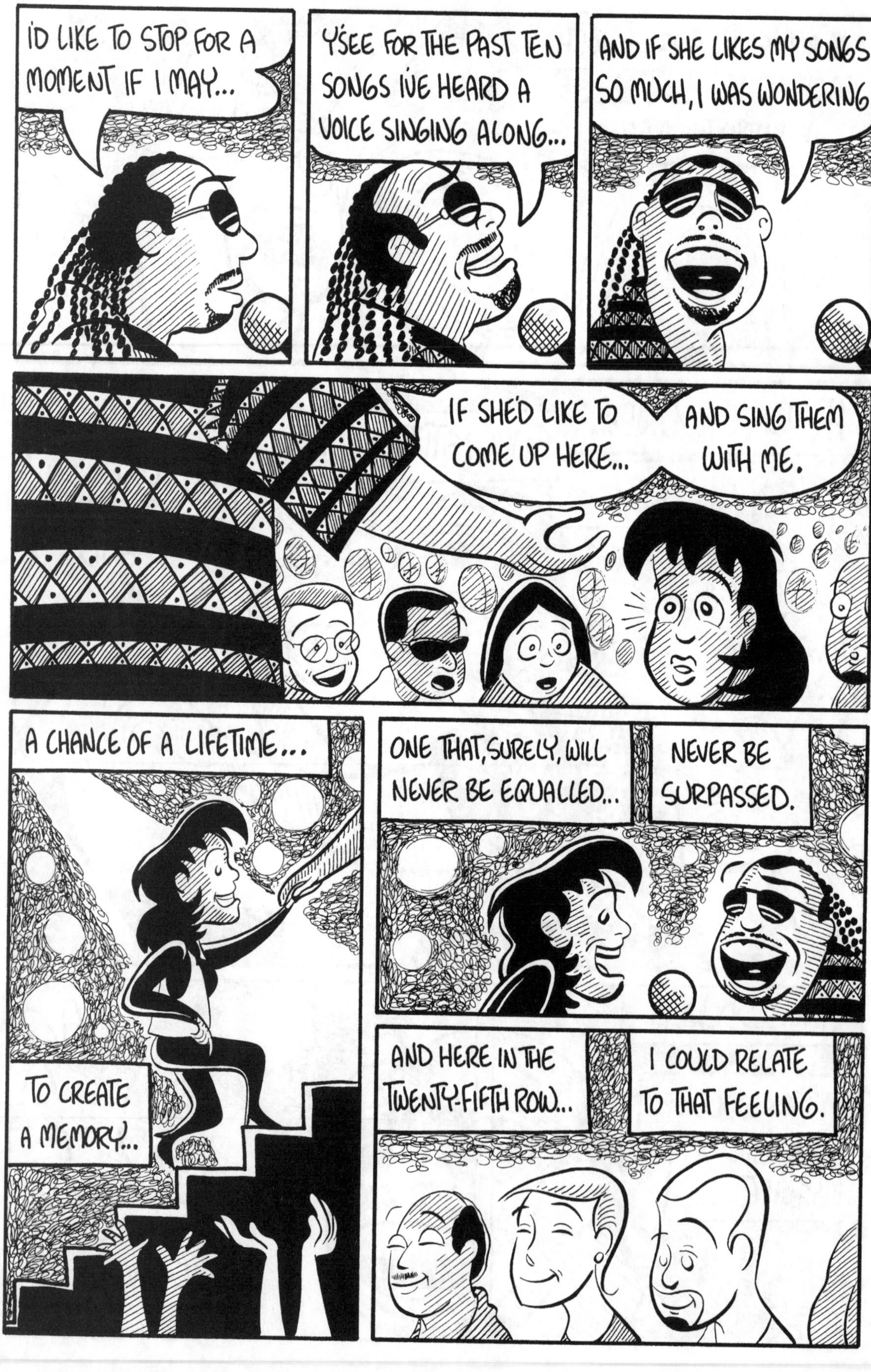

I'D LIKE TO STOP FOR A MOMENT IF I MAY...
Y'SEE FOR THE PAST TEN SONGS I'VE HEARD A VOICE SINGING ALONG...
AND IF SHE LIKES MY SONGS SO MUCH, I WAS WONDERING
IF SHE'D LIKE TO COME UP HERE...
AND SING THEM WITH ME.
A CHANCE OF A LIFETIME...
TO CREATE A MEMORY...
ONE THAT, SURELY, WILL NEVER BE EQUALLED...
NEVER BE SURPASSED.
AND HERE IN THE TWENTY-FIFTH ROW...
I COULD RELATE TO THAT FEELING.

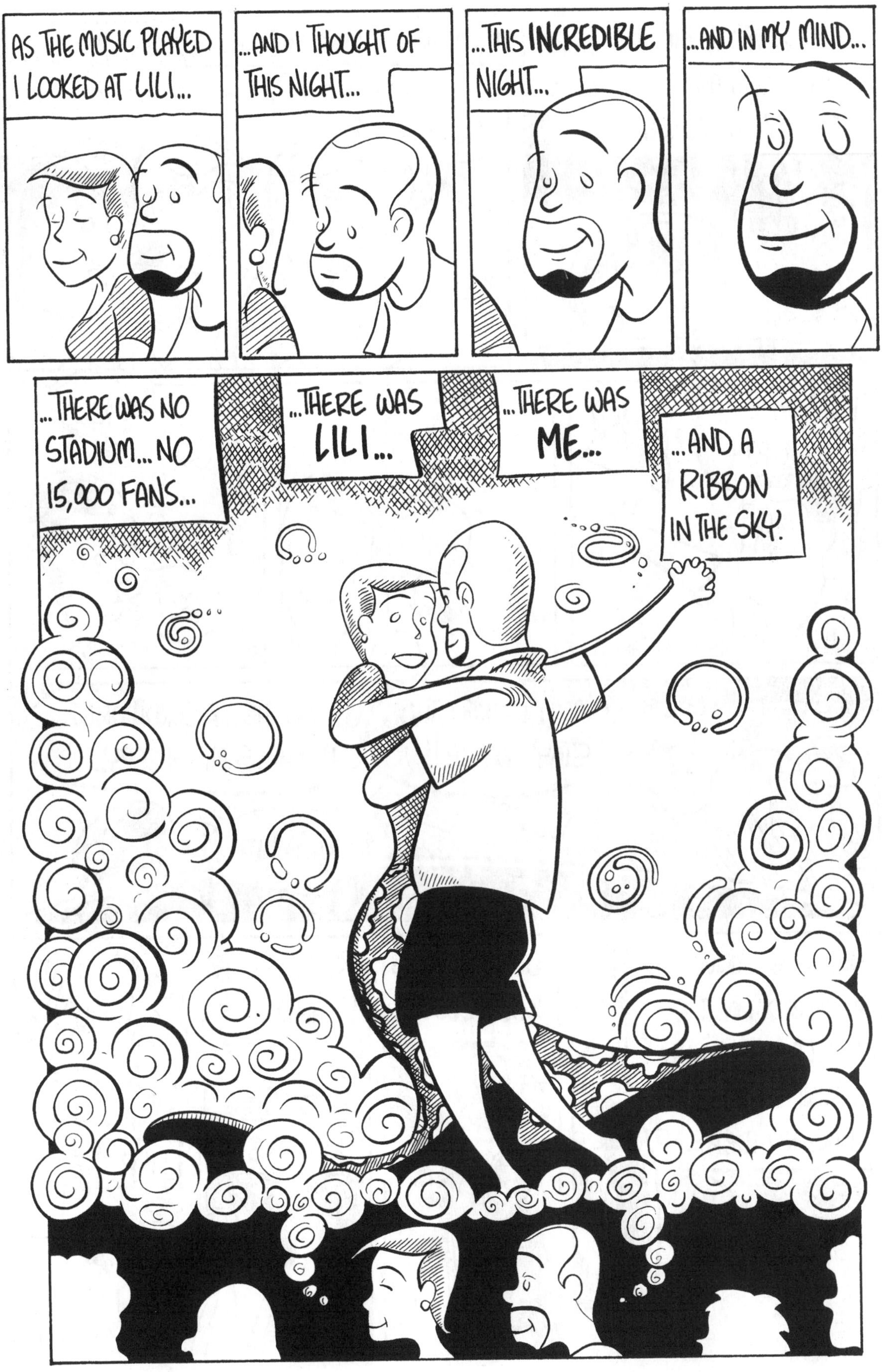
AS THE MUSIC PLAYED I LOOKED AT LILI...
...AND I THOUGHT OF THIS NIGHT...
...THIS INCREDIBLE NIGHT...
...AND IN MY MIND...
...THERE WAS NO STADIUM... NO 15,000 FANS...
...THERE WAS LILI...
...THERE WAS ME...
...AND A RIBBON IN THE SKY.

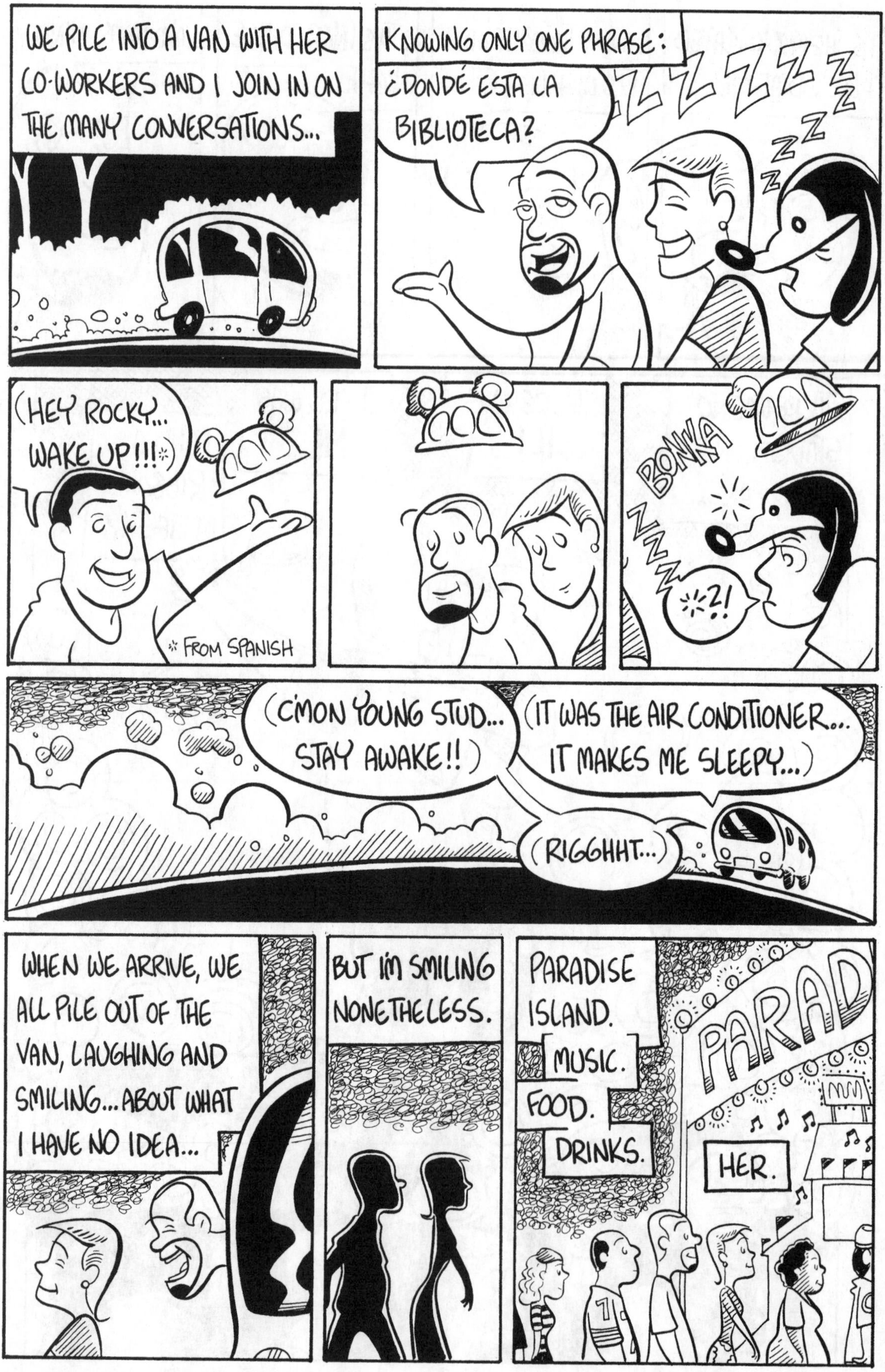
WE PILE INTO A VAN WITH HER CO-WORKERS AND I JOIN IN ON THE MANY CONVERSATIONS...
KNOWING ONLY ONE PHRASE:
¿DONDÉ ESTA LA BIBLIOTECA?
ZZZZZZ ZZZ
(HEY ROCKY... WAKE UP!!!*)
* FROM SPANISH
BONKA
ZZZZ
!?!
(C'MON YOUNG STUD... STAY AWAKE!!)
(IT WAS THE AIR CONDITIONER... IT MAKES ME SLEEPY...)
(RIGGHHT...)
WHEN WE ARRIVE, WE ALL PILE OUT OF THE VAN, LAUGHING AND SMILING... ABOUT WHAT I HAVE NO IDEA...
BUT I'M SMILING NONETHELESS.
PARADISE ISLAND.
MUSIC.
FOOD.
DRINKS.
HER.
PARAD

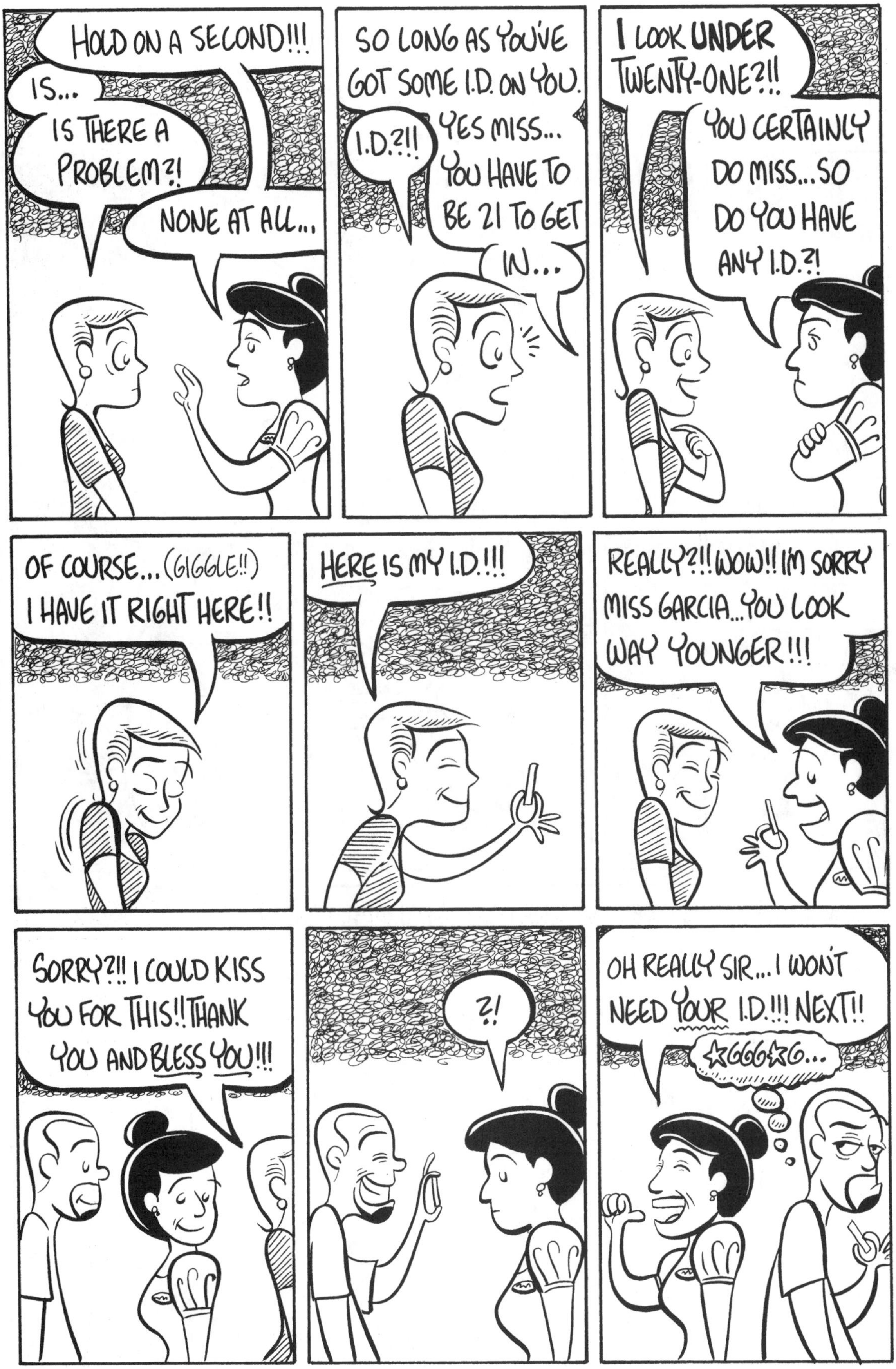
HOLD ON A SECOND!!!
IS...
IS THERE A PROBLEM?!
NONE AT ALL...
SO LONG AS YOU'VE GOT SOME I.D. ON YOU.
I.D.?!!
YES MISS... YOU HAVE TO BE 21 TO GET IN...
I LOOK UNDER TWENTY-ONE?!!
YOU CERTAINLY DO MISS...SO DO YOU HAVE ANY I.D.?!
OF COURSE...(GIGGLE!!) I HAVE IT RIGHT HERE!!
HERE IS MY I.D.!!!
REALLY?!! WOW!! I'M SORRY MISS GARCIA...YOU LOOK WAY YOUNGER!!!
SORRY?!! I COULD KISS YOU FOR THIS!! THANK YOU AND BLESS YOU!!!
?!
OH REALLY SIR...I WON'T NEED YOUR I.D.!!! NEXT!!
☆GGG☆G...

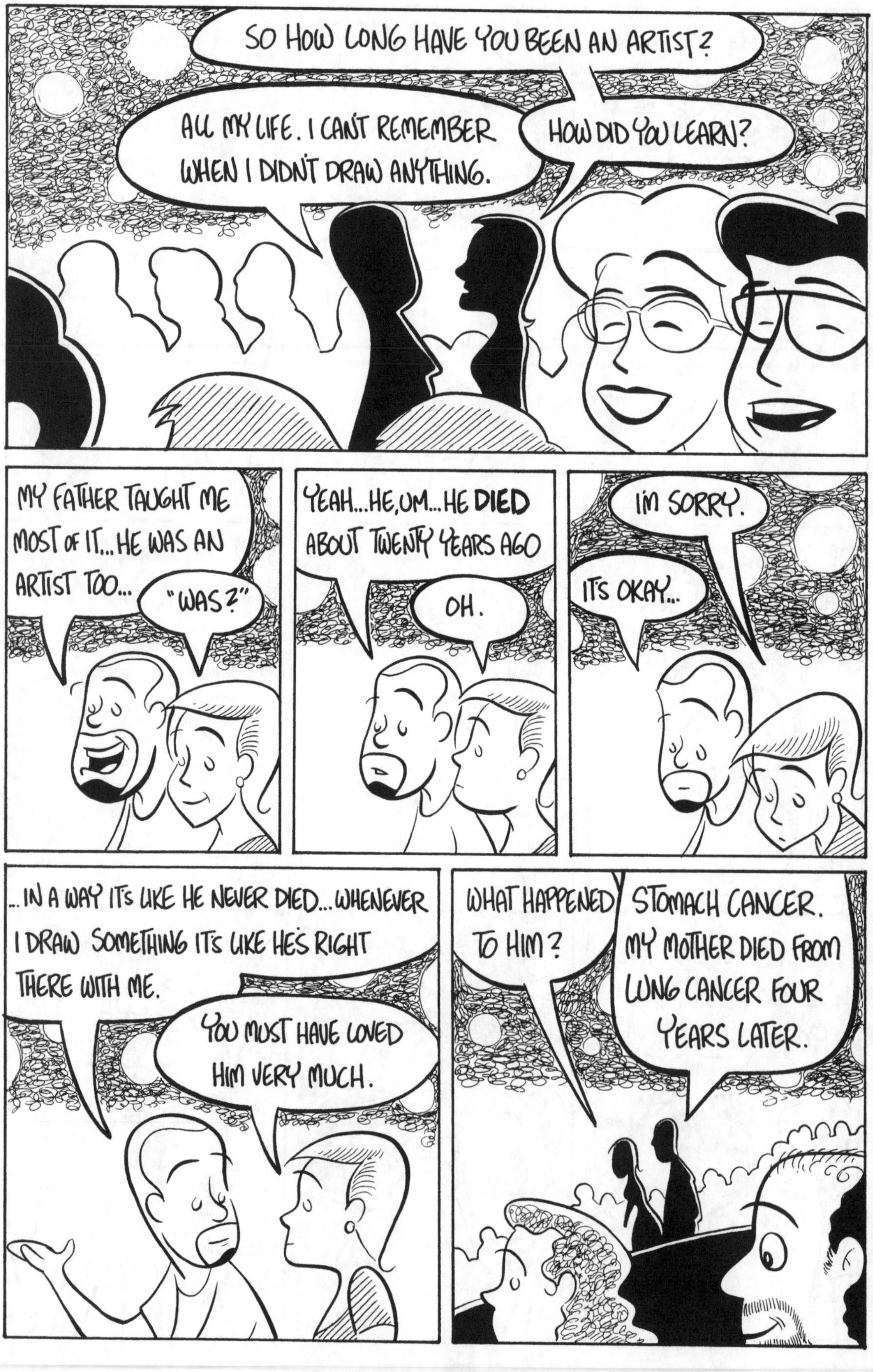
SO HOW LONG HAVE YOU BEEN AN ARTIST?
ALL MY LIFE. I CAN'T REMEMBER WHEN I DIDN'T DRAW ANYTHING.
HOW DID YOU LEARN?
MY FATHER TAUGHT ME MOST OF IT... HE WAS AN ARTIST TOO...
"WAS?"
YEAH... HE, UM... HE **DIED** ABOUT TWENTY YEARS AGO
OH.
I'M SORRY.
IT'S OKAY...
...IN A WAY IT'S LIKE HE NEVER DIED... WHENEVER I DRAW SOMETHING IT'S LIKE HE'S RIGHT THERE WITH ME.
YOU MUST HAVE LOVED HIM VERY MUCH.
WHAT HAPPENED TO HIM?
STOMACH CANCER. MY MOTHER DIED FROM LUNG CANCER FOUR YEARS LATER.

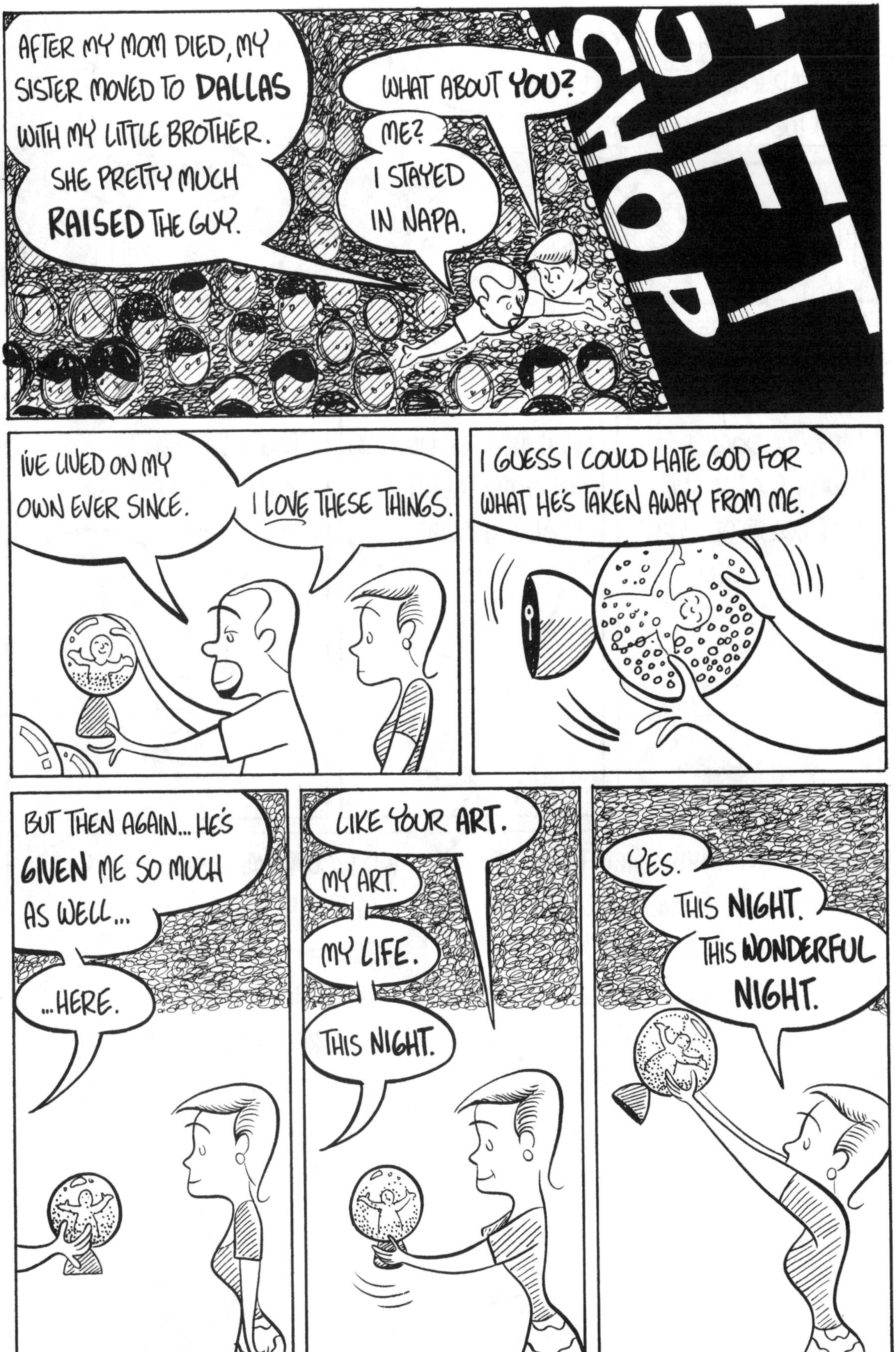
AFTER MY MOM DIED, MY SISTER MOVED TO DALLAS WITH MY LITTLE BROTHER.
SHE PRETTY MUCH RAISED THE GUY.
WHAT ABOUT YOU?
ME?
I STAYED IN NAPA.
GIFT SHOP
I'VE LIVED ON MY OWN EVER SINCE.
I LOVE THESE THINGS.
I GUESS I COULD HATE GOD FOR WHAT HE'S TAKEN AWAY FROM ME.
BUT THEN AGAIN... HE'S GIVEN ME SO MUCH AS WELL...
...HERE.
LIKE YOUR ART.
MY ART.
MY LIFE.
THIS NIGHT.
YES.
THIS NIGHT.
THIS WONDERFUL NIGHT.

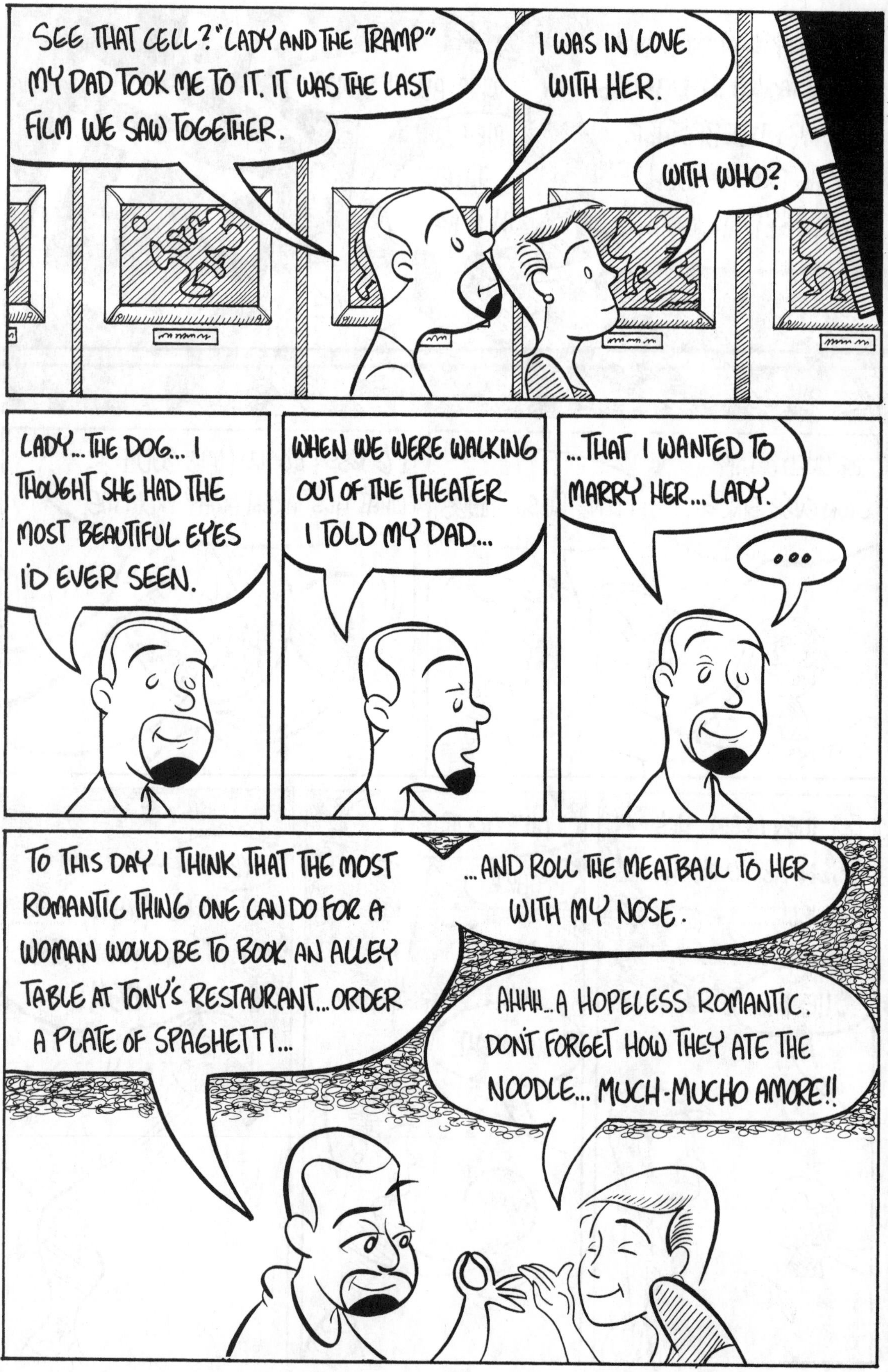
SEE THAT CELL? "LADY AND THE TRAMP" MY DAD TOOK ME TO IT. IT WAS THE LAST FILM WE SAW TOGETHER.
I WAS IN LOVE WITH HER.
WITH WHO?
LADY... THE DOG... I THOUGHT SHE HAD THE MOST BEAUTIFUL EYES I'D EVER SEEN.
WHEN WE WERE WALKING OUT OF THE THEATER I TOLD MY DAD...
...THAT I WANTED TO MARRY HER... LADY.
...
TO THIS DAY I THINK THAT THE MOST ROMANTIC THING ONE CAN DO FOR A WOMAN WOULD BE TO BOOK AN ALLEY TABLE AT TONY'S RESTAURANT... ORDER A PLATE OF SPAGHETTI...
...AND ROLL THE MEATBALL TO HER WITH MY NOSE.
AHHH... A HOPELESS ROMANTIC. DON'T FORGET HOW THEY ATE THE NOODLE... MUCH-MUCHO AMORE!!

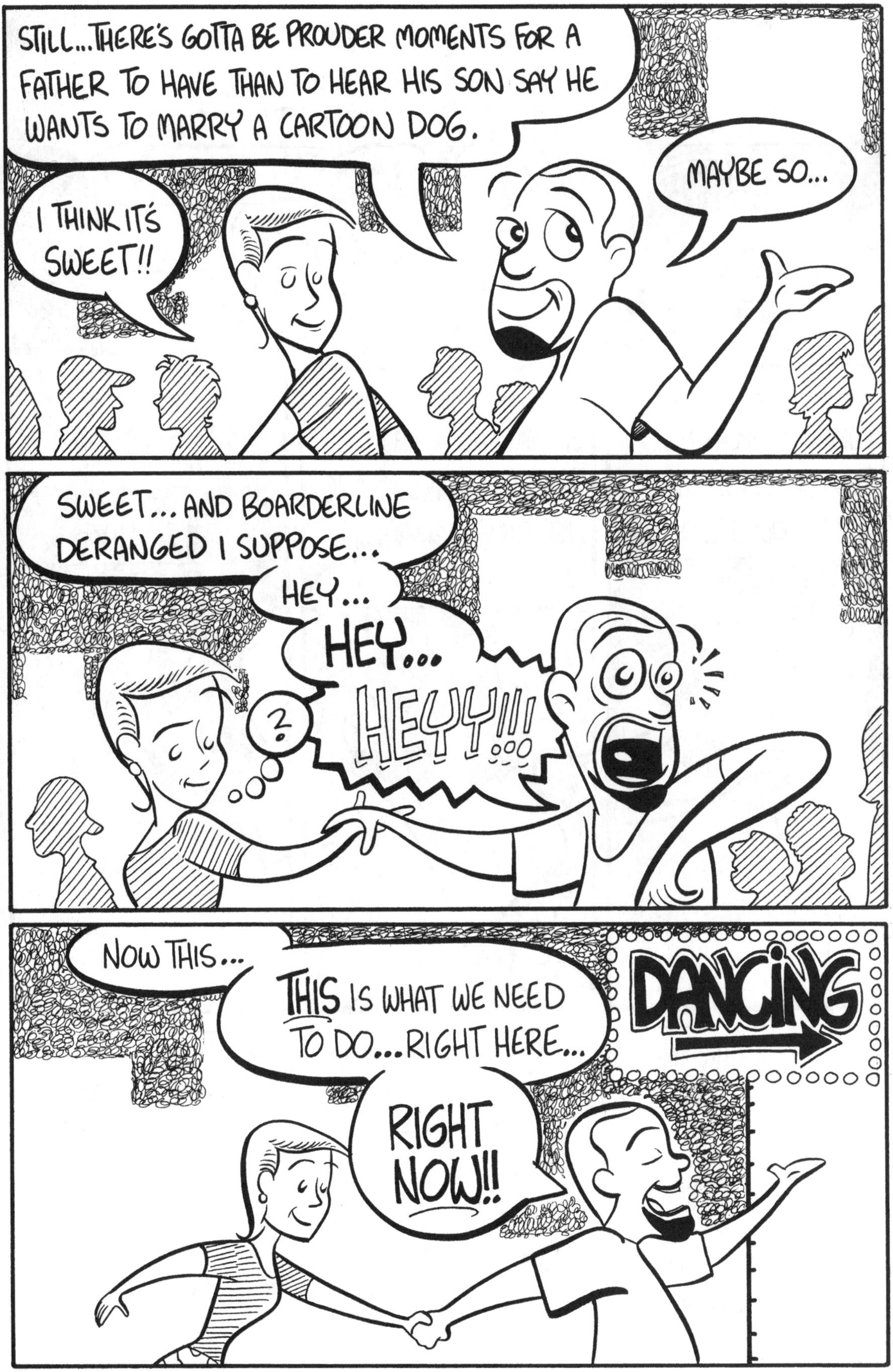
STILL...THERE'S GOTTA BE PROUDER MOMENTS FOR A FATHER TO HAVE THAN TO HEAR HIS SON SAY HE WANTS TO MARRY A CARTOON DOG.
I THINK IT'S SWEET!!
MAYBE SO...
SWEET... AND BOARDERLINE DERANGED I SUPPOSE...
HEY...
HEY...
?
HEYY!!!
NOW THIS...
THIS IS WHAT WE NEED TO DO...RIGHT HERE...
RIGHT NOW!!
DANCING

"GOOD." IT'S SUCH A SMALL WORD THAT USED TO MEAN SO VERY MUCH.

TO SAY THAT THIS IS SUCH A "GOOD" NIGHT MAKES IT ALL SEEM SO...SO...

...ORDINARY.

HARDLY.

I CAN'T TELL YOU WHAT SONGS ARE PLAYING... WHO CARES? I WAS A BIT TOO PREOCCUPIED...

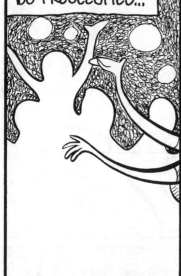

...DANCING WITH THE WOMAN WHO WILL END UP ON MY HEART THROB HALL OF FAME LIST. SHE'S EVERYTHING THAT'S ON MY LIST...

...AND SHE'S HERE.

WITH ME.

SMILING.

YOU'D THINK THAT WE WERE NEWLYWEDS, WE'RE SO GIDDY...

...MAYBE WE ARE. AGAIN...WHO CARES?! LET THEM LOOK, WE JUST DON'T CARE.

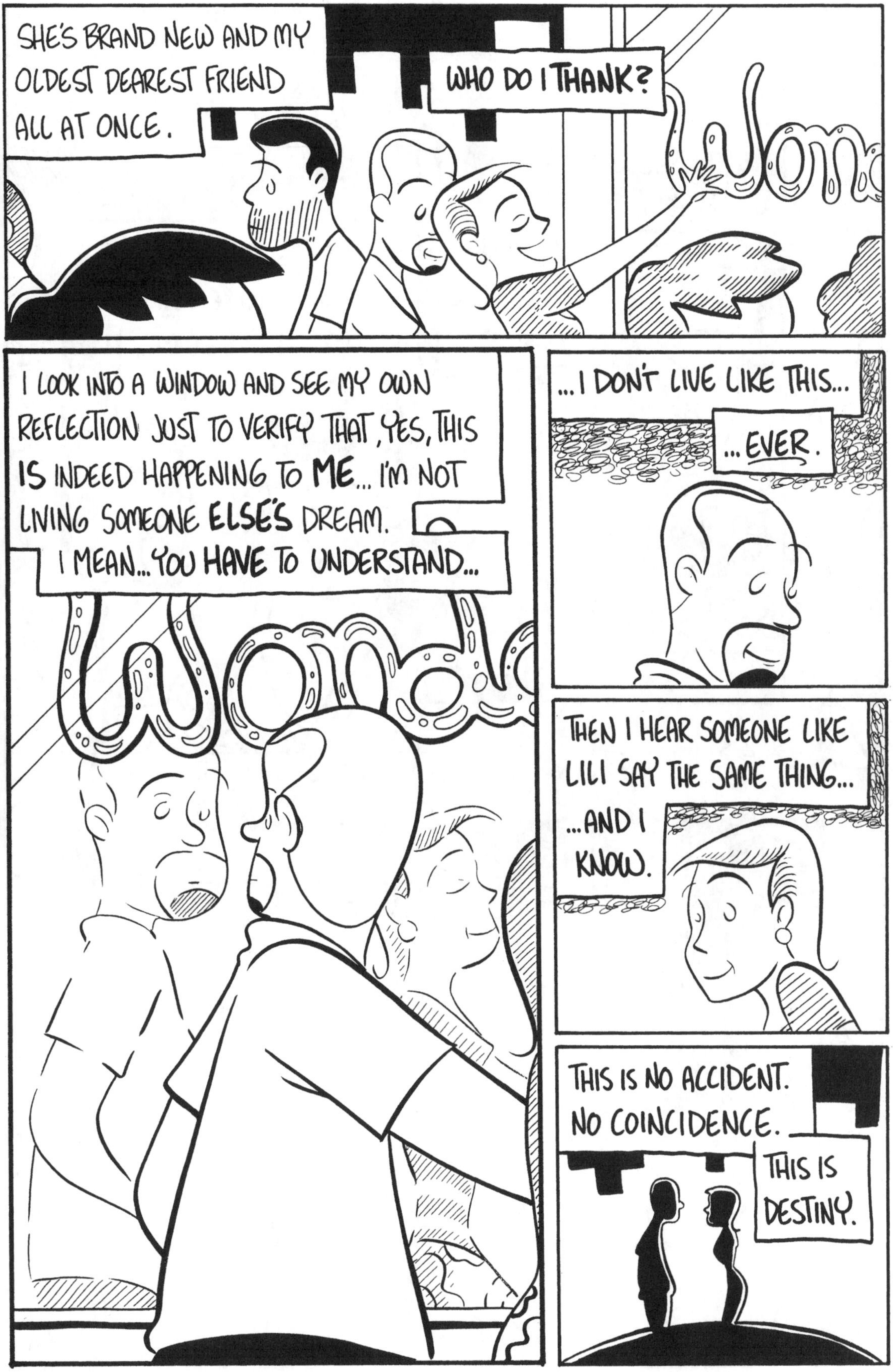
SHE'S BRAND NEW AND MY OLDEST DEAREST FRIEND ALL AT ONCE.
WHO DO I THANK?
I LOOK INTO A WINDOW AND SEE MY OWN REFLECTION JUST TO VERIFY THAT, YES, THIS IS INDEED HAPPENING TO ME... I'M NOT LIVING SOMEONE ELSE'S DREAM.
I MEAN... YOU HAVE TO UNDERSTAND...
...I DON'T LIVE LIKE THIS...
...EVER.
THEN I HEAR SOMEONE LIKE LILI SAY THE SAME THING...
...AND I KNOW.
THIS IS NO ACCIDENT. NO COINCIDENCE.
THIS IS DESTINY.

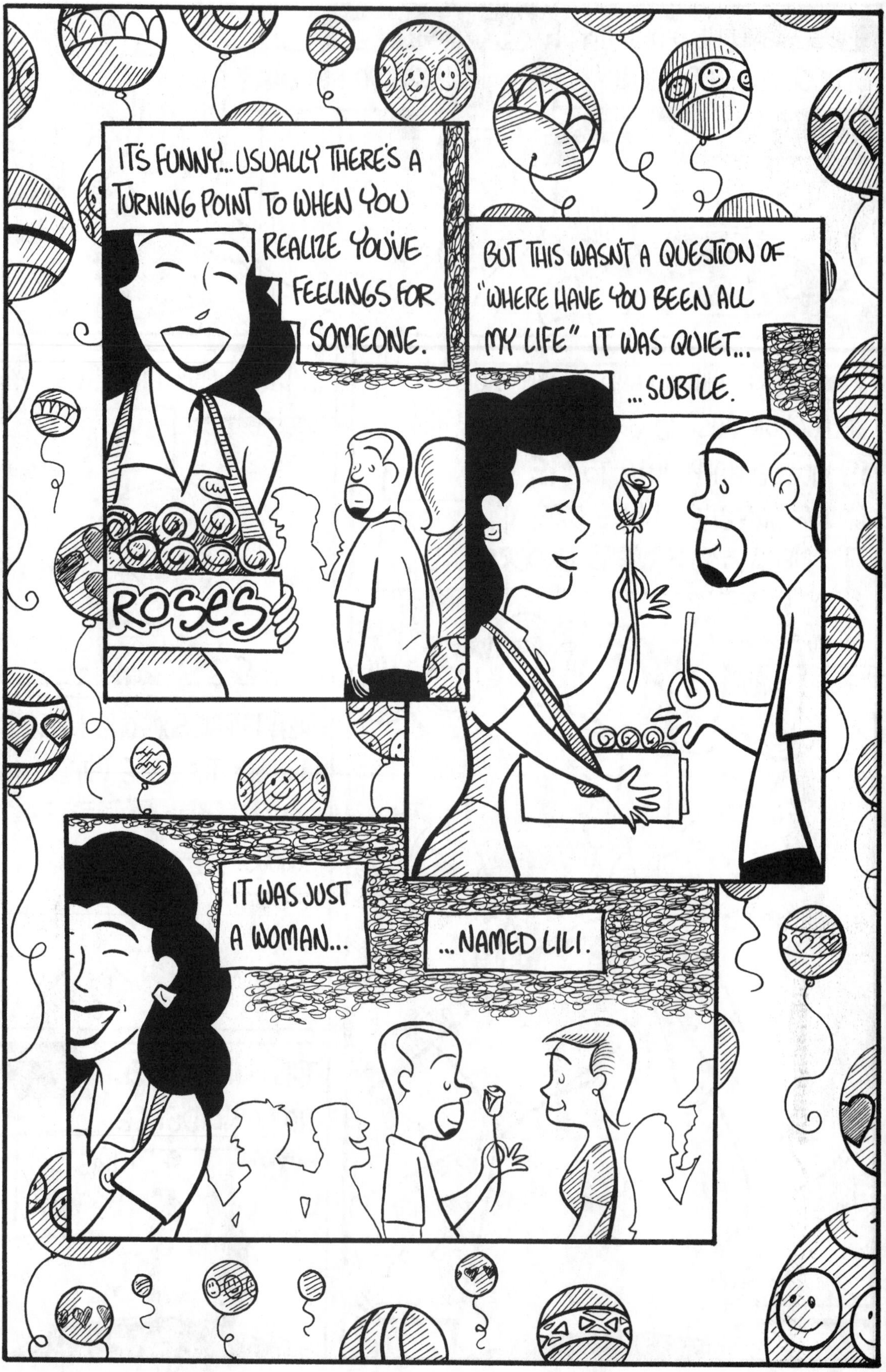

IT'S FUNNY... USUALLY THERE'S A TURNING POINT TO WHEN YOU REALIZE YOU'VE FEELINGS FOR SOMEONE.
ROSES
BUT THIS WASN'T A QUESTION OF "WHERE HAVE YOU BEEN ALL MY LIFE" IT WAS QUIET...
...SUBTLE.
IT WAS JUST A WOMAN...
...NAMED LILI.

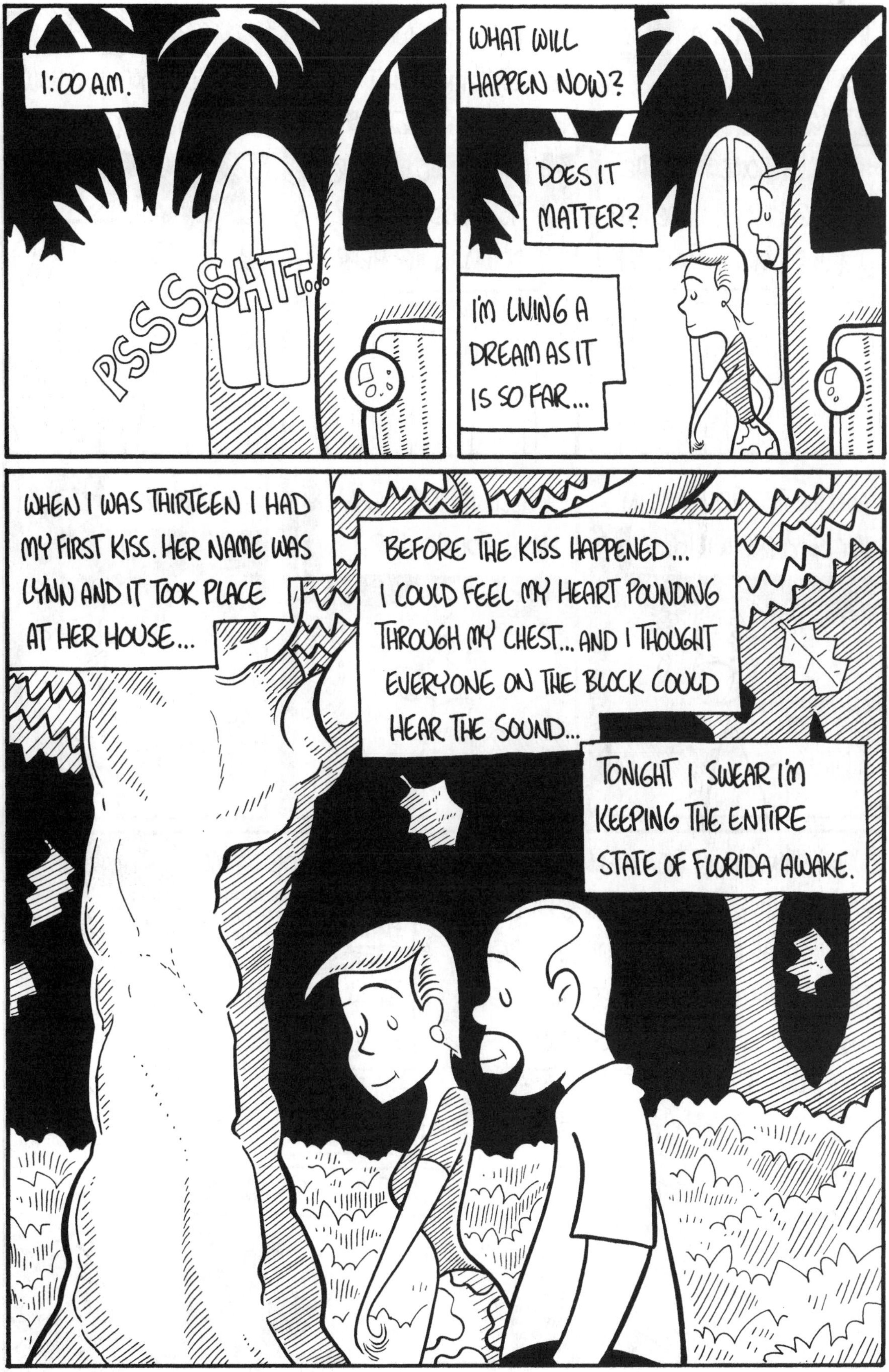
1:00 A.M.
PSSSSHTT...
WHAT WILL HAPPEN NOW?
DOES IT MATTER?
I'M LIVING A DREAM AS IT IS SO FAR...
WHEN I WAS THIRTEEN I HAD MY FIRST KISS. HER NAME WAS LYNN AND IT TOOK PLACE AT HER HOUSE...
BEFORE THE KISS HAPPENED... I COULD FEEL MY HEART POUNDING THROUGH MY CHEST... AND I THOUGHT EVERYONE ON THE BLOCK COULD HEAR THE SOUND...
TONIGHT I SWEAR I'M KEEPING THE ENTIRE STATE OF FLORIDA AWAKE.

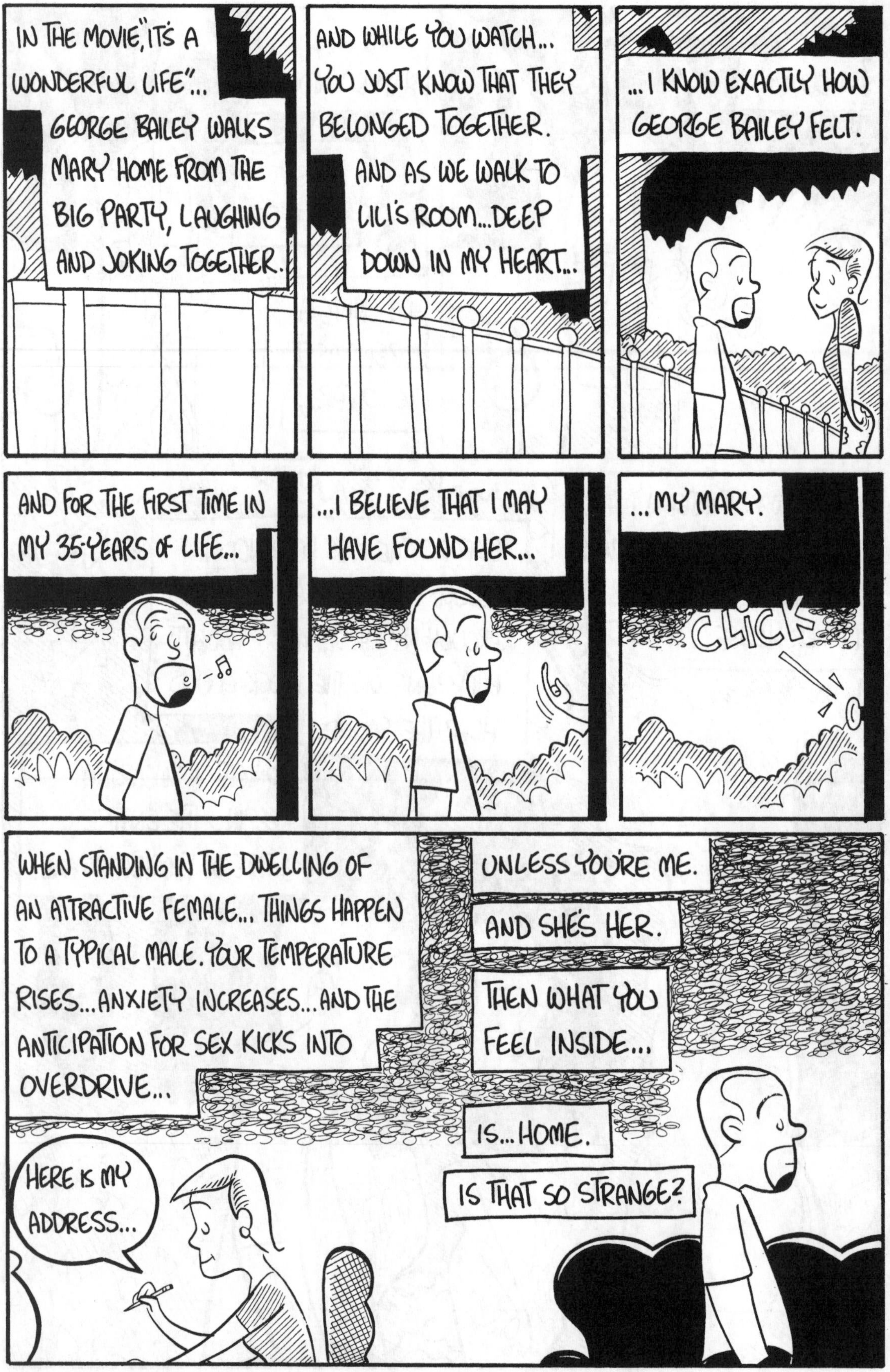
IN THE MOVIE, "IT'S A WONDERFUL LIFE"...
GEORGE BAILEY WALKS MARY HOME FROM THE BIG PARTY, LAUGHING AND JOKING TOGETHER.
AND WHILE YOU WATCH... YOU JUST KNOW THAT THEY BELONGED TOGETHER.
AND AS WE WALK TO LILI'S ROOM...DEEP DOWN IN MY HEART...
...I KNOW EXACTLY HOW GEORGE BAILEY FELT.
AND FOR THE FIRST TIME IN MY 35 YEARS OF LIFE...
...I BELIEVE THAT I MAY HAVE FOUND HER...
...MY MARY.
CLICK
WHEN STANDING IN THE DWELLING OF AN ATTRACTIVE FEMALE... THINGS HAPPEN TO A TYPICAL MALE. YOUR TEMPERATURE RISES...ANXIETY INCREASES...AND THE ANTICIPATION FOR SEX KICKS INTO OVERDRIVE...
UNLESS YOU'RE ME.
AND SHE'S HER.
THEN WHAT YOU FEEL INSIDE...
IS...HOME.
IS THAT SO STRANGE?
HERE IS MY ADDRESS...

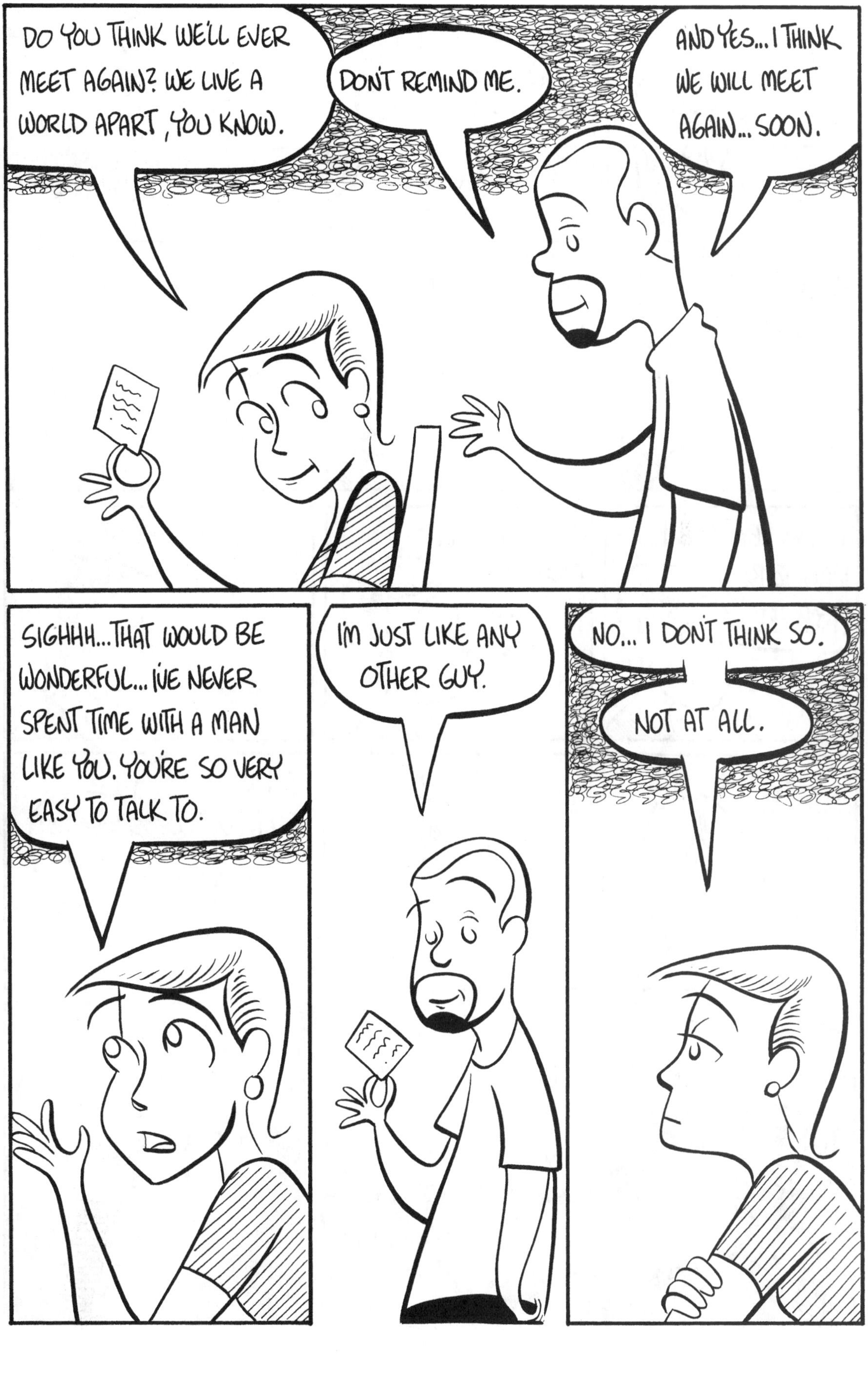
DO YOU THINK WE'LL EVER MEET AGAIN? WE LIVE A WORLD APART, YOU KNOW.
DON'T REMIND ME.
AND YES... I THINK WE WILL MEET AGAIN... SOON.
SIGHHH... THAT WOULD BE WONDERFUL... I'VE NEVER SPENT TIME WITH A MAN LIKE YOU. YOU'RE SO VERY EASY TO TALK TO.
I'M JUST LIKE ANY OTHER GUY.
NO... I DON'T THINK SO.
NOT AT ALL.

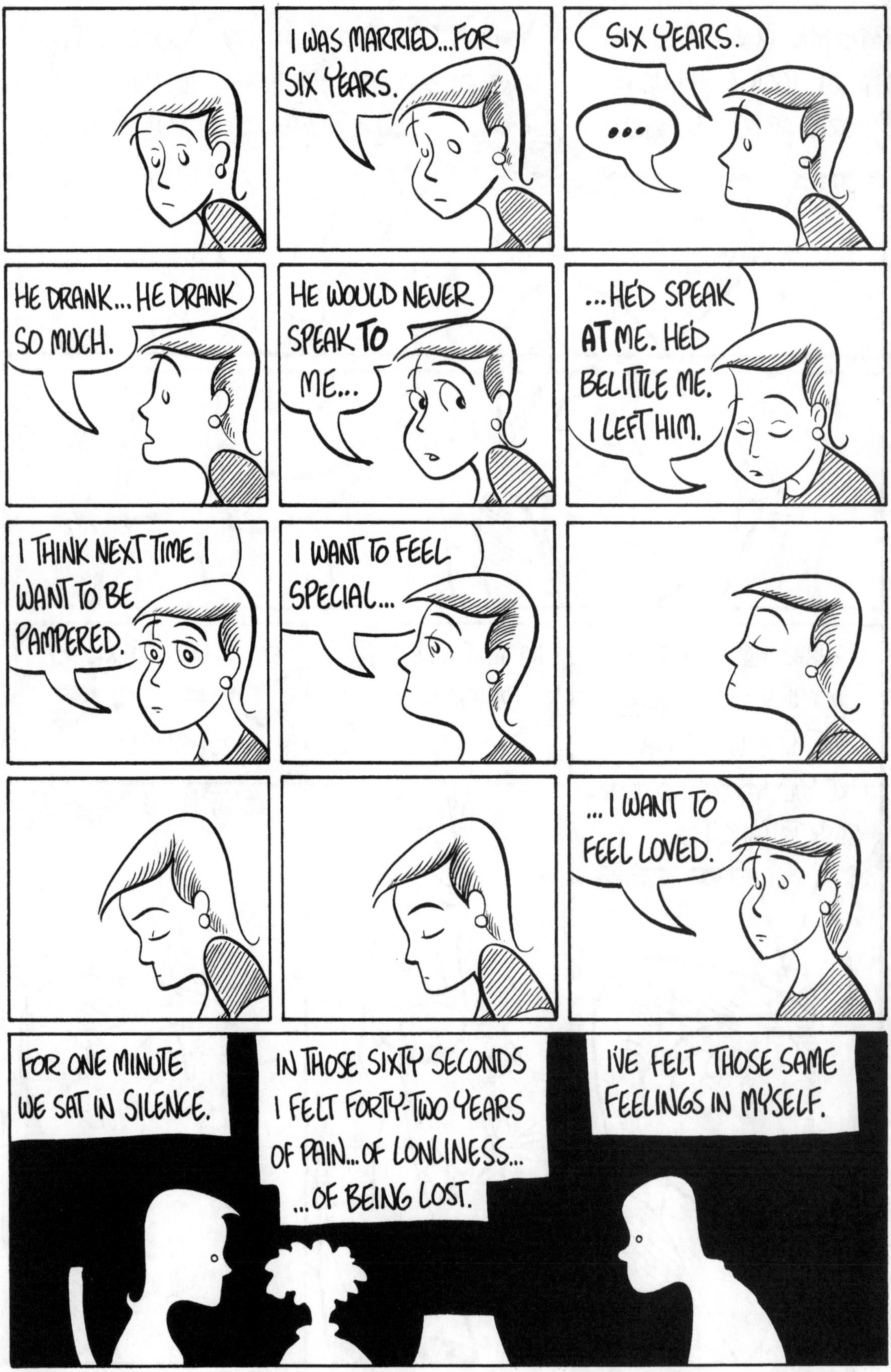
I WAS MARRIED...FOR SIX YEARS.
SIX YEARS.
...
HE DRANK... HE DRANK SO MUCH.
HE WOULD NEVER SPEAK TO ME...
...HE'D SPEAK AT ME. HE'D BELITTLE ME. I LEFT HIM.
I THINK NEXT TIME I WANT TO BE PAMPERED.
I WANT TO FEEL SPECIAL...
...I WANT TO FEEL LOVED.
FOR ONE MINUTE WE SAT IN SILENCE.
IN THOSE SIXTY SECONDS I FELT FORTY-TWO YEARS OF PAIN...OF LONLINESS... ...OF BEING LOST.
I'VE FELT THOSE SAME FEELINGS IN MYSELF.

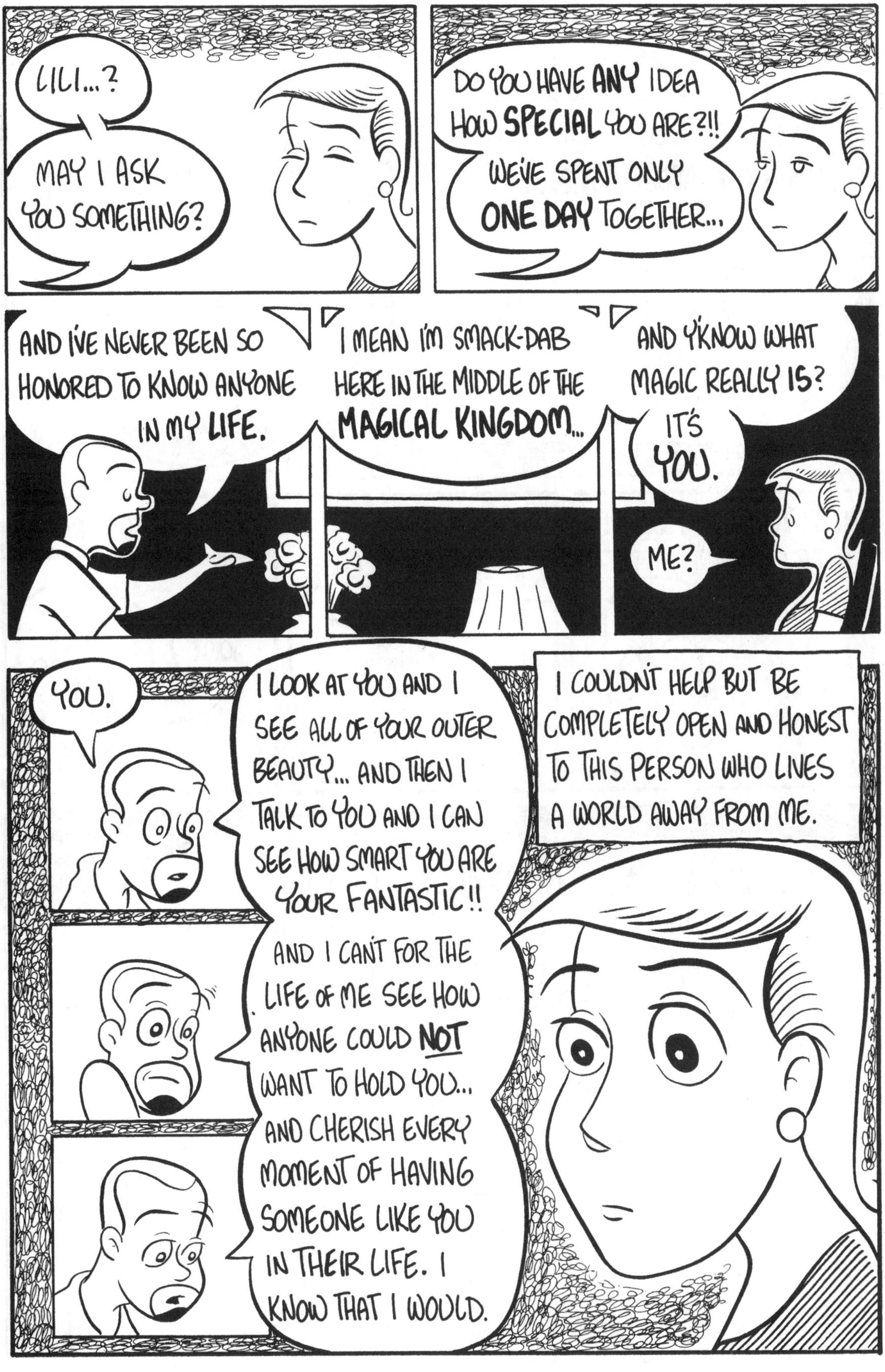
LILI...?
MAY I ASK YOU SOMETHING?
DO YOU HAVE ANY IDEA HOW SPECIAL YOU ARE?!!
WE'VE SPENT ONLY ONE DAY TOGETHER...
AND I'VE NEVER BEEN SO HONORED TO KNOW ANYONE IN MY LIFE.
I MEAN I'M SMACK-DAB HERE IN THE MIDDLE OF THE MAGICAL KINGDOM...
AND Y'KNOW WHAT MAGIC REALLY IS?
IT'S YOU.
ME?
YOU.
I LOOK AT YOU AND I SEE ALL OF YOUR OUTER BEAUTY... AND THEN I TALK TO YOU AND I CAN SEE HOW SMART YOU ARE YOUR FANTASTIC!!
AND I CAN'T FOR THE LIFE OF ME SEE HOW ANYONE COULD NOT WANT TO HOLD YOU... AND CHERISH EVERY MOMENT OF HAVING SOMEONE LIKE YOU IN THEIR LIFE. I KNOW THAT I WOULD.
I COULDN'T HELP BUT BE COMPLETELY OPEN AND HONEST TO THIS PERSON WHO LIVES A WORLD AWAY FROM ME.

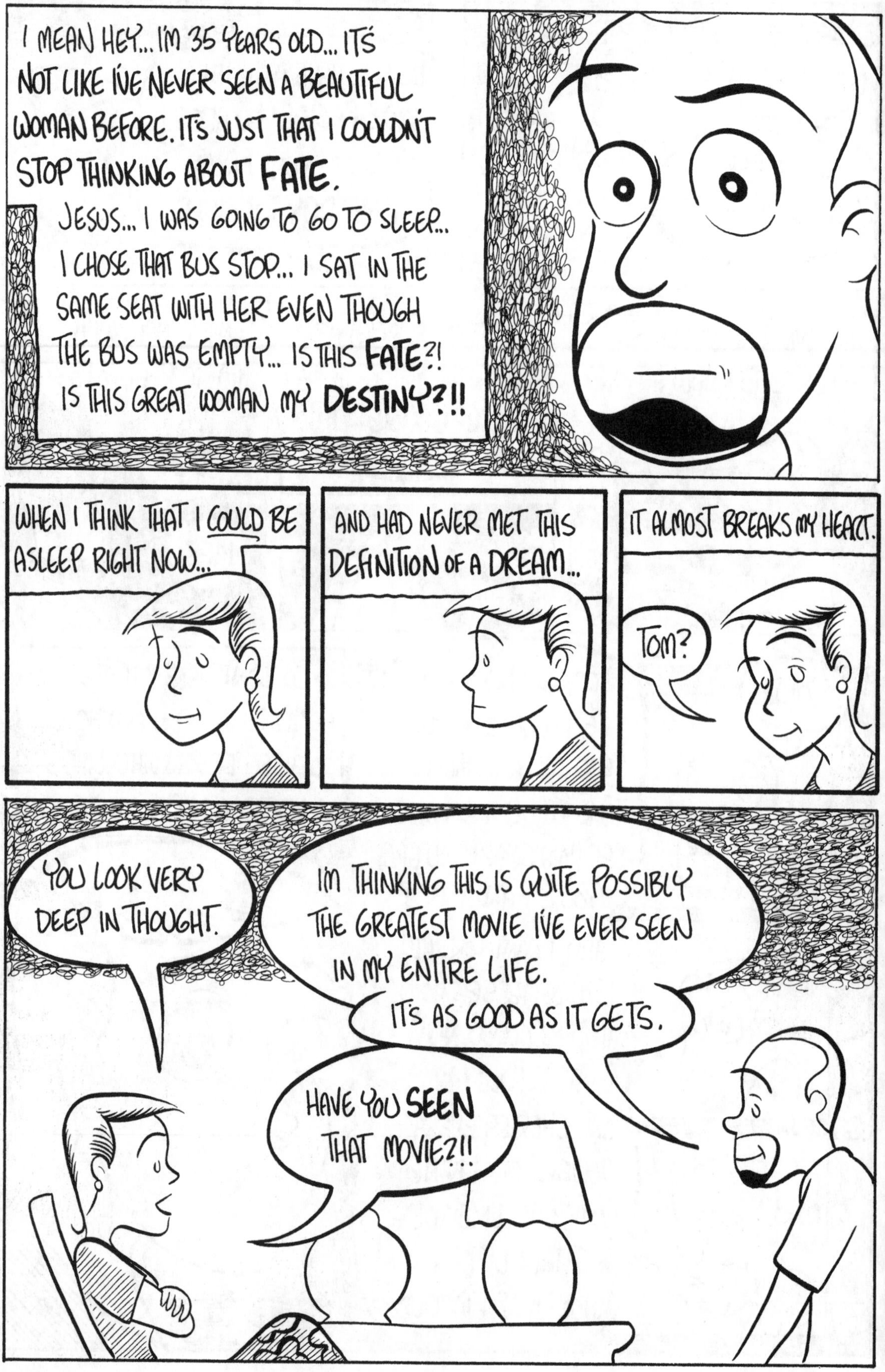
I MEAN HEY... I'M 35 YEARS OLD... IT'S NOT LIKE I'VE NEVER SEEN A BEAUTIFUL WOMAN BEFORE. IT'S JUST THAT I COULDN'T STOP THINKING ABOUT FATE.
JESUS... I WAS GOING TO GO TO SLEEP... I CHOSE THAT BUS STOP... I SAT IN THE SAME SEAT WITH HER EVEN THOUGH THE BUS WAS EMPTY... IS THIS FATE?! IS THIS GREAT WOMAN MY DESTINY?!!
WHEN I THINK THAT I COULD BE ASLEEP RIGHT NOW...
AND HAD NEVER MET THIS DEFINITION OF A DREAM...
IT ALMOST BREAKS MY HEART.
TOM?
YOU LOOK VERY DEEP IN THOUGHT.
I'M THINKING THIS IS QUITE POSSIBLY THE GREATEST MOVIE I'VE EVER SEEN IN MY ENTIRE LIFE.
IT'S AS GOOD AS IT GETS.
HAVE YOU SEEN THAT MOVIE?!!

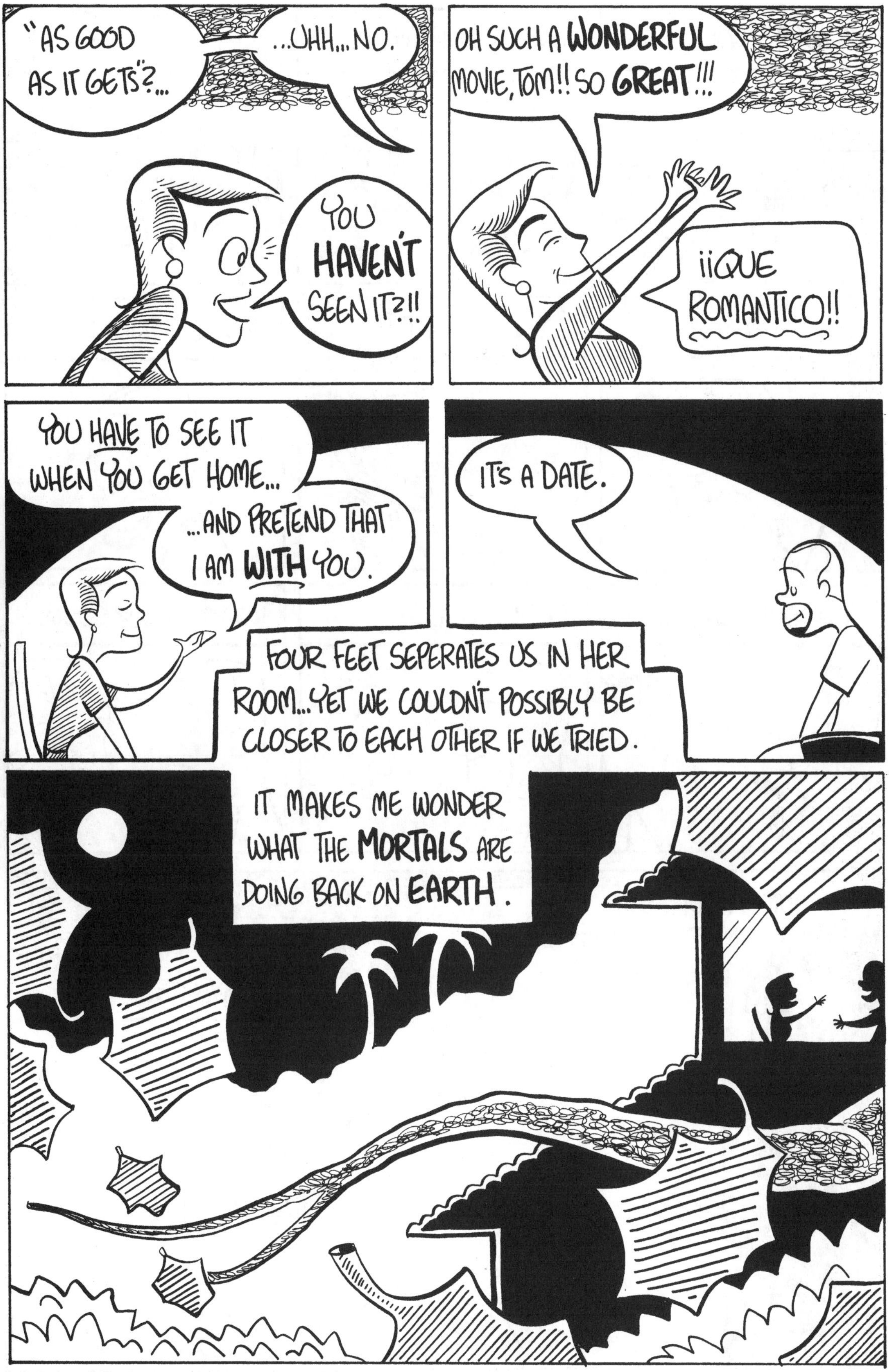

"AS GOOD AS IT GETS"?...
...UHH... NO.
YOU HAVEN'T SEEN IT?!!
OH SUCH A WONDERFUL MOVIE, TOM!! SO GREAT!!!
¡¡QUE ROMANTICO!!
YOU HAVE TO SEE IT WHEN YOU GET HOME...
...AND PRETEND THAT I AM WITH YOU.
IT'S A DATE.
FOUR FEET SEPERATES US IN HER ROOM... YET WE COULDN'T POSSIBLY BE CLOSER TO EACH OTHER IF WE TRIED.
IT MAKES ME WONDER WHAT THE MORTALS ARE DOING BACK ON EARTH.

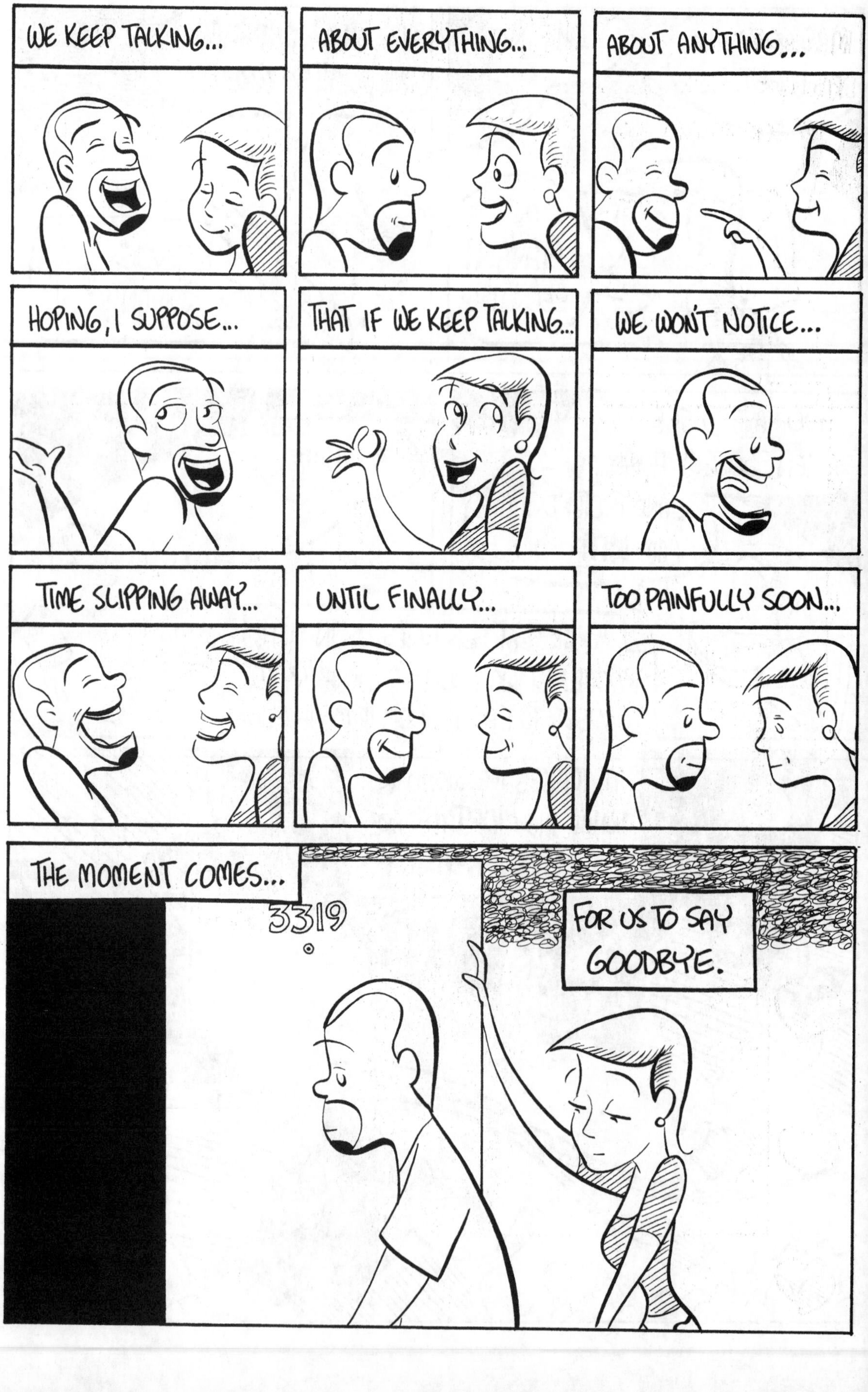
WE KEEP TALKING...
ABOUT EVERYTHING...
ABOUT ANYTHING...
HOPING, I SUPPOSE...
THAT IF WE KEEP TALKING...
WE WON'T NOTICE...
TIME SLIPPING AWAY...
UNTIL FINALLY...
TOO PAINFULLY SOON...
THE MOMENT COMES...
3319
FOR US TO SAY GOODBYE.

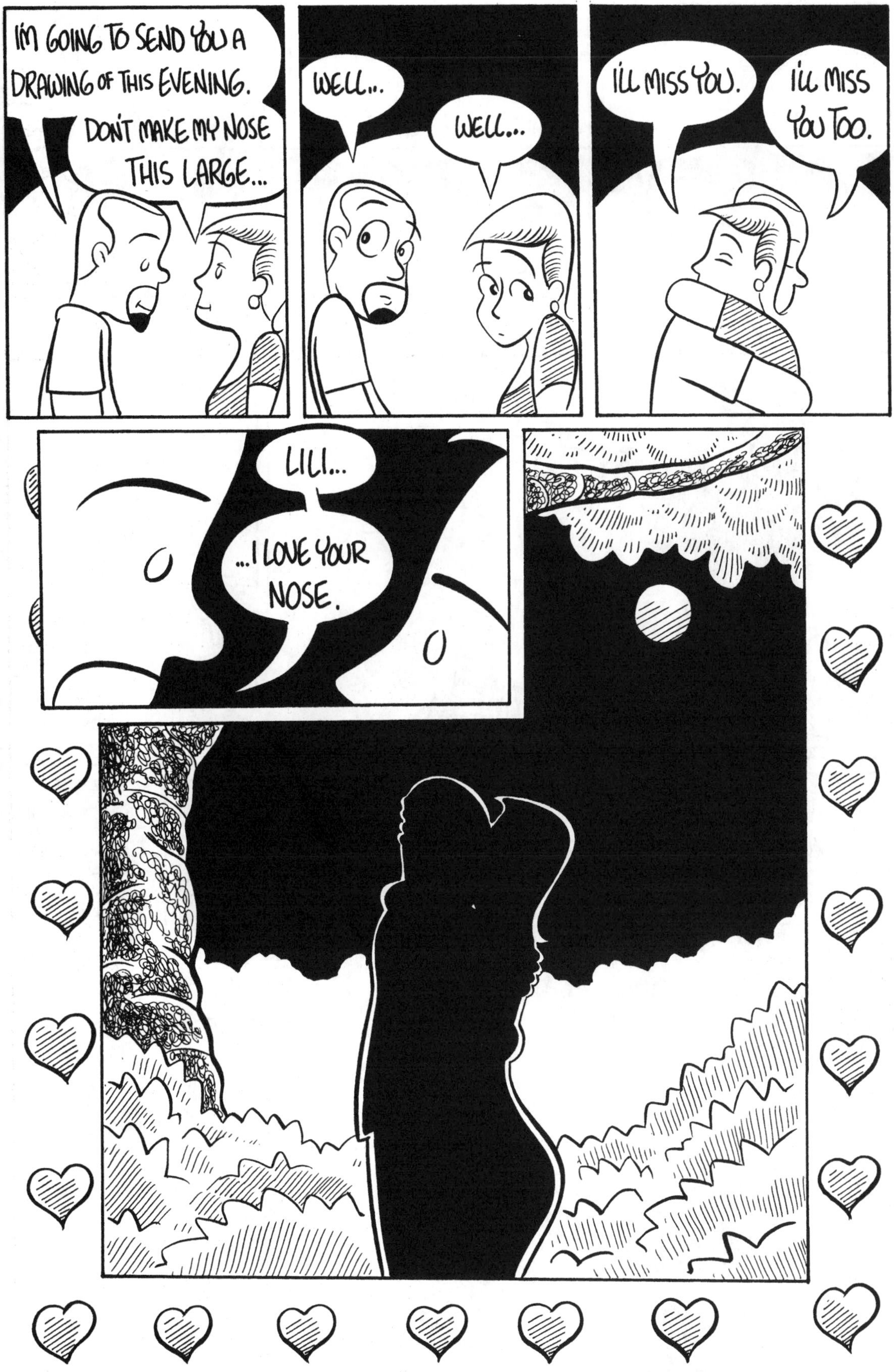
I'M GOING TO SEND YOU A DRAWING OF THIS EVENING.
DON'T MAKE MY NOSE THIS LARGE...
WELL...
WELL...
I'LL MISS YOU.
I'LL MISS YOU TOO.
LILI...
...I LOVE YOUR NOSE.

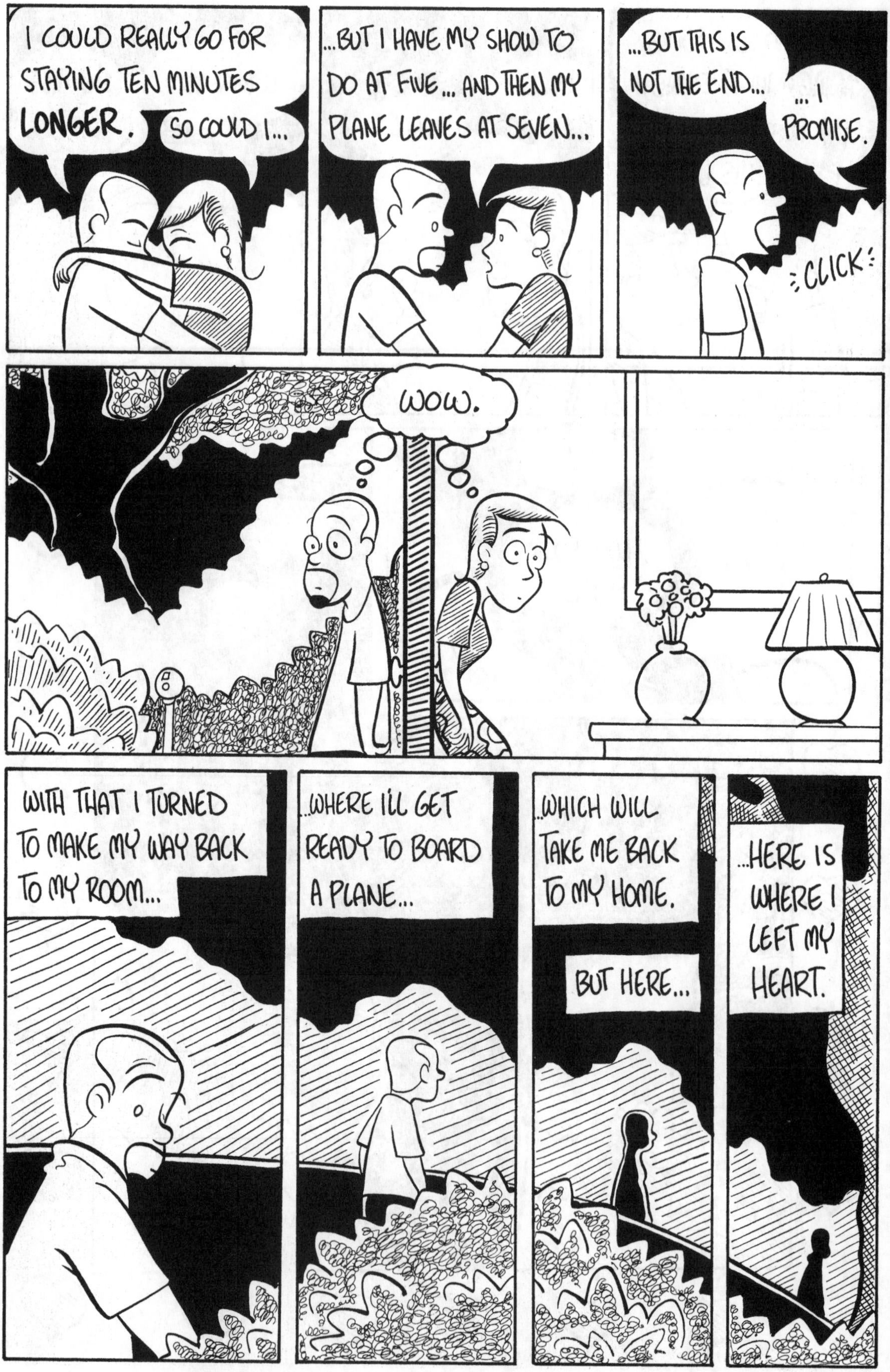
I COULD REALLY GO FOR STAYING TEN MINUTES **LONGER**.
SO COULD I...
...BUT I HAVE MY SHOW TO DO AT FIVE... AND THEN MY PLANE LEAVES AT SEVEN...
...BUT THIS IS NOT THE END...
...I PROMISE.
CLICK
WOW.
WITH THAT I TURNED TO MAKE MY WAY BACK TO MY ROOM...
...WHERE I'LL GET READY TO BOARD A PLANE...
...WHICH WILL TAKE ME BACK TO MY HOME.
BUT HERE...
...HERE IS WHERE I LEFT MY HEART.

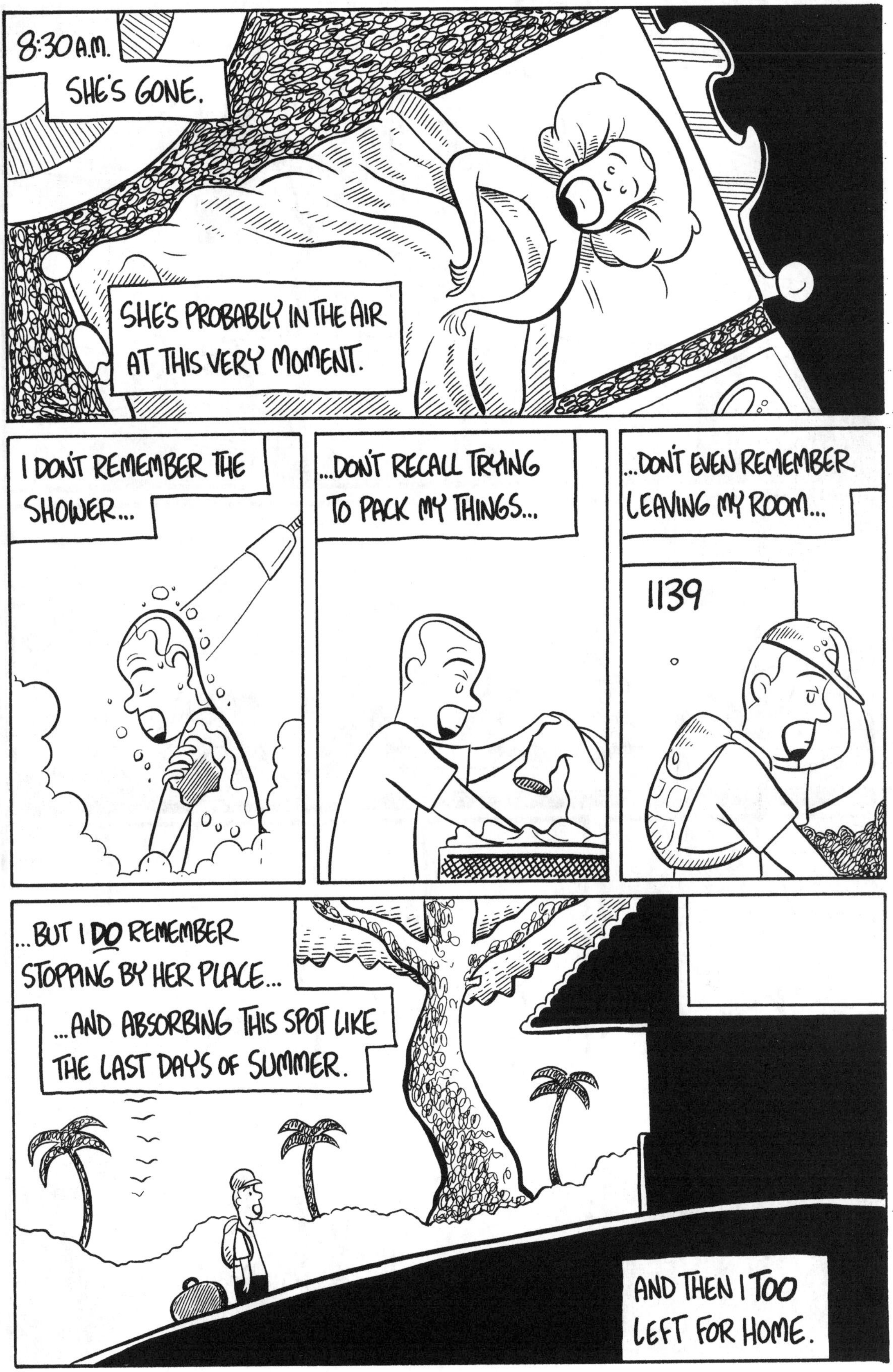
8:30 A.M.
SHE'S GONE.
SHE'S PROBABLY IN THE AIR AT THIS VERY MOMENT.
I DON'T REMEMBER THE SHOWER...
...DON'T RECALL TRYING TO PACK MY THINGS...
...DON'T EVEN REMEMBER LEAVING MY ROOM...
1139
...BUT I DO REMEMBER STOPPING BY HER PLACE...
...AND ABSORBING THIS SPOT LIKE THE LAST DAYS OF SUMMER.
AND THEN I TOO LEFT FOR HOME.

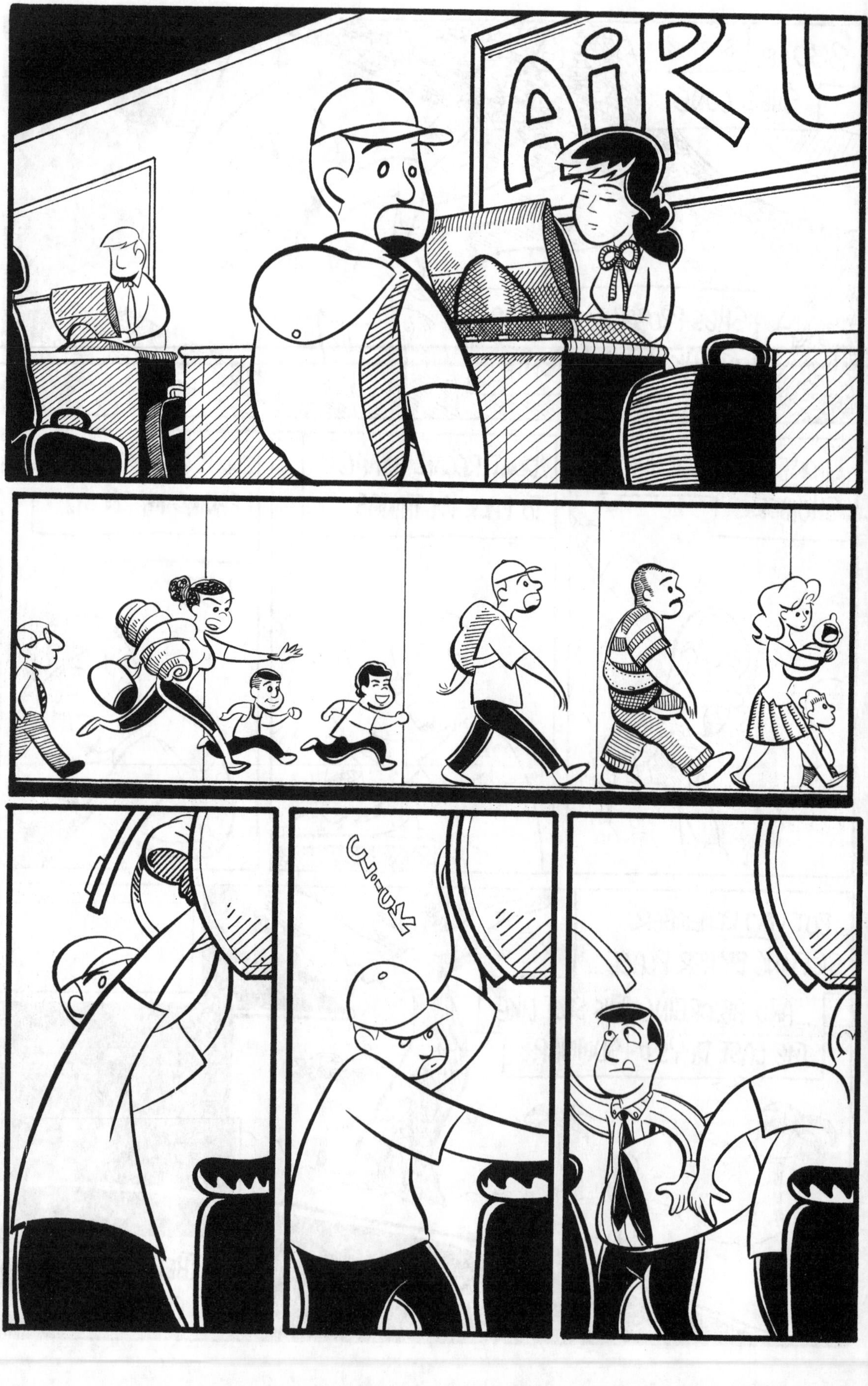
AiR U
CL-UNK

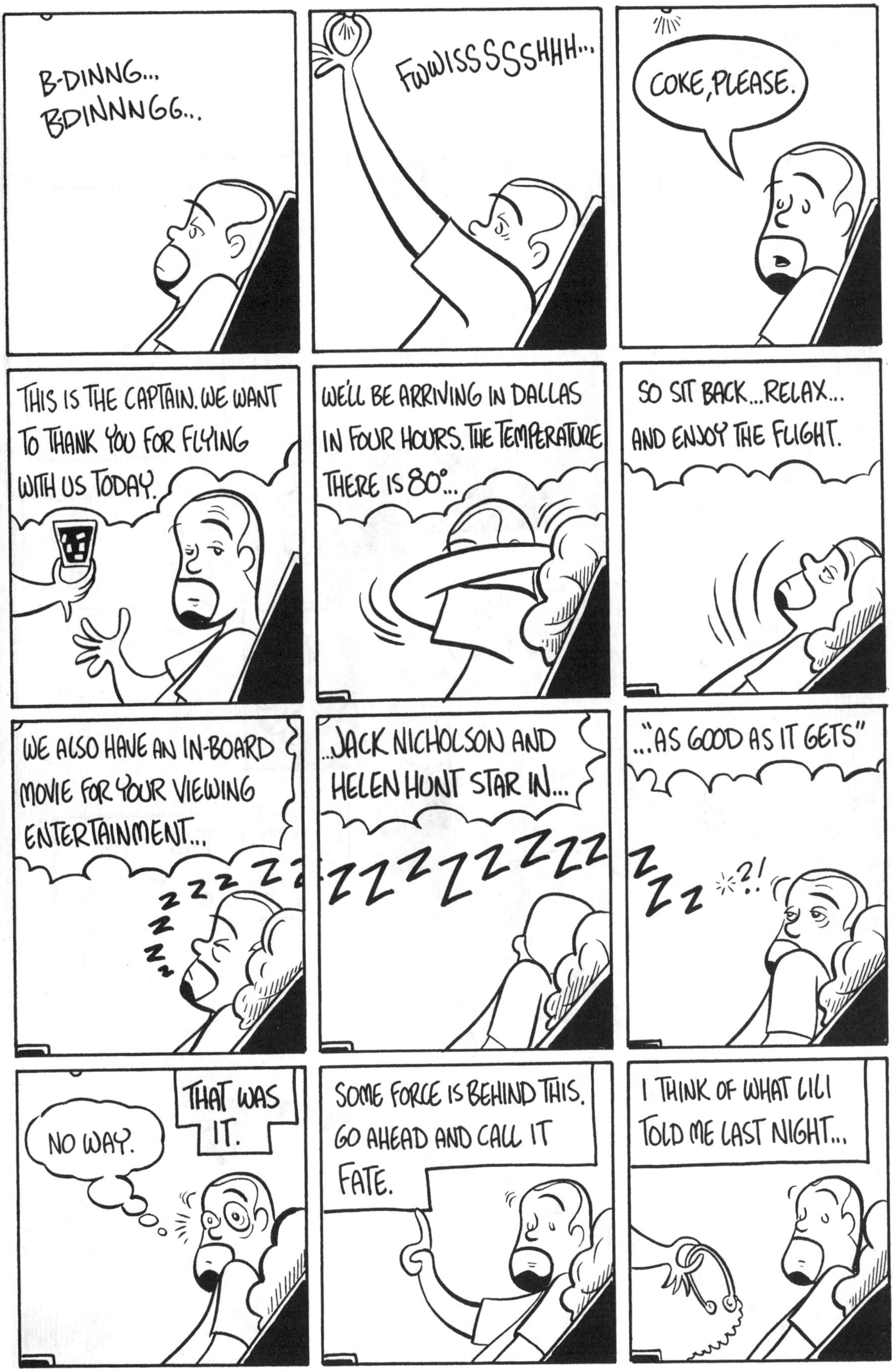

B-DINNG...
BDINNNGG...
FWWISSSSSHHH...
COKE, PLEASE.
THIS IS THE CAPTAIN. WE WANT TO THANK YOU FOR FLYING WITH US TODAY.
WE'LL BE ARRIVING IN DALLAS IN FOUR HOURS. THE TEMPERATURE THERE IS 80°...
SO SIT BACK...RELAX... AND ENJOY THE FLIGHT.
WE ALSO HAVE AN IN-BOARD MOVIE FOR YOUR VIEWING ENTERTAINMENT...
ZZZZZ
...JACK NICHOLSON AND HELEN HUNT STAR IN...
ZZZZZZZZZ
..."AS GOOD AS IT GETS"
ZZZ
?!
THAT WAS IT.
NO WAY.
SOME FORCE IS BEHIND THIS. GO AHEAD AND CALL IT FATE.
I THINK OF WHAT LILI TOLD ME LAST NIGHT...

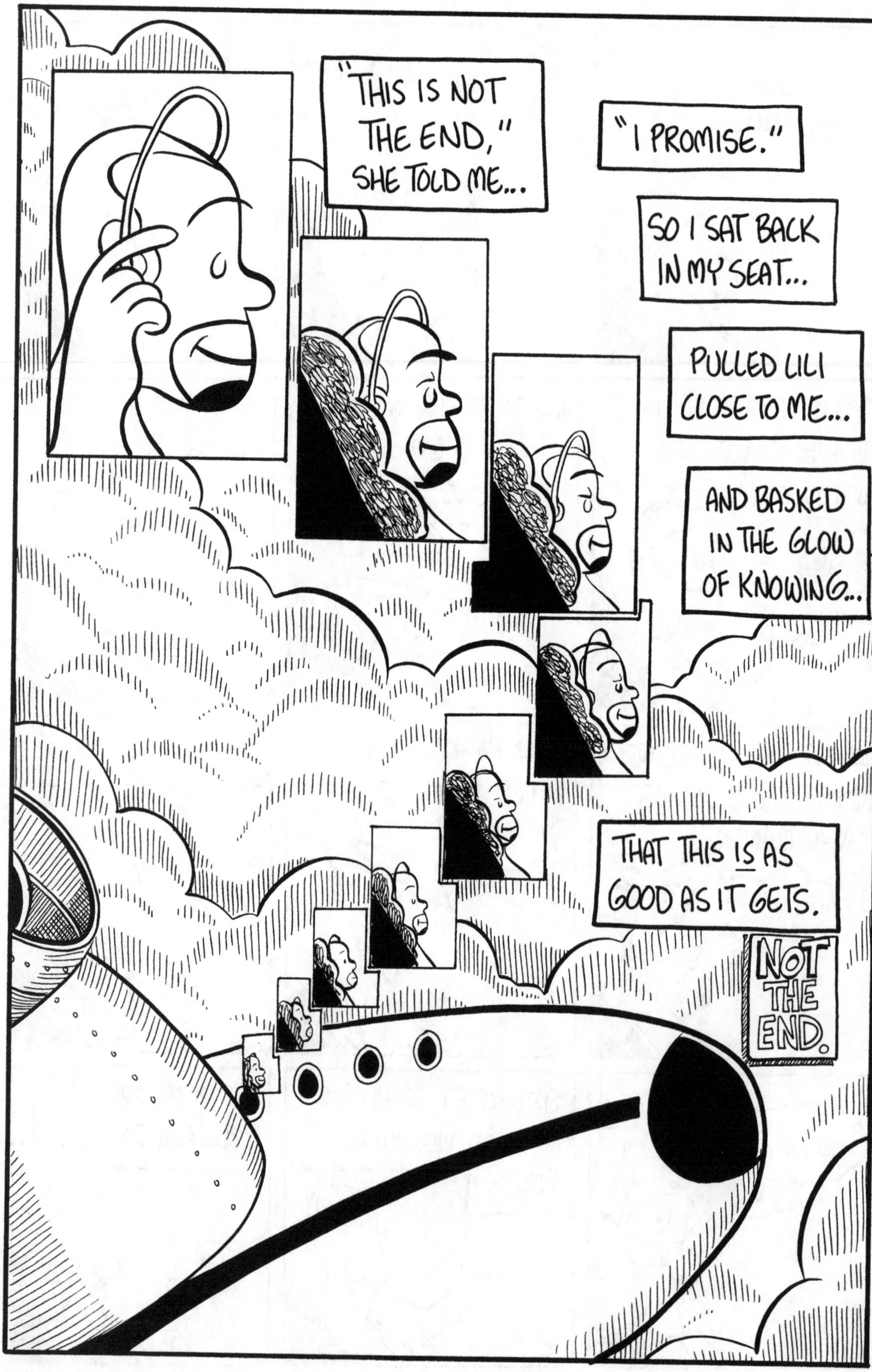

"THIS IS NOT THE END," SHE TOLD ME...
"I PROMISE."
SO I SAT BACK IN MY SEAT...
PULLED LILI CLOSE TO ME...
AND BASKED IN THE GLOW OF KNOWING...
THAT THIS IS AS GOOD AS IT GETS.
NOT THE END.

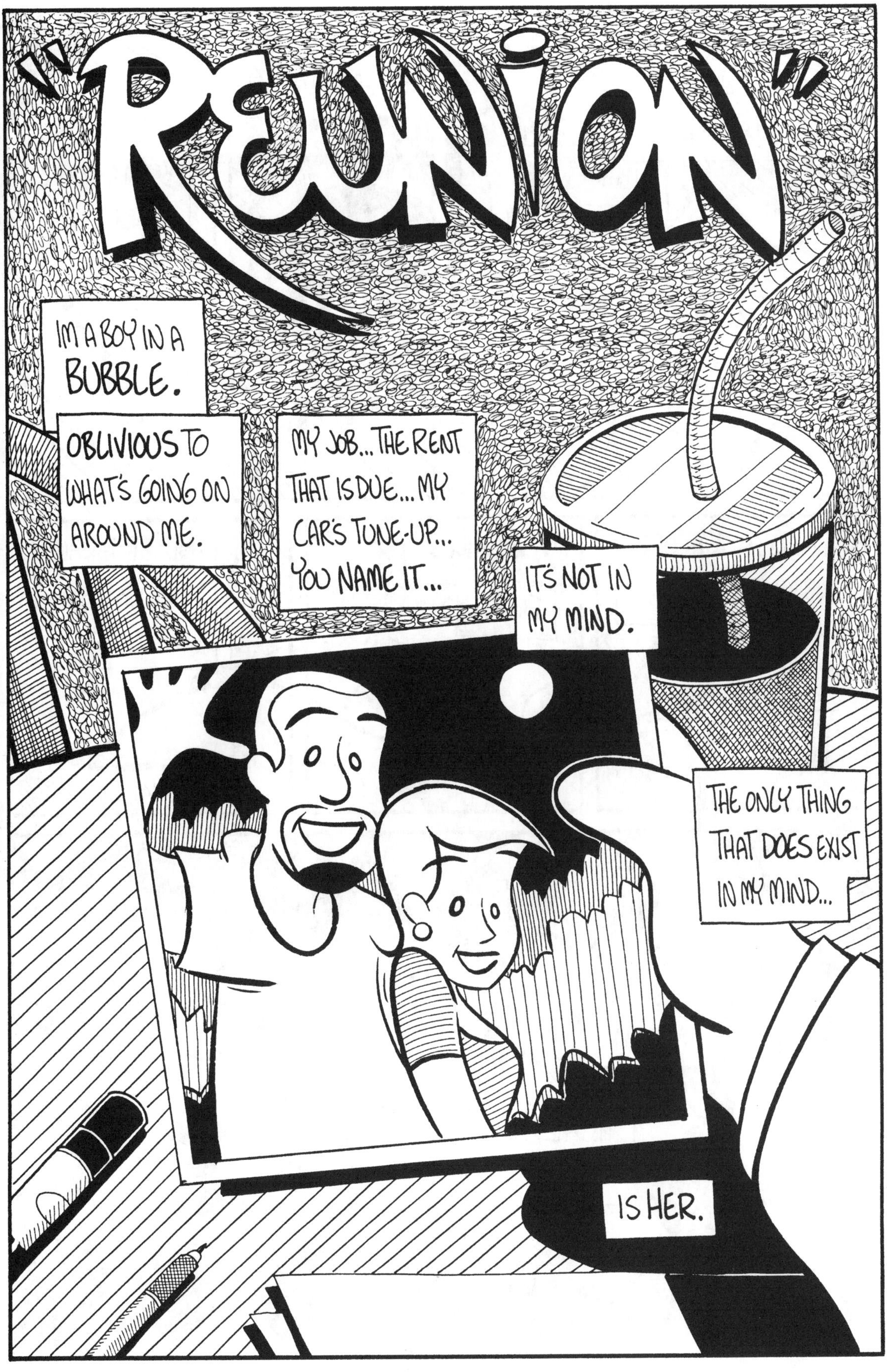
"REUNION"
IM A BOY IN A BUBBLE.
OBLIVIOUS TO WHAT'S GOING ON AROUND ME.
MY JOB... THE RENT THAT IS DUE... MY CAR'S TUNE-UP... YOU NAME IT...
IT'S NOT IN MY MIND.
THE ONLY THING THAT DOES EXIST IN MY MIND...
IS HER.

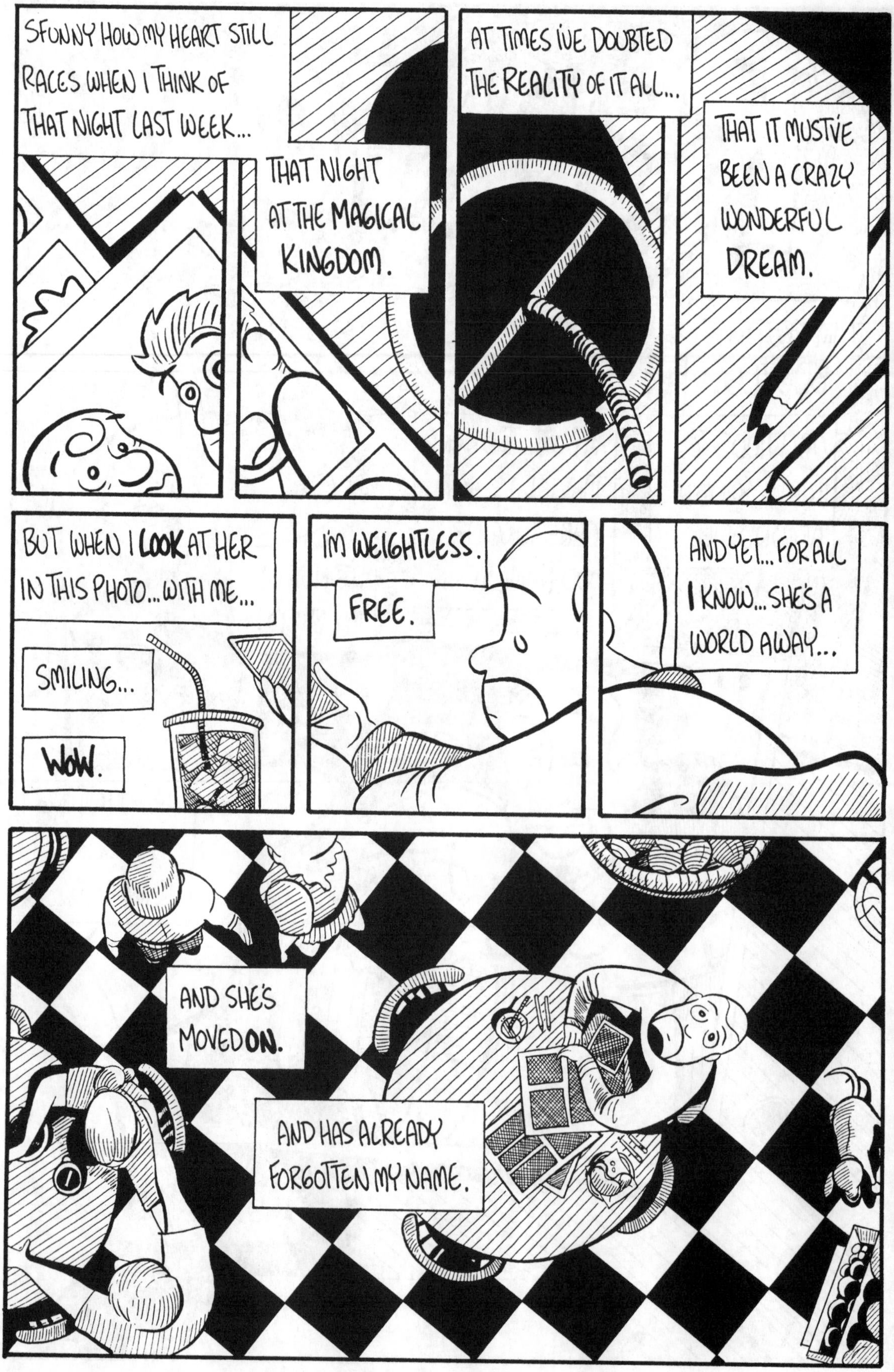
SFUNNY HOW MY HEART STILL RACES WHEN I THINK OF THAT NIGHT LAST WEEK...
THAT NIGHT AT THE MAGICAL KINGDOM.
AT TIMES IVE DOUBTED THE REALITY OF IT ALL...
THAT IT MUSTVE BEEN A CRAZY WONDERFUL DREAM.
BUT WHEN I LOOK AT HER IN THIS PHOTO... WITH ME...
SMILING...
WOW.
I'M WEIGHTLESS.
FREE.
AND YET... FOR ALL I KNOW... SHE'S A WORLD AWAY...
AND SHE'S MOVED ON.
AND HAS ALREADY FORGOTTEN MY NAME.

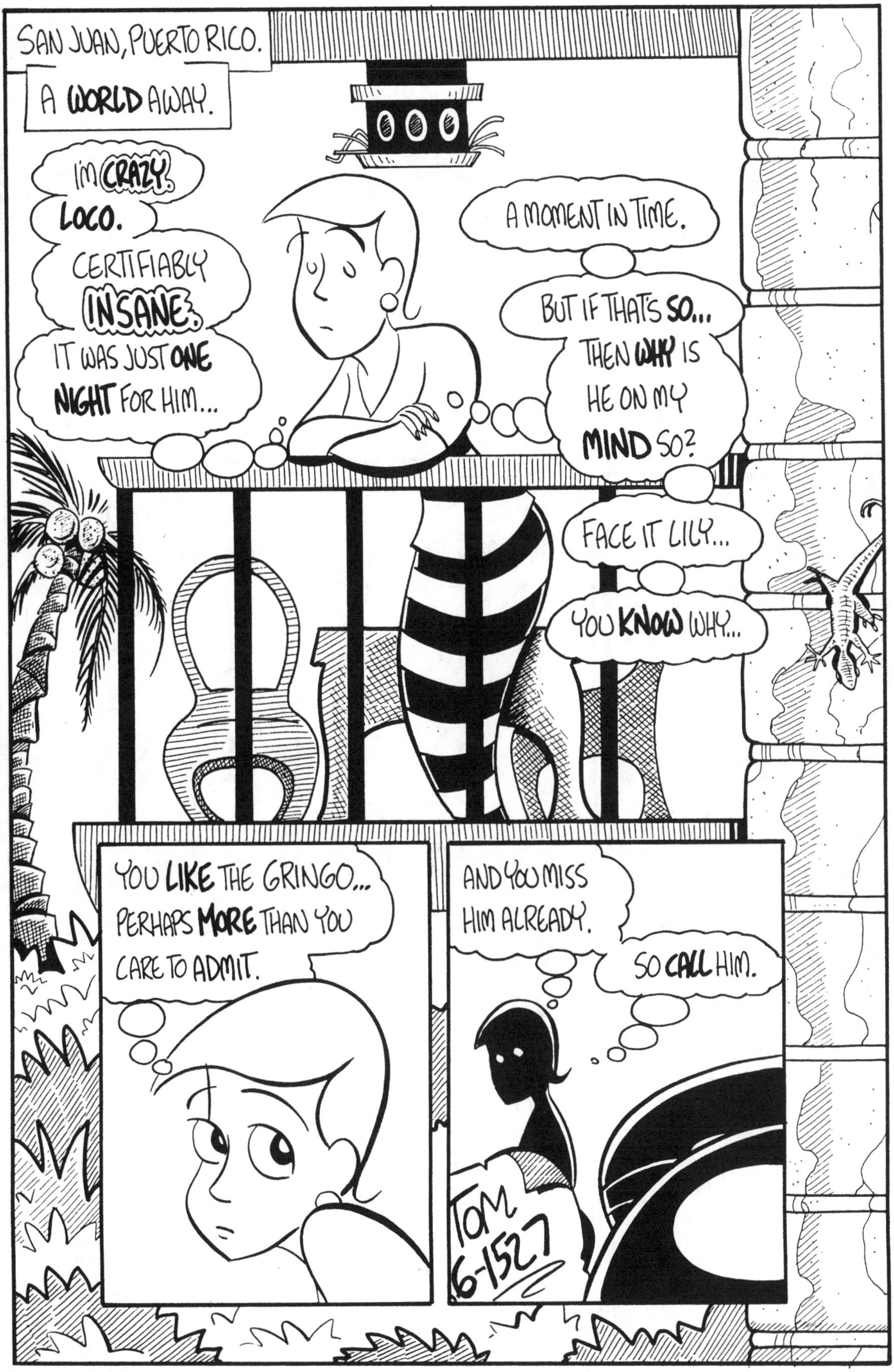
SAN JUAN, PUERTO RICO.
A WORLD AWAY.
I'M CRAZY.
LOCO.
CERTIFIABLY INSANE.
IT WAS JUST ONE NIGHT FOR HIM...
A MOMENT IN TIME.
BUT IF THAT'S SO... THEN WHY IS HE ON MY MIND SO?
FACE IT LILY...
YOU KNOW WHY...
YOU LIKE THE GRINGO... PERHAPS MORE THAN YOU CARE TO ADMIT.
AND YOU MISS HIM ALREADY.
SO CALL HIM.
TOM 6-1527

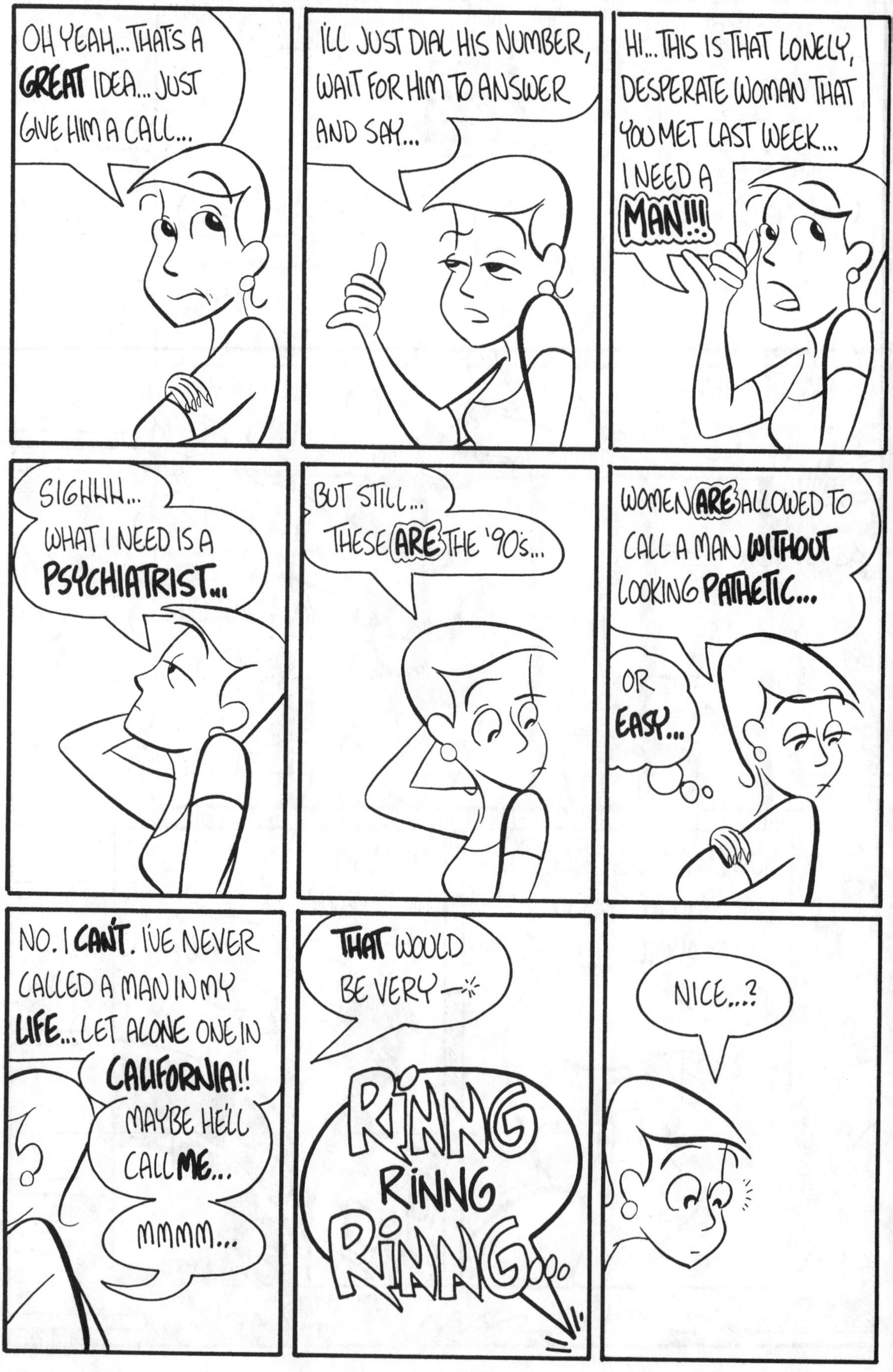
OH YEAH... THAT'S A GREAT IDEA... JUST GIVE HIM A CALL...
I'LL JUST DIAL HIS NUMBER, WAIT FOR HIM TO ANSWER AND SAY...
HI... THIS IS THAT LONELY, DESPERATE WOMAN THAT YOU MET LAST WEEK... I NEED A MAN!!!
SIGHHH... WHAT I NEED IS A PSYCHIATRIST...
BUT STILL... THESE ARE THE '90's...
WOMEN ARE ALLOWED TO CALL A MAN WITHOUT LOOKING PATHETIC...
OR EASY...
NO. I CAN'T. I'VE NEVER CALLED A MAN IN MY LIFE... LET ALONE ONE IN CALIFORNIA!!
MAYBE HE'LL CALL ME...
MMMM...
THAT WOULD BE VERY—
RINNG RINNG RINNG...
NICE...?

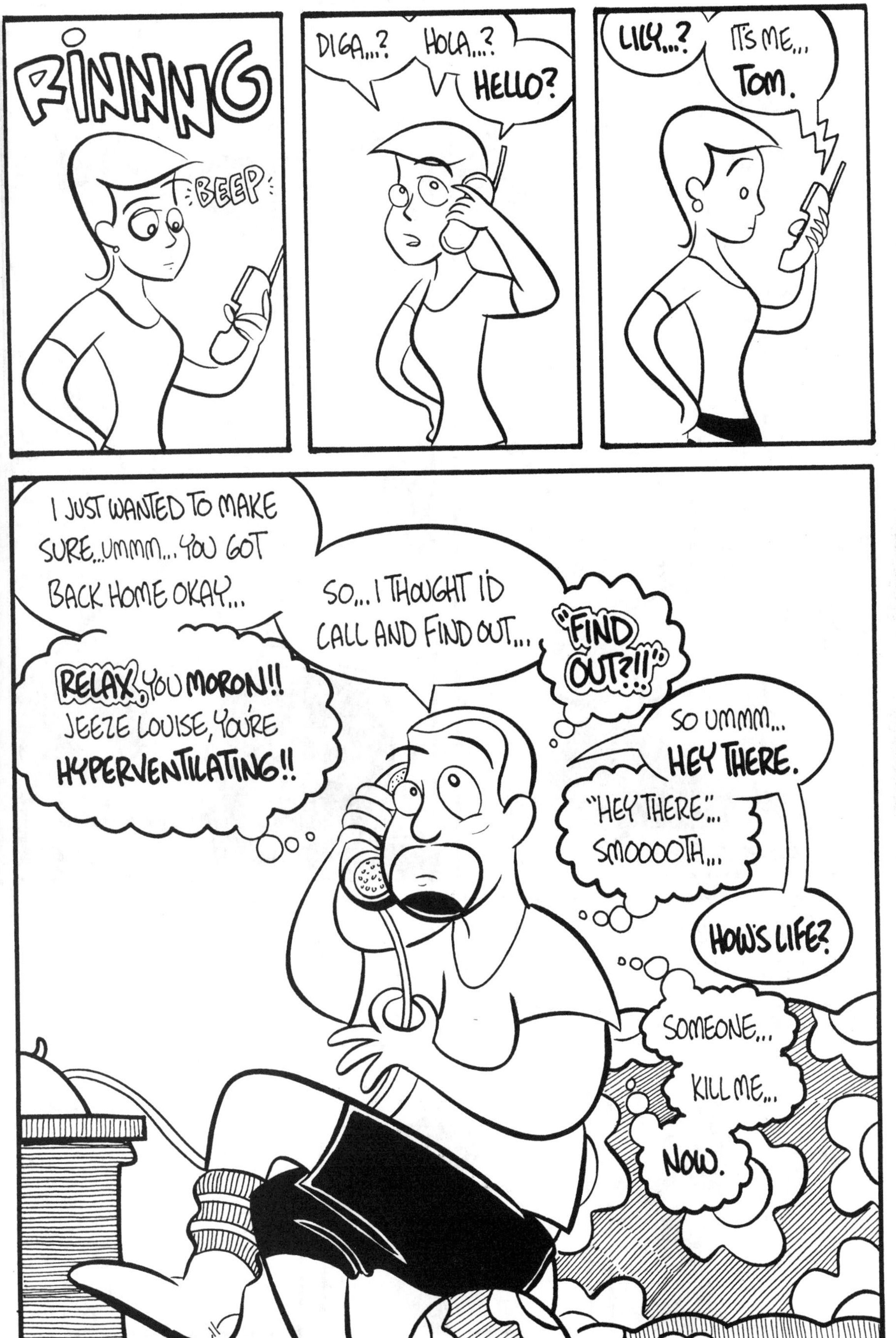

RINNNG
BEEP
DIGA...?
HOLA...?
HELLO?
LILY...?
IT'S ME...
TOM.
I JUST WANTED TO MAKE SURE...UMMM... YOU GOT BACK HOME OKAY...
RELAX, YOU MORON!! JEEZE LOUISE, YOU'RE HYPERVENTILATING!!
SO... I THOUGHT I'D CALL AND FIND OUT...
"FIND OUT?!!"
SO UMMM... HEY THERE.
"HEY THERE"... SMOOOOTH...
HOW'S LIFE?
SOMEONE...
KILL ME...
NOW.

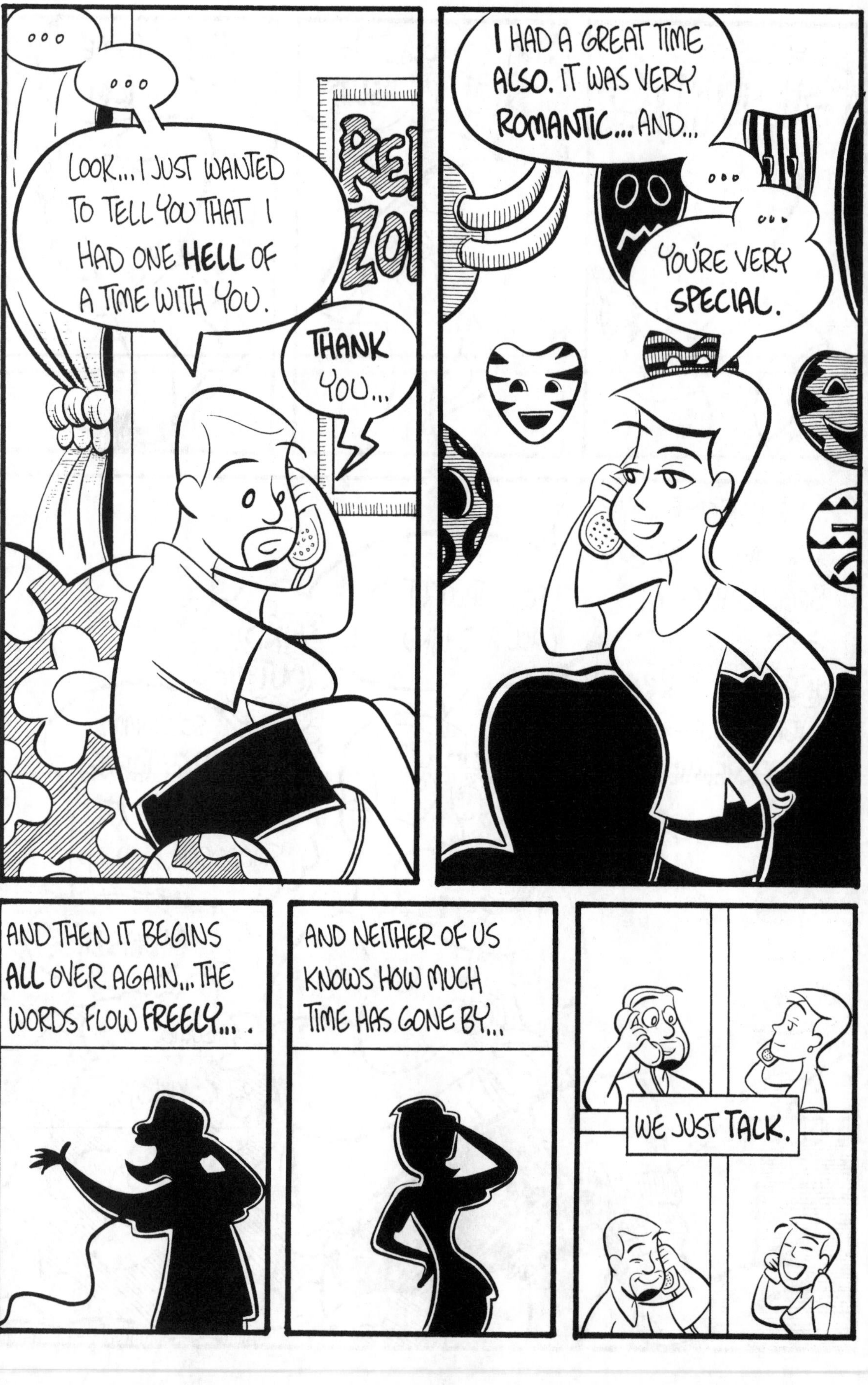

...
...
LOOK... I JUST WANTED TO TELL YOU THAT I HAD ONE HELL OF A TIME WITH YOU.
THANK YOU...
I HAD A GREAT TIME ALSO. IT WAS VERY ROMANTIC... AND...
...
...
YOU'RE VERY SPECIAL.
AND THEN IT BEGINS ALL OVER AGAIN... THE WORDS FLOW FREELY... .
AND NEITHER OF US KNOWS HOW MUCH TIME HAS GONE BY...
WE JUST TALK.

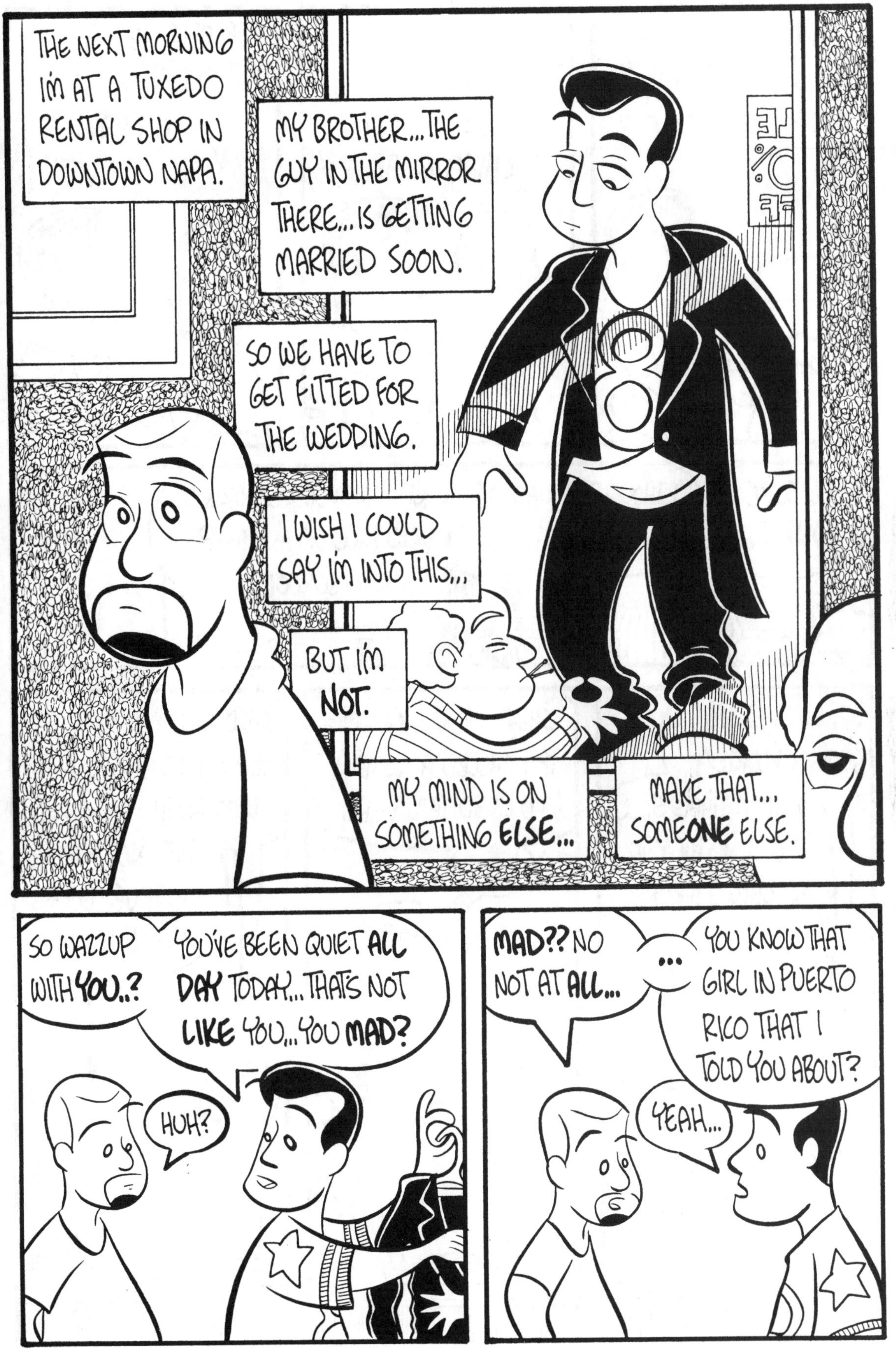
THE NEXT MORNING I'M AT A TUXEDO RENTAL SHOP IN DOWNTOWN NAPA.
MY BROTHER... THE GUY IN THE MIRROR THERE... IS GETTING MARRIED SOON.
SO WE HAVE TO GET FITTED FOR THE WEDDING.
I WISH I COULD SAY I'M INTO THIS...
BUT I'M NOT.
MY MIND IS ON SOMETHING ELSE...
MAKE THAT... SOMEONE ELSE.
SO WAZZUP WITH YOU..?
YOU'VE BEEN QUIET ALL DAY TODAY... THAT'S NOT LIKE YOU... YOU MAD?
HUH?
MAD?? NO NOT AT ALL...
...
YOU KNOW THAT GIRL IN PUERTO RICO THAT I TOLD YOU ABOUT?
YEAH...

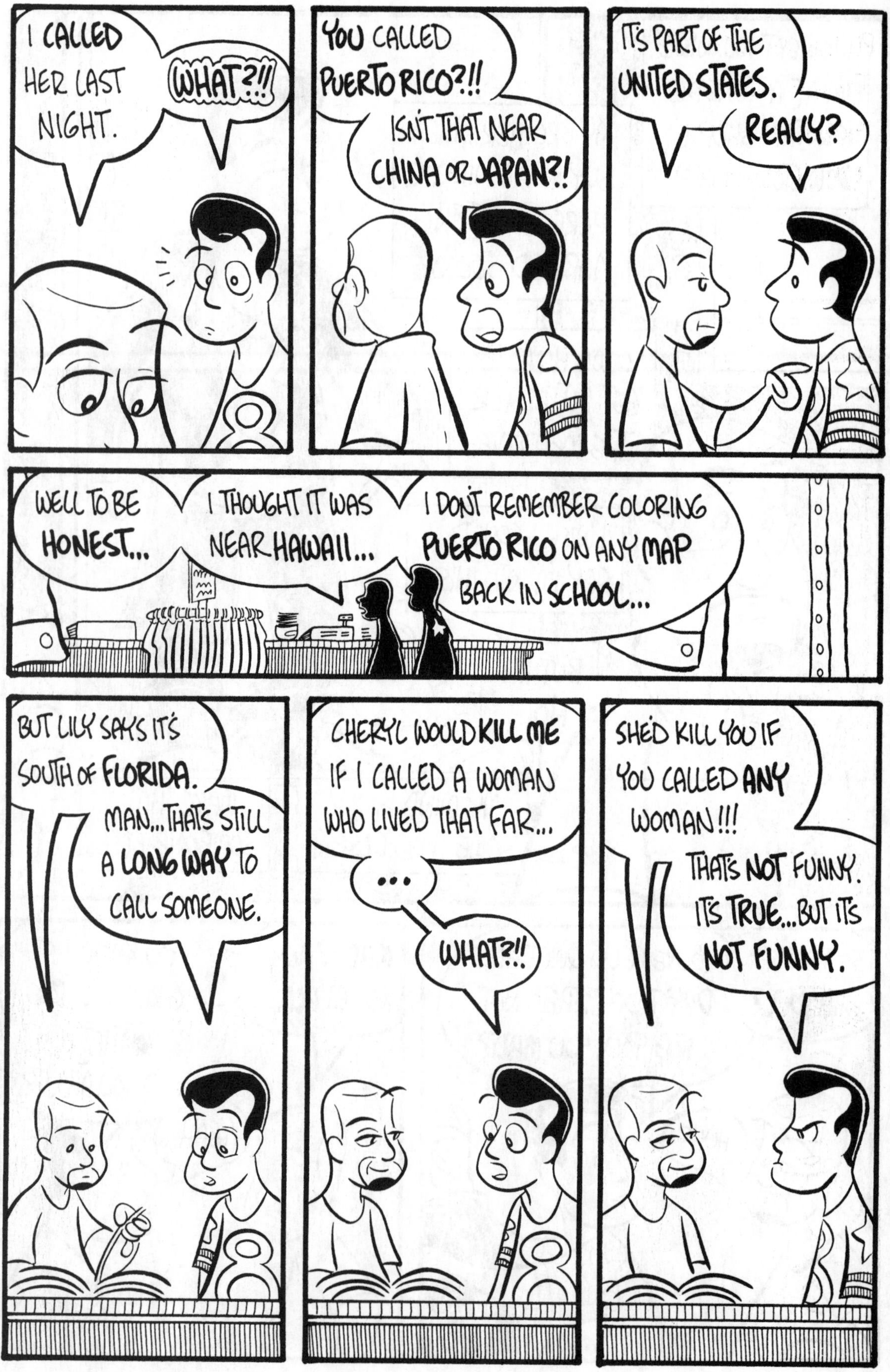
I CALLED HER LAST NIGHT.
WHAT?!!
YOU CALLED PUERTO RICO?!!
ISN'T THAT NEAR CHINA OR JAPAN?!
IT'S PART OF THE UNITED STATES.
REALLY?
WELL TO BE HONEST...
I THOUGHT IT WAS NEAR HAWAII...
I DON'T REMEMBER COLORING PUERTO RICO ON ANY MAP BACK IN SCHOOL...
BUT LILY SAYS IT'S SOUTH OF FLORIDA.
MAN... THAT'S STILL A LONG WAY TO CALL SOMEONE.
CHERYL WOULD KILL ME IF I CALLED A WOMAN WHO LIVED THAT FAR...
...
WHAT?!!
SHE'D KILL YOU IF YOU CALLED ANY WOMAN!!!
THAT'S NOT FUNNY. IT'S TRUE... BUT IT'S NOT FUNNY.

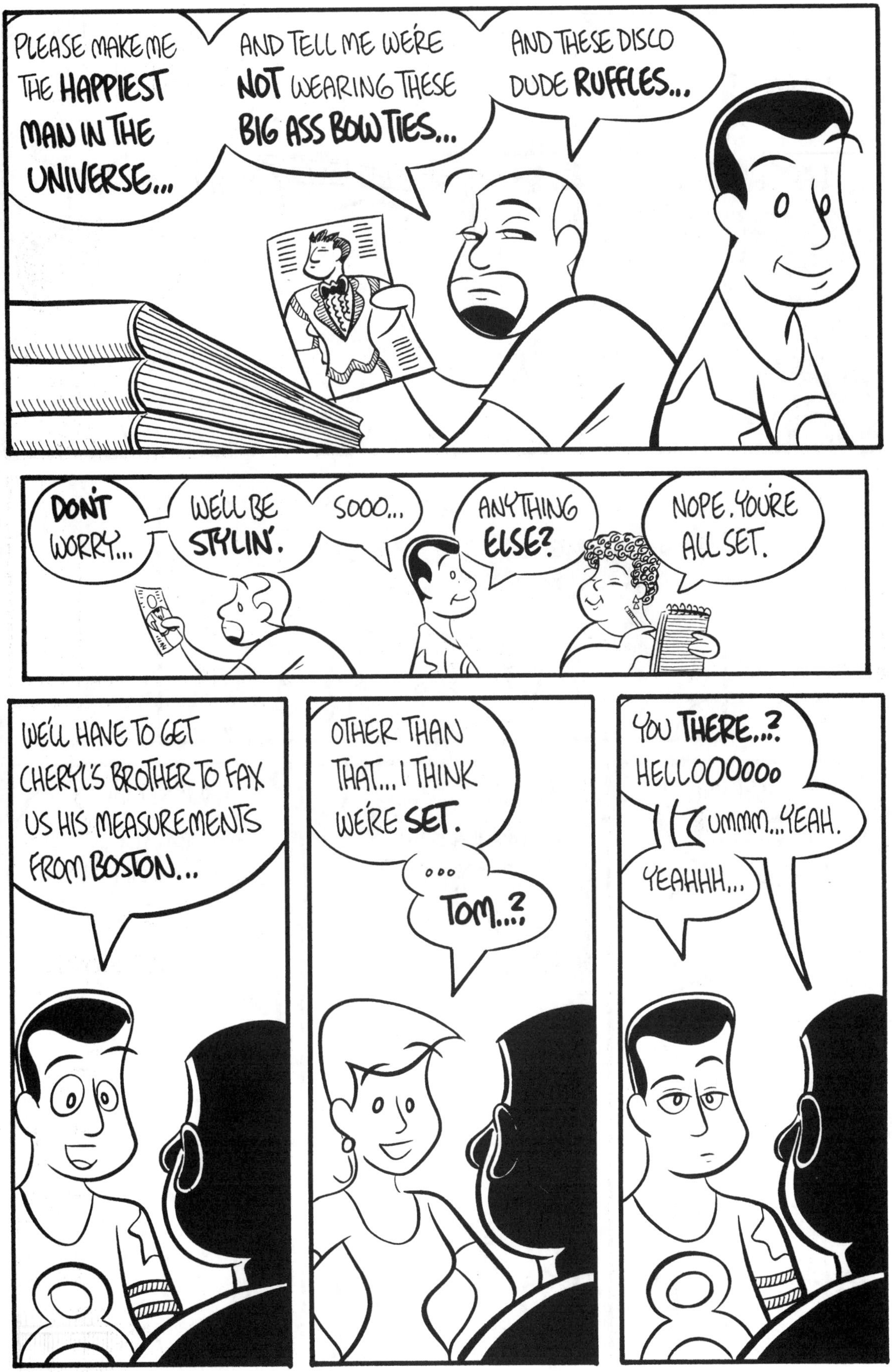
PLEASE MAKE ME THE HAPPIEST MAN IN THE UNIVERSE...
AND TELL ME WE'RE NOT WEARING THESE BIG ASS BOW TIES...
AND THESE DISCO DUDE RUFFLES...
DON'T WORRY...
WE'LL BE STYLIN'.
SOOO...
ANYTHING ELSE?
NOPE. YOU'RE ALL SET.
WE'LL HAVE TO GET CHERYL'S BROTHER TO FAX US HIS MEASUREMENTS FROM BOSTON...
OTHER THAN THAT... I THINK WE'RE SET.
...
TOM...?
YOU THERE...?
HELLOOOOOO
UMMM... YEAH.
YEAHHH...

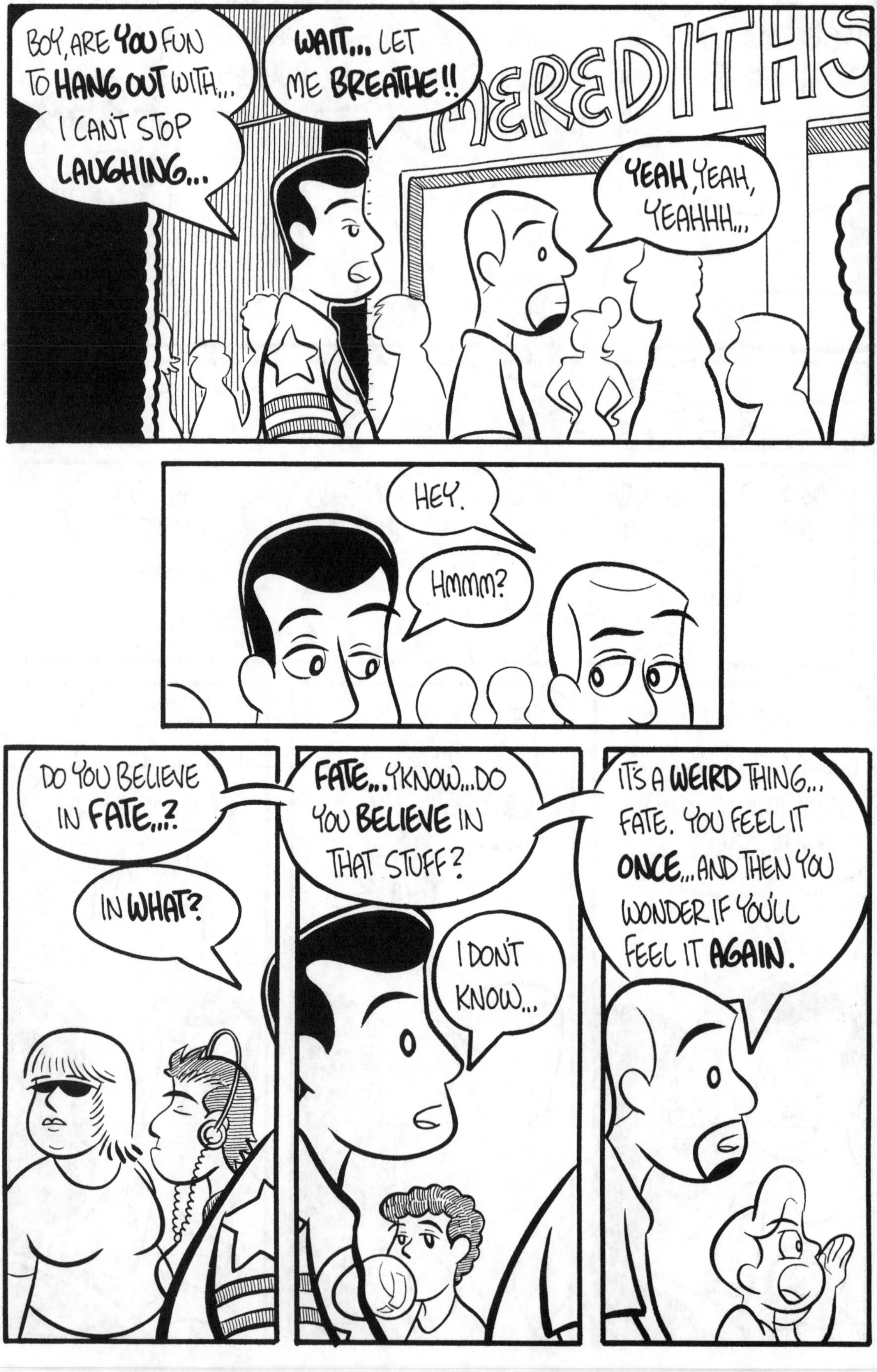
MEREDITHS
BOY, ARE YOU FUN TO HANG OUT WITH... I CAN'T STOP LAUGHING...
WAIT... LET ME BREATHE!!
YEAH, YEAH, YEAHHH...
HEY.
Hmmm?
DO YOU BELIEVE IN FATE...?
IN WHAT?
FATE... Y'KNOW... DO YOU BELIEVE IN THAT STUFF?
I DON'T KNOW...
IT'S A WEIRD THING... FATE. YOU FEEL IT ONCE... AND THEN YOU WONDER IF YOU'LL FEEL IT AGAIN.

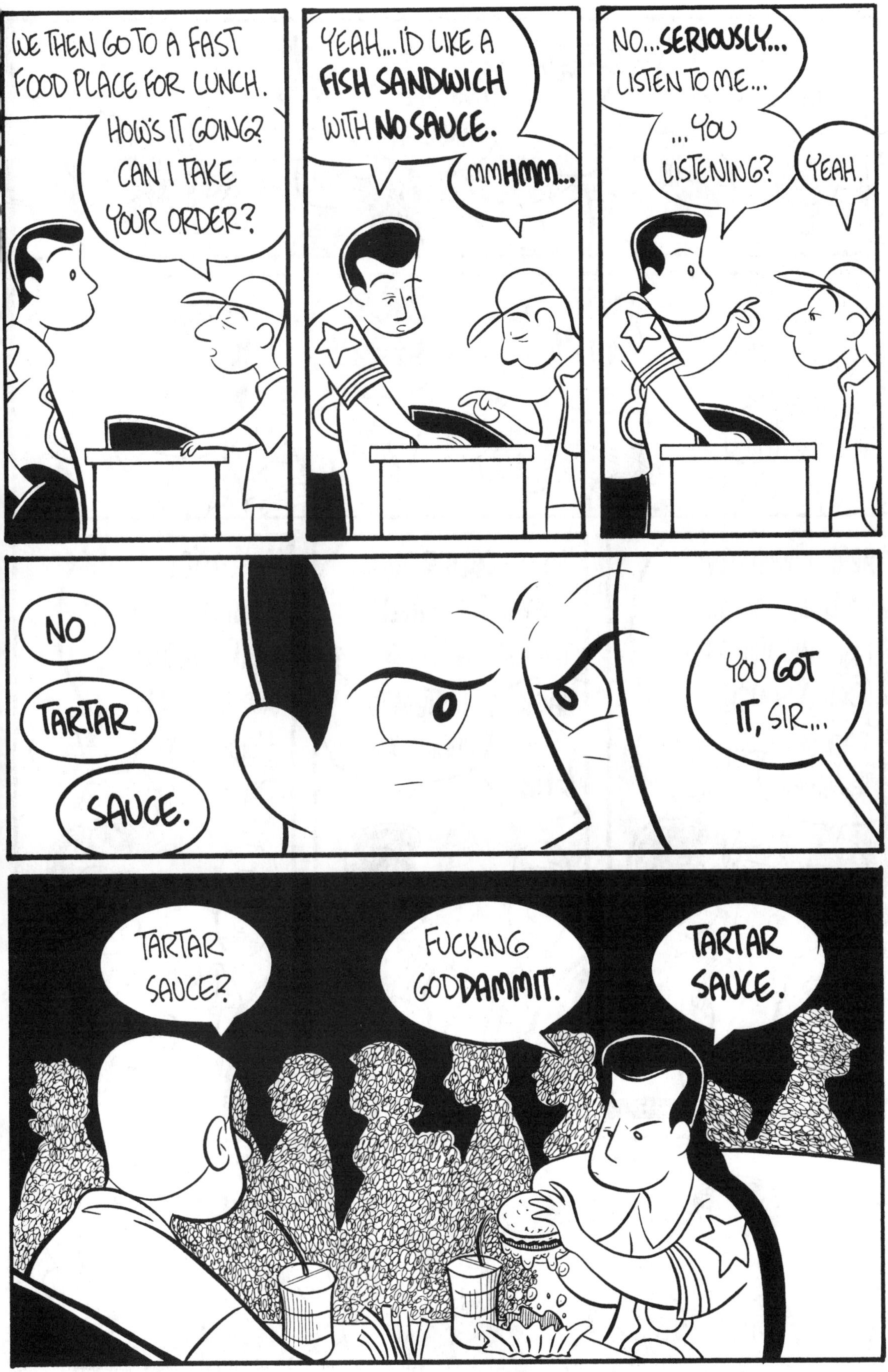
WE THEN GO TO A FAST FOOD PLACE FOR LUNCH.
HOW'S IT GOING? CAN I TAKE YOUR ORDER?
YEAH...I'D LIKE A FISH SANDWICH WITH NO SAUCE.
MMHMM...
NO...SERIOUSLY... LISTEN TO ME...
...YOU LISTENING?
YEAH.
NO
TARTAR
SAUCE.
YOU GOT IT, SIR...
TARTAR SAUCE?
FUCKING GODDAMMIT.
TARTAR SAUCE.

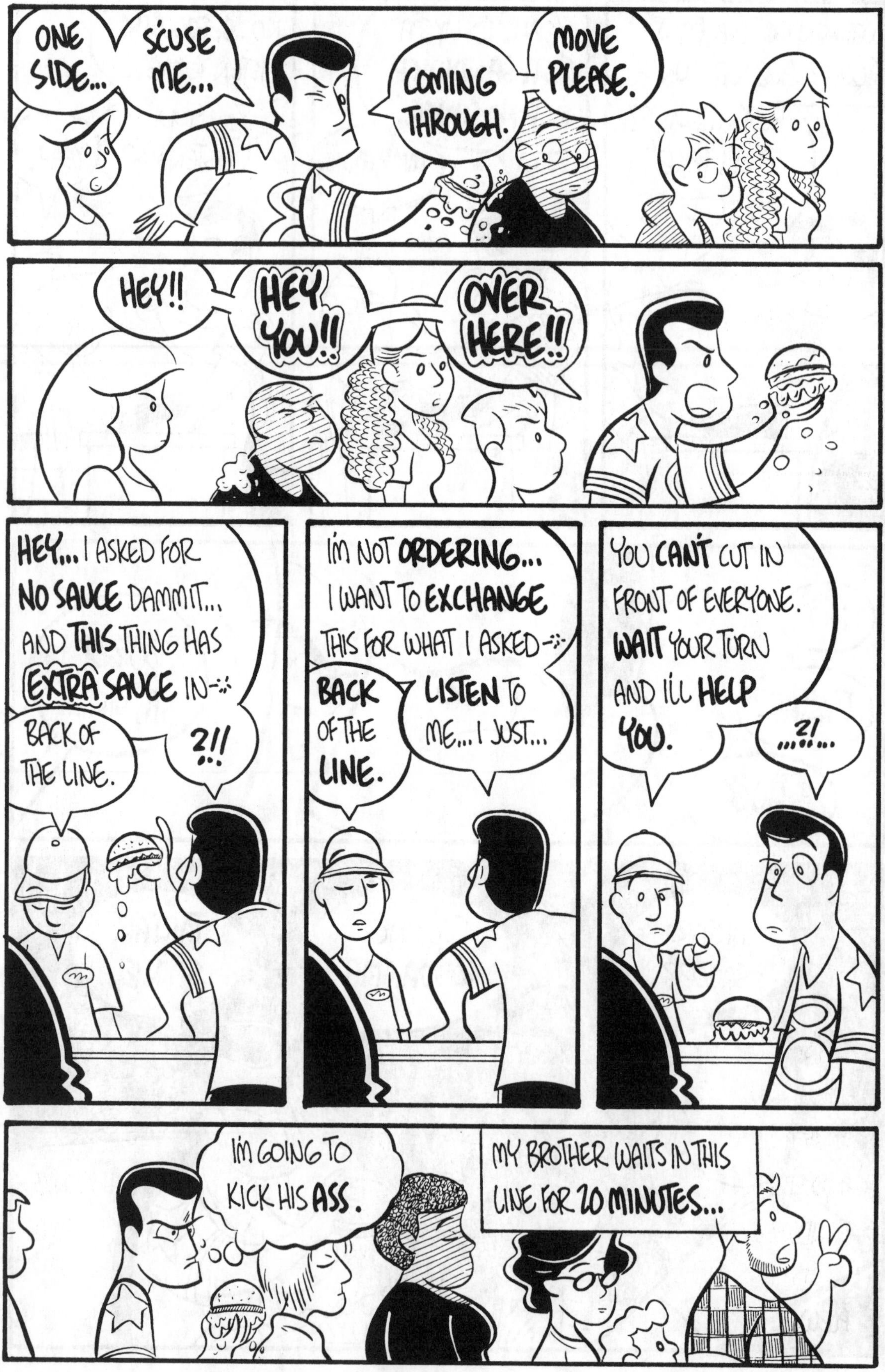
ONE SIDE...
S'CUSE ME...
COMING THROUGH.
MOVE PLEASE.
HEY!!
HEY YOU!!
OVER HERE!!
HEY... I ASKED FOR NO SAUCE DAMMIT... AND THIS THING HAS EXTRA SAUCE IN-
BACK OF THE LINE.
?!!
I'M NOT ORDERING... I WANT TO EXCHANGE THIS FOR WHAT I ASKED-
BACK OF THE LINE.
LISTEN TO ME... I JUST...
YOU CAN'T CUT IN FRONT OF EVERYONE. WAIT YOUR TURN AND I'LL HELP YOU.
...?!...
I'M GOING TO KICK HIS ASS.
MY BROTHER WAITS IN THIS LINE FOR 20 MINUTES...

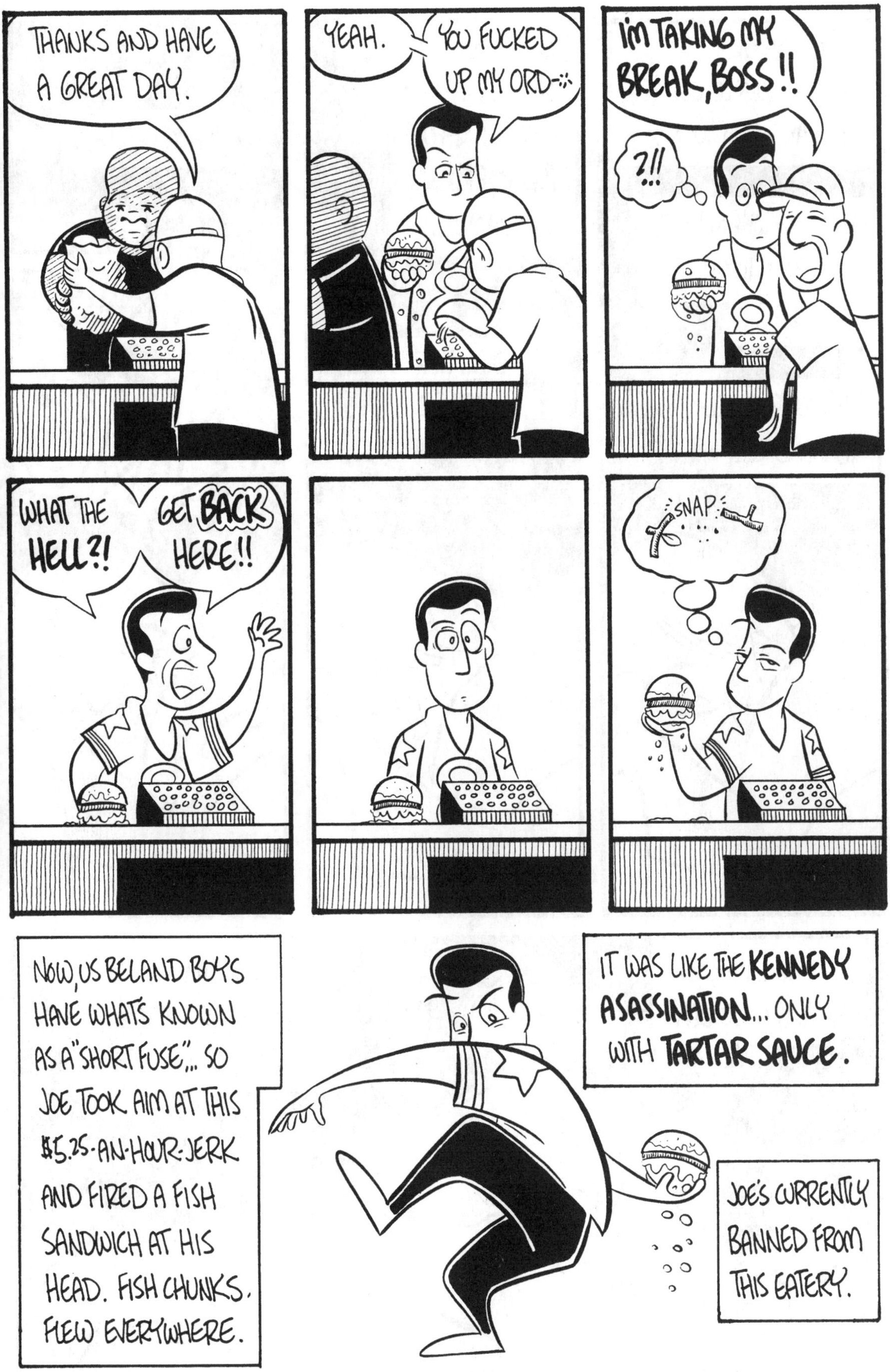
THANKS AND HAVE A GREAT DAY.
YEAH.
YOU FUCKED UP MY ORD-
I'M TAKING MY BREAK, BOSS!!
?!!...
WHAT THE HELL?!
GET BACK HERE!!
SNAP
NOW, US BELAND BOYS HAVE WHAT'S KNOWN AS A "SHORT FUSE"... SO JOE TOOK AIM AT THIS $5.25-AN-HOUR-JERK AND FIRED A FISH SANDWICH AT HIS HEAD. FISH CHUNKS FLEW EVERYWHERE.
IT WAS LIKE THE KENNEDY ASASSINATION... ONLY WITH TARTAR SAUCE.
JOE'S CURRENTLY BANNED FROM THIS EATERY.

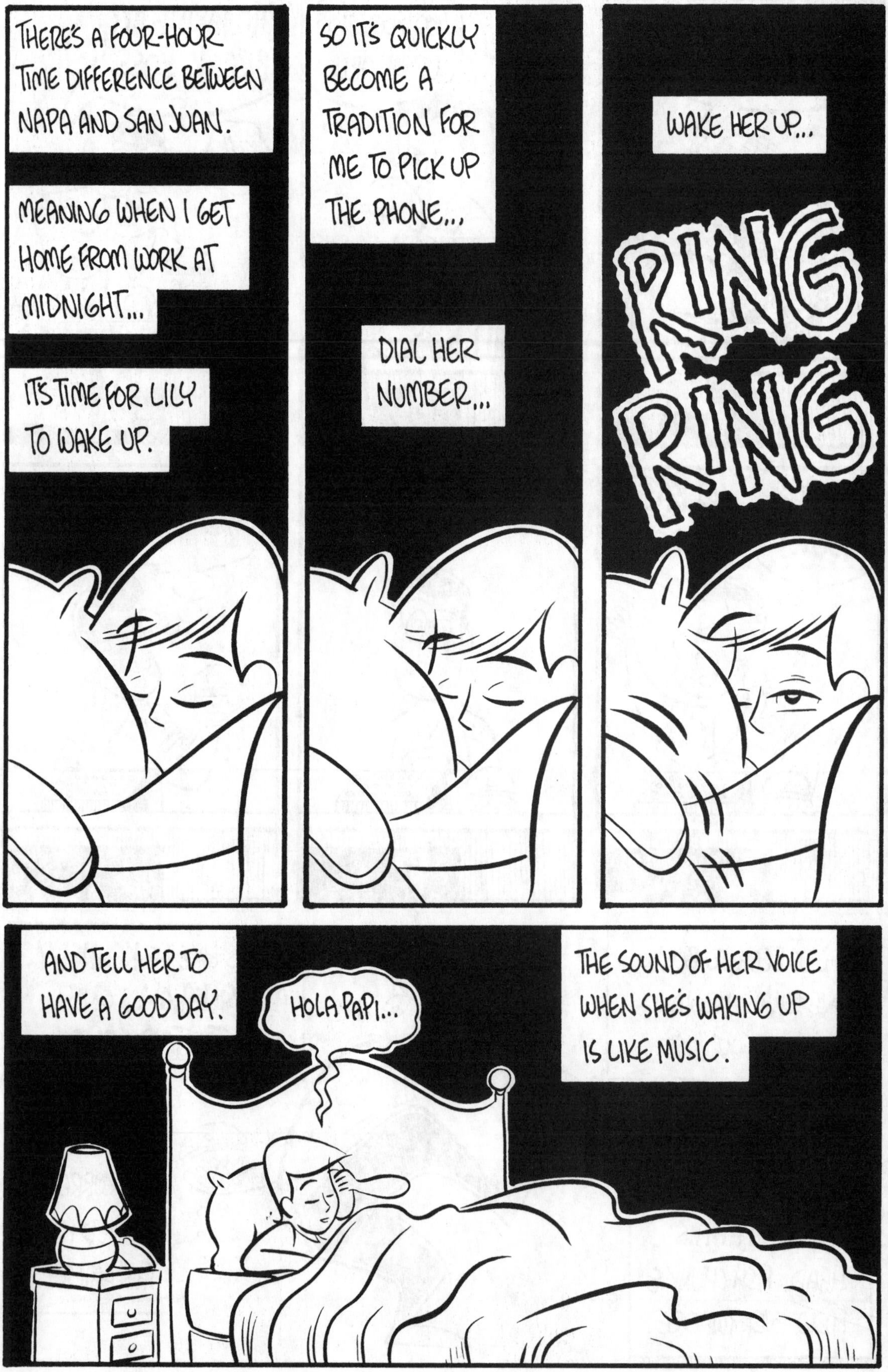
THERE'S A FOUR-HOUR TIME DIFFERENCE BETWEEN NAPA AND SAN JUAN.
MEANING WHEN I GET HOME FROM WORK AT MIDNIGHT...
IT'S TIME FOR LILY TO WAKE UP.
SO IT'S QUICKLY BECOME A TRADITION FOR ME TO PICK UP THE PHONE...
DIAL HER NUMBER...
WAKE HER UP...
RING RING
AND TELL HER TO HAVE A GOOD DAY.
HOLA PAPI...
THE SOUND OF HER VOICE WHEN SHE'S WAKING UP IS LIKE MUSIC.

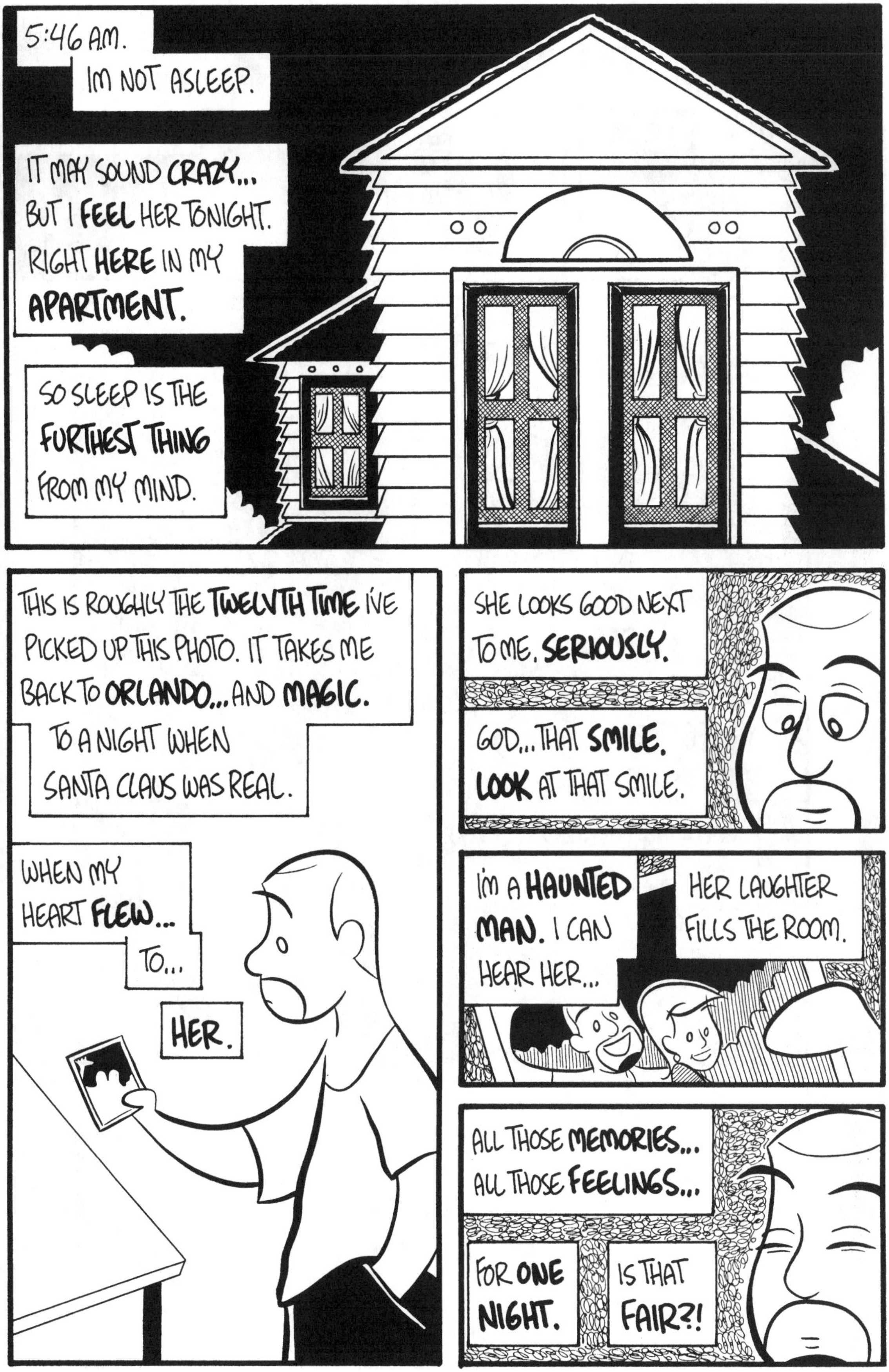
5:46 A.M.
I'M NOT ASLEEP.
IT MAY SOUND **CRAZY...** BUT I **FEEL** HER TONIGHT. RIGHT **HERE** IN MY **APARTMENT.**
SO SLEEP IS THE **FURTHEST THING** FROM MY MIND.
THIS IS ROUGHLY THE **TWELVTH TIME** I'VE PICKED UP THIS PHOTO. IT TAKES ME BACK TO **ORLANDO...** AND **MAGIC.**
TO A NIGHT WHEN SANTA CLAUS WAS REAL.
WHEN MY HEART **FLEW...**
TO...
HER.
SHE LOOKS GOOD NEXT TO ME. **SERIOUSLY.**
GOD... THAT **SMILE. LOOK** AT THAT SMILE.
I'M A **HAUNTED MAN.** I CAN HEAR HER...
HER LAUGHTER FILLS THE ROOM.
ALL THOSE **MEMORIES...** ALL THOSE **FEELINGS...**
FOR **ONE NIGHT.**
IS THAT **FAIR?!**

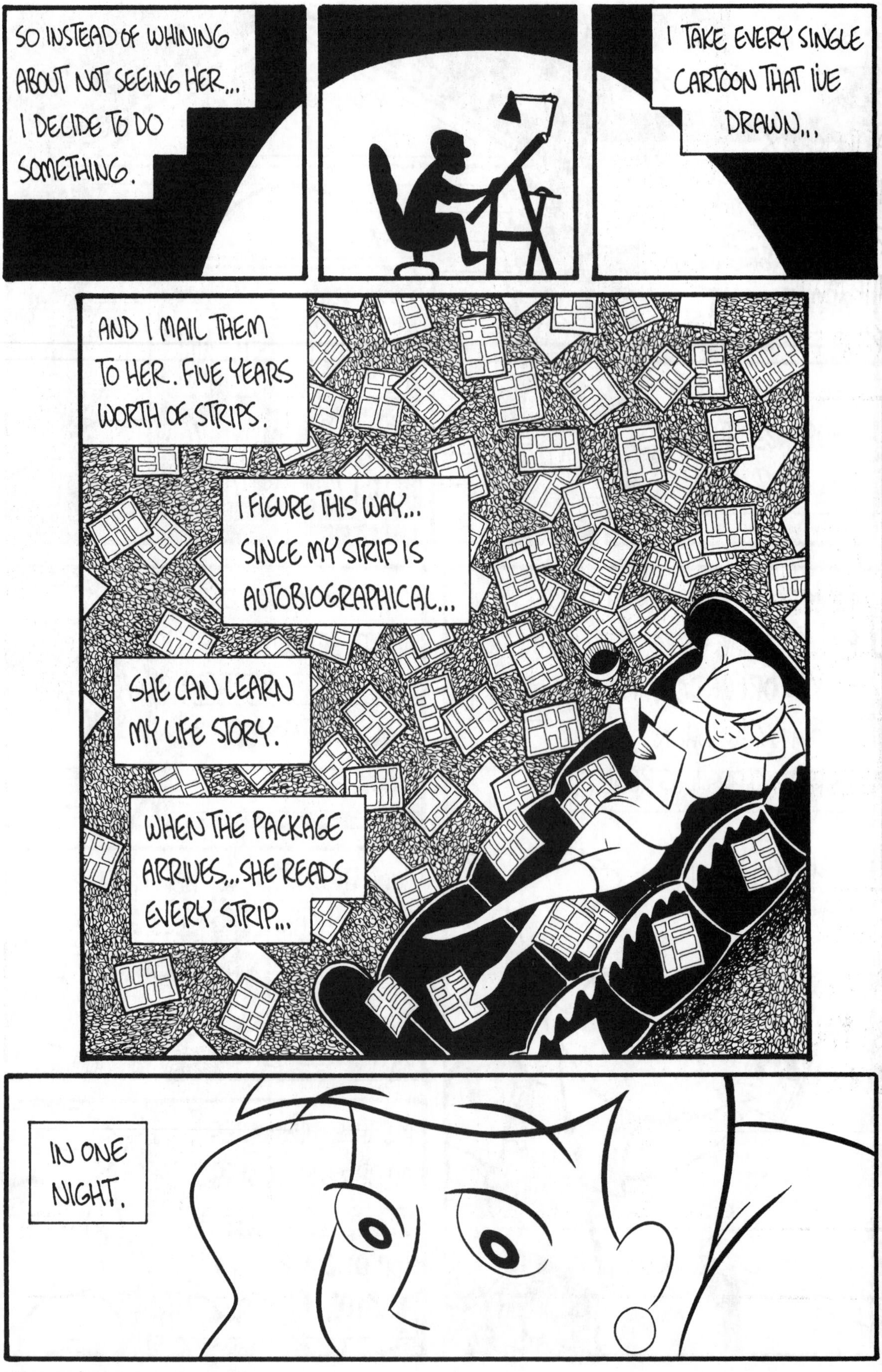
SO INSTEAD OF WHINING ABOUT NOT SEEING HER... I DECIDE TO DO SOMETHING.
I TAKE EVERY SINGLE CARTOON THAT I'VE DRAWN...
AND I MAIL THEM TO HER. FIVE YEARS WORTH OF STRIPS.
I FIGURE THIS WAY... SINCE MY STRIP IS AUTOBIOGRAPHICAL...
SHE CAN LEARN MY LIFE STORY.
WHEN THE PACKAGE ARRIVES... SHE READS EVERY STRIP...
IN ONE NIGHT.

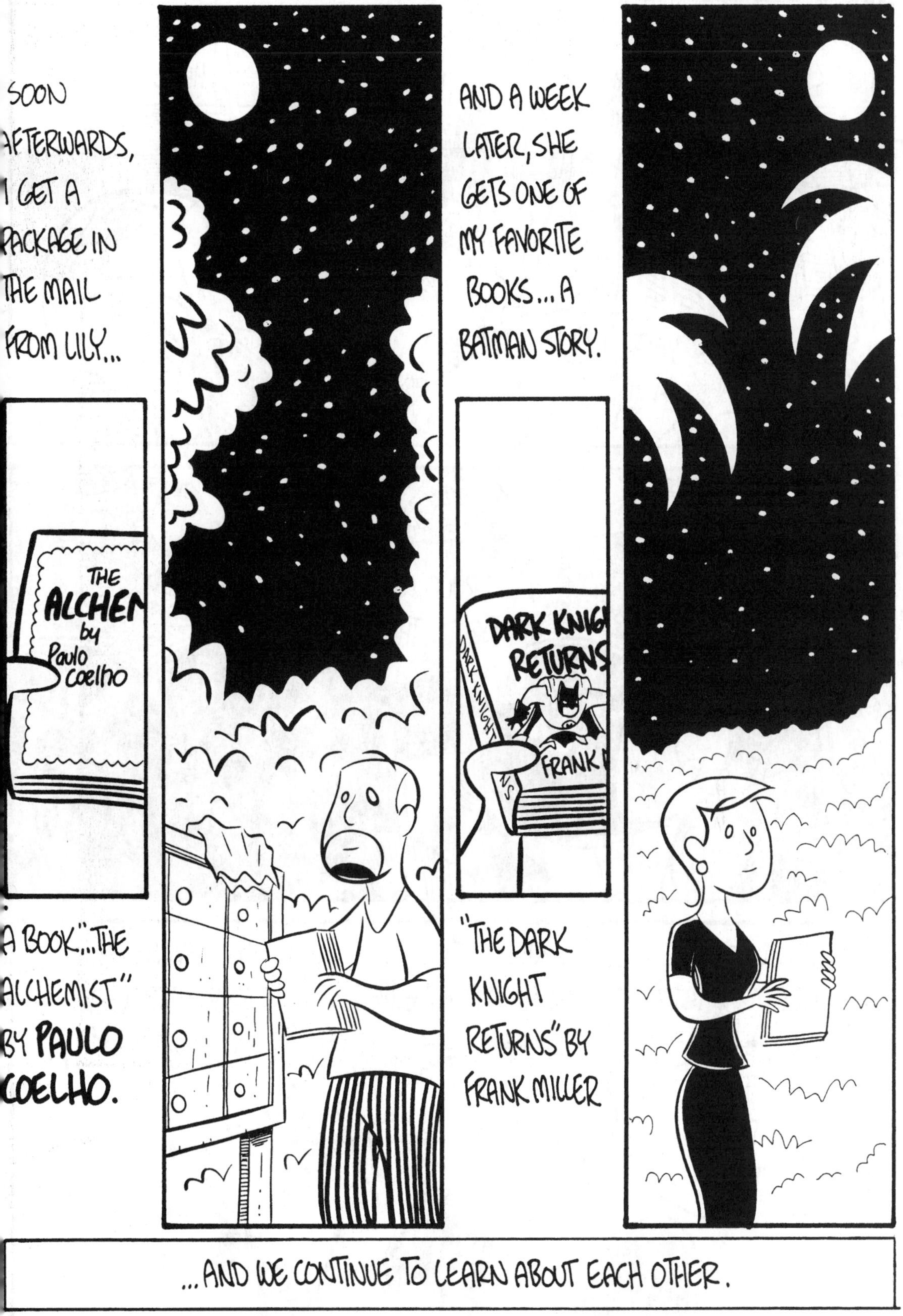

SOON AFTERWARDS, I GET A PACKAGE IN THE MAIL FROM LILY...
THE ALCHEM by Paulo coelho
A BOOK..."THE ALCHEMIST" BY PAULO COELHO.
AND A WEEK LATER, SHE GETS ONE OF MY FAVORITE BOOKS... A BATMAN STORY.
DARK KNIGH RETURNS FRANK
"THE DARK KNIGHT RETURNS" BY FRANK MILLER
...AND WE CONTINUE TO LEARN ABOUT EACH OTHER.

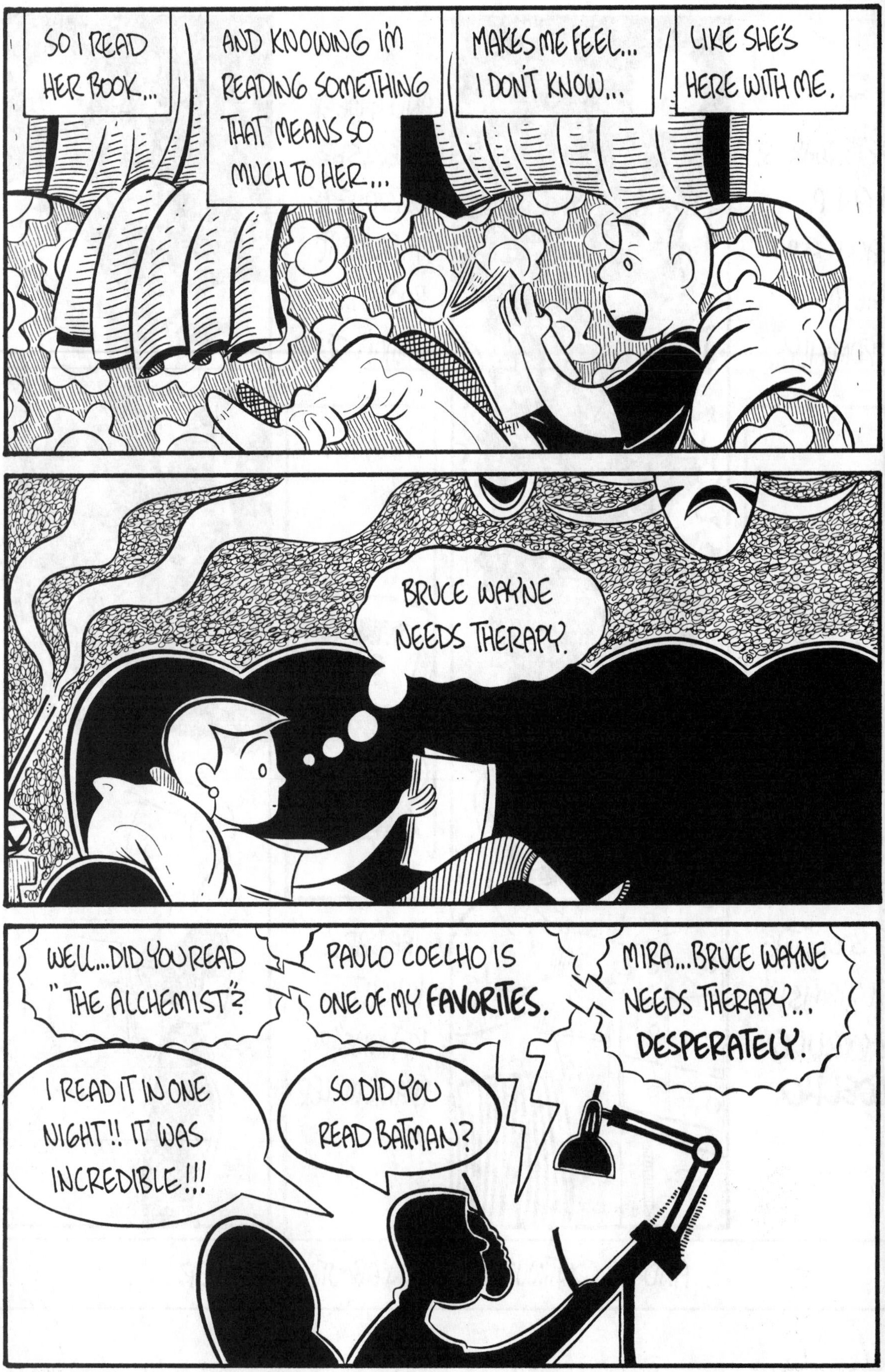
SO I READ HER BOOK...
AND KNOWING I'M READING SOMETHING THAT MEANS SO MUCH TO HER...
MAKES ME FEEL... I DON'T KNOW...
LIKE SHE'S HERE WITH ME.
BRUCE WAYNE NEEDS THERAPY.
WELL...DID YOU READ "THE ALCHEMIST"?
PAULO COELHO IS ONE OF MY FAVORITES.
MIRA...BRUCE WAYNE NEEDS THERAPY... DESPERATELY.
I READ IT IN ONE NIGHT!! IT WAS INCREDIBLE!!!
SO DID YOU READ BATMAN?

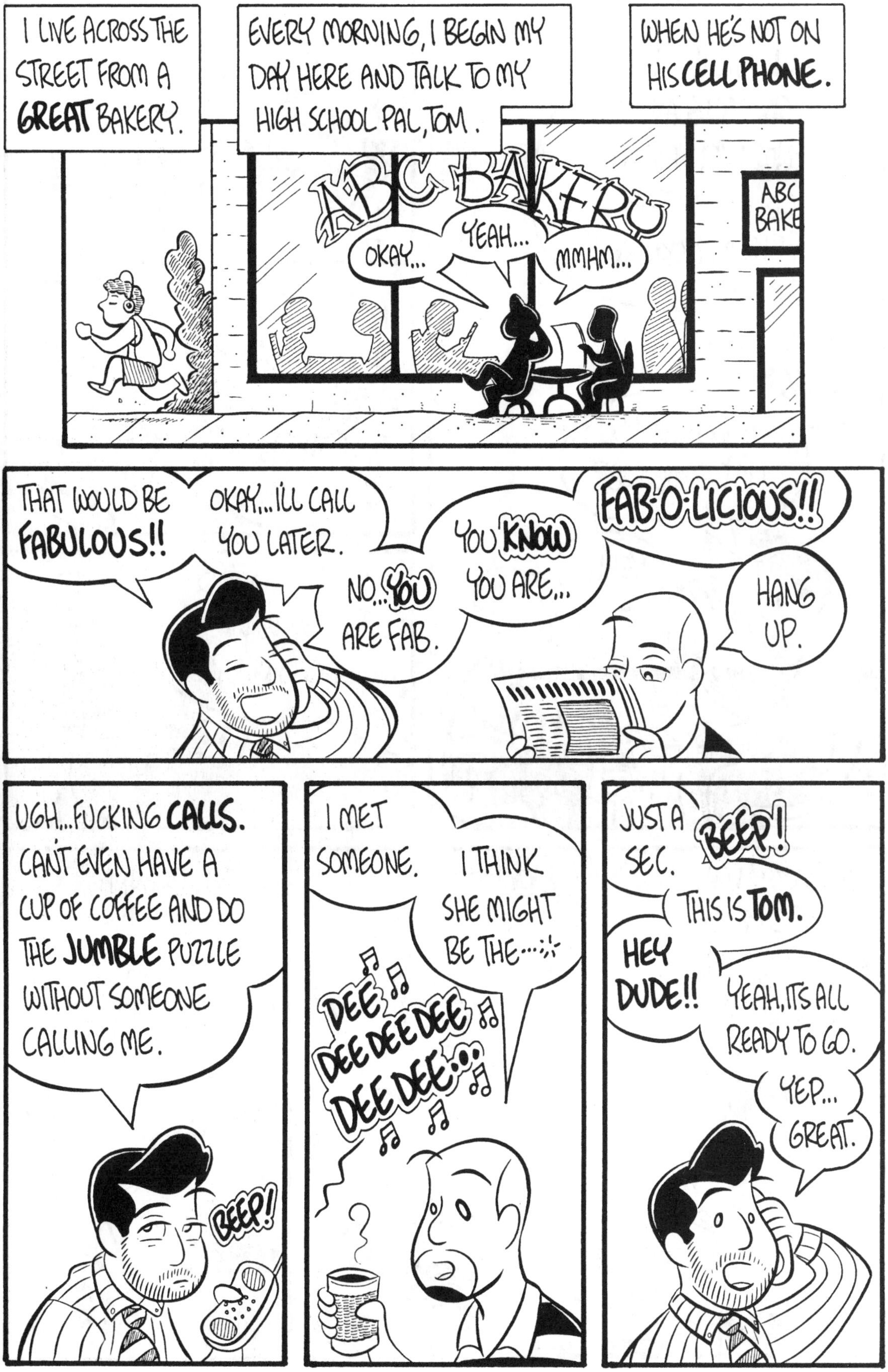
I LIVE ACROSS THE STREET FROM A GREAT BAKERY.
EVERY MORNING, I BEGIN MY DAY HERE AND TALK TO MY HIGH SCHOOL PAL, TOM.
WHEN HE'S NOT ON HIS CELL PHONE.
ABC BAKERY
ABC BAKE
OKAY...
YEAH...
MMHM...
THAT WOULD BE FABULOUS!!
OKAY... I'LL CALL YOU LATER.
NO... YOU ARE FAB.
YOU KNOW YOU ARE...
FAB-O-LICIOUS!!
HANG UP.
UGH... FUCKING CALLS. CAN'T EVEN HAVE A CUP OF COFFEE AND DO THE JUMBLE PUZZLE WITHOUT SOMEONE CALLING ME.
BEEP!
I MET SOMEONE.
I THINK SHE MIGHT BE THE...
DEE DEE DEE DEE DEE DEE...
?
JUST A SEC.
BEEP!
THIS IS TOM.
HEY DUDE!!
YEAH, ITS ALL READY TO GO.
YEP... GREAT.

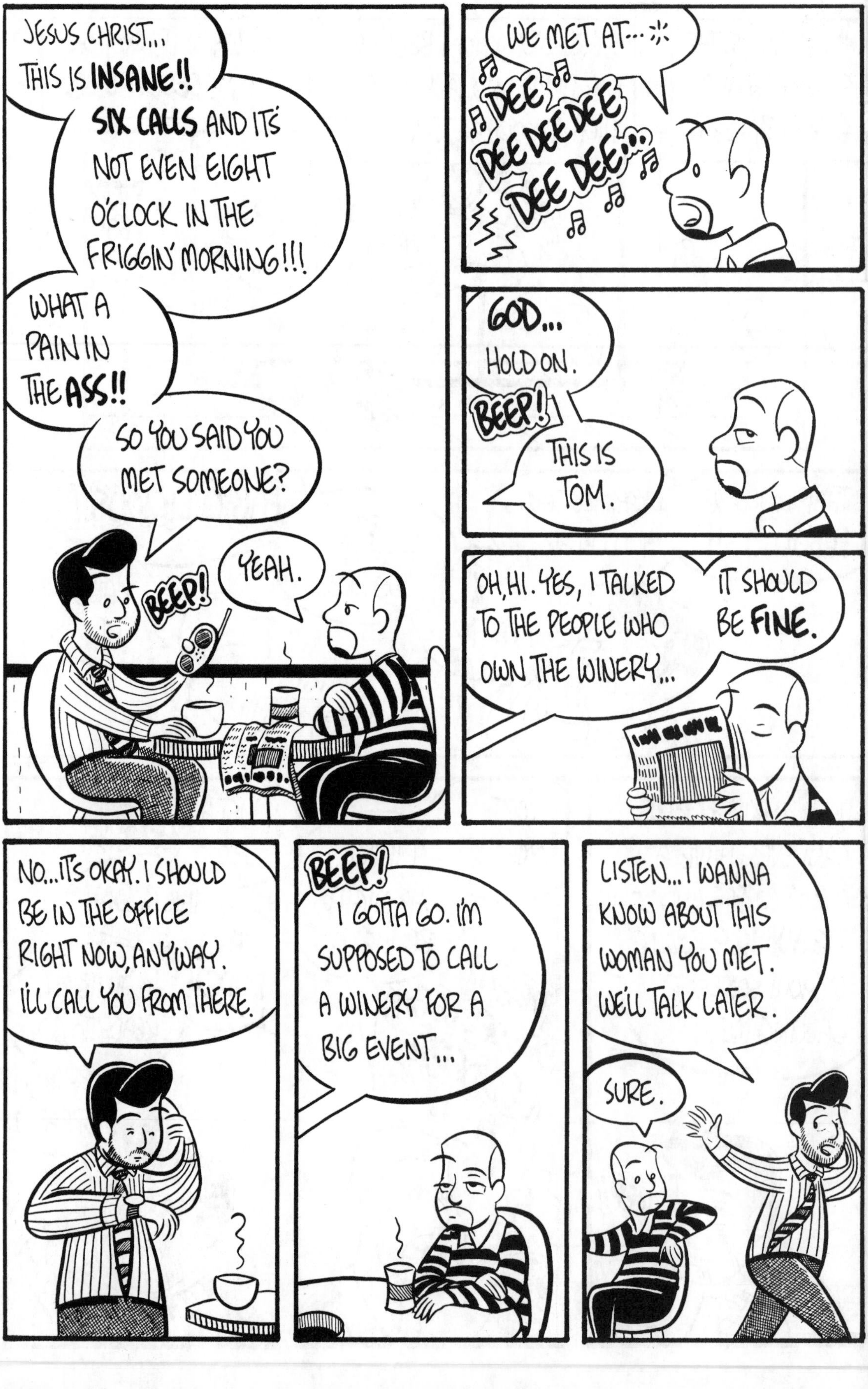
JESUS CHRIST... THIS IS INSANE!!
SIX CALLS AND IT'S NOT EVEN EIGHT O'CLOCK IN THE FRIGGIN' MORNING!!!
WHAT A PAIN IN THE ASS!!
SO YOU SAID YOU MET SOMEONE?
BEEP!
YEAH.
WE MET AT...
DEE DEE DEE DEE DEE DEE...
GOD... HOLD ON.
BEEP!
THIS IS TOM.
OH, HI. YES, I TALKED TO THE PEOPLE WHO OWN THE WINERY...
IT SHOULD BE FINE.
NO... IT'S OKAY. I SHOULD BE IN THE OFFICE RIGHT NOW, ANYWAY. I'LL CALL YOU FROM THERE.
BEEP!
I GOTTA GO. I'M SUPPOSED TO CALL A WINERY FOR A BIG EVENT...
LISTEN... I WANNA KNOW ABOUT THIS WOMAN YOU MET. WE'LL TALK LATER.
SURE.

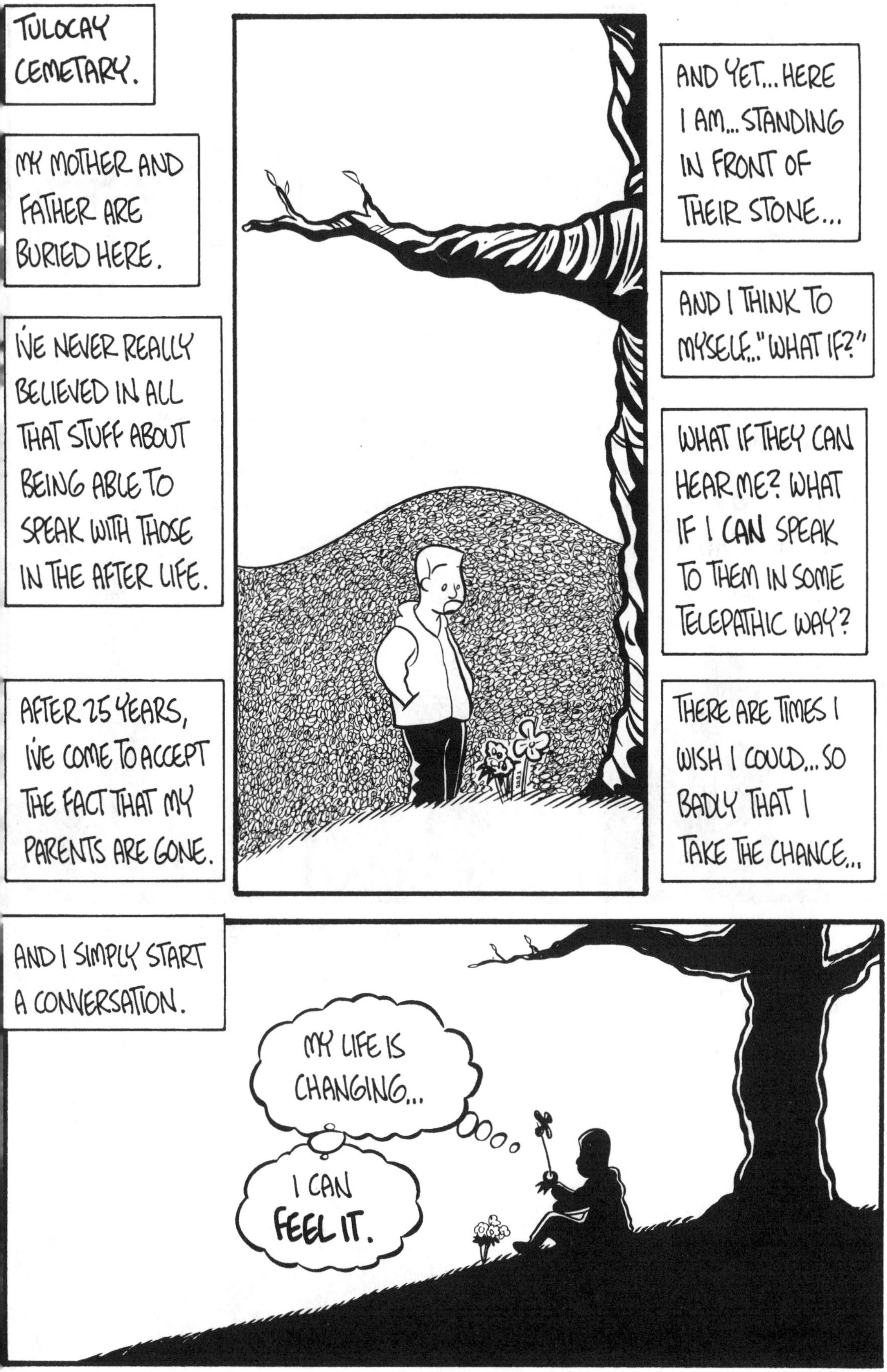
TULOCAY CEMETARY.
MY MOTHER AND FATHER ARE BURIED HERE.
I'VE NEVER REALLY BELIEVED IN ALL THAT STUFF ABOUT BEING ABLE TO SPEAK WITH THOSE IN THE AFTER LIFE.
AFTER 25 YEARS, I'VE COME TO ACCEPT THE FACT THAT MY PARENTS ARE GONE.
AND YET... HERE I AM... STANDING IN FRONT OF THEIR STONE...
AND I THINK TO MYSELF..."WHAT IF?"
WHAT IF THEY CAN HEAR ME? WHAT IF I CAN SPEAK TO THEM IN SOME TELEPATHIC WAY?
THERE ARE TIMES I WISH I COULD... SO BADLY THAT I TAKE THE CHANCE...
AND I SIMPLY START A CONVERSATION.
MY LIFE IS CHANGING...
I CAN FEEL IT.

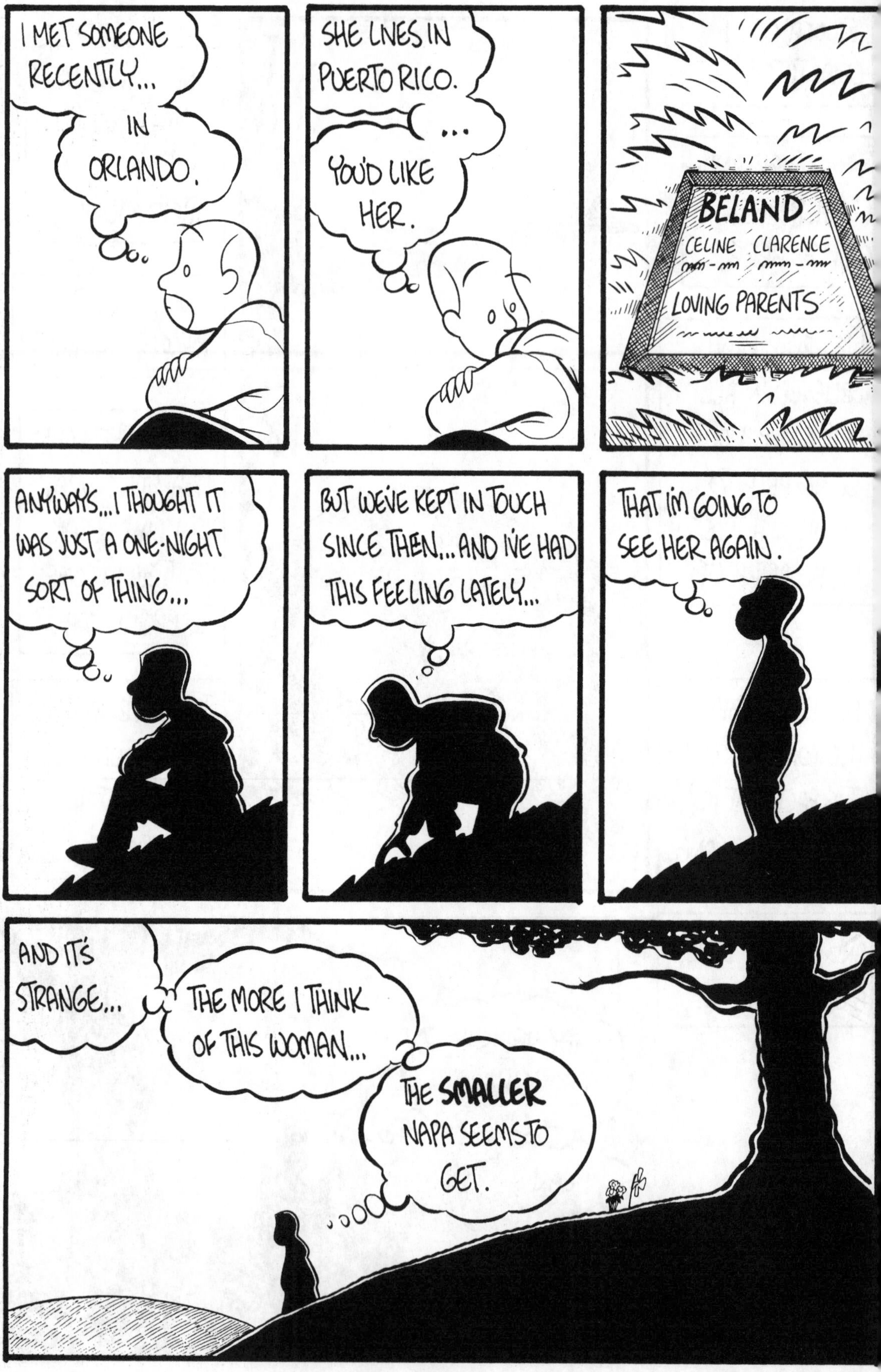

I MET SOMEONE RECENTLY...
IN ORLANDO.
SHE LIVES IN PUERTO RICO.
...
YOU'D LIKE HER.
BELAND
CELINE CLARENCE
LOVING PARENTS
ANYWAYS... I THOUGHT IT WAS JUST A ONE-NIGHT SORT OF THING...
BUT WE'VE KEPT IN TOUCH SINCE THEN... AND I'VE HAD THIS FEELING LATELY...
THAT I'M GOING TO SEE HER AGAIN.
AND IT'S STRANGE...
THE MORE I THINK OF THIS WOMAN...
THE SMALLER NAPA SEEMS TO GET.

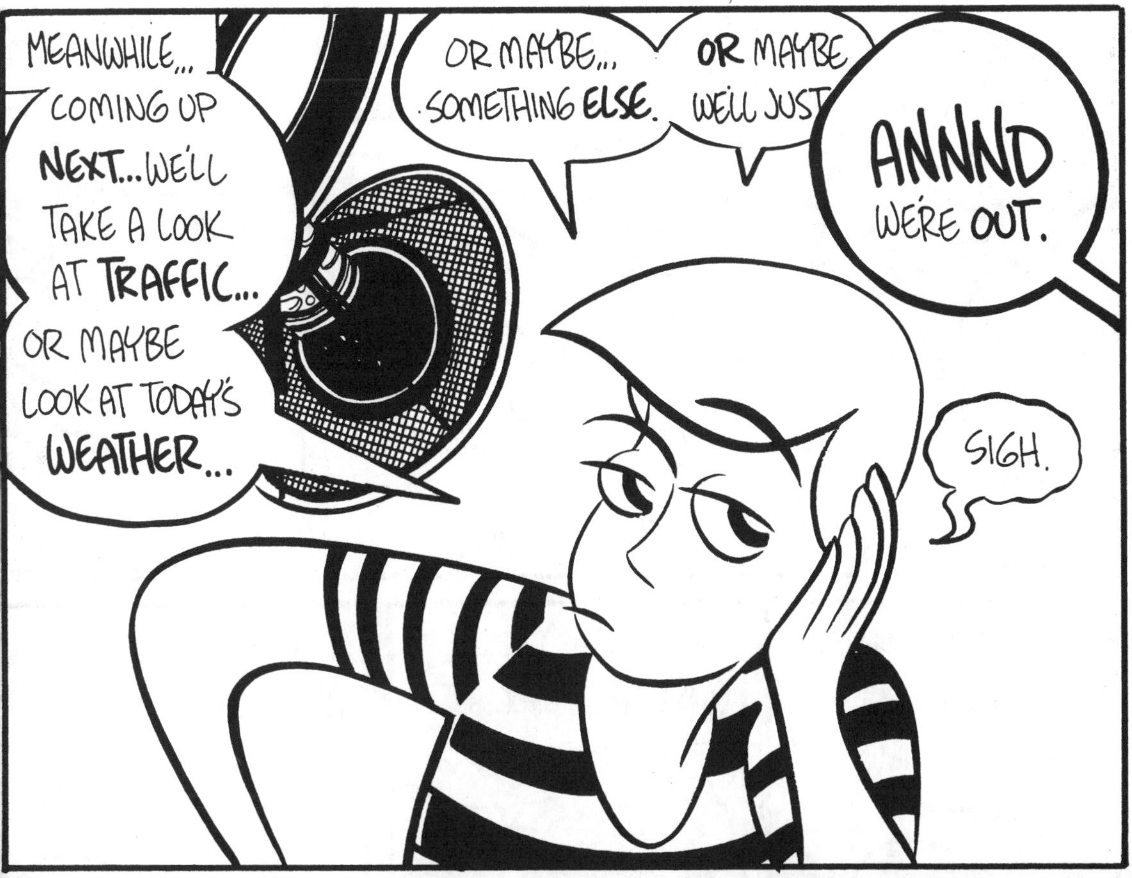
MEANWHILE... COMING UP NEXT... WE'LL TAKE A LOOK AT TRAFFIC...
OR MAYBE LOOK AT TODAY'S WEATHER...
OR MAYBE... SOMETHING ELSE.
OR MAYBE WE'LL JUST
ANNND WE'RE OUT.
SIGH.

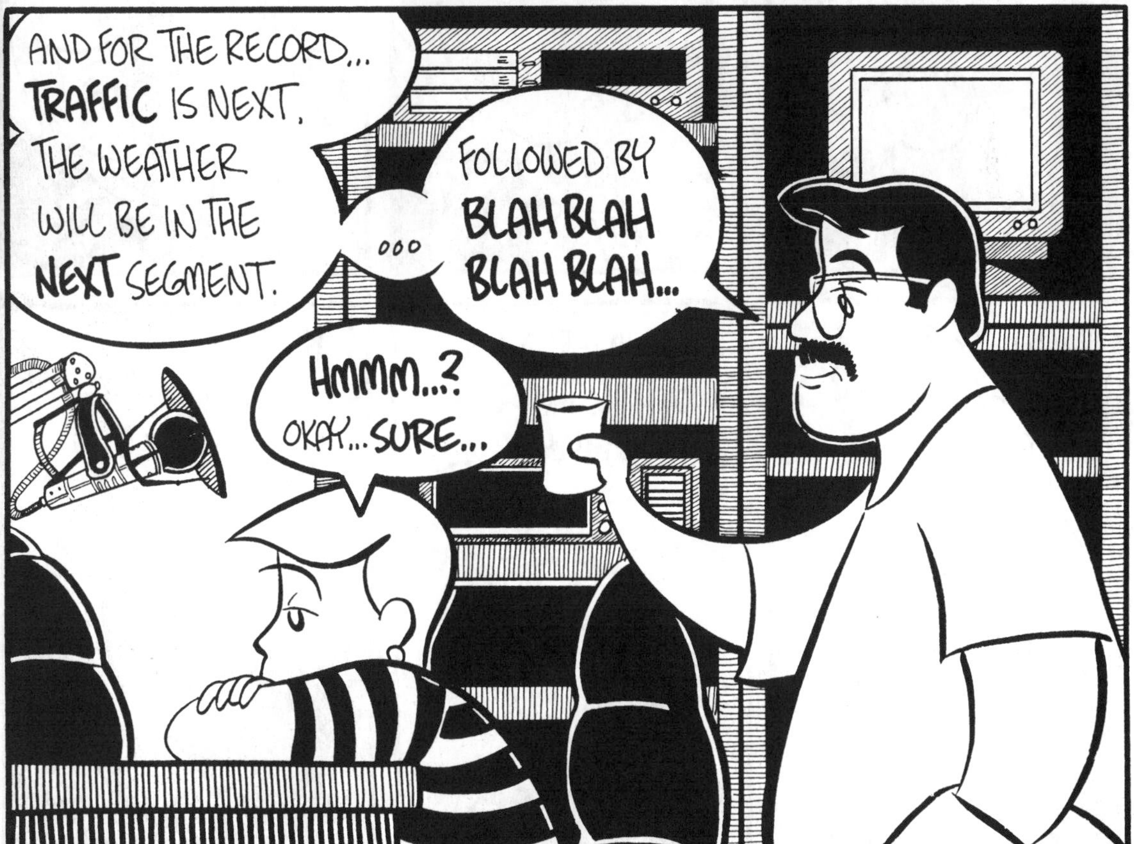
AND FOR THE RECORD... TRAFFIC IS NEXT, THE WEATHER WILL BE IN THE NEXT SEGMENT.
...
FOLLOWED BY BLAH BLAH BLAH BLAH...
HMMM...? OKAY... SURE...

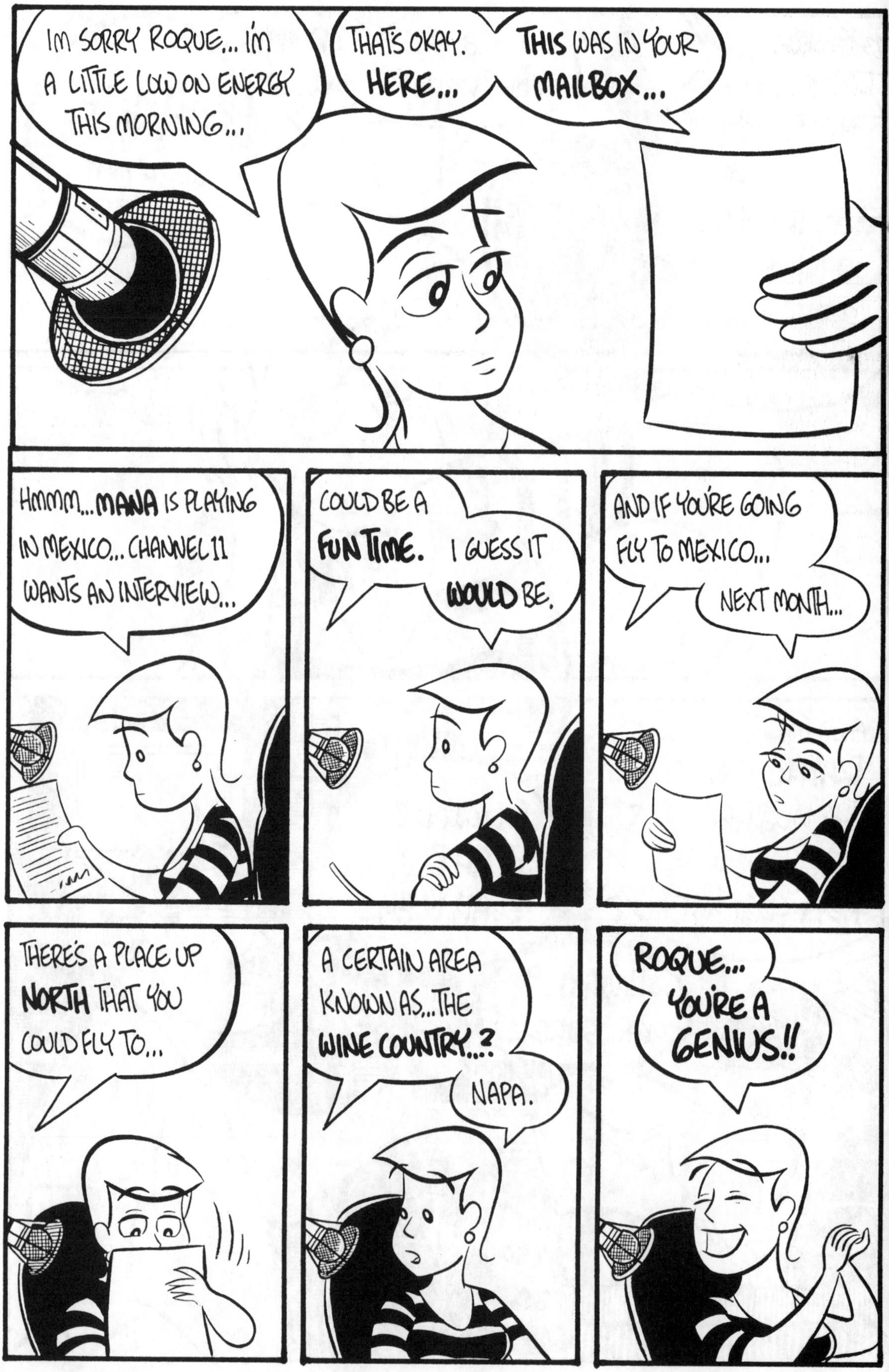
IM SORRY ROQUE... I'M A LITTLE LOW ON ENERGY THIS MORNING...
THAT'S OKAY. HERE...
THIS WAS IN YOUR MAILBOX...
HMMM... MANA IS PLAYING IN MEXICO... CHANNEL 11 WANTS AN INTERVIEW...
COULD BE A FUN TIME.
I GUESS IT WOULD BE.
AND IF YOU'RE GOING FLY TO MEXICO...
NEXT MONTH...
THERE'S A PLACE UP NORTH THAT YOU COULD FLY TO...
A CERTAIN AREA KNOWN AS... THE WINE COUNTRY...?
NAPA.
ROQUE... YOU'RE A GENIUS!!

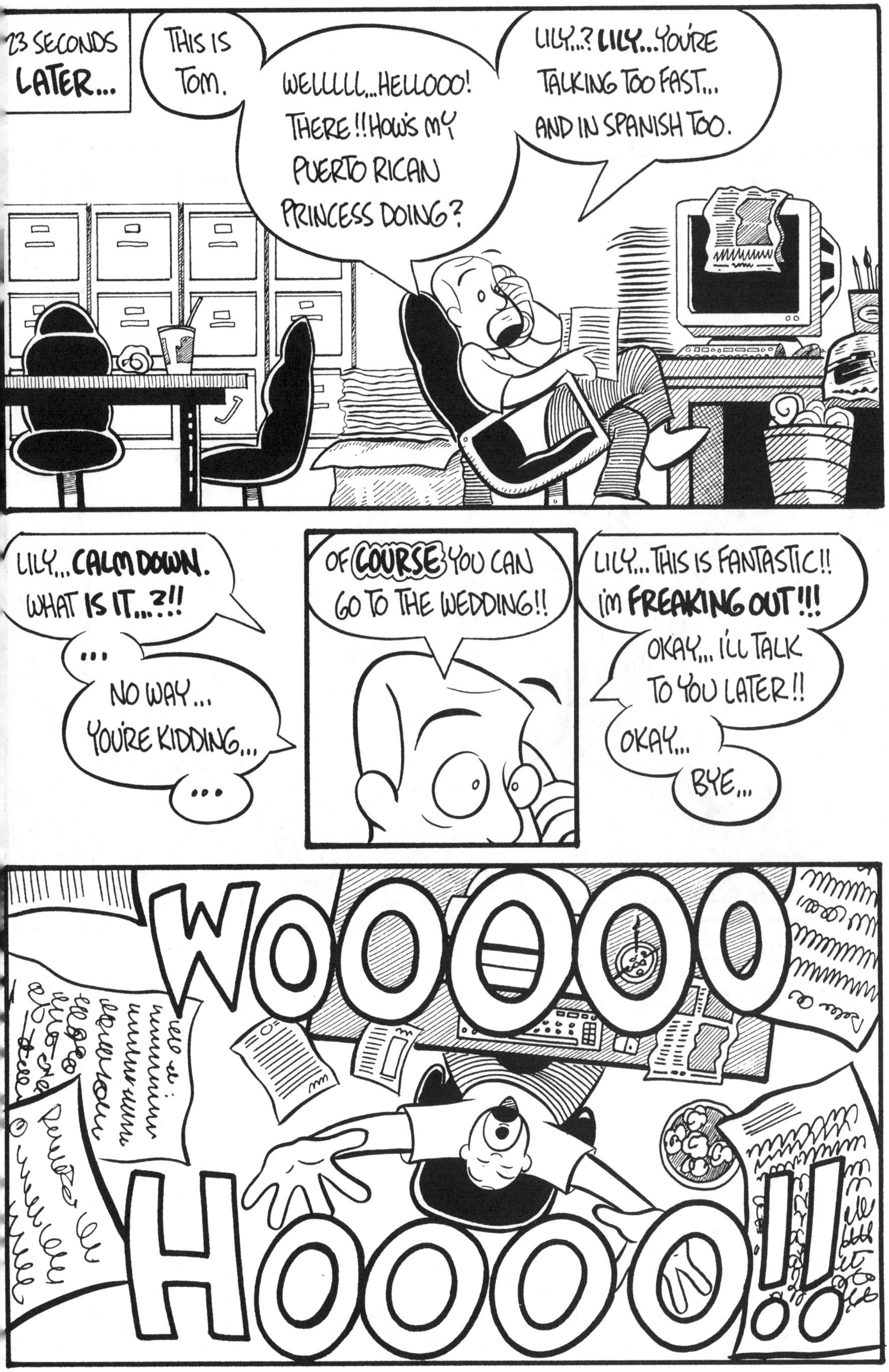
23 SECONDS LATER...
THIS IS TOM.
WELLLLL...HELLOOO! THERE!! HOW'S MY PUERTO RICAN PRINCESS DOING?
LILY...? LILY...YOU'RE TALKING TOO FAST... AND IN SPANISH TOO.
LILY... CALM DOWN. WHAT IS IT...?!!
...
NO WAY... YOU'RE KIDDING...
...
OF COURSE YOU CAN GO TO THE WEDDING!!
LILY... THIS IS FANTASTIC!! I'M FREAKING OUT!!!
OKAY... I'LL TALK TO YOU LATER!!
OKAY...
BYE...
WOOOOO
HOOOO!!

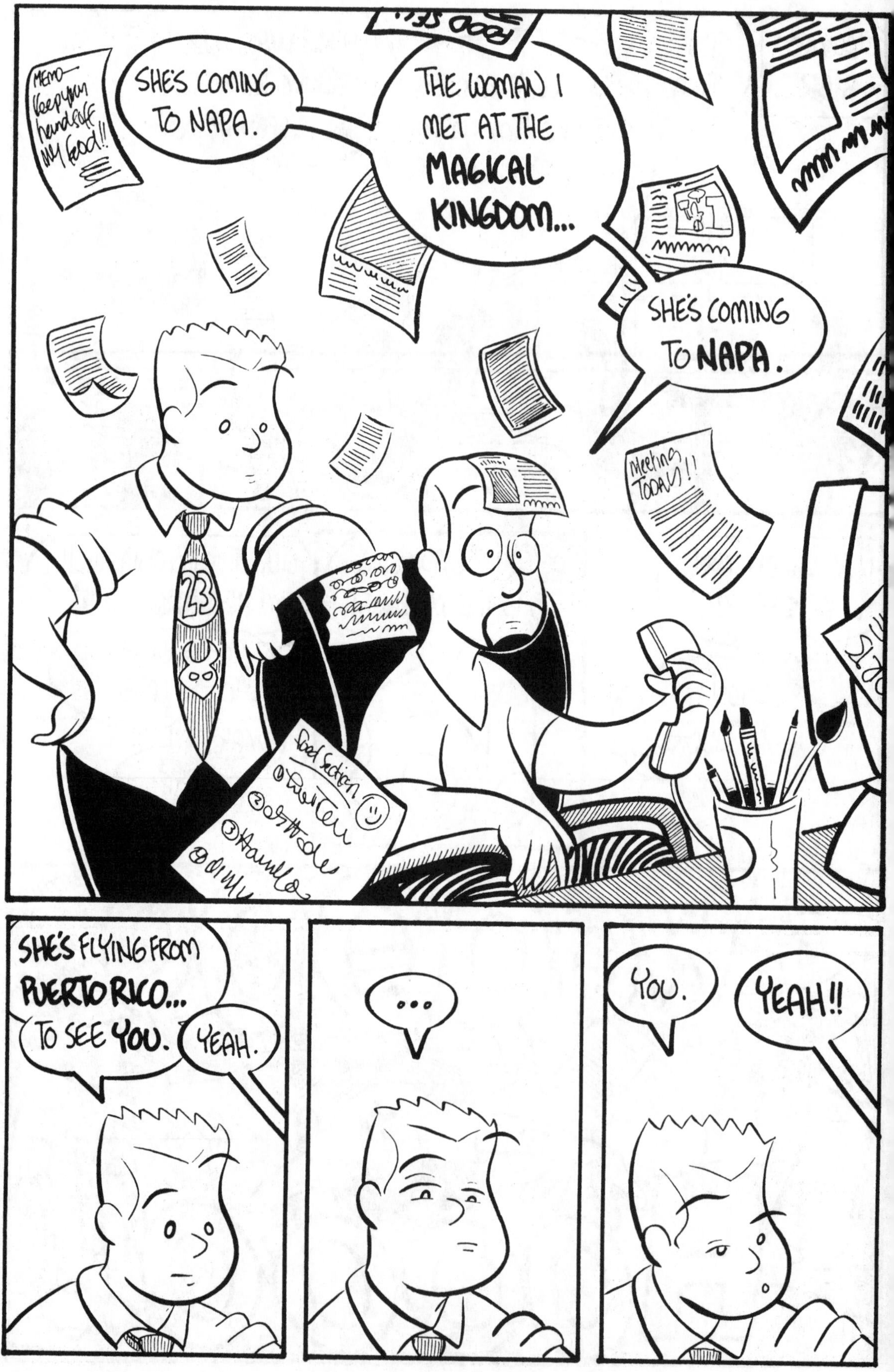
MEMO
Keep your hands off MY food!!
SHE'S COMING TO NAPA.
THE WOMAN I MET AT THE MAGICAL KINGDOM...
SHE'S COMING TO NAPA.
Meeting TODAY!!
Food Section
SHE'S FLYING FROM PUERTO RICO...
TO SEE YOU.
YEAH.
...
YOU.
YEAH!!

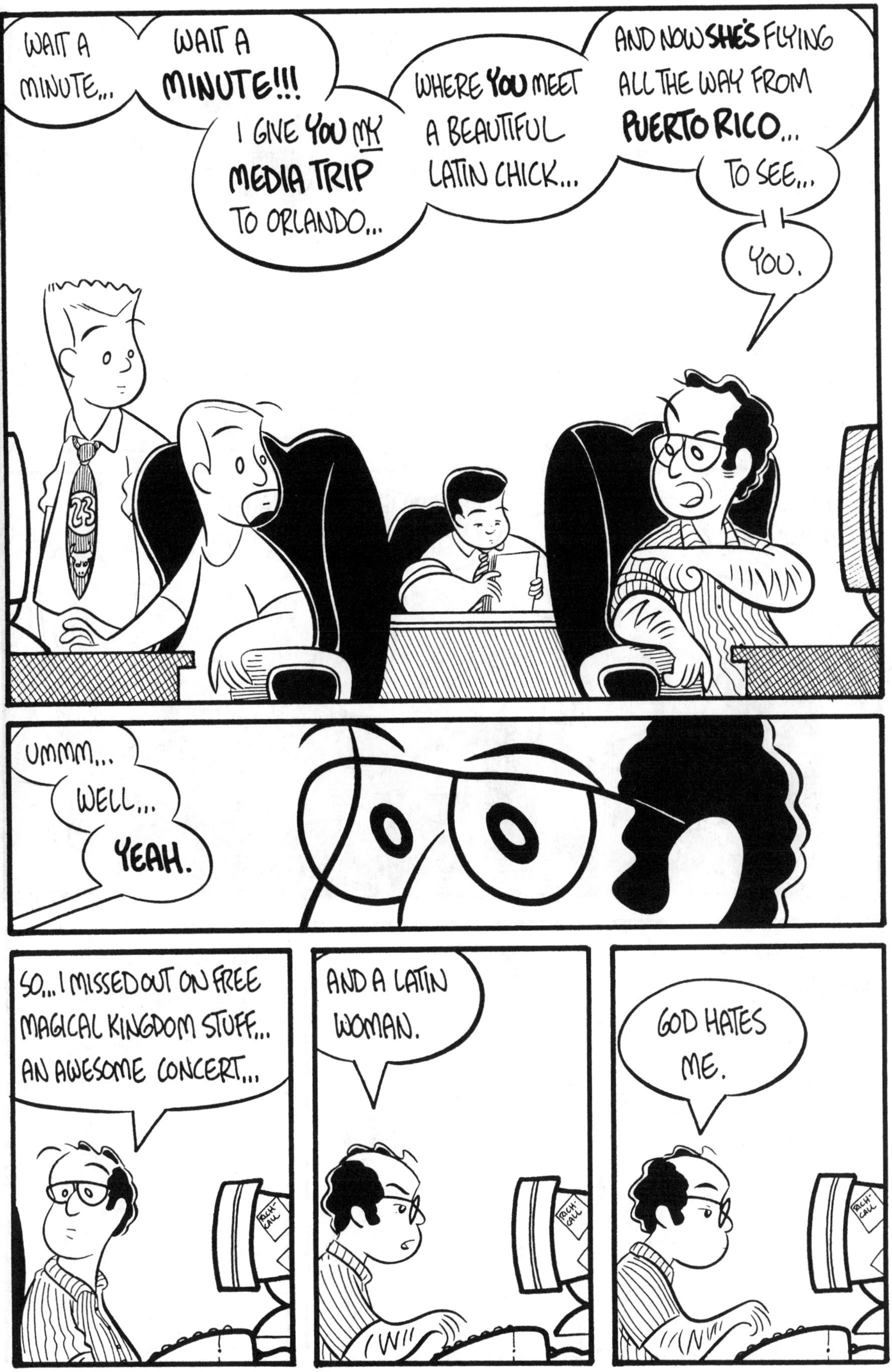
WAIT A MINUTE...
WAIT A MINUTE!!!
I GIVE YOU MY MEDIA TRIP TO ORLANDO...
WHERE YOU MEET A BEAUTIFUL LATIN CHICK...
AND NOW SHE'S FLYING ALL THE WAY FROM PUERTO RICO...
TO SEE...
YOU.
UMMM...
WELL...
YEAH.
SO... I MISSED OUT ON FREE MAGICAL KINGDOM STUFF... AN AWESOME CONCERT...
AND A LATIN WOMAN.
GOD HATES ME.

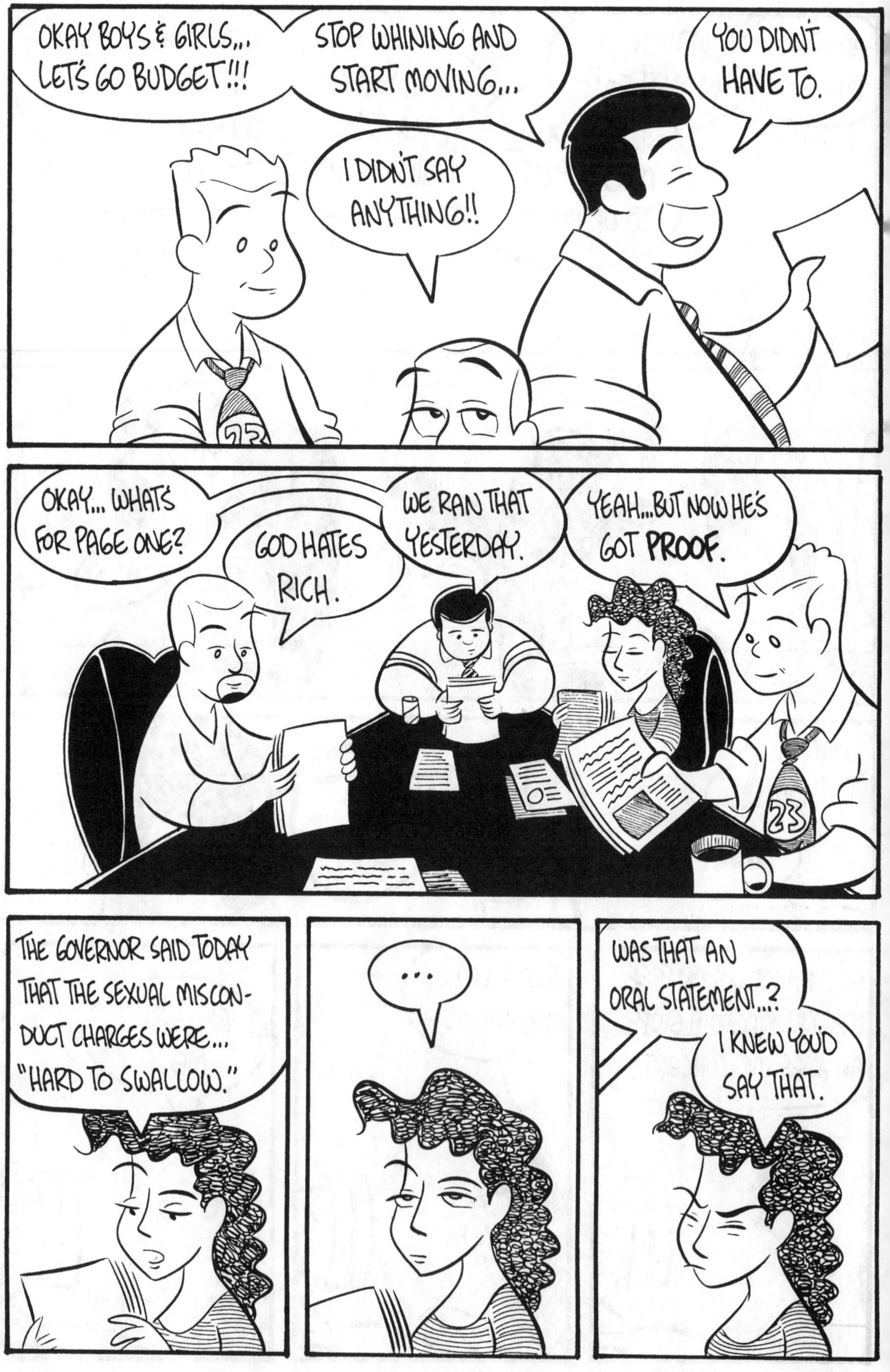
OKAY BOYS & GIRLS... LET'S GO BUDGET!!!
STOP WHINING AND START MOVING...
I DIDN'T SAY ANYTHING!!
YOU DIDN'T HAVE TO.
23
OKAY... WHAT'S FOR PAGE ONE?
GOD HATES RICH.
WE RAN THAT YESTERDAY.
YEAH...BUT NOW HE'S GOT **PROOF**.
23
THE GOVERNOR SAID TODAY THAT THE SEXUAL MISCON-DUCT CHARGES WERE... "HARD TO SWALLOW."
...
WAS THAT AN ORAL STATEMENT...?
I KNEW YOU'D SAY THAT.

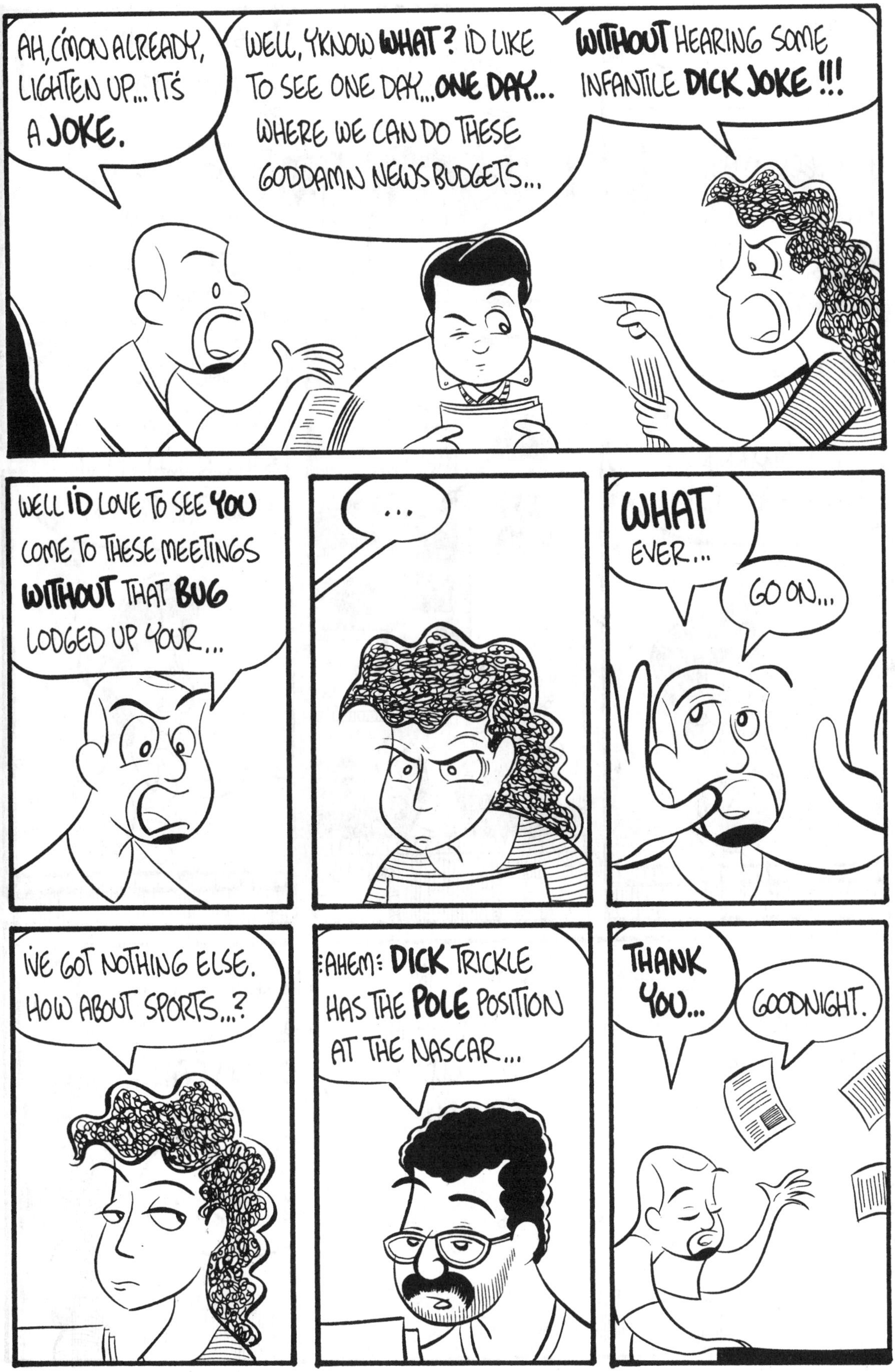
AH, C'MON ALREADY, LIGHTEN UP... IT'S A JOKE.
WELL, Y'KNOW WHAT? I'D LIKE TO SEE ONE DAY... ONE DAY... WHERE WE CAN DO THESE GODDAMN NEWS BUDGETS...
WITHOUT HEARING SOME INFANTILE DICK JOKE !!!
WELL I'D LOVE TO SEE YOU COME TO THESE MEETINGS WITHOUT THAT BUG LODGED UP YOUR...
...
WHAT EVER...
GO ON...
I'VE GOT NOTHING ELSE. HOW ABOUT SPORTS...?
:AHEM: DICK TRICKLE HAS THE POLE POSITION AT THE NASCAR...
THANK YOU...
GOODNIGHT.

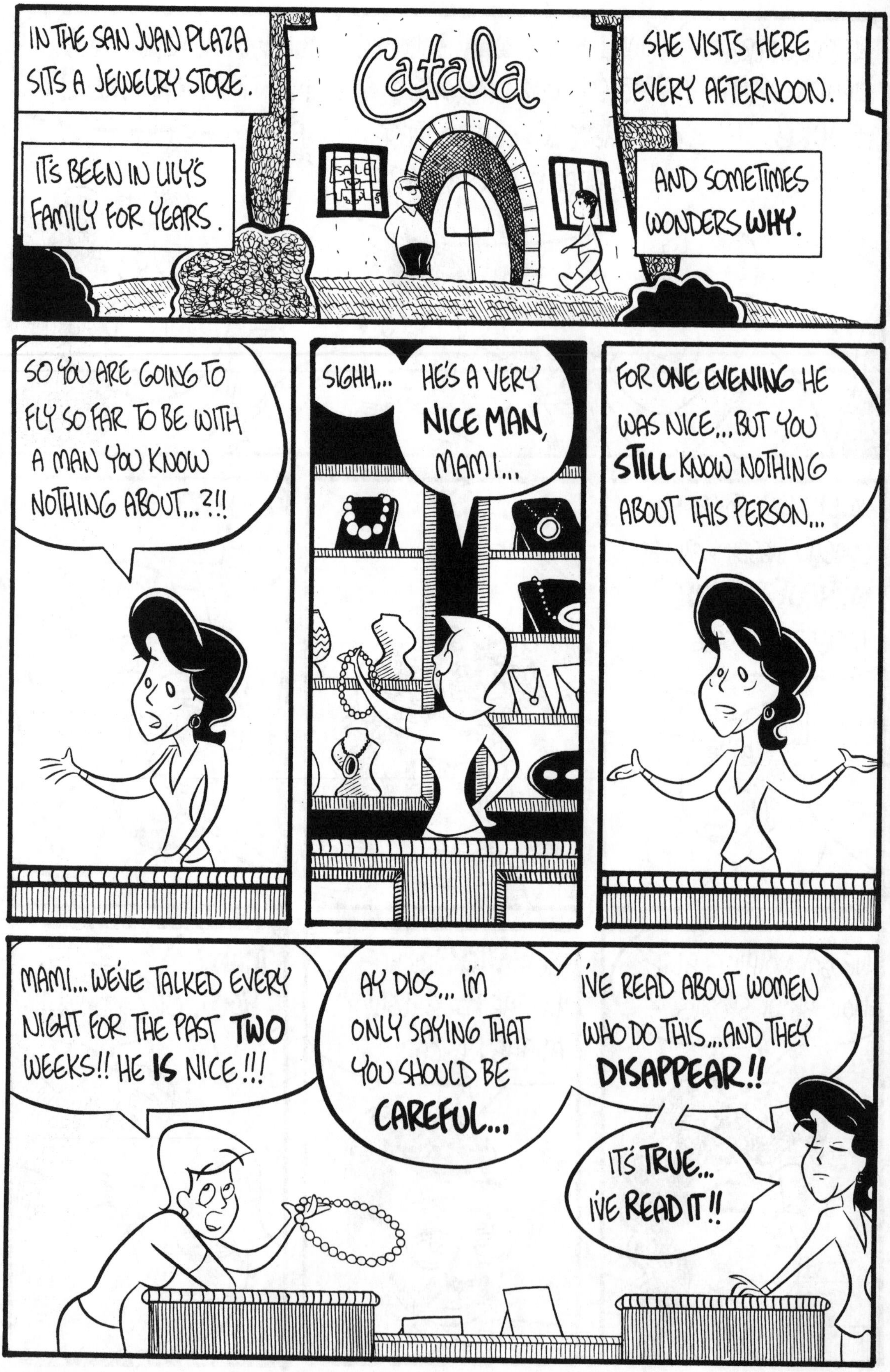
IN THE SAN JUAN PLAZA SITS A JEWELRY STORE.
IT'S BEEN IN LILY'S FAMILY FOR YEARS.
Catala
SALE
SHE VISITS HERE EVERY AFTERNOON.
AND SOMETIMES WONDERS **WHY**.
SO YOU ARE GOING TO FLY SO FAR TO BE WITH A MAN YOU KNOW NOTHING ABOUT...?!!
SIGHH...
HE'S A VERY **NICE MAN**, MAMI...
FOR **ONE EVENING** HE WAS NICE... BUT YOU **STILL** KNOW NOTHING ABOUT THIS PERSON...
MAMI... WE'VE TALKED EVERY NIGHT FOR THE PAST **TWO** WEEKS!! HE **IS** NICE!!!
AY DIOS... I'M ONLY SAYING THAT YOU SHOULD BE **CAREFUL...**
I'VE READ ABOUT WOMEN WHO DO THIS... AND THEY **DISAPPEAR!!**
IT'S **TRUE...** I'VE **READ IT!!**

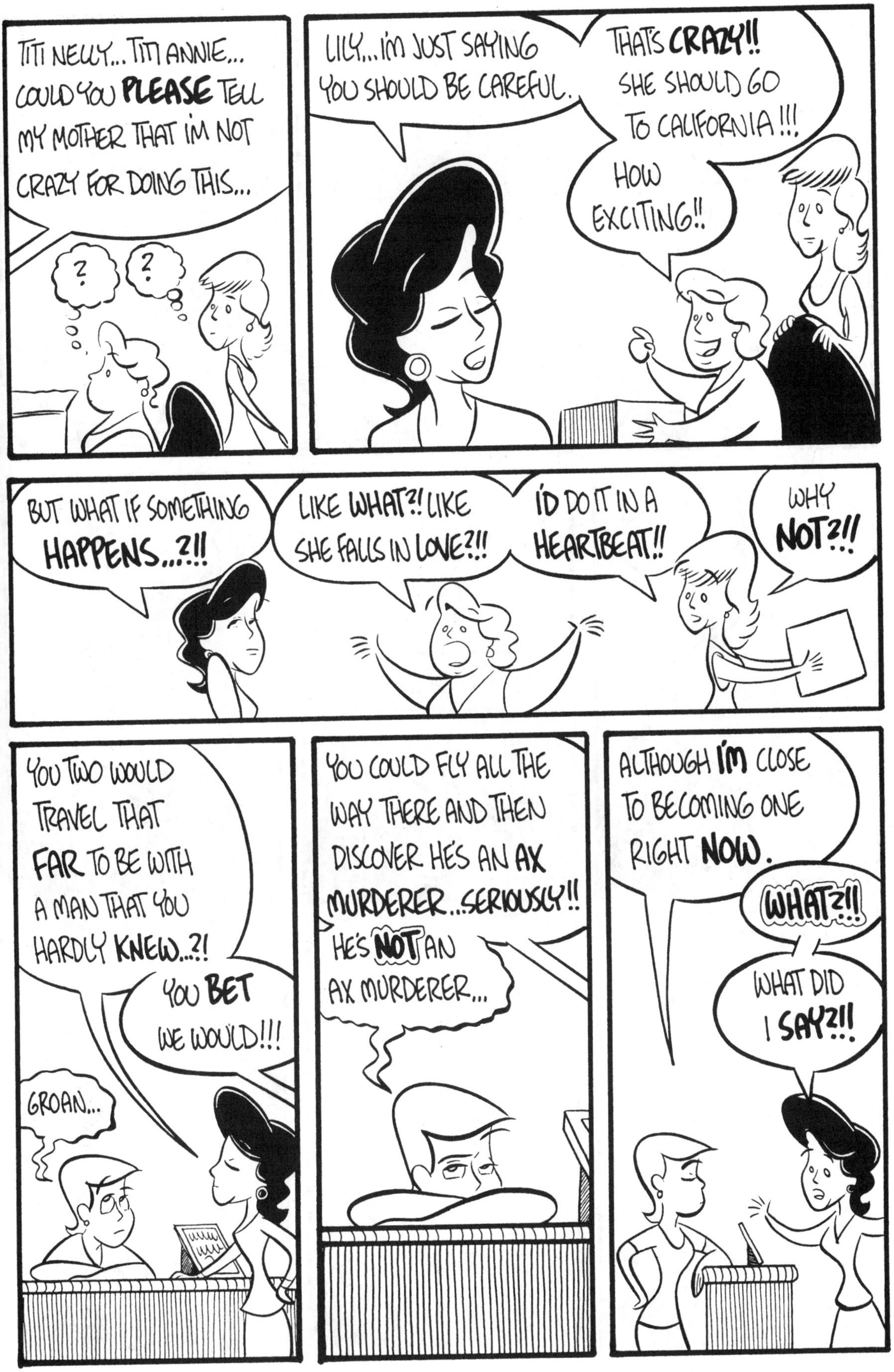
TITI NELLY... TITI ANNIE... COULD YOU PLEASE TELL MY MOTHER THAT I'M NOT CRAZY FOR DOING THIS...
?
?
LILY... I'M JUST SAYING YOU SHOULD BE CAREFUL.
THAT'S CRAZY!! SHE SHOULD GO TO CALIFORNIA!!!
HOW EXCITING!!
BUT WHAT IF SOMETHING HAPPENS...?!!
LIKE WHAT?! LIKE SHE FALLS IN LOVE?!!
I'D DO IT IN A HEARTBEAT!!
WHY NOT?!!
YOU TWO WOULD TRAVEL THAT FAR TO BE WITH A MAN THAT YOU HARDLY KNEW...?!
YOU BET WE WOULD!!!
GROAN...
YOU COULD FLY ALL THE WAY THERE AND THEN DISCOVER HE'S AN AX MURDERER... SERIOUSLY!!
HE'S NOT AN AX MURDERER...
ALTHOUGH I'M CLOSE TO BECOMING ONE RIGHT NOW.
WHAT?!!
WHAT DID I SAY?!!

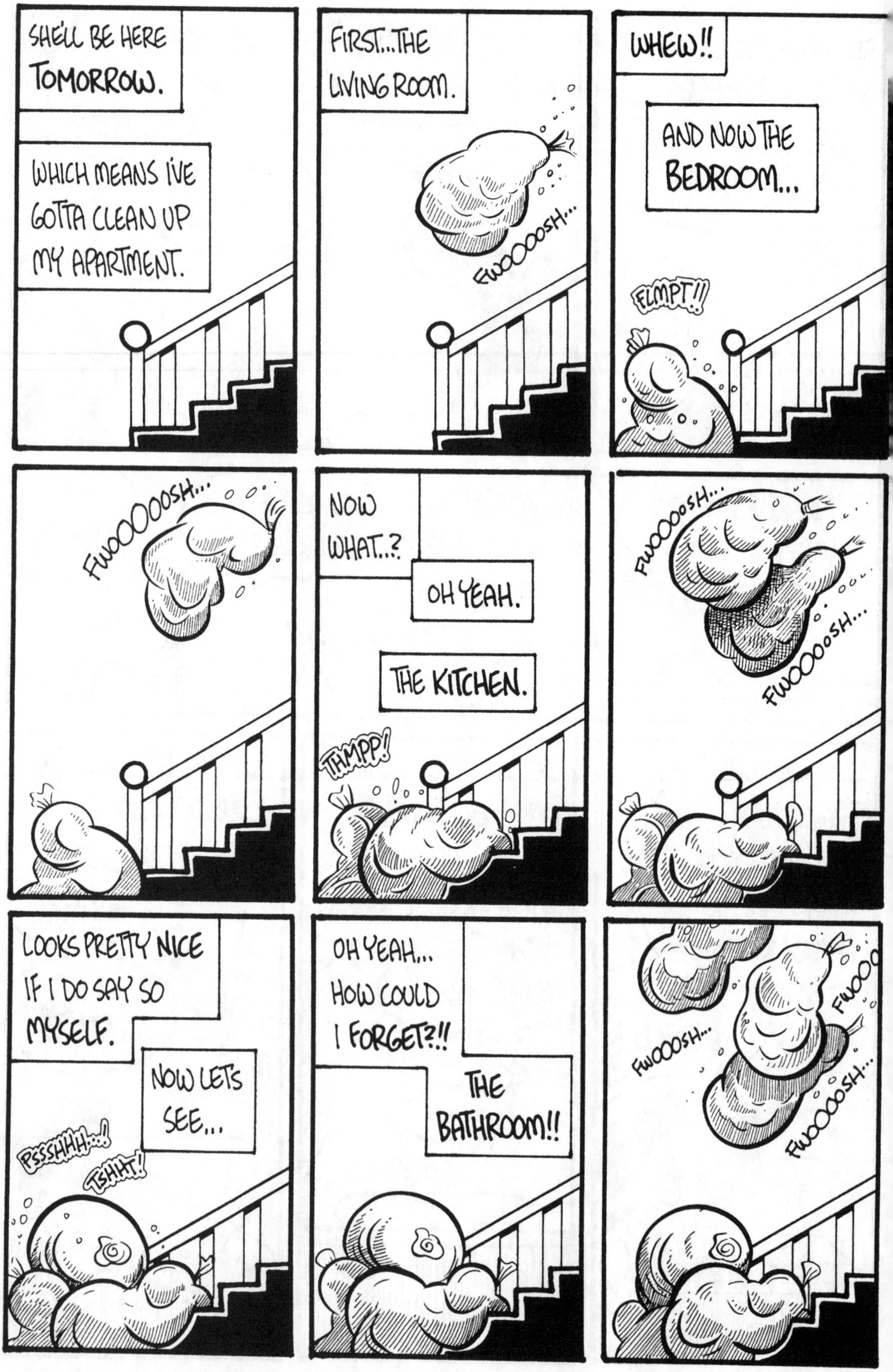
SHE'LL BE HERE TOMORROW.
WHICH MEANS I'VE GOTTA CLEAN UP MY APARTMENT.
FIRST...THE LIVING ROOM.
FWOOOOSH...
WHEW!!
AND NOW THE BEDROOM...
FLMPT!!
FWOOOOOSH...
NOW WHAT..?
OH YEAH.
THE KITCHEN.
THMPP!
FWOOOOOSH...
FWOOOOOSH...
LOOKS PRETTY NICE IF I DO SAY SO MYSELF.
NOW LET'S SEE...
PSSSHHH...!
TSHHT!
OH YEAH... HOW COULD I FORGET?!!
THE BATHROOM!!
FWOOOSH...
FWOOOOOSH...

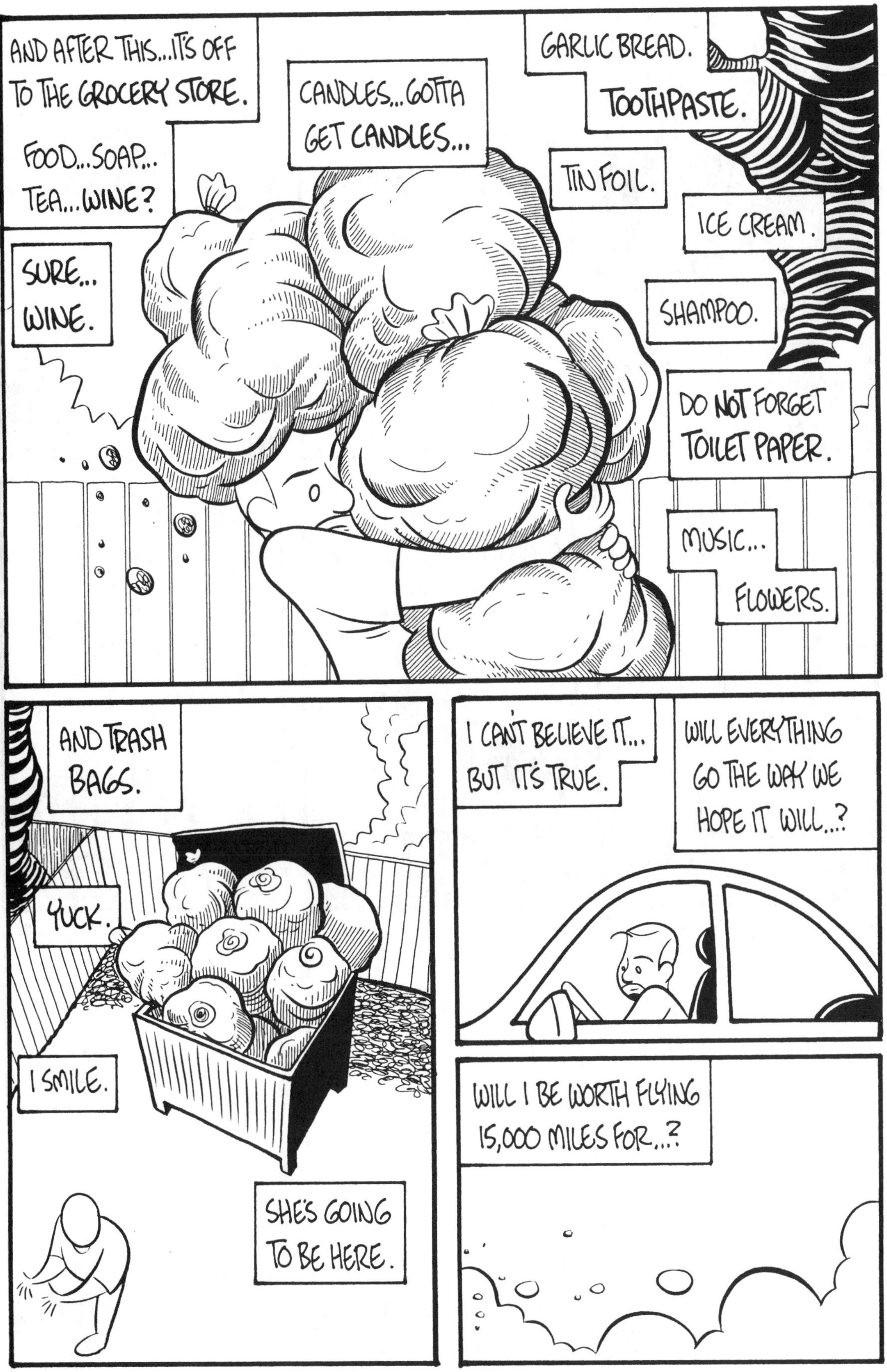

AND AFTER THIS...IT'S OFF TO THE GROCERY STORE.
FOOD...SOAP... TEA...WINE?
SURE... WINE.
CANDLES...GOTTA GET CANDLES...
GARLIC BREAD.
TOOTHPASTE.
TIN FOIL.
ICE CREAM.
SHAMPOO.
DO NOT FORGET TOILET PAPER.
MUSIC...
FLOWERS.
AND TRASH BAGS.
YUCK.
I SMILE.
SHE'S GOING TO BE HERE.
I CAN'T BELIEVE IT... BUT IT'S TRUE.
WILL EVERYTHING GO THE WAY WE HOPE IT WILL...?
WILL I BE WORTH FLYING 15,000 MILES FOR...?

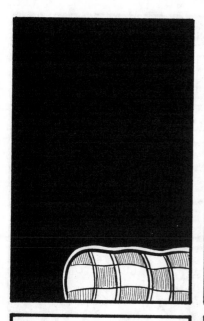

I THOUGHT ABOUT A CONVERSATION I HAD WITH MY GOOD FRIEND, CARLOS, LAST MONTH.

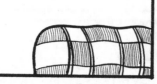
click

I TOLD HIM THAT I'D JUST MET A GRINGO AT THE MAGICAL KINGDOM.

BUT SINCE HE WAS IN CALIFORNIA...

I'D NEVER SEE HIM AGAIN.

"BUT YOU'VE READ 'THE ALCHEMIST' HAVEN'T YOU?" HE ASKED.

"THE BOOK SAYS TO JUST THROW YOUR WISHES OUT THERE AND ALLOW THE UNIVERSE TO MAKE THEM COME TRUE."

"NEVER UNDERESTIMATE THE UNIVERSE," CARLOS ADDED. "BECAUSE WHEN THINGS ARE MEANT TO HAPPEN... THEY WILL."

AND TOMORROW I FLY TO NAPA VALLEY...

TO SEE THE GRINGO.

THE UNIVERSE IS A BEAUTIFUL THING.

ZZZZZZZZZZ...

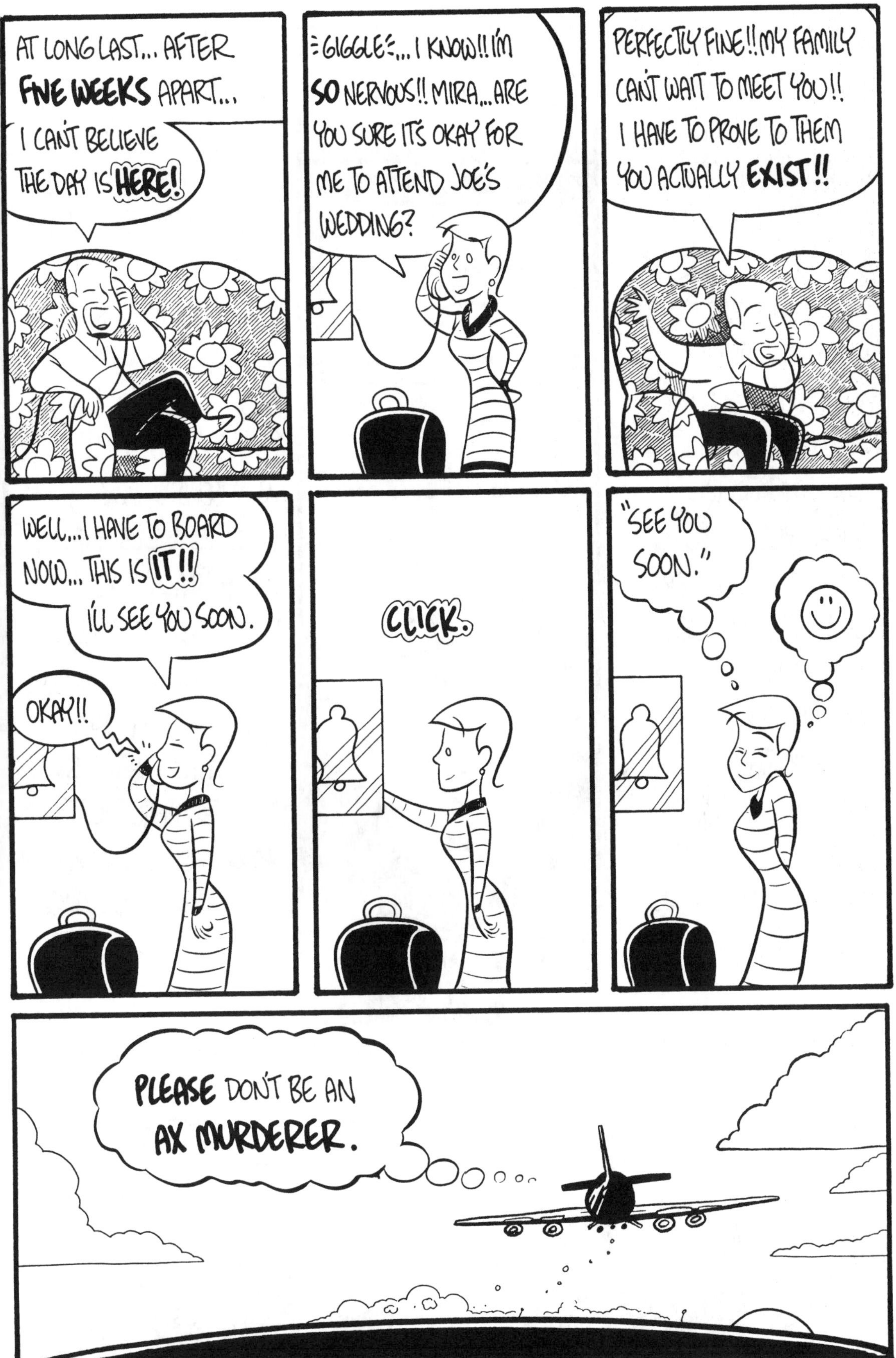
AT LONG LAST... AFTER FIVE WEEKS APART...
I CAN'T BELIEVE THE DAY IS HERE!
GIGGLE... I KNOW!! I'M SO NERVOUS!! MIRA... ARE YOU SURE IT'S OKAY FOR ME TO ATTEND JOE'S WEDDING?
PERFECTLY FINE!! MY FAMILY CAN'T WAIT TO MEET YOU!! I HAVE TO PROVE TO THEM YOU ACTUALLY EXIST!!
WELL... I HAVE TO BOARD NOW... THIS IS IT!! I'LL SEE YOU SOON.
OKAY!!
CLICK.
"SEE YOU SOON."
PLEASE DON'T BE AN AX MURDERER.

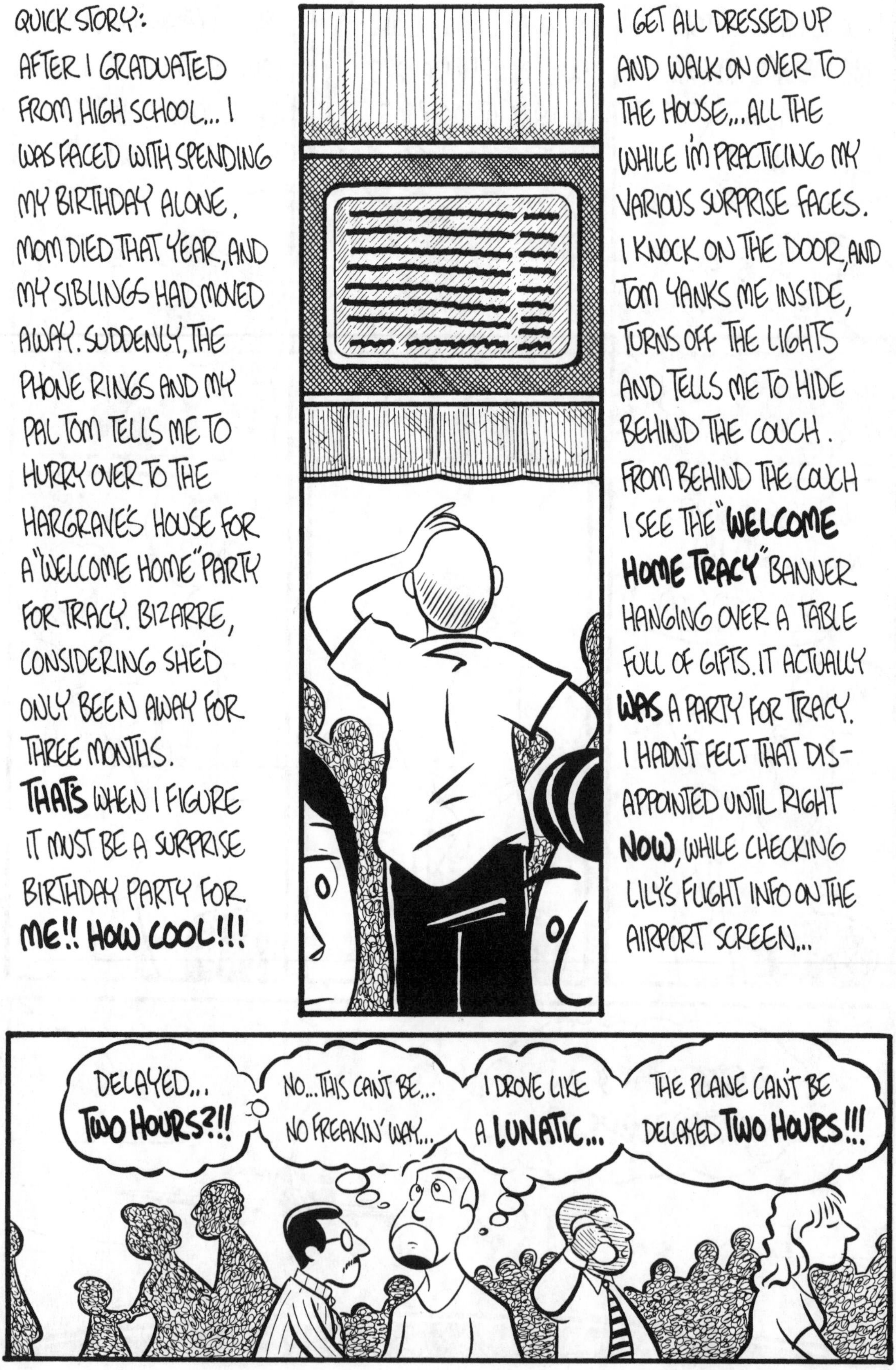
QUICK STORY:
AFTER I GRADUATED FROM HIGH SCHOOL... I WAS FACED WITH SPENDING MY BIRTHDAY ALONE. MOM DIED THAT YEAR, AND MY SIBLINGS HAD MOVED AWAY. SUDDENLY, THE PHONE RINGS AND MY PAL TOM TELLS ME TO HURRY OVER TO THE HARGRAVE'S HOUSE FOR A "WELCOME HOME" PARTY FOR TRACY. BIZARRE, CONSIDERING SHE'D ONLY BEEN AWAY FOR THREE MONTHS.
THAT'S WHEN I FIGURE IT MUST BE A SURPRISE BIRTHDAY PARTY FOR **ME!! HOW COOL!!!**
I GET ALL DRESSED UP AND WALK ON OVER TO THE HOUSE... ALL THE WHILE I'M PRACTICING MY VARIOUS SURPRISE FACES.
I KNOCK ON THE DOOR, AND TOM YANKS ME INSIDE, TURNS OFF THE LIGHTS AND TELLS ME TO HIDE BEHIND THE COUCH.
FROM BEHIND THE COUCH I SEE THE "**WELCOME HOME TRACY**" BANNER HANGING OVER A TABLE FULL OF GIFTS. IT ACTUALLY **WAS** A PARTY FOR TRACY.
I HADN'T FELT THAT DIS-APPOINTED UNTIL RIGHT **NOW**, WHILE CHECKING LILY'S FLIGHT INFO ON THE AIRPORT SCREEN...
DELAYED... **TWO HOURS?!!**
NO... THIS CAN'T BE... NO FREAKIN' WAY...
I DROVE LIKE A **LUNATIC...**
THE PLANE CAN'T BE DELAYED **TWO HOURS!!!**

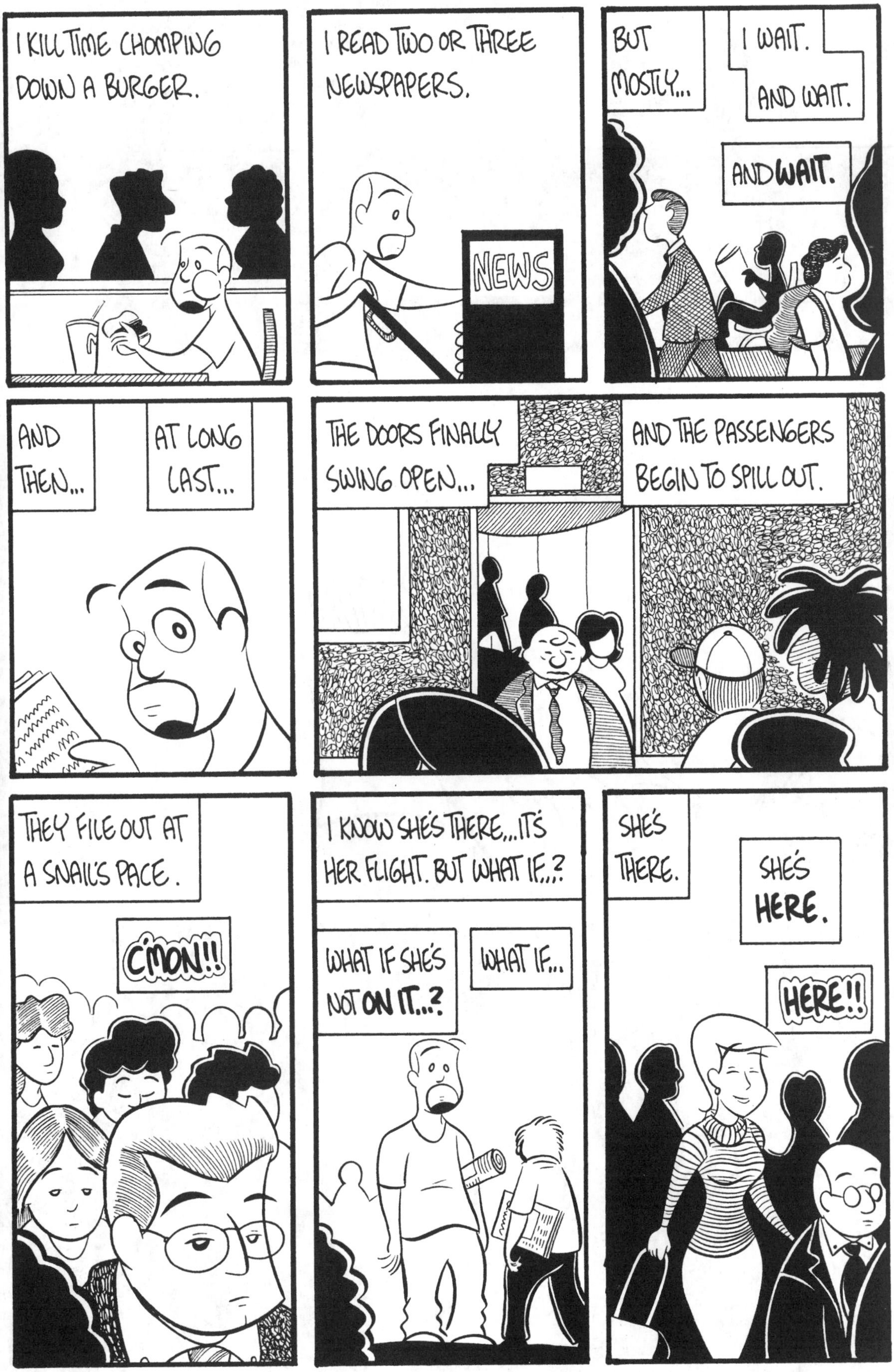
I KILL TIME CHOMPING DOWN A BURGER.
I READ TWO OR THREE NEWSPAPERS.
NEWS
BUT MOSTLY...
I WAIT.
AND WAIT.
AND WAIT.
AND THEN...
AT LONG LAST...
THE DOORS FINALLY SWING OPEN...
AND THE PASSENGERS BEGIN TO SPILL OUT.
THEY FILE OUT AT A SNAIL'S PACE.
C'MON!!
I KNOW SHE'S THERE,...IT'S HER FLIGHT. BUT WHAT IF...?
WHAT IF SHE'S NOT ON IT...?
WHAT IF...
SHE'S THERE.
SHE'S HERE.
HERE!!

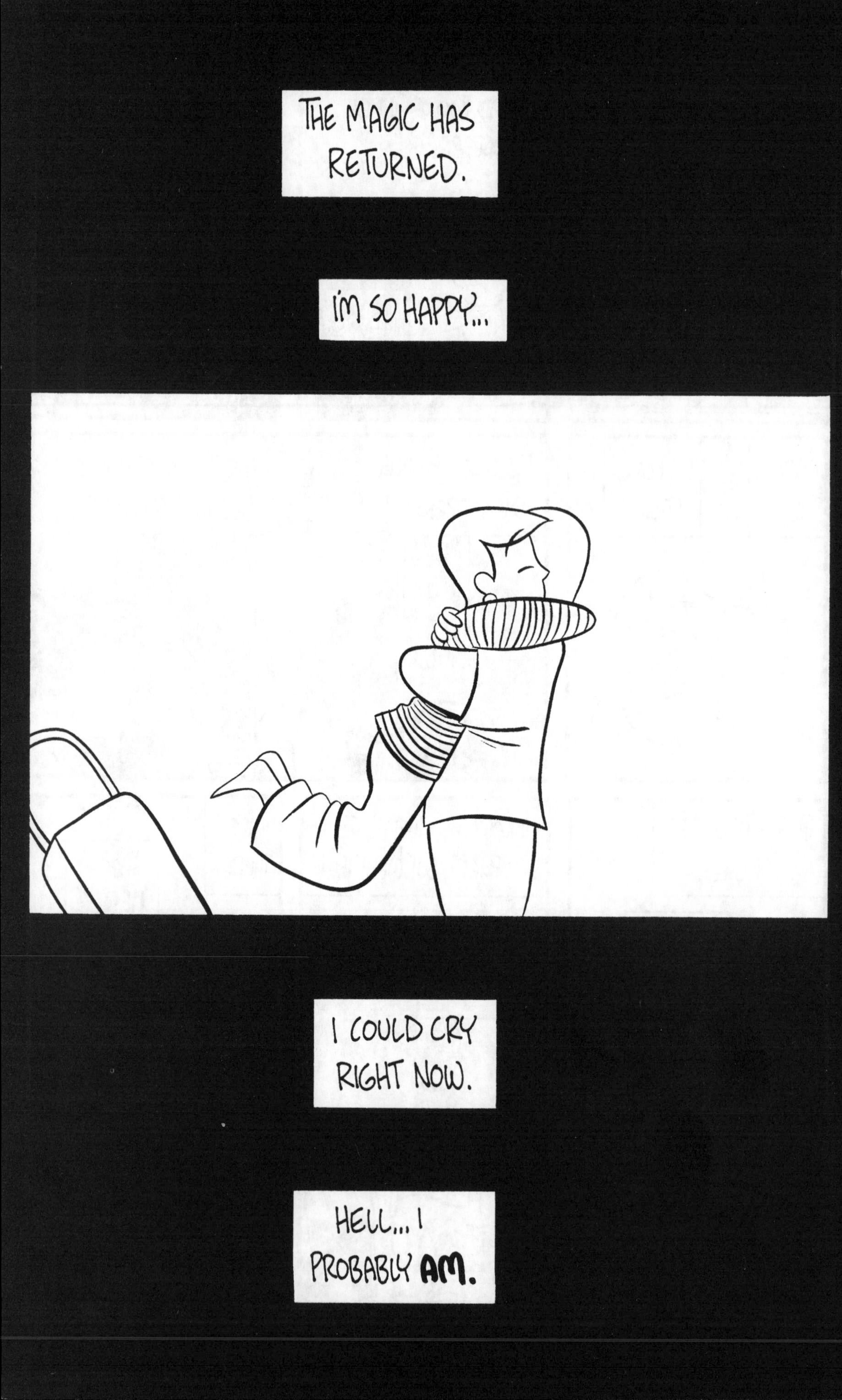
THE MAGIC HAS RETURNED.
I'M SO HAPPY...
I COULD CRY RIGHT NOW.
HELL... I PROBABLY AM.

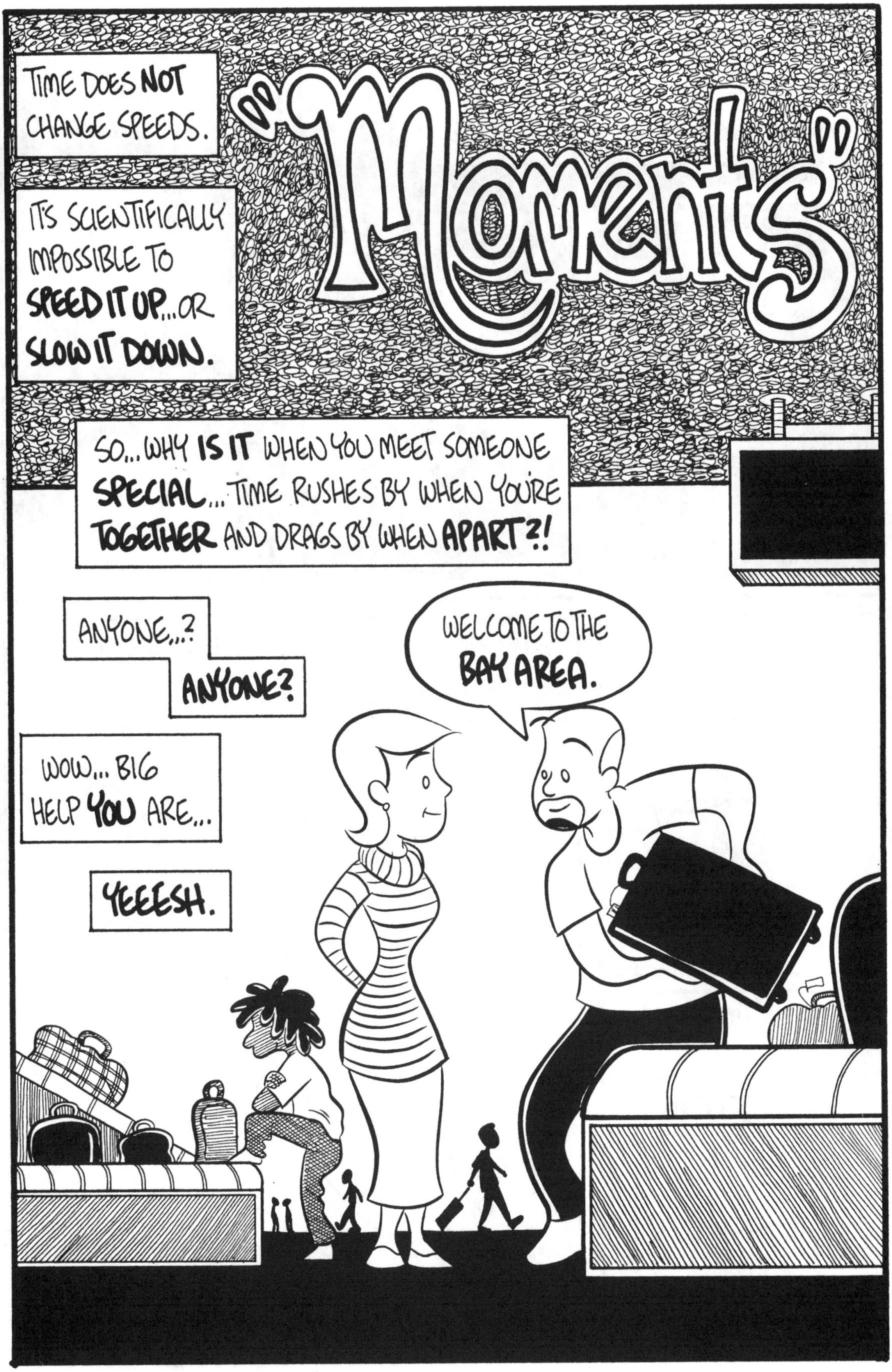

TIME DOES NOT CHANGE SPEEDS.
IT'S SCIENTIFICALLY IMPOSSIBLE TO SPEED IT UP...OR SLOW IT DOWN.
"Moments"
SO... WHY IS IT WHEN YOU MEET SOMEONE SPECIAL... TIME RUSHES BY WHEN YOU'RE TOGETHER AND DRAGS BY WHEN APART?!
ANYONE...?
ANYONE?
WELCOME TO THE BAY AREA.
WOW... BIG HELP YOU ARE...
YEEESH.

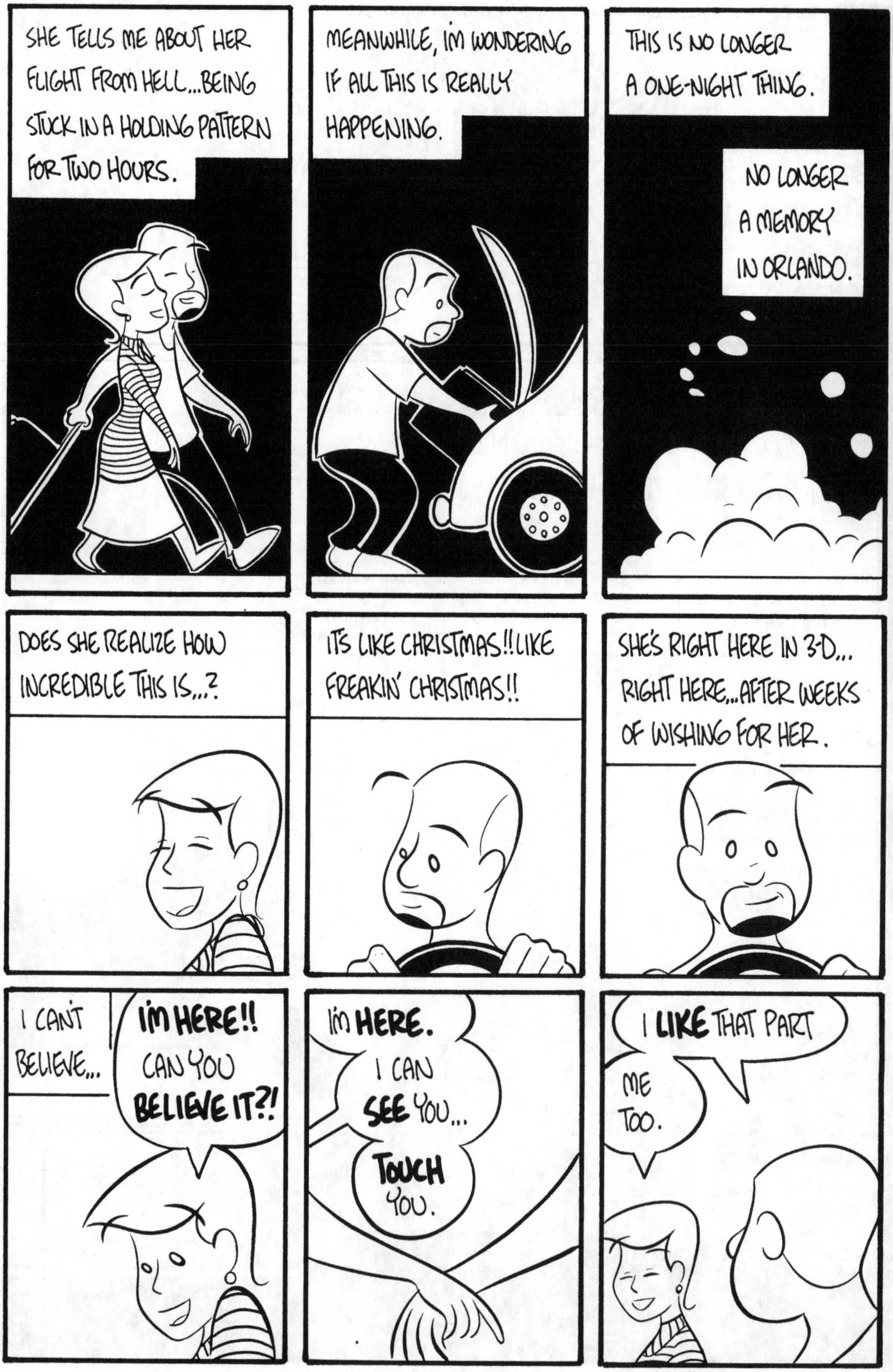
SHE TELLS ME ABOUT HER FLIGHT FROM HELL...BEING STUCK IN A HOLDING PATTERN FOR TWO HOURS.
MEANWHILE, I'M WONDERING IF ALL THIS IS REALLY HAPPENING.
THIS IS NO LONGER A ONE-NIGHT THING.
NO LONGER A MEMORY IN ORLANDO.
DOES SHE REALIZE HOW INCREDIBLE THIS IS...?
IT'S LIKE CHRISTMAS!! LIKE FREAKIN' CHRISTMAS!!
SHE'S RIGHT HERE IN 3-D... RIGHT HERE... AFTER WEEKS OF WISHING FOR HER.
I CAN'T BELIEVE...
I'M HERE!! CAN YOU BELIEVE IT?!
I'M HERE.
I CAN SEE YOU...
TOUCH YOU.
I LIKE THAT PART
ME TOO.

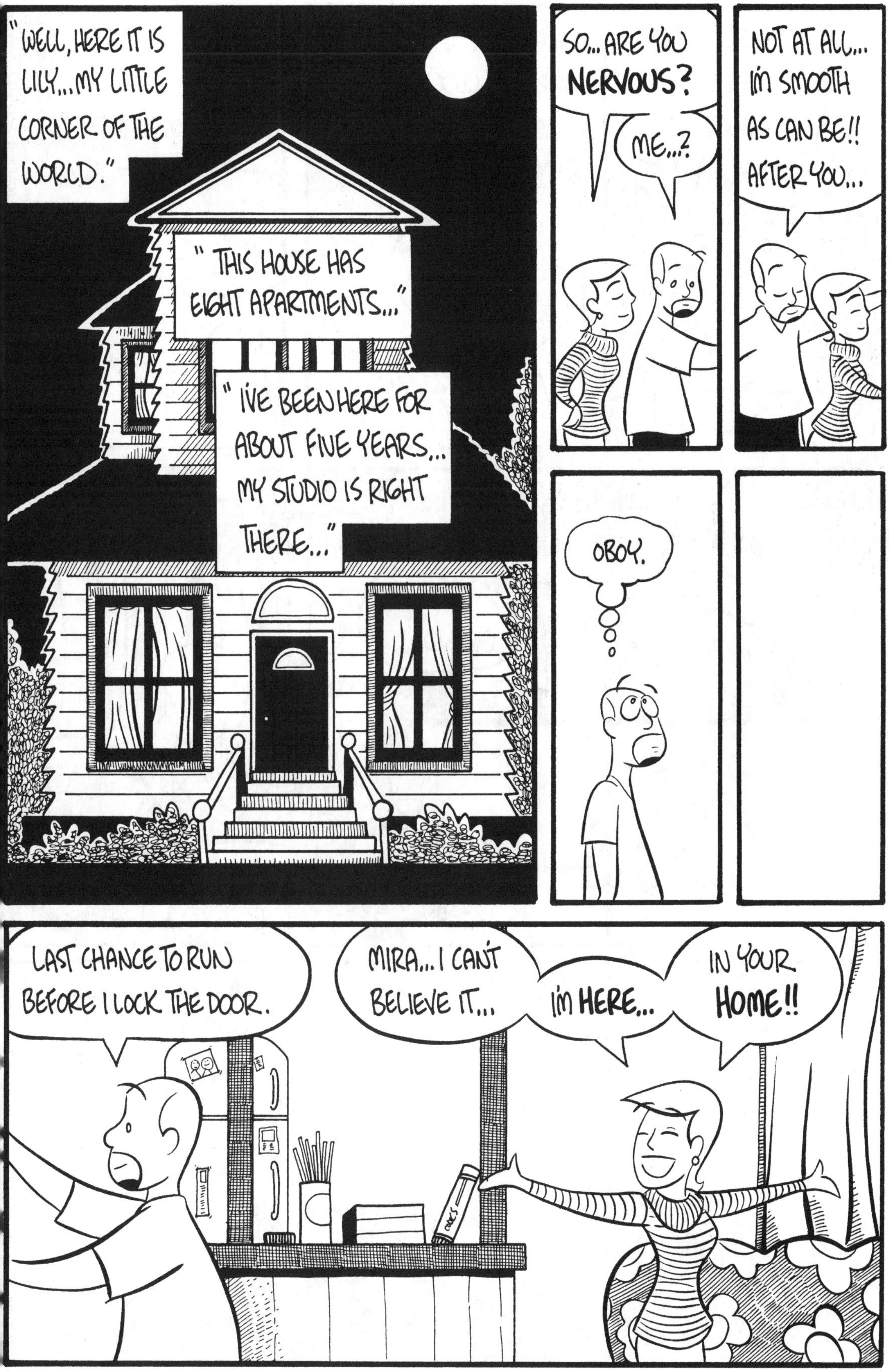
"WELL, HERE IT IS LILY... MY LITTLE CORNER OF THE WORLD."
" THIS HOUSE HAS EIGHT APARTMENTS..."
" I'VE BEEN HERE FOR ABOUT FIVE YEARS... MY STUDIO IS RIGHT THERE..."
SO... ARE YOU NERVOUS?
ME...?
NOT AT ALL... I'M SMOOTH AS CAN BE!! AFTER YOU...
OBOY.
LAST CHANCE TO RUN BEFORE I LOCK THE DOOR.
MIRA... I CAN'T BELIEVE IT...
I'M HERE...
IN YOUR HOME!!

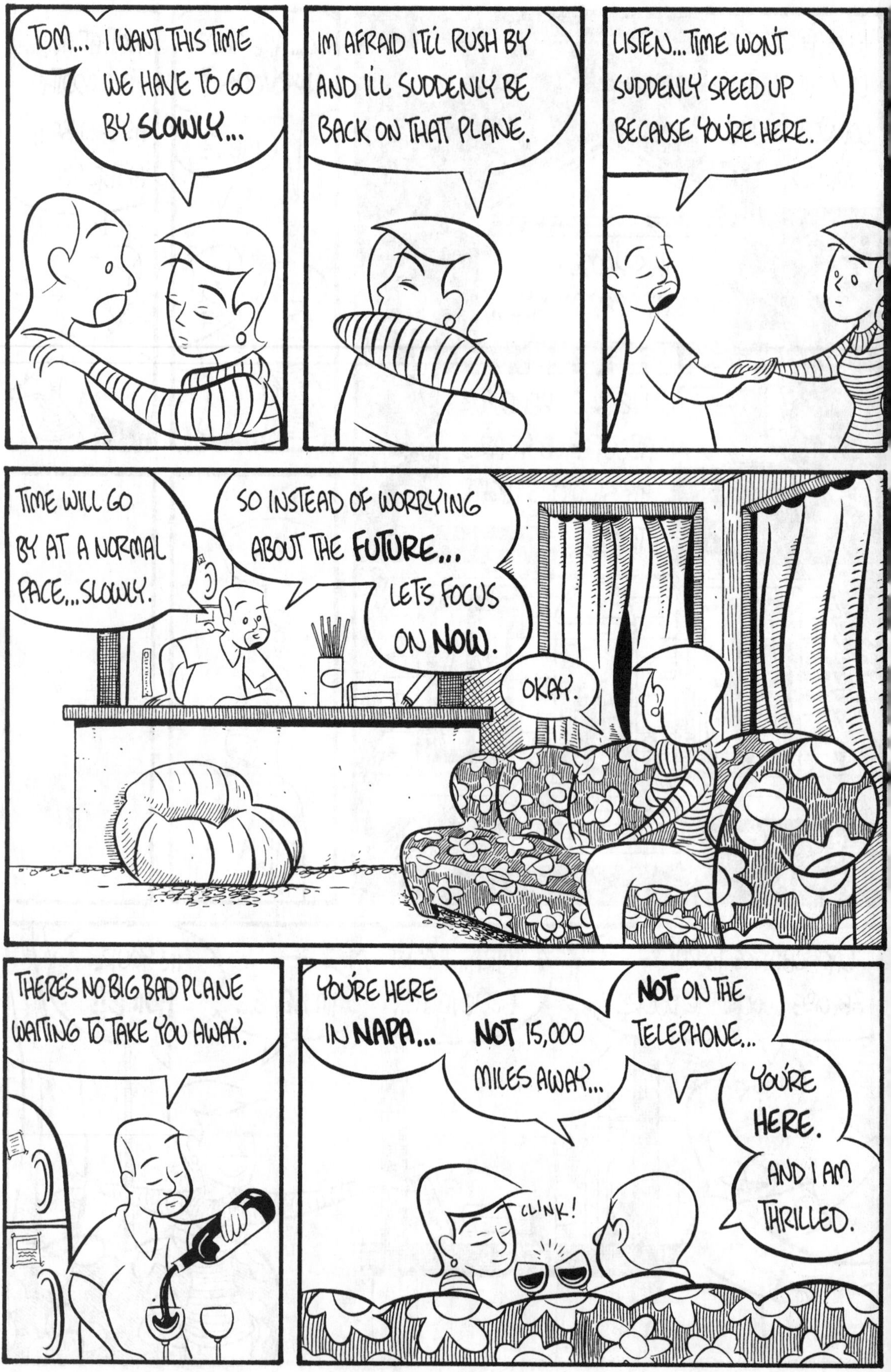
TOM... I WANT THIS TIME WE HAVE TO GO BY **SLOWLY**...
IM AFRAID IT'LL RUSH BY AND I'LL SUDDENLY BE BACK ON THAT PLANE.
LISTEN... TIME WON'T SUDDENLY SPEED UP BECAUSE YOU'RE HERE.
TIME WILL GO BY AT A NORMAL PACE... SLOWLY.
SO INSTEAD OF WORRYING ABOUT THE **FUTURE**... LET'S FOCUS ON **NOW**.
OKAY.
THERE'S NO BIG BAD PLANE WAITING TO TAKE YOU AWAY.
YOU'RE HERE IN **NAPA**...
NOT 15,000 MILES AWAY...
NOT ON THE TELEPHONE...
YOU'RE **HERE**.
AND I AM THRILLED.
CLINK!

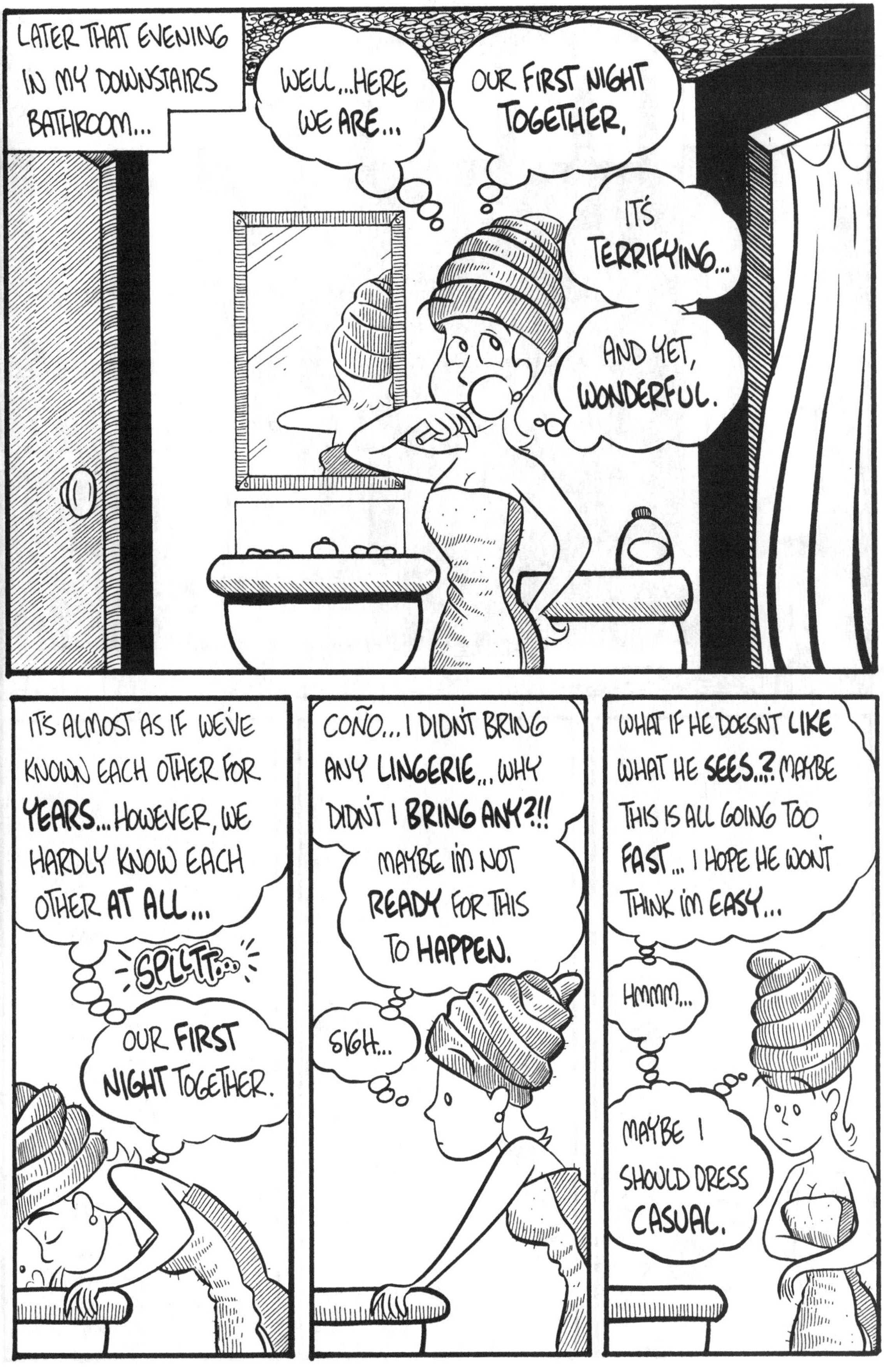
LATER THAT EVENING IN MY DOWNSTAIRS BATHROOM...
WELL...HERE WE ARE...
OUR FIRST NIGHT TOGETHER,
IT'S TERRIFYING...
AND YET, WONDERFUL.
IT'S ALMOST AS IF WE'VE KNOWN EACH OTHER FOR YEARS...HOWEVER, WE HARDLY KNOW EACH OTHER AT ALL...
SPLLTT...
OUR FIRST NIGHT TOGETHER.
COÑO...I DIDN'T BRING ANY LINGERIE...WHY DIDN'T I BRING ANY?!!
MAYBE I'M NOT READY FOR THIS TO HAPPEN.
SIGH...
WHAT IF HE DOESN'T LIKE WHAT HE SEES..? MAYBE THIS IS ALL GOING TOO FAST... I HOPE HE WON'T THINK I'M EASY...
HMMM...
MAYBE I SHOULD DRESS CASUAL.

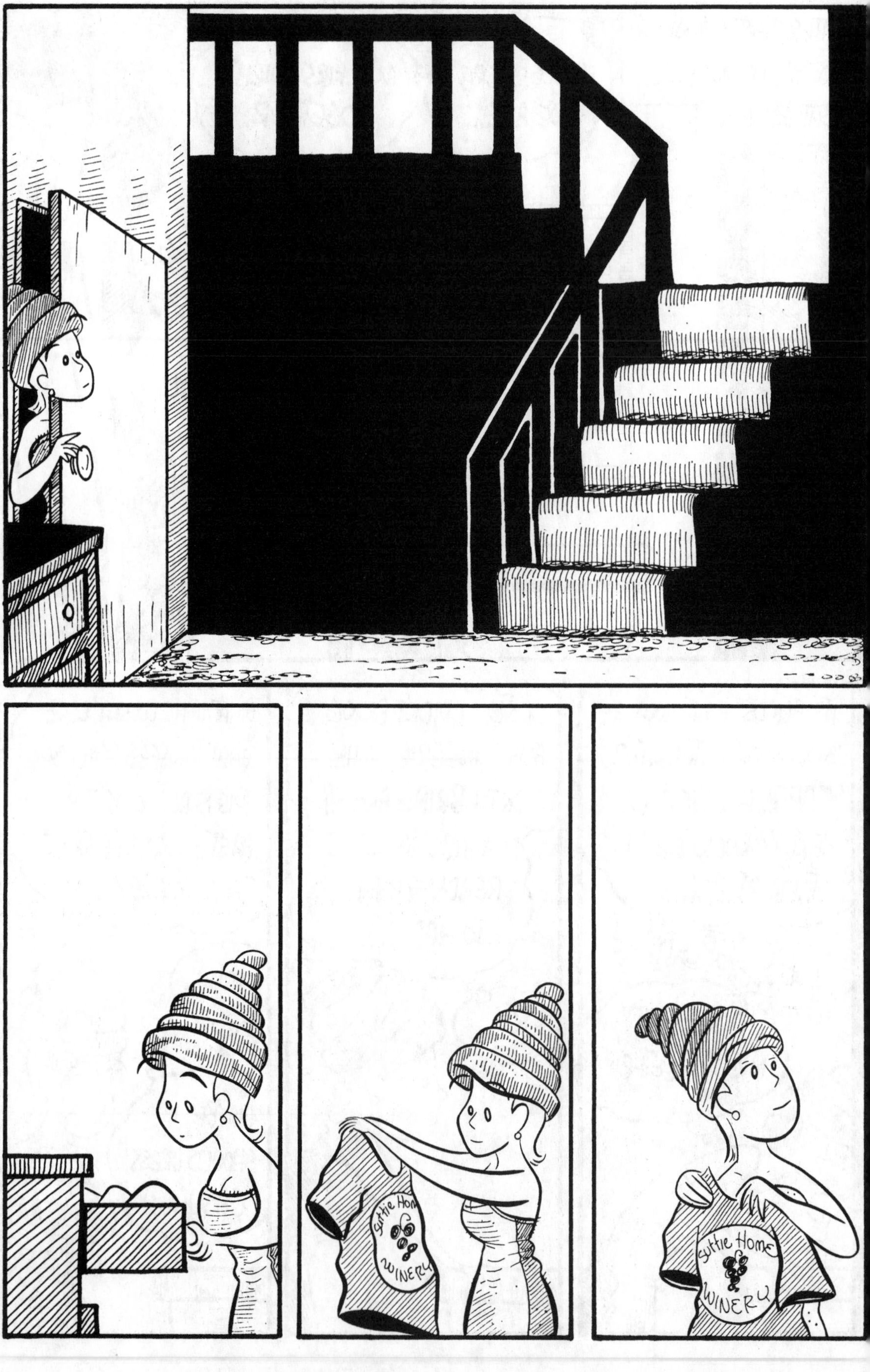
suttie Home
WINERY
suttie Home
WINERY

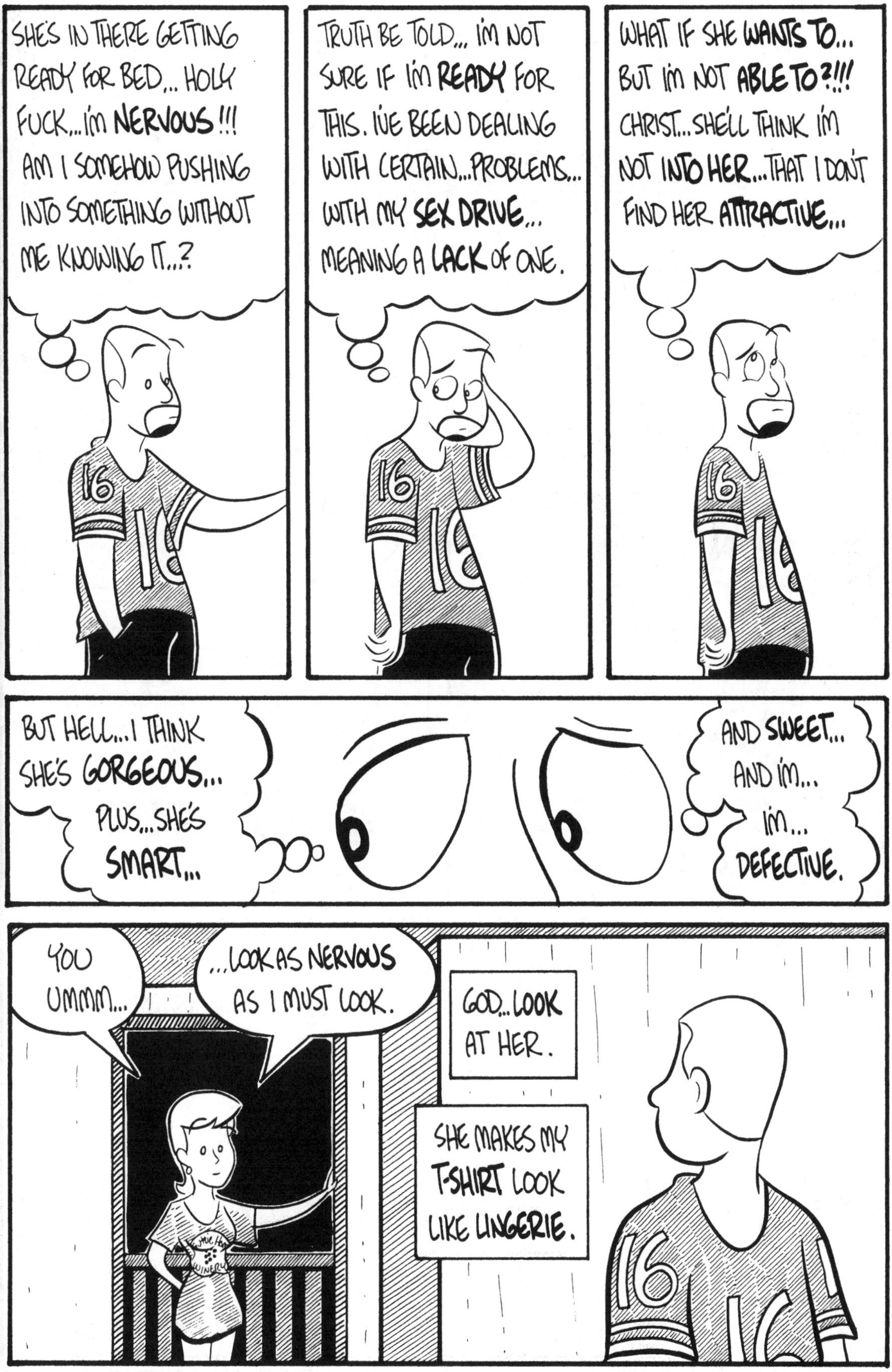
SHE'S IN THERE GETTING READY FOR BED... HOLY FUCK...I'M **NERVOUS**!!! AM I SOMEHOW PUSHING INTO SOMETHING WITHOUT ME KNOWING IT...?
TRUTH BE TOLD... I'M NOT SURE IF I'M **READY** FOR THIS. I'VE BEEN DEALING WITH CERTAIN...PROBLEMS... WITH MY **SEX DRIVE**... MEANING A **LACK** OF ONE.
WHAT IF SHE **WANTS TO**... BUT I'M NOT **ABLE TO**?!!! CHRIST...SHE'LL THINK I'M NOT **INTO HER**...THAT I DON'T FIND HER **ATTRACTIVE**...
BUT HELL...I THINK SHE'S **GORGEOUS**... PLUS...SHE'S **SMART**...
AND **SWEET**... AND I'M... I'M... **DEFECTIVE**.
YOU UMMM...
...LOOK AS **NERVOUS** AS I MUST LOOK.
GOD...**LOOK** AT HER.
SHE MAKES MY **T-SHIRT** LOOK LIKE **LINGERIE**.

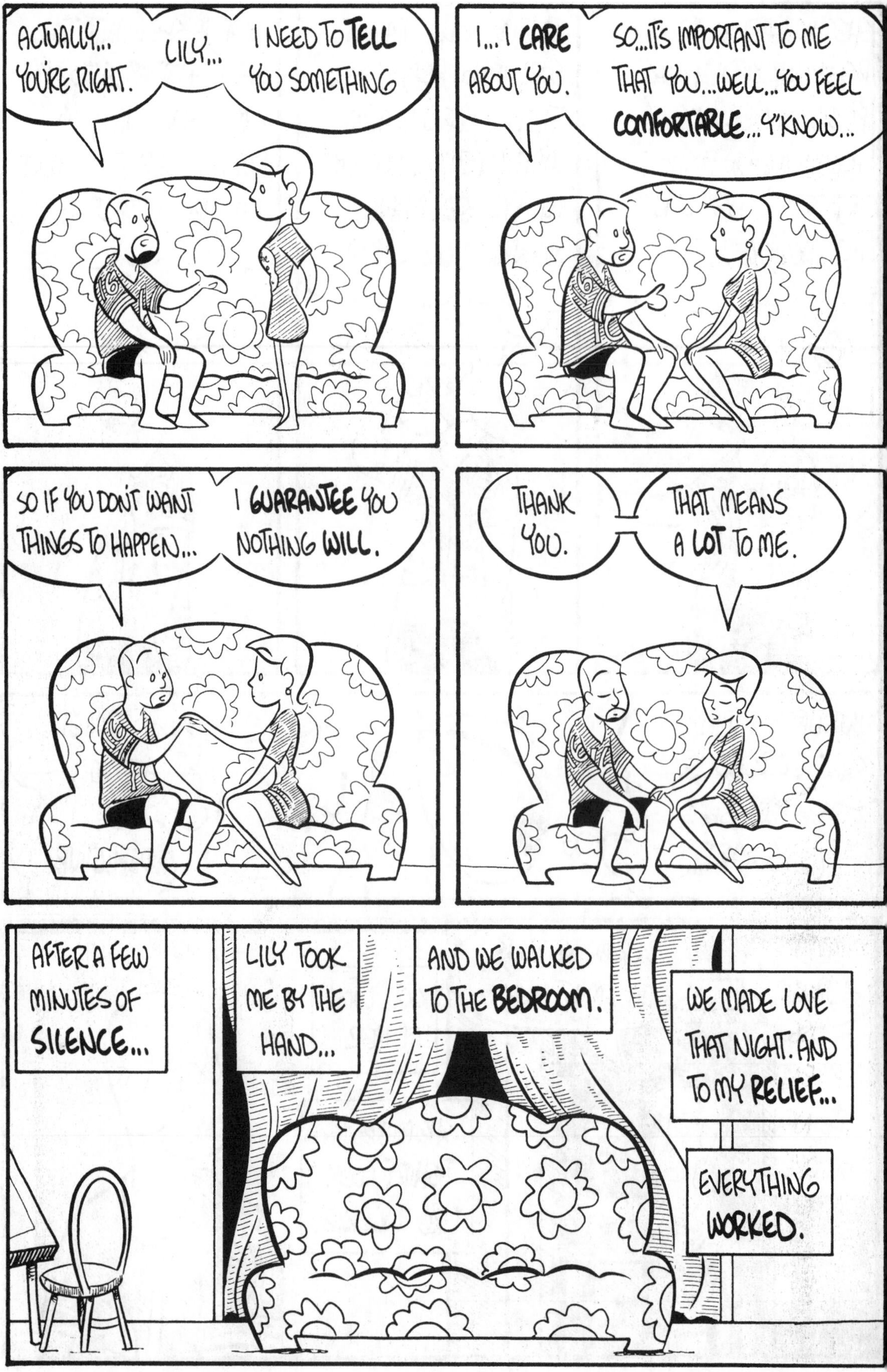
ACTUALLY... YOU'RE RIGHT.
LILY...
I NEED TO TELL YOU SOMETHING
I... I CARE ABOUT YOU.
SO...IT'S IMPORTANT TO ME THAT YOU...WELL...YOU FEEL COMFORTABLE...Y'KNOW...
SO IF YOU DON'T WANT THINGS TO HAPPEN...
I GUARANTEE YOU NOTHING WILL.
THANK YOU.
THAT MEANS A LOT TO ME.
AFTER A FEW MINUTES OF SILENCE...
LILY TOOK ME BY THE HAND...
AND WE WALKED TO THE BEDROOM.
WE MADE LOVE THAT NIGHT. AND TO MY RELIEF...
EVERYTHING WORKED.

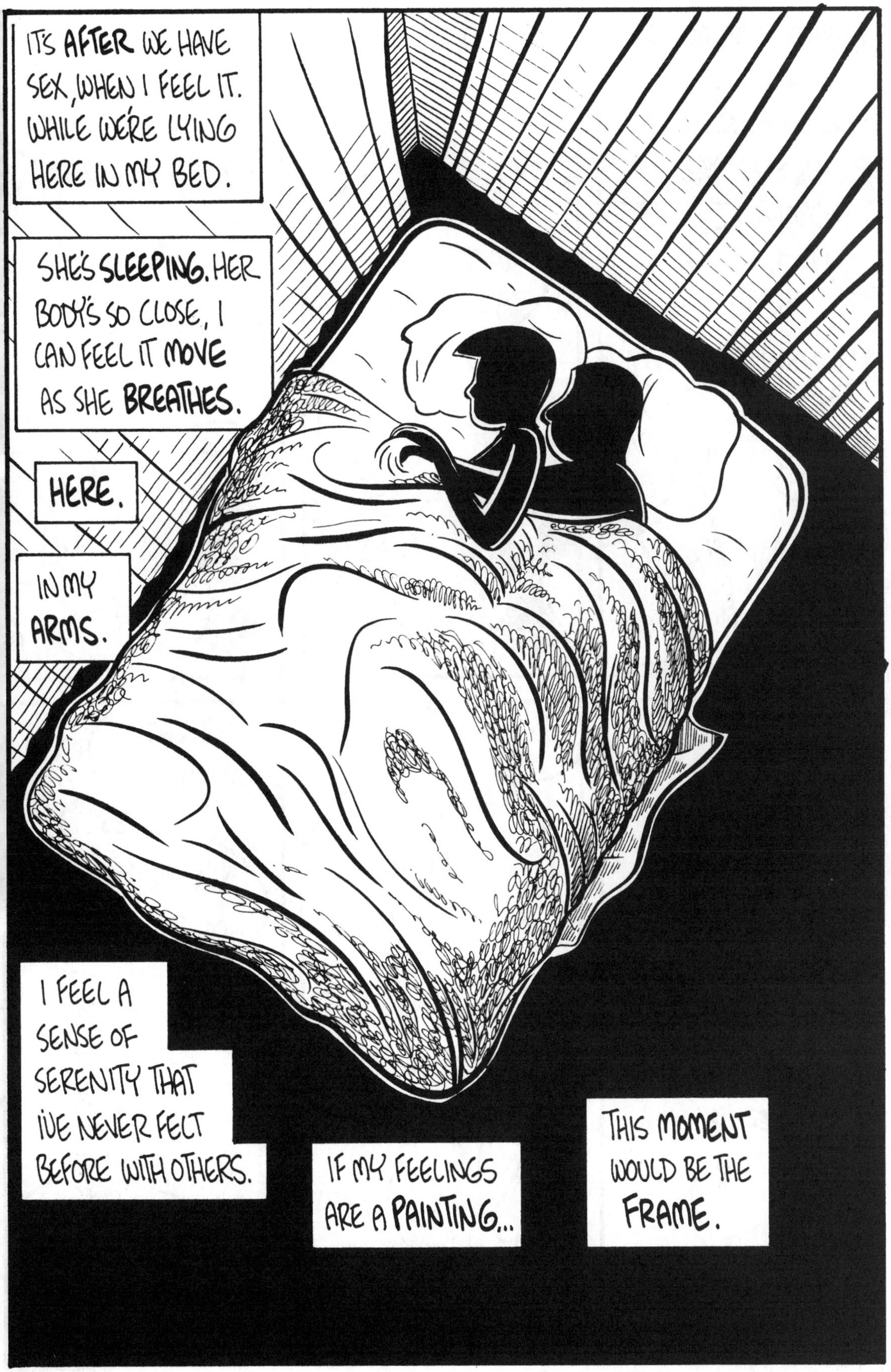
IT'S AFTER WE HAVE SEX, WHEN I FEEL IT. WHILE WE'RE LYING HERE IN MY BED.
SHE'S SLEEPING. HER BODY'S SO CLOSE, I CAN FEEL IT MOVE AS SHE BREATHES.
HERE.
IN MY ARMS.
I FEEL A SENSE OF SERENITY THAT I'VE NEVER FELT BEFORE WITH OTHERS.
IF MY FEELINGS ARE A PAINTING...
THIS MOMENT WOULD BE THE FRAME.

SURPRISINGLY, THE MORNING IS **AWKWARD-FREE**. WE HAVE BREAKFAST...OMLETS AND ORANGE JUICE.

SOOOOoo...

YES...?

I'M CURIOUS.

ABOUT...?

ABOUT... THIS. US. UMM...

I'M CURIOUS ABOUT WHAT IT IS WE **HAVE HERE**.

Hmm...

WELL...ID SAY WE HAVE SOMETHING VERY... **GOOD**.

I THINK WE'RE A VERY **GOOD THING**.

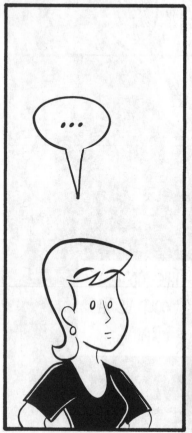

...

SOOOOOO...

THAT MEANS WE...**DO HAVE** SOMETHING...

IT'S NOT JUST **ME**.

NO,...IT'S **NOT** JUST YOU.

AND **YES** WE **HAVE** SOMETHING. SOMETHING...**GOOD**.

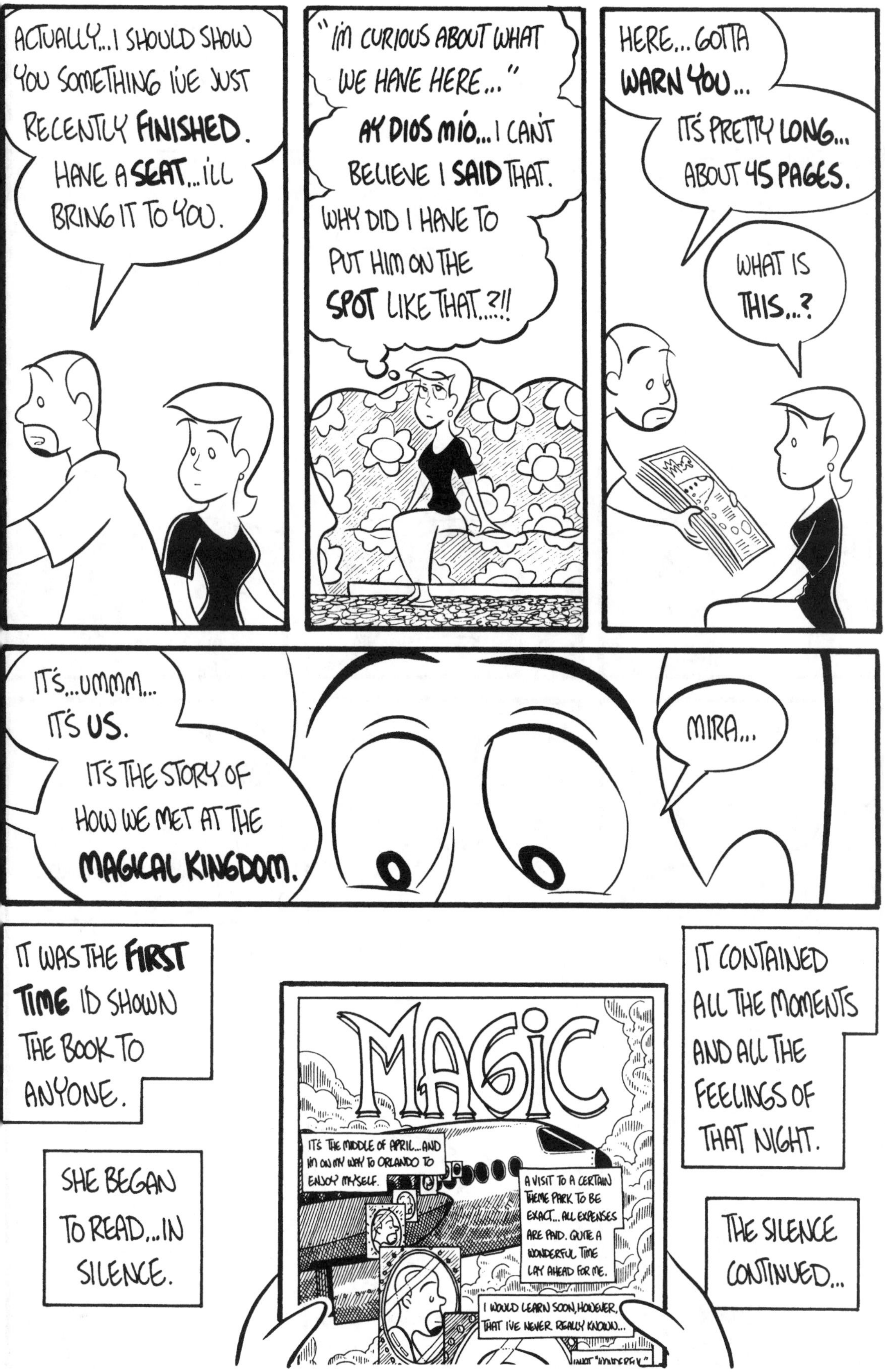
ACTUALLY...I SHOULD SHOW YOU SOMETHING I'VE JUST RECENTLY FINISHED. HAVE A SEAT...I'LL BRING IT TO YOU.
"I'M CURIOUS ABOUT WHAT WE HAVE HERE..."
AY DIOS MÍO...I CAN'T BELIEVE I SAID THAT.
WHY DID I HAVE TO PUT HIM ON THE SPOT LIKE THAT..?!!
HERE... GOTTA WARN YOU...
IT'S PRETTY LONG... ABOUT 45 PAGES.
WHAT IS THIS...?
IT'S...UMMM... IT'S US.
IT'S THE STORY OF HOW WE MET AT THE MAGICAL KINGDOM.
MIRA...
IT WAS THE FIRST TIME I'D SHOWN THE BOOK TO ANYONE.
SHE BEGAN TO READ...IN SILENCE.
MAGIC
IT'S THE MIDDLE OF APRIL...AND I'M ON MY WAY TO ORLANDO TO ENJOY MYSELF.
A VISIT TO A CERTAIN THEME PARK TO BE EXACT... ALL EXPENSES ARE PAID. QUITE A WONDERFUL TIME LAY AHEAD FOR ME.
I WOULD LEARN SOON, HOWEVER, THAT I'VE NEVER REALLY KNOWN...
IT CONTAINED ALL THE MOMENTS AND ALL THE FEELINGS OF THAT NIGHT.
THE SILENCE CONTINUED...

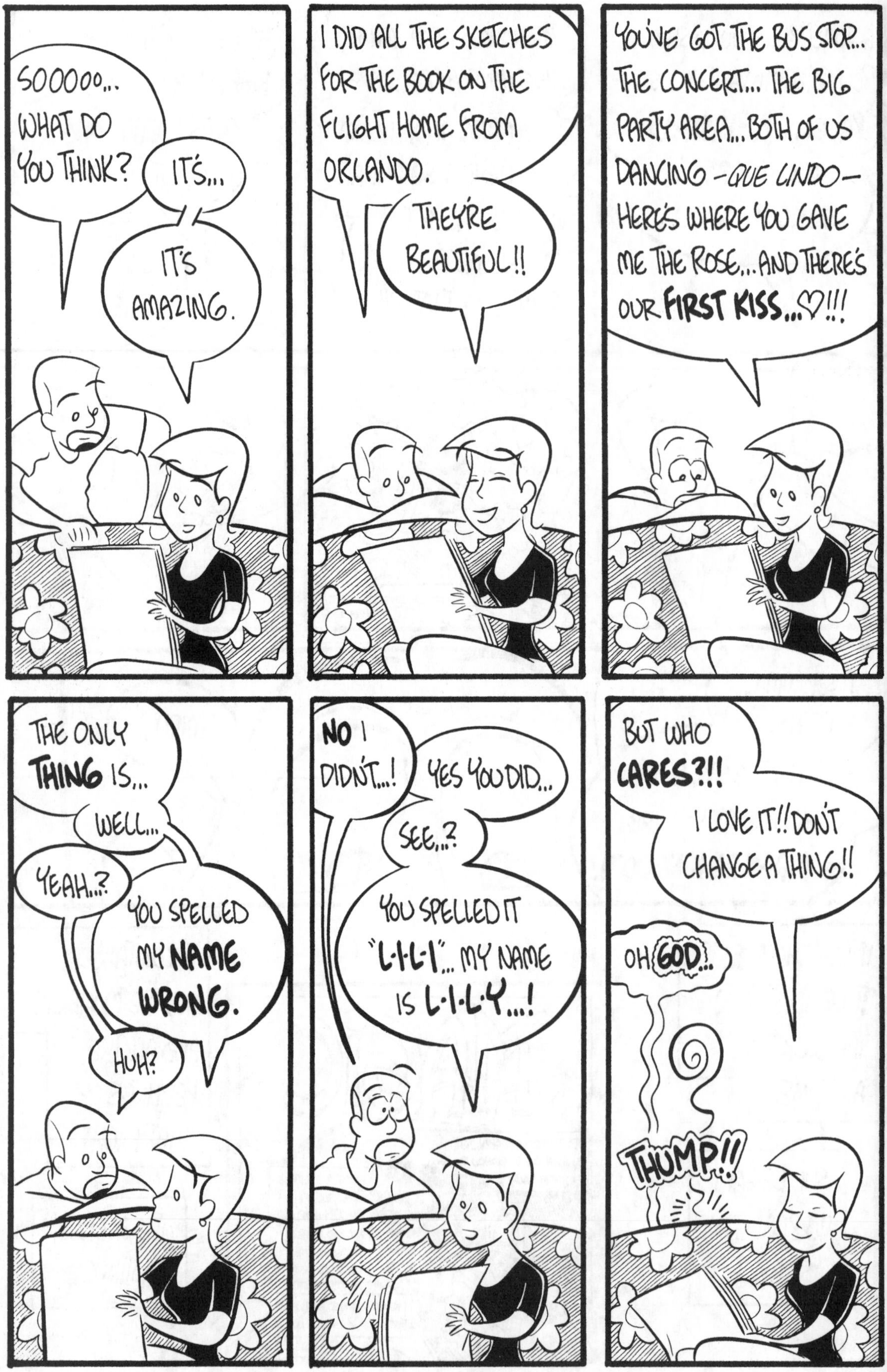
SOOOOo... WHAT DO YOU THINK?
IT'S...
IT'S AMAZING.
I DID ALL THE SKETCHES FOR THE BOOK ON THE FLIGHT HOME FROM ORLANDO.
THEY'RE BEAUTIFUL!!
YOU'VE GOT THE BUS STOP... THE CONCERT... THE BIG PARTY AREA... BOTH OF US DANCING -QUE LINDO- HERE'S WHERE YOU GAVE ME THE ROSE... AND THERE'S OUR FIRST KISS...♡!!!
THE ONLY THING IS...
WELL...
YEAH...?
YOU SPELLED MY NAME WRONG.
HUH?
NO I DIDN'T...!
YES YOU DID...
SEE...?
YOU SPELLED IT "L·I·L·I"... MY NAME IS L·I·L·Y...!
BUT WHO CARES?!!
I LOVE IT!! DON'T CHANGE A THING!!
OH GOD...
THUMP!!

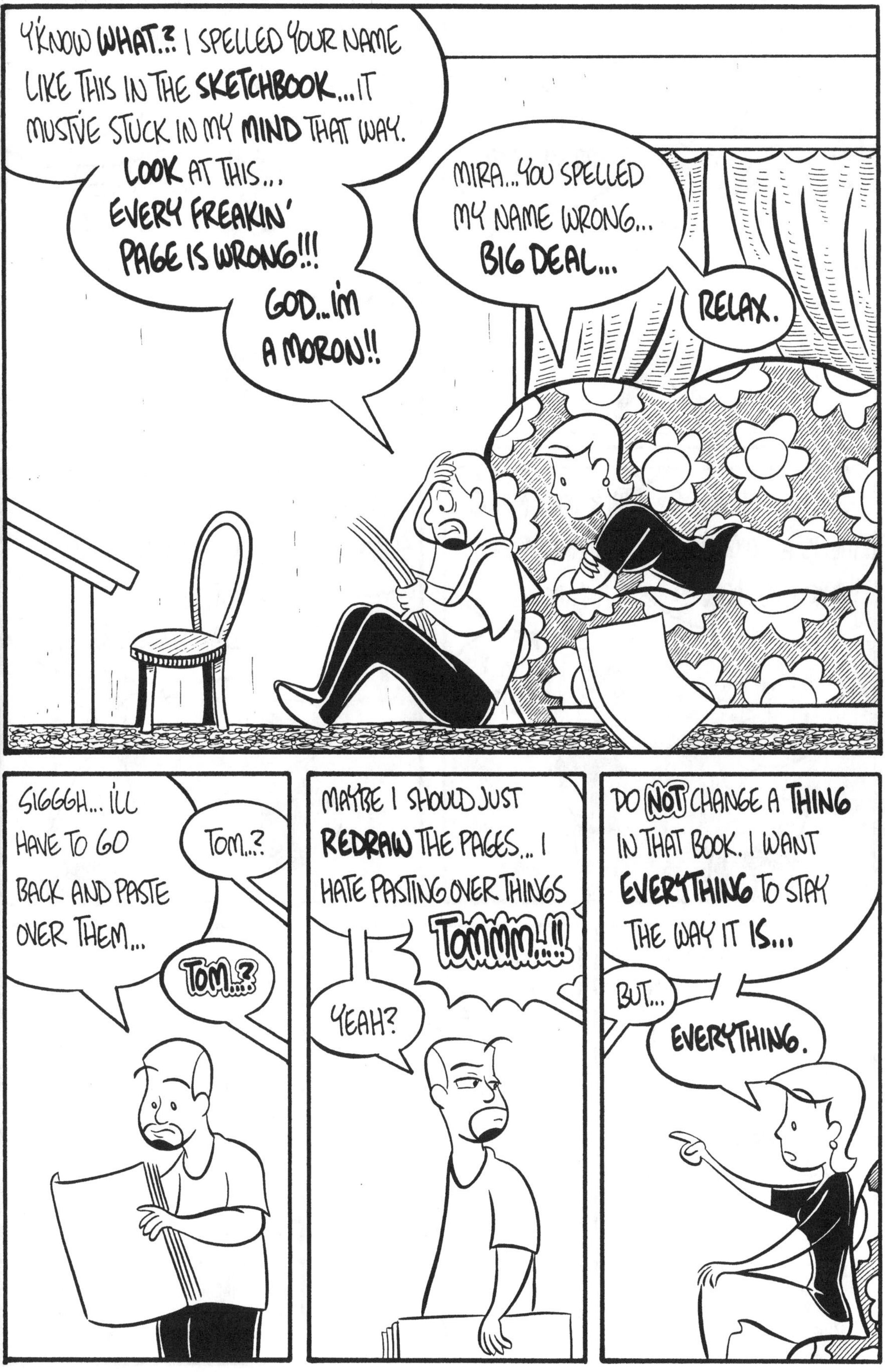

Y'KNOW WHAT..?! I SPELLED YOUR NAME LIKE THIS IN THE SKETCHBOOK...IT MUST'VE STUCK IN MY MIND THAT WAY.
LOOK AT THIS... EVERY FREAKIN' PAGE IS WRONG!!!
GOD...I'M A MORON!!
MIRA...YOU SPELLED MY NAME WRONG... BIG DEAL...
RELAX.
SIGGGH... I'LL HAVE TO GO BACK AND PASTE OVER THEM...
TOM..?
TOM...?
MAYBE I SHOULD JUST REDRAW THE PAGES... I HATE PASTING OVER THINGS
TOMMM..!!
YEAH?
DO NOT CHANGE A THING IN THAT BOOK. I WANT EVERYTHING TO STAY THE WAY IT IS...
BUT...
EVERYTHING.

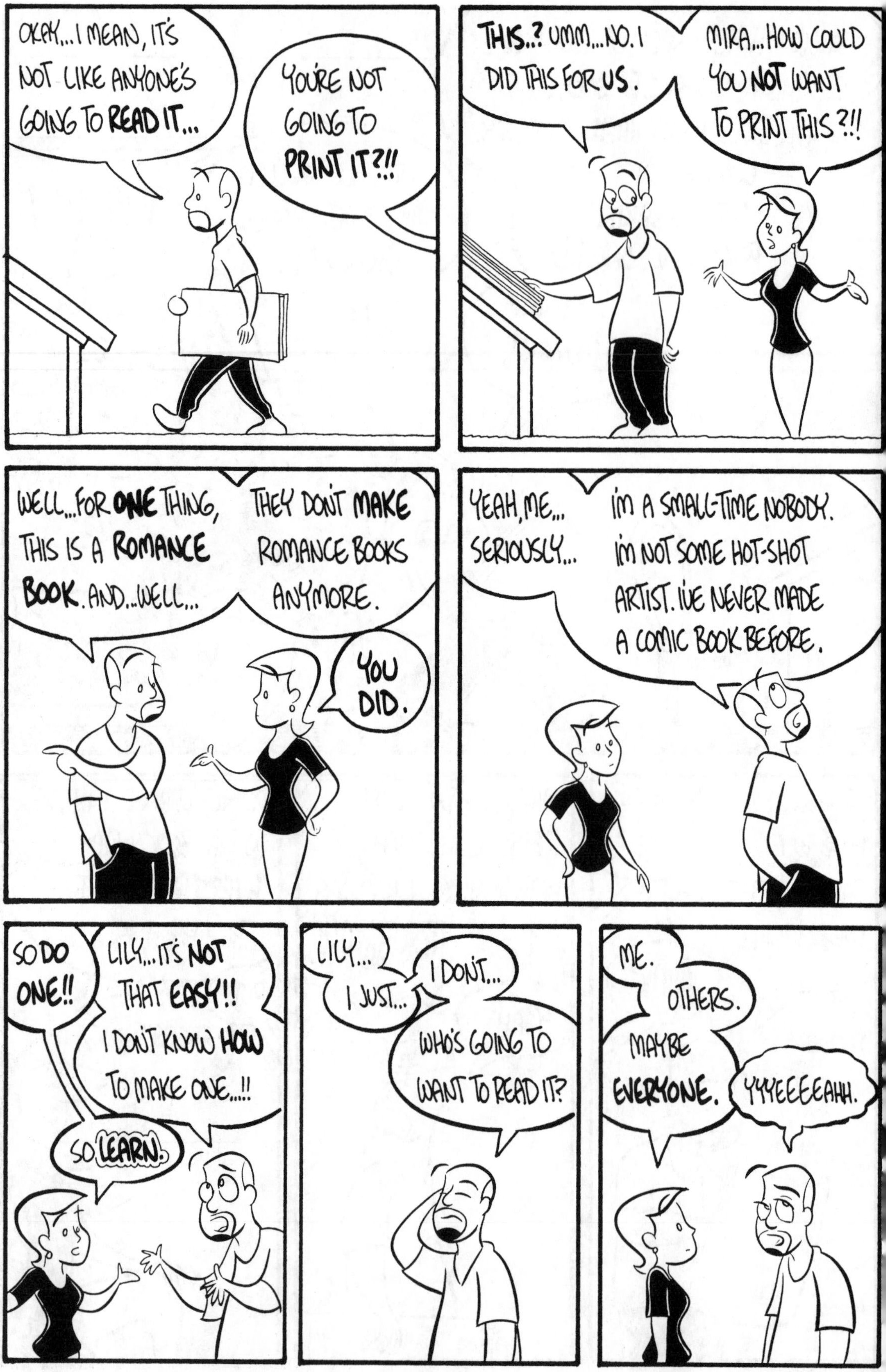
OKAY... I MEAN, IT'S NOT LIKE ANYONE'S GOING TO READ IT...
YOU'RE NOT GOING TO PRINT IT?!!
THIS..? UMM... NO. I DID THIS FOR US.
MIRA... HOW COULD YOU NOT WANT TO PRINT THIS?!!
WELL... FOR ONE THING, THIS IS A ROMANCE BOOK. AND... WELL...
THEY DON'T MAKE ROMANCE BOOKS ANYMORE.
YOU DID.
YEAH, ME... SERIOUSLY...
I'M A SMALL-TIME NOBODY. I'M NOT SOME HOT-SHOT ARTIST. I'VE NEVER MADE A COMIC BOOK BEFORE.
SO DO ONE!!
LILY... IT'S NOT THAT EASY!! I DON'T KNOW HOW TO MAKE ONE...!!
SO LEARN.
LILY... I JUST...
I DON'T...
WHO'S GOING TO WANT TO READ IT?
ME.
OTHERS.
MAYBE EVERYONE.
YYYEEEEAHH.

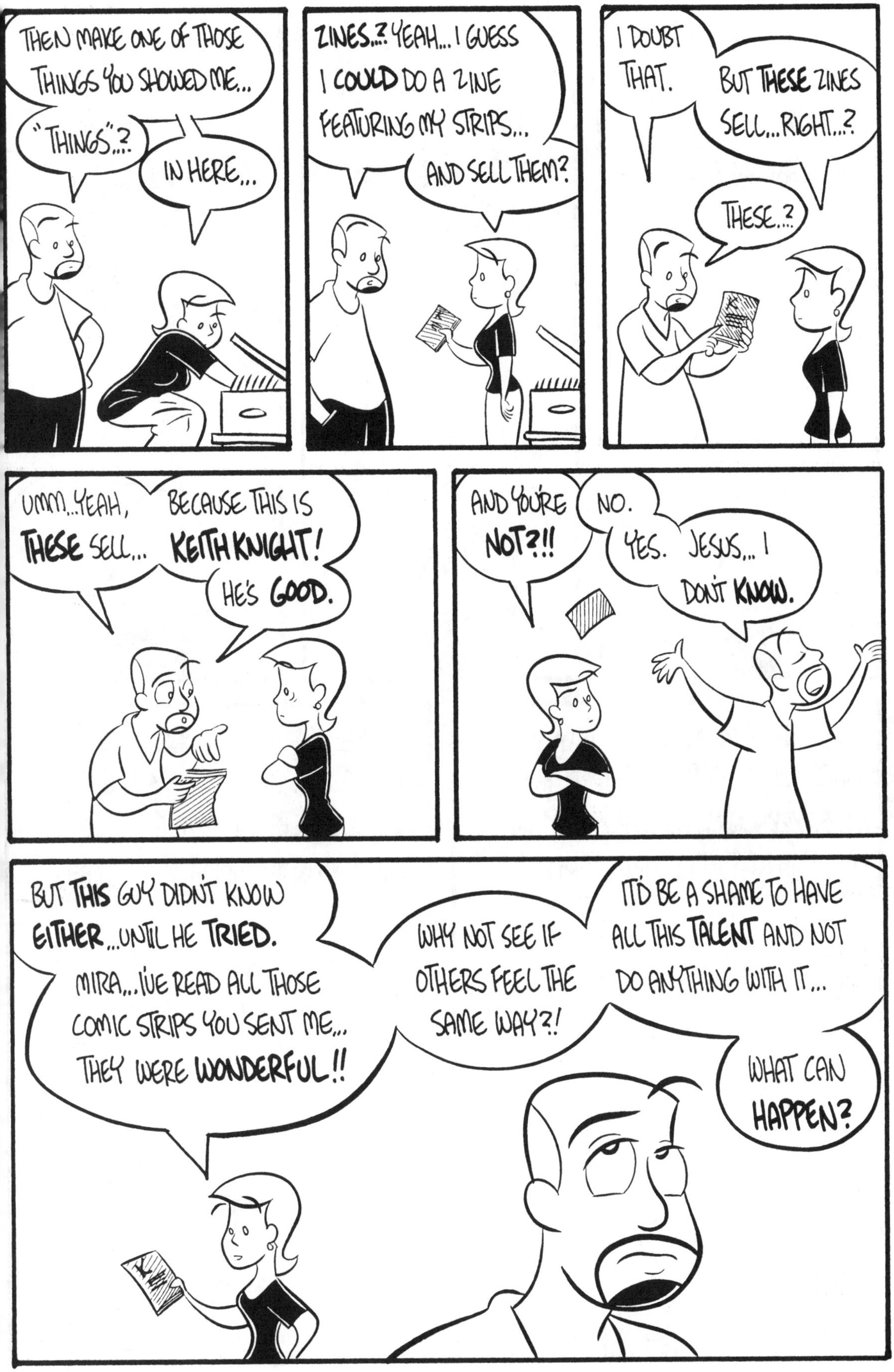
THEN MAKE ONE OF THOSE THINGS YOU SHOWED ME...
"THINGS"...?
IN HERE...
ZINES...? YEAH... I GUESS I COULD DO A ZINE FEATURING MY STRIPS...
AND SELL THEM?
I DOUBT THAT.
BUT THESE ZINES SELL... RIGHT...?
THESE...?
UMM...YEAH, THESE SELL...
BECAUSE THIS IS KEITH KNIGHT!
HE'S GOOD.
AND YOU'RE NOT?!!
NO.
YES. JESUS... I DON'T KNOW.
BUT THIS GUY DIDN'T KNOW EITHER...UNTIL HE TRIED.
MIRA... I'VE READ ALL THOSE COMIC STRIPS YOU SENT ME... THEY WERE WONDERFUL!!
WHY NOT SEE IF OTHERS FEEL THE SAME WAY?!
IT'D BE A SHAME TO HAVE ALL THIS TALENT AND NOT DO ANYTHING WITH IT...
WHAT CAN HAPPEN?

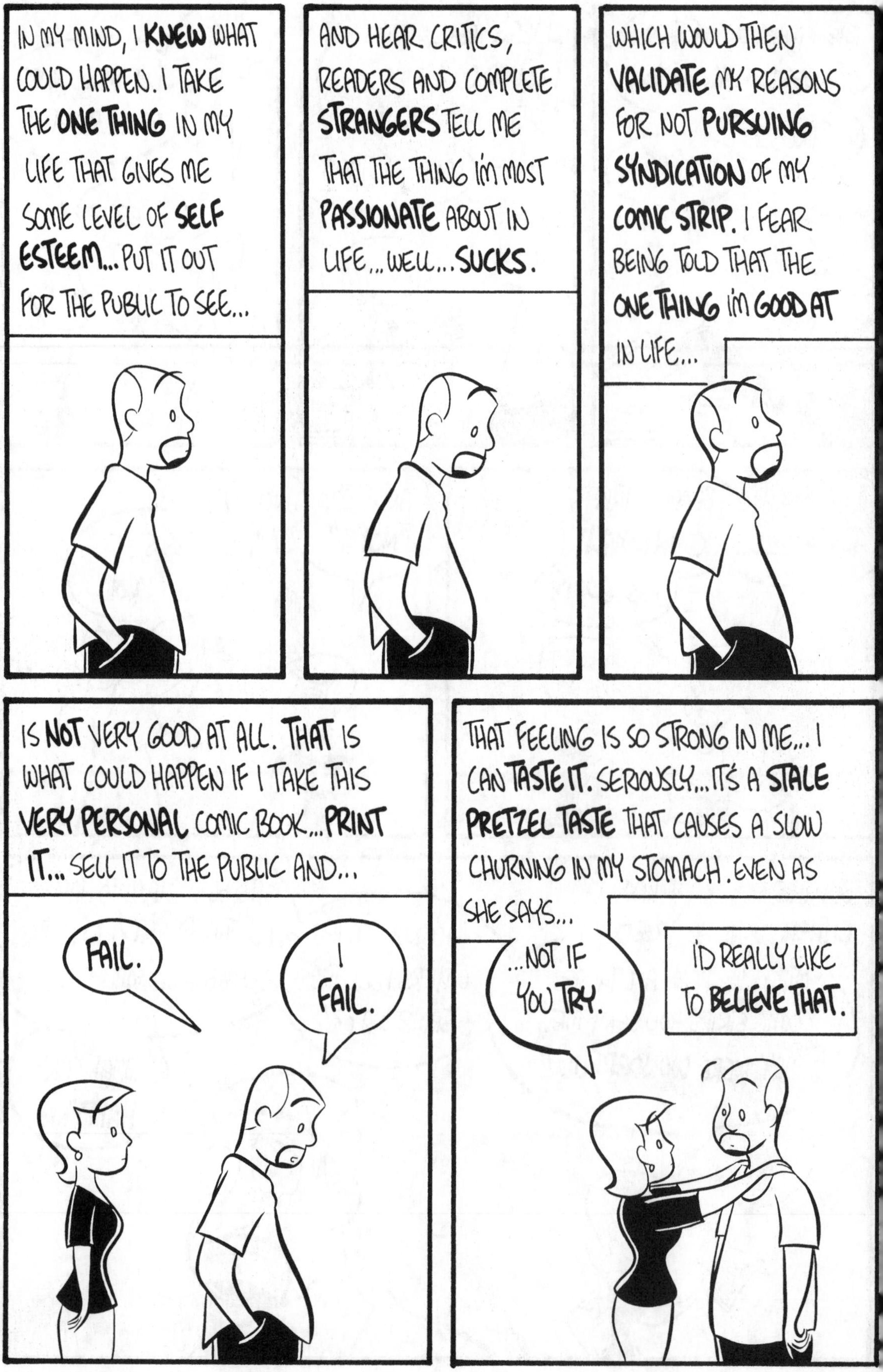
IN MY MIND, I KNEW WHAT COULD HAPPEN. I TAKE THE ONE THING IN MY LIFE THAT GIVES ME SOME LEVEL OF SELF ESTEEM... PUT IT OUT FOR THE PUBLIC TO SEE...
AND HEAR CRITICS, READERS AND COMPLETE STRANGERS TELL ME THAT THE THING I'M MOST PASSIONATE ABOUT IN LIFE... WELL... SUCKS.
WHICH WOULD THEN VALIDATE MY REASONS FOR NOT PURSUING SYNDICATION OF MY COMIC STRIP. I FEAR BEING TOLD THAT THE ONE THING I'M GOOD AT IN LIFE...
IS NOT VERY GOOD AT ALL. THAT IS WHAT COULD HAPPEN IF I TAKE THIS VERY PERSONAL COMIC BOOK... PRINT IT... SELL IT TO THE PUBLIC AND...
FAIL.
I FAIL.
THAT FEELING IS SO STRONG IN ME... I CAN TASTE IT. SERIOUSLY... IT'S A STALE PRETZEL TASTE THAT CAUSES A SLOW CHURNING IN MY STOMACH. EVEN AS SHE SAYS...
...NOT IF YOU TRY.
I'D REALLY LIKE TO BELIEVE THAT.

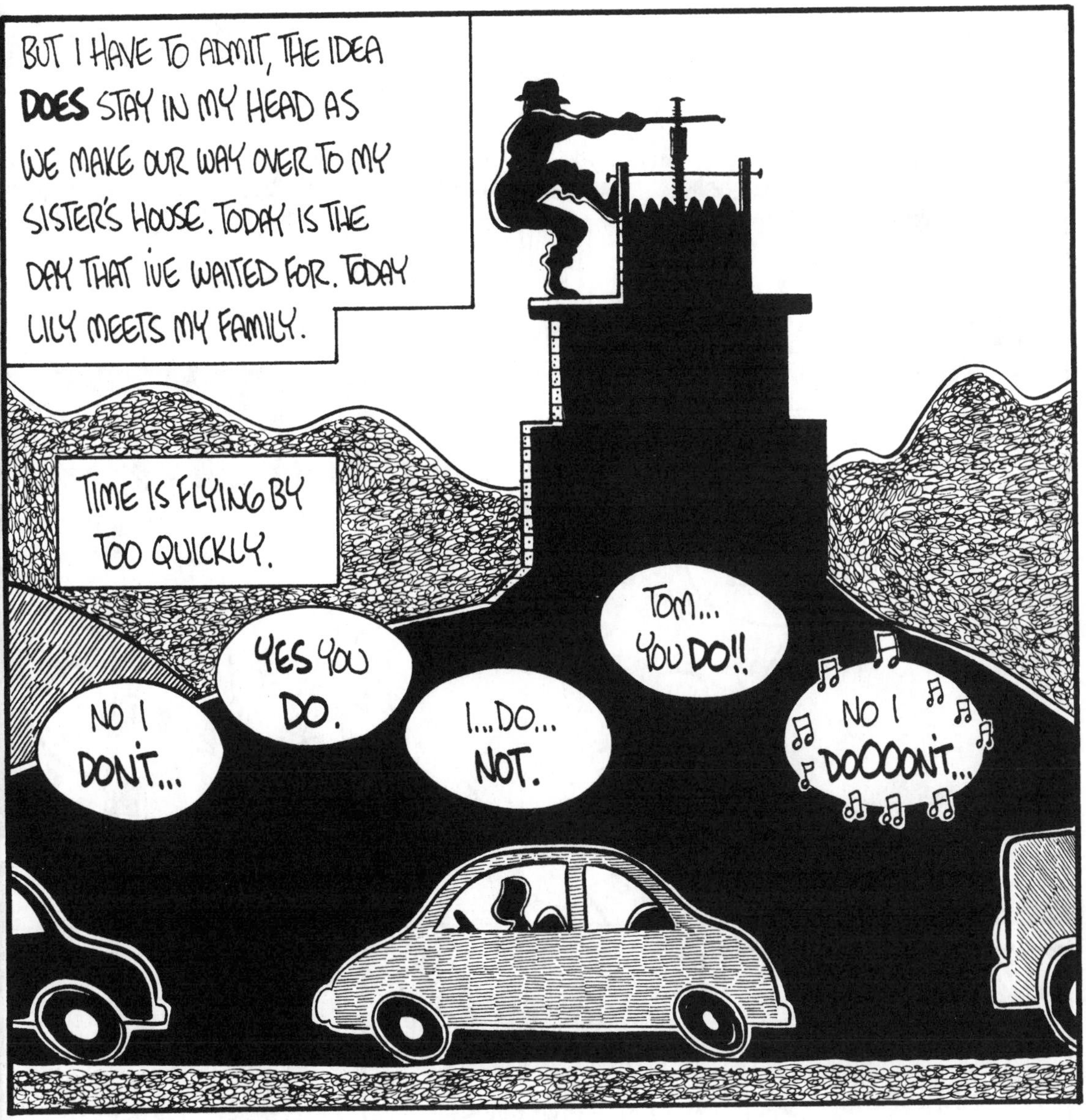
BUT I HAVE TO ADMIT, THE IDEA **DOES** STAY IN MY HEAD AS WE MAKE OUR WAY OVER TO MY SISTER'S HOUSE. TODAY IS THE DAY THAT I'VE WAITED FOR. TODAY LILY MEETS MY FAMILY.
TIME IS FLYING BY TOO QUICKLY.
NO I DON'T...
YES YOU DO.
I...DO... NOT.
TOM... YOU DO!!
NO I DOOOON'T...

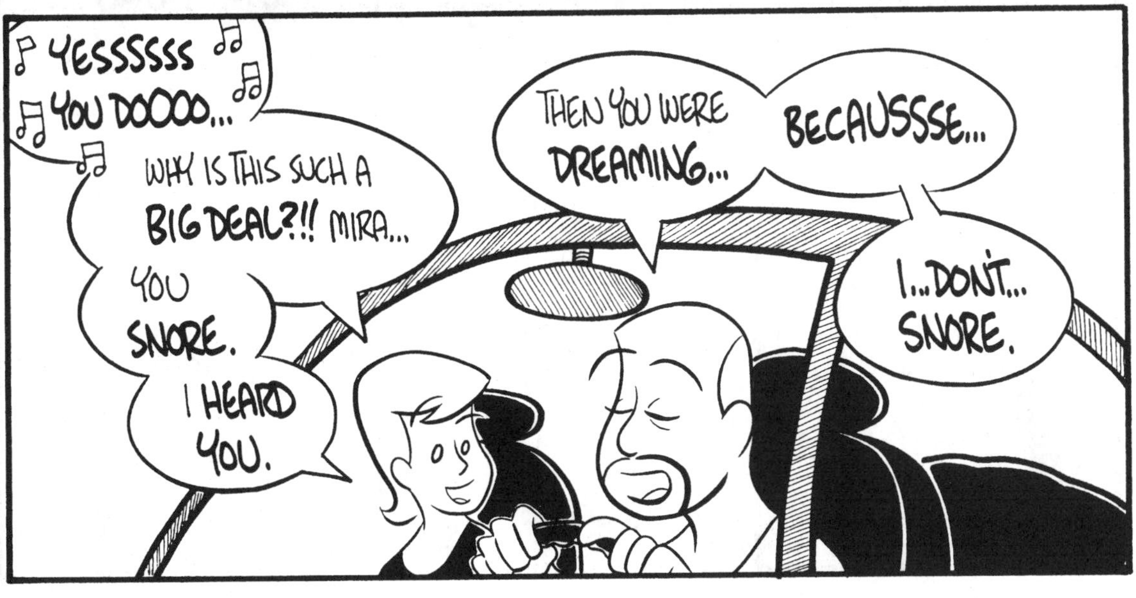
YESSSSSS YOU DOOOO...
WHY IS THIS SUCH A BIG DEAL?!! MIRA...
YOU SNORE.
I HEARD YOU.
THEN YOU WERE DREAMING...
BECAUSSSE...
I...DON'T... SNORE.

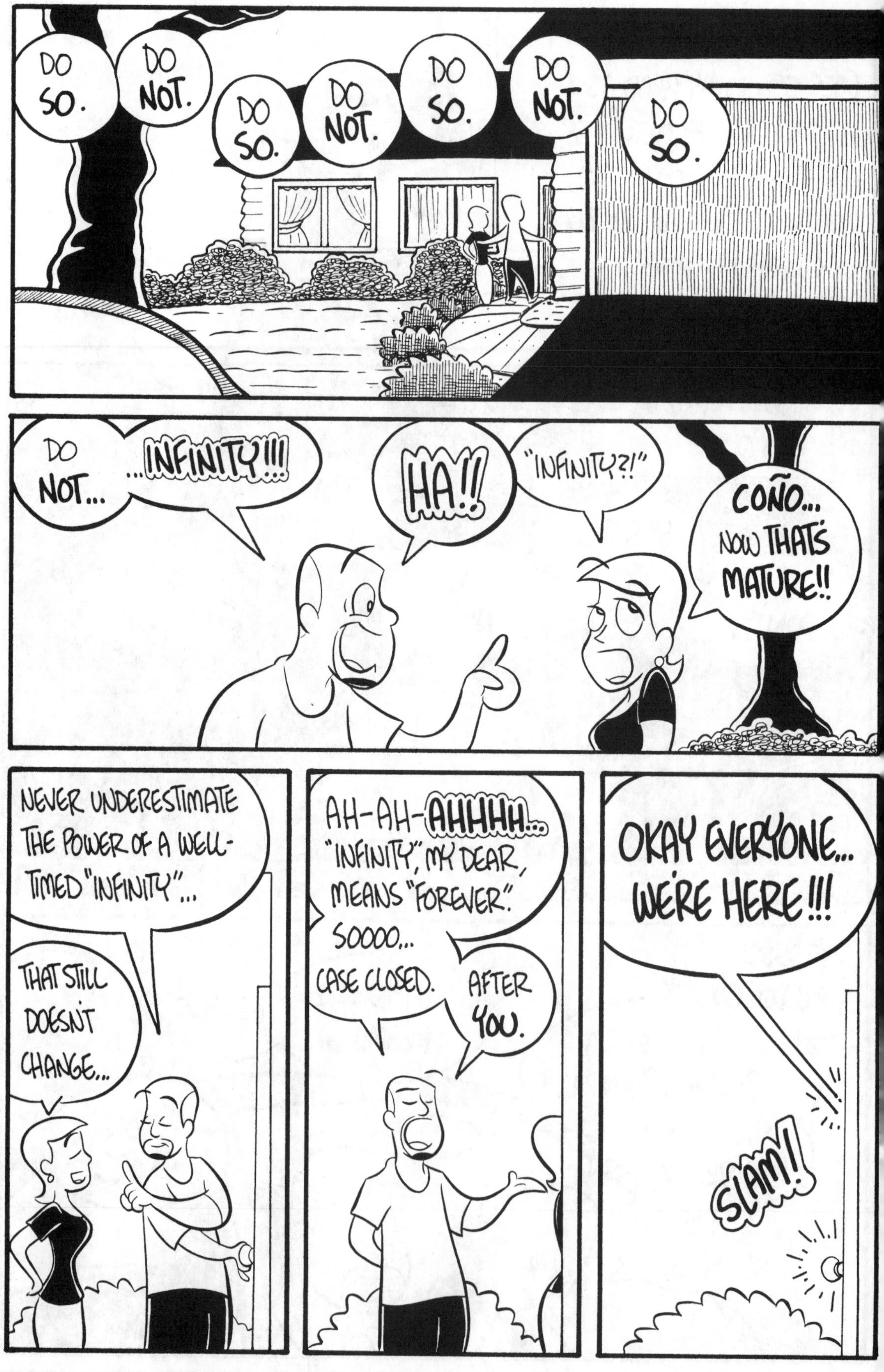
DO SO.
DO NOT.
DO SO.
DO NOT.
DO SO.
DO NOT.
DO SO.
DO NOT...
...INFINITY!!!
HA!!
"INFINITY?!"
COÑO... NOW THAT'S MATURE!!
NEVER UNDERESTIMATE THE POWER OF A WELL-TIMED "INFINITY"...
THAT STILL DOESN'T CHANGE...
AH-AH-AHHHH... "INFINITY", MY DEAR, MEANS "FOREVER". SOOOO... CASE CLOSED.
AFTER YOU.
OKAY EVERYONE... WE'RE HERE!!!
SLAM!

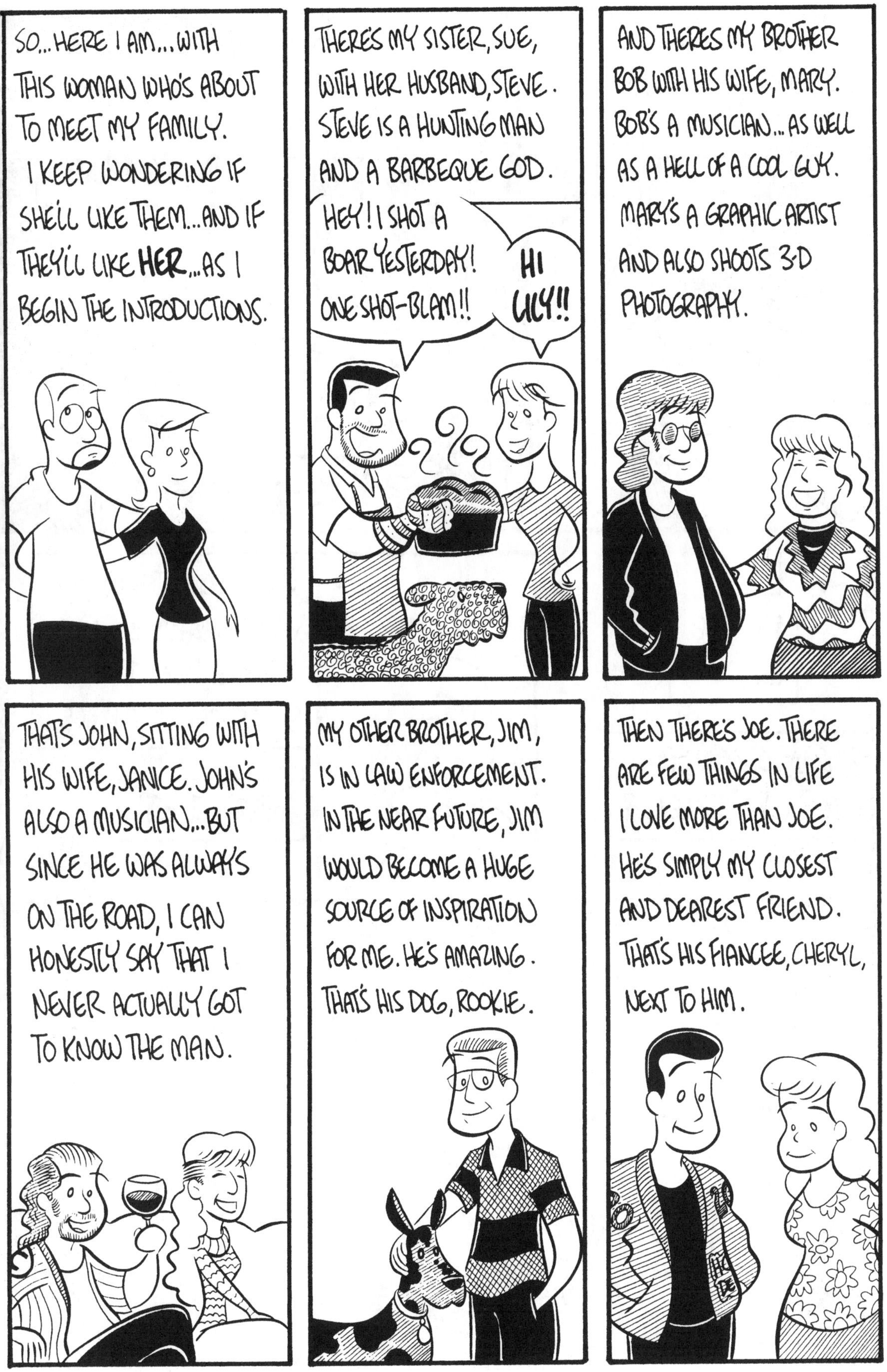
SO... HERE I AM... WITH THIS WOMAN WHO'S ABOUT TO MEET MY FAMILY. I KEEP WONDERING IF SHE'LL LIKE THEM... AND IF THEY'LL LIKE HER... AS I BEGIN THE INTRODUCTIONS.
THERE'S MY SISTER, SUE, WITH HER HUSBAND, STEVE. STEVE IS A HUNTING MAN AND A BARBEQUE GOD.
HEY! I SHOT A BOAR YESTERDAY! ONE SHOT-BLAM!!
HI LILY!!
AND THERE'S MY BROTHER BOB WITH HIS WIFE, MARY. BOB'S A MUSICIAN... AS WELL AS A HELL OF A COOL GUY. MARY'S A GRAPHIC ARTIST AND ALSO SHOOTS 3-D PHOTOGRAPHY.
THAT'S JOHN, SITTING WITH HIS WIFE, JANICE. JOHN'S ALSO A MUSICIAN... BUT SINCE HE WAS ALWAYS ON THE ROAD, I CAN HONESTLY SAY THAT I NEVER ACTUALLY GOT TO KNOW THE MAN.
MY OTHER BROTHER, JIM, IS IN LAW ENFORCEMENT. IN THE NEAR FUTURE, JIM WOULD BECOME A HUGE SOURCE OF INSPIRATION FOR ME. HE'S AMAZING. THAT'S HIS DOG, ROOKIE.
THEN THERE'S JOE. THERE ARE FEW THINGS IN LIFE I LOVE MORE THAN JOE. HE'S SIMPLY MY CLOSEST AND DEAREST FRIEND. THAT'S HIS FIANCEE, CHERYL, NEXT TO HIM.

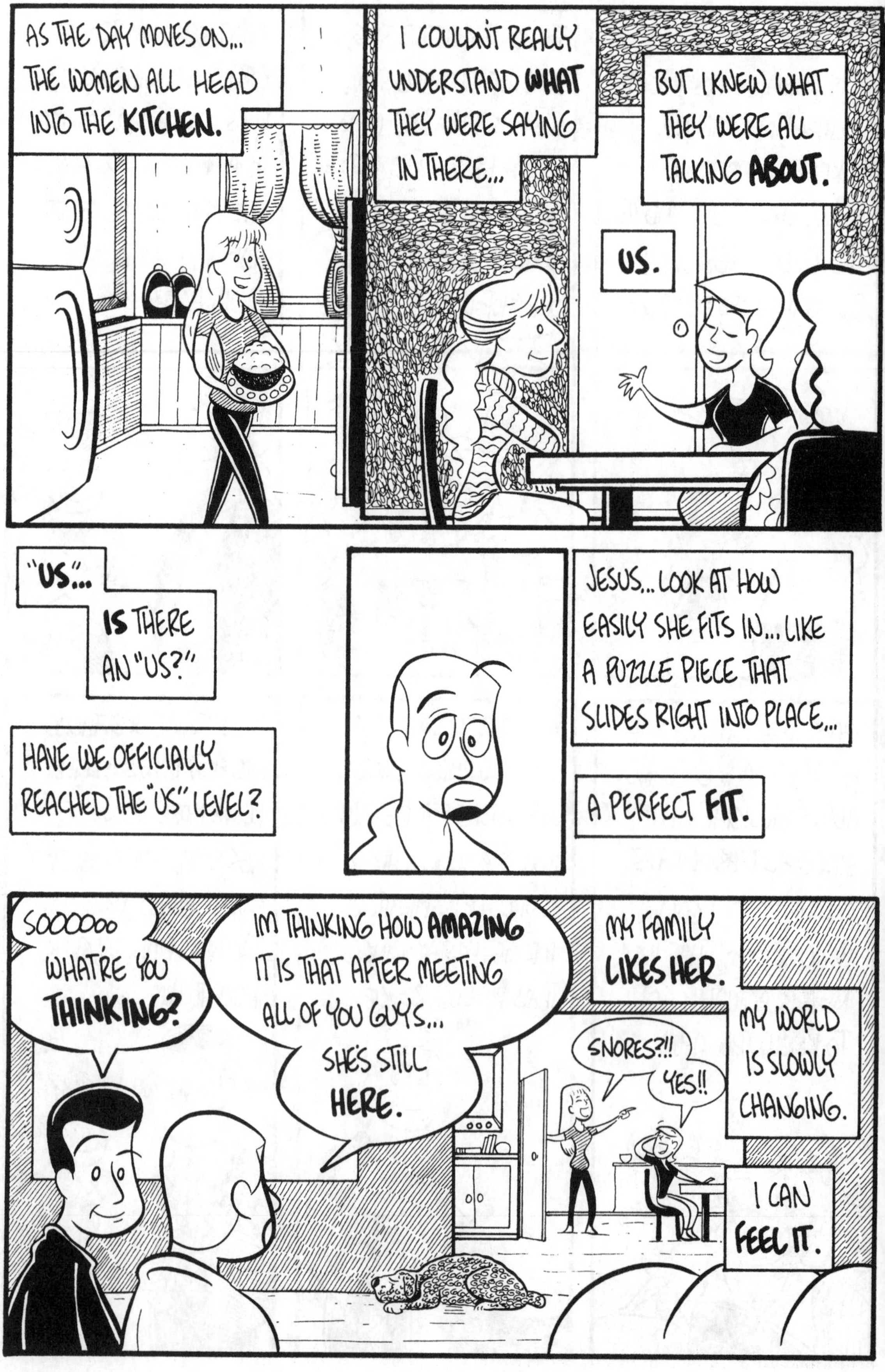
AS THE DAY MOVES ON... THE WOMEN ALL HEAD INTO THE **KITCHEN.**
I COULDN'T REALLY UNDERSTAND **WHAT** THEY WERE SAYING IN THERE...
BUT I KNEW WHAT THEY WERE ALL TALKING **ABOUT.**
US.
"US"...
IS THERE AN "US?"
HAVE WE OFFICIALLY REACHED THE "US" LEVEL?
JESUS... LOOK AT HOW EASILY SHE FITS IN... LIKE A PUZZLE PIECE THAT SLIDES RIGHT INTO PLACE...
A PERFECT **FIT.**
SOOOOOOO WHAT'RE YOU **THINKING?**
IM THINKING HOW **AMAZING** IT IS THAT AFTER MEETING ALL OF YOU GUYS... SHE'S STILL **HERE.**
MY FAMILY **LIKES HER.**
MY WORLD IS SLOWLY CHANGING.
SNORES?!!
YES!!
I CAN **FEEL IT.**

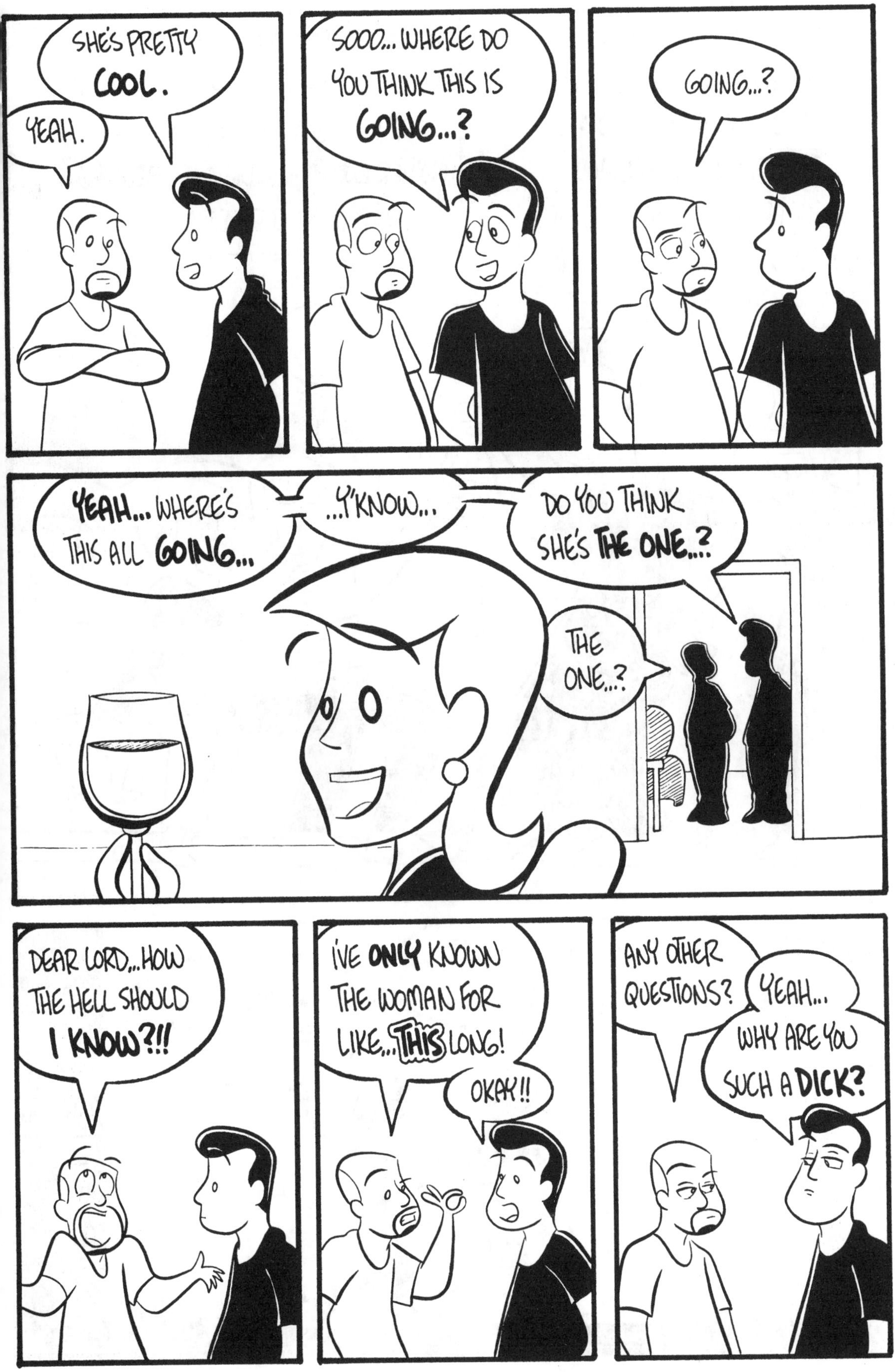
SHE'S PRETTY COOL.
YEAH.
SOOO... WHERE DO YOU THINK THIS IS GOING...?
GOING...?
YEAH... WHERE'S THIS ALL GOING...
...Y'KNOW...
DO YOU THINK SHE'S THE ONE...?
THE ONE...?
DEAR LORD... HOW THE HELL SHOULD I KNOW?!!
I'VE ONLY KNOWN THE WOMAN FOR LIKE... THIS LONG!
OKAY!!
ANY OTHER QUESTIONS?
YEAH... WHY ARE YOU SUCH A DICK?

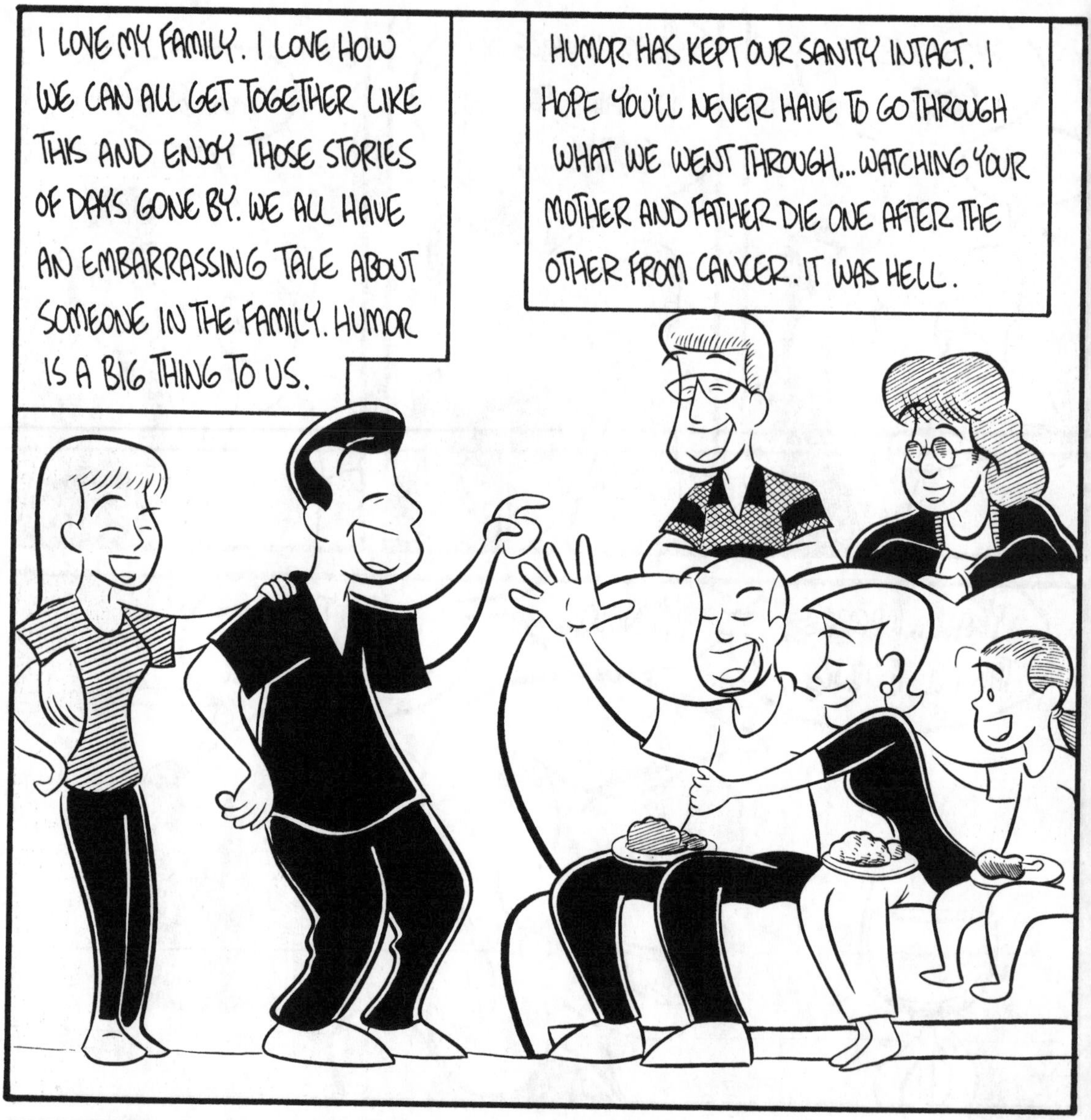
I LOVE MY FAMILY. I LOVE HOW WE CAN ALL GET TOGETHER LIKE THIS AND ENJOY THOSE STORIES OF DAYS GONE BY. WE ALL HAVE AN EMBARRASSING TALE ABOUT SOMEONE IN THE FAMILY. HUMOR IS A BIG THING TO US.
HUMOR HAS KEPT OUR SANITY INTACT. I HOPE YOU'LL NEVER HAVE TO GO THROUGH WHAT WE WENT THROUGH... WATCHING YOUR MOTHER AND FATHER DIE ONE AFTER THE OTHER FROM CANCER. IT WAS HELL.

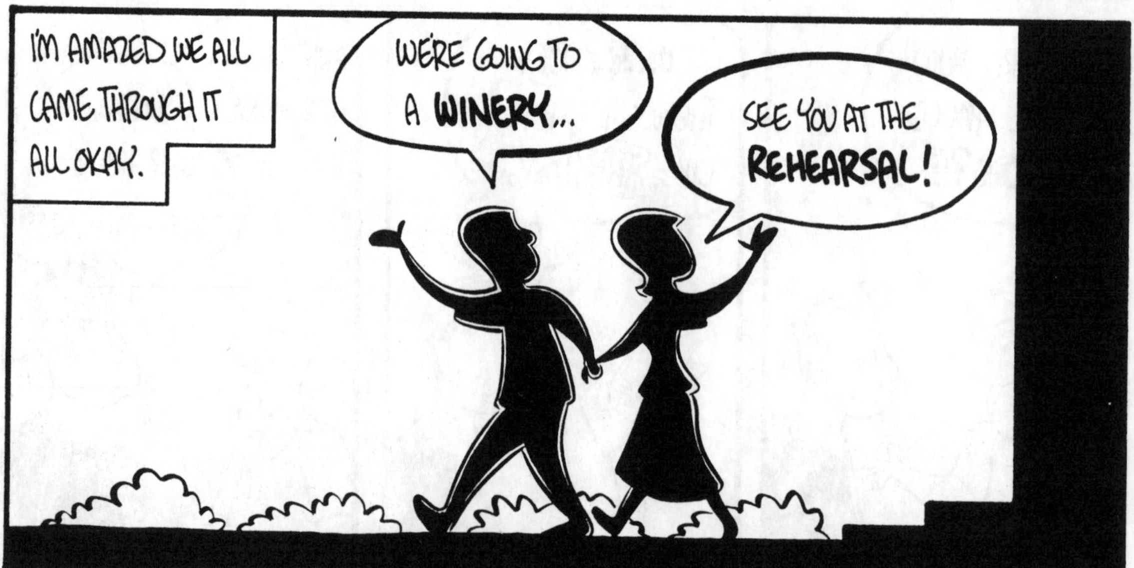
I'M AMAZED WE ALL CAME THROUGH IT ALL OKAY.
WE'RE GOING TO A **WINERY**...
SEE YOU AT THE **REHEARSAL!**

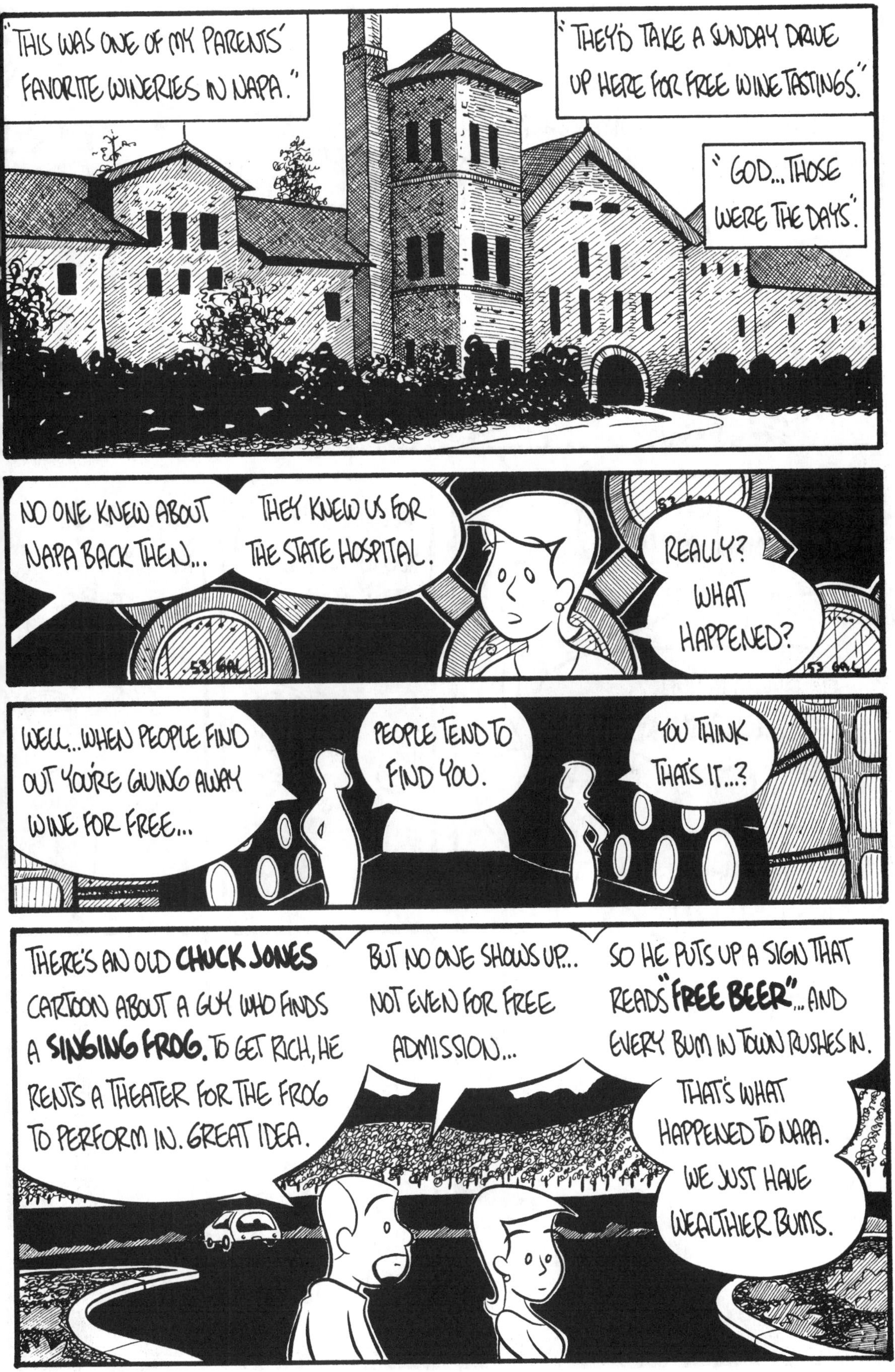
"THIS WAS ONE OF MY PARENTS' FAVORITE WINERIES IN NAPA."
"THEY'D TAKE A SUNDAY DRIVE UP HERE FOR FREE WINE TASTINGS."
"GOD... THOSE WERE THE DAYS."
NO ONE KNEW ABOUT NAPA BACK THEN...
THEY KNEW US FOR THE STATE HOSPITAL.
REALLY? WHAT HAPPENED?
53 GAL
WELL...WHEN PEOPLE FIND OUT YOU'RE GIVING AWAY WINE FOR FREE...
PEOPLE TEND TO FIND YOU.
YOU THINK THAT'S IT...?
THERE'S AN OLD CHUCK JONES CARTOON ABOUT A GUY WHO FINDS A SINGING FROG. TO GET RICH, HE RENTS A THEATER FOR THE FROG TO PERFORM IN. GREAT IDEA.
BUT NO ONE SHOWS UP... NOT EVEN FOR FREE ADMISSION...
SO HE PUTS UP A SIGN THAT READS "FREE BEER"... AND EVERY BUM IN TOWN RUSHES IN.
THAT'S WHAT HAPPENED TO NAPA. WE JUST HAVE WEALTHIER BUMS.

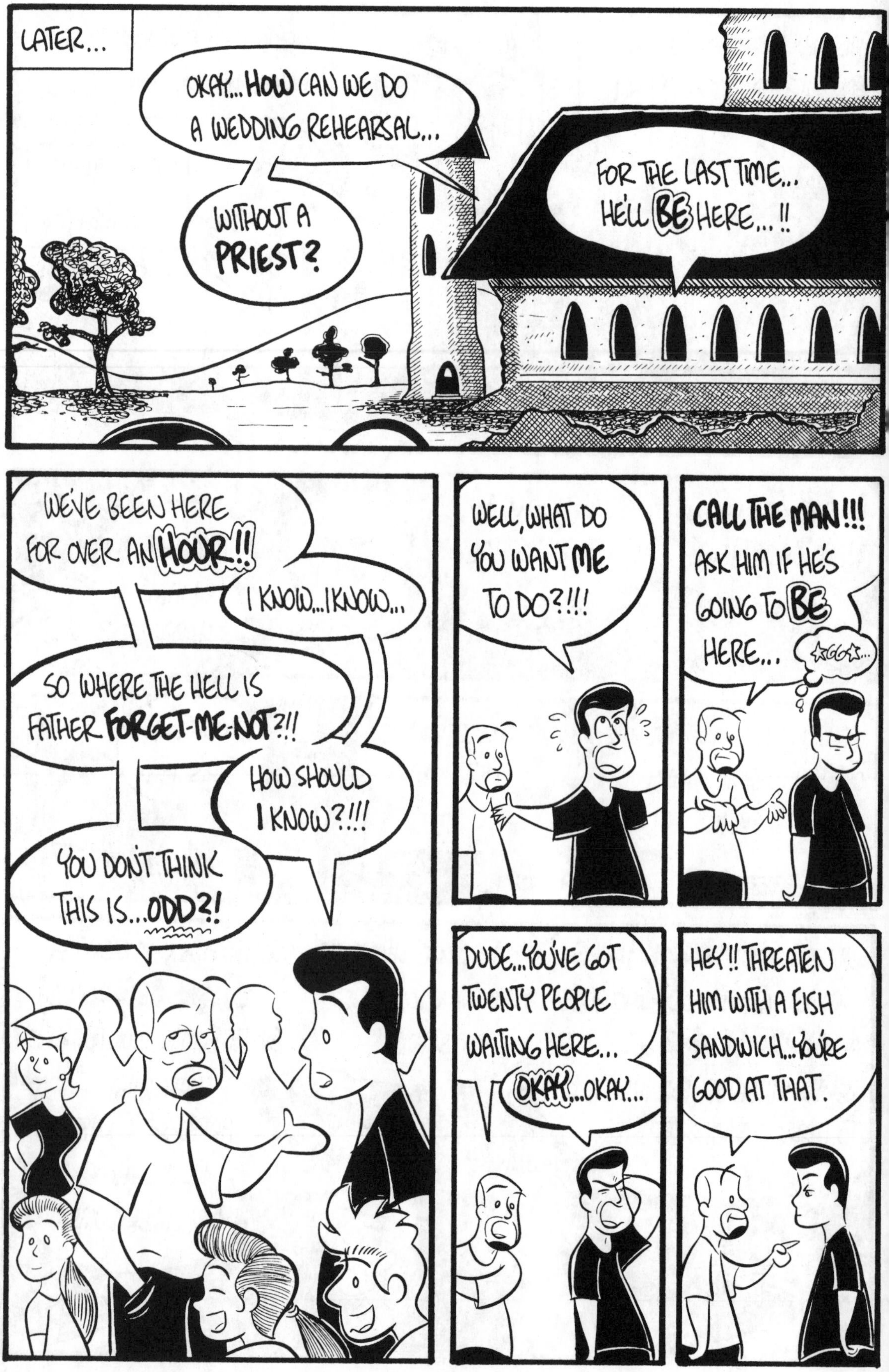
LATER...
OKAY... HOW CAN WE DO A WEDDING REHEARSAL...
WITHOUT A PRIEST?
FOR THE LAST TIME... HE'LL BE HERE...!!
WE'VE BEEN HERE FOR OVER AN HOUR!!
I KNOW...I KNOW...
SO WHERE THE HELL IS FATHER FORGET-ME-NOT?!!
HOW SHOULD I KNOW?!!!
YOU DON'T THINK THIS IS...ODD?!
WELL, WHAT DO YOU WANT ME TO DO?!!!
CALL THE MAN!!! ASK HIM IF HE'S GOING TO BE HERE...
DUDE... YOU'VE GOT TWENTY PEOPLE WAITING HERE...
OKAY!...OKAY...
HEY!! THREATEN HIM WITH A FISH SANDWICH... YOU'RE GOOD AT THAT.

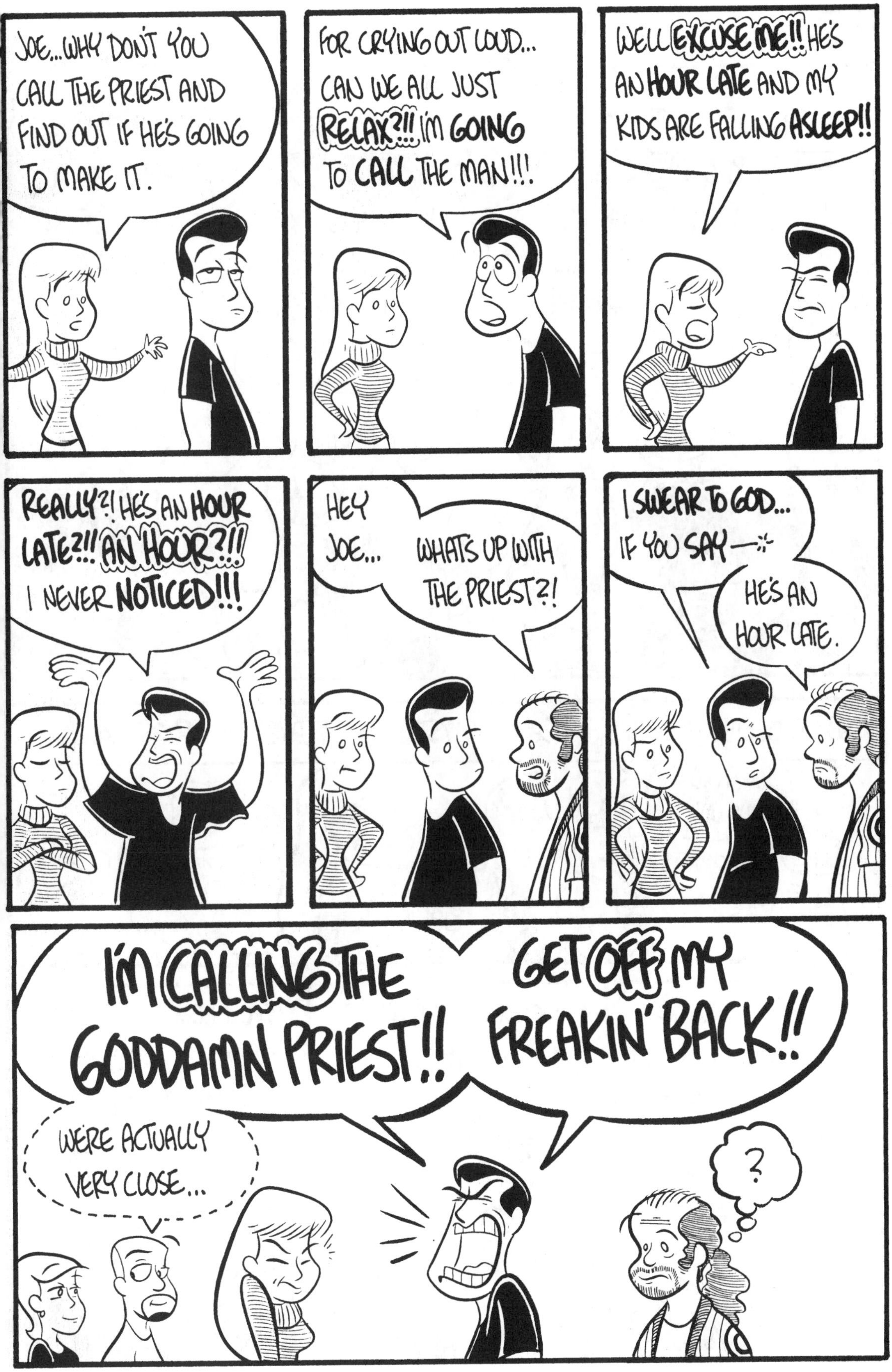
JOE... WHY DON'T YOU CALL THE PRIEST AND FIND OUT IF HE'S GOING TO MAKE IT.
FOR CRYING OUT LOUD... CAN WE ALL JUST RELAX?!! I'M GOING TO CALL THE MAN!!!
WELL EXCUSE ME!! HE'S AN HOUR LATE AND MY KIDS ARE FALLING ASLEEP!!
REALLY?! HE'S AN HOUR LATE?!! AN HOUR?!! I NEVER NOTICED!!!
HEY JOE... WHAT'S UP WITH THE PRIEST?!
I SWEAR TO GOD... IF YOU SAY—
HE'S AN HOUR LATE.
I'M CALLING THE GODDAMN PRIEST!!
GET OFF MY FREAKIN' BACK!!
WE'RE ACTUALLY VERY CLOSE...
?

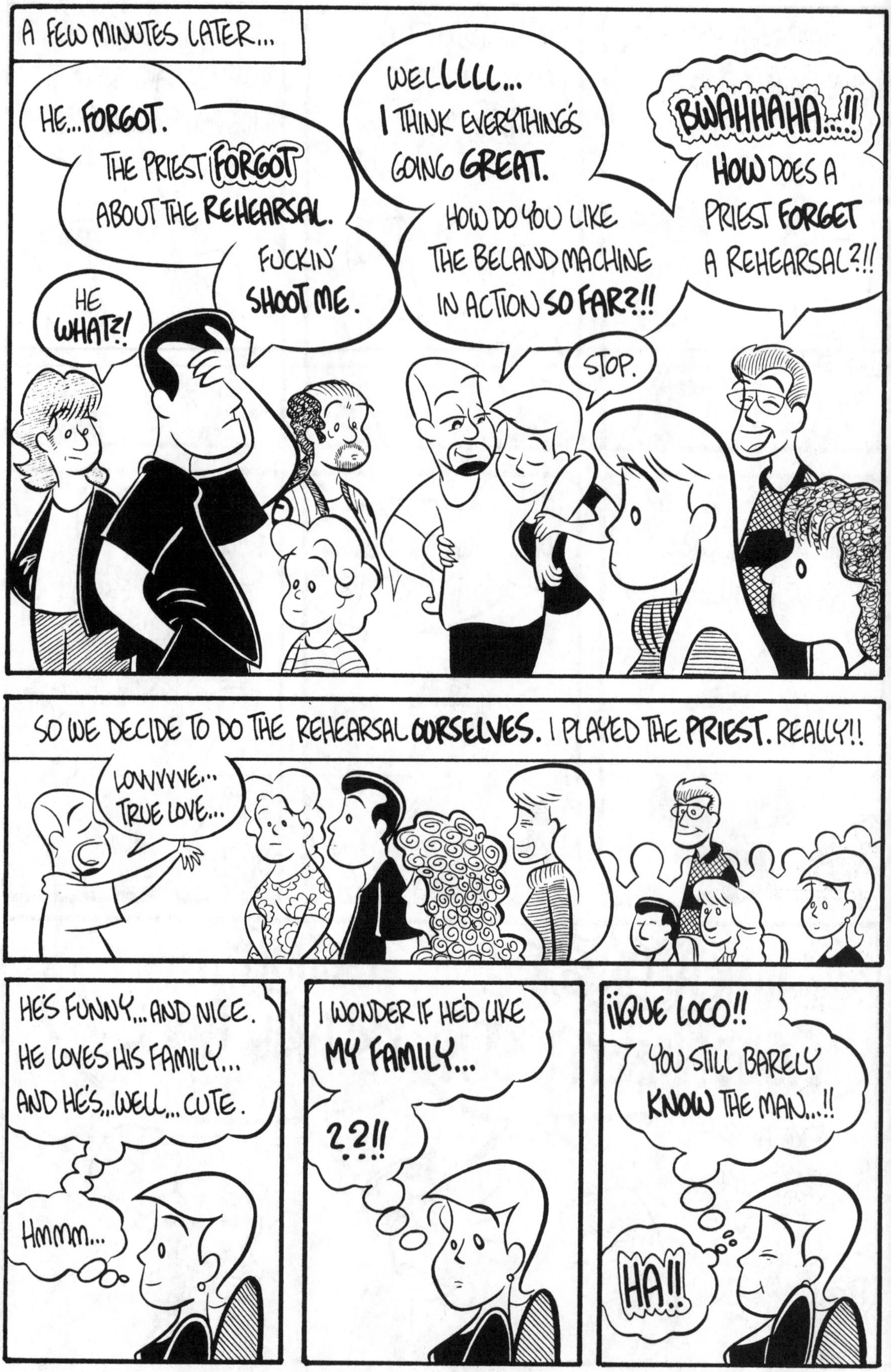
A FEW MINUTES LATER...
HE... FORGOT. THE PRIEST FORGOT ABOUT THE REHEARSAL.
FUCKIN' SHOOT ME.
HE WHAT?!
WELLLLL... I THINK EVERYTHING'S GOING GREAT.
HOW DO YOU LIKE THE BELAND MACHINE IN ACTION SO FAR?!!
STOP.
BWAHHHAHA...!!
HOW DOES A PRIEST FORGET A REHEARSAL?!!
SO WE DECIDE TO DO THE REHEARSAL OURSELVES. I PLAYED THE PRIEST. REALLY!!
LOVVVVVE... TRUE LOVE...
HE'S FUNNY... AND NICE. HE LOVES HIS FAMILY... AND HE'S... WELL... CUTE.
Hmmm...
I WONDER IF HE'D LIKE MY FAMILY...
??!!
¡¡QUE LOCO!!
YOU STILL BARELY KNOW THE MAN...!!
HA!!

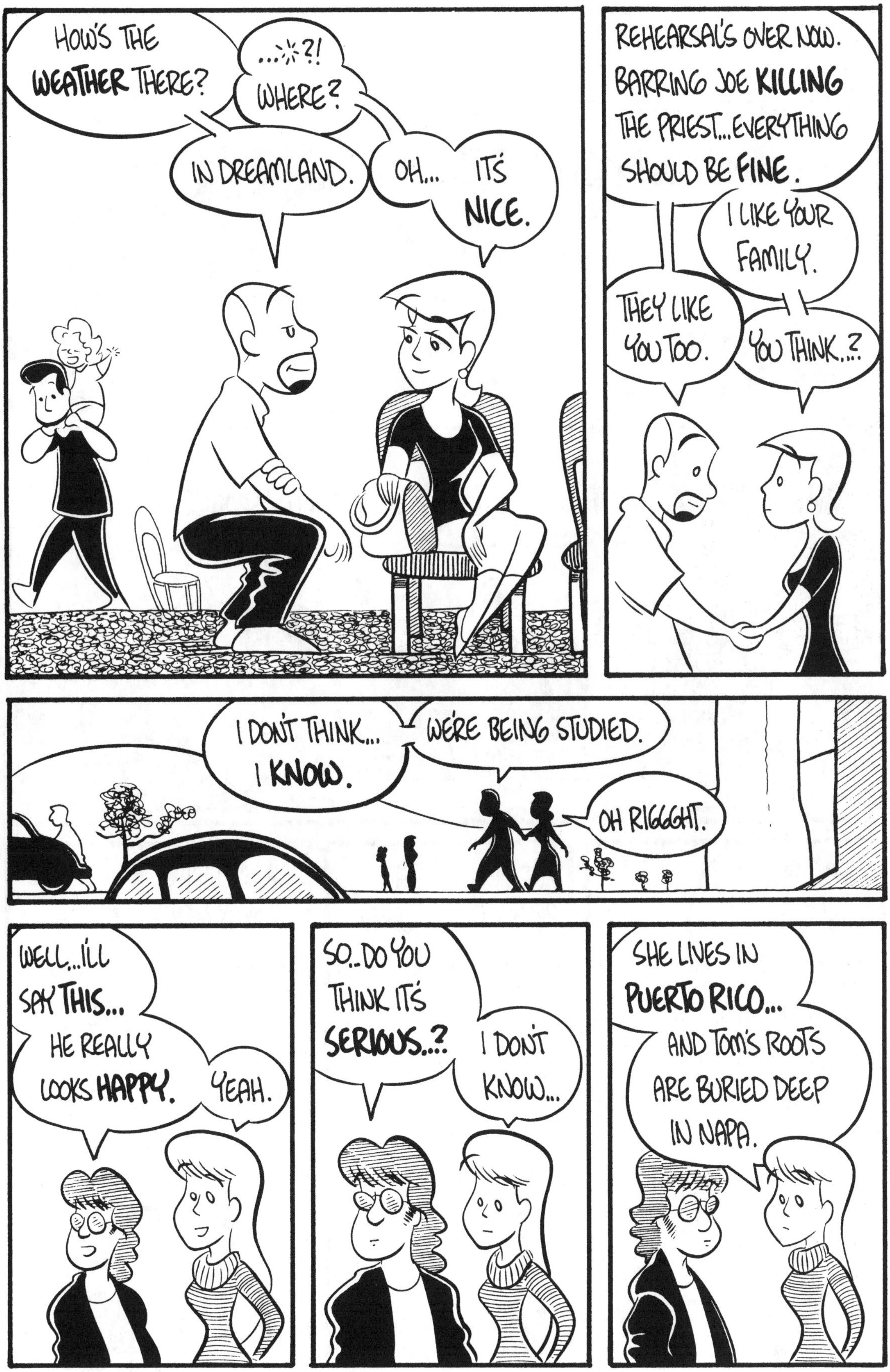
HOW'S THE WEATHER THERE?
...?!
WHERE?
IN DREAMLAND.
OH... IT'S NICE.
REHEARSAL'S OVER NOW. BARRING JOE KILLING THE PRIEST... EVERYTHING SHOULD BE FINE.
I LIKE YOUR FAMILY.
THEY LIKE YOU TOO.
YOU THINK...?
I DON'T THINK... I KNOW.
WE'RE BEING STUDIED.
OH RIGGGHT.
WELL... I'LL SAY THIS... HE REALLY LOOKS HAPPY.
YEAH.
SO... DO YOU THINK IT'S SERIOUS...?
I DON'T KNOW...
SHE LIVES IN PUERTO RICO...
AND TOM'S ROOTS ARE BURIED DEEP IN NAPA.

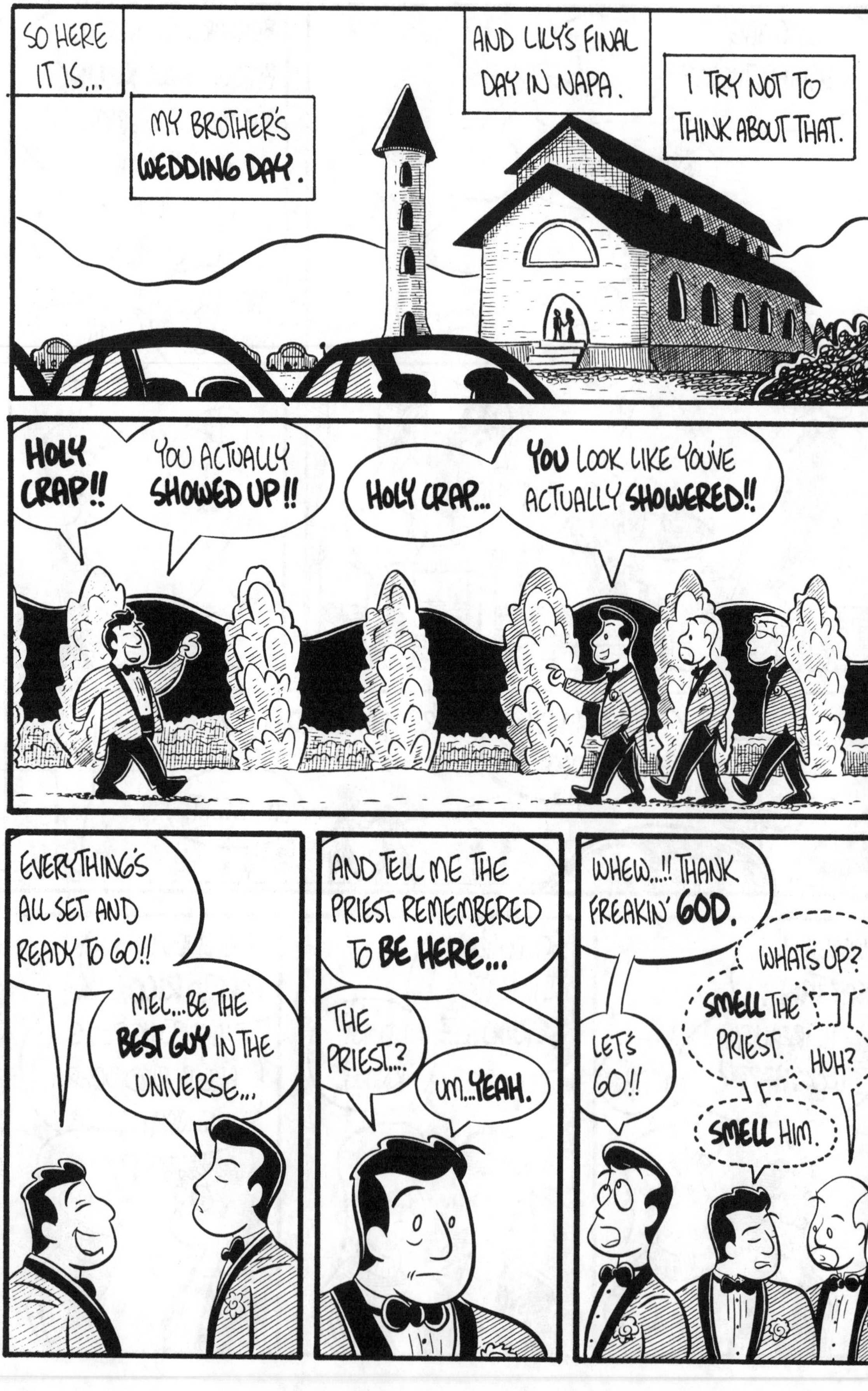
SO HERE IT IS...
MY BROTHER'S WEDDING DAY.
AND LILY'S FINAL DAY IN NAPA.
I TRY NOT TO THINK ABOUT THAT.
HOLY CRAP!!
YOU ACTUALLY SHOWED UP!!
HOLY CRAP...
YOU LOOK LIKE YOU'VE ACTUALLY SHOWERED!!
EVERYTHING'S ALL SET AND READY TO GO!!
MEL...BE THE BEST GUY IN THE UNIVERSE...
AND TELL ME THE PRIEST REMEMBERED TO BE HERE...
THE PRIEST...?
UM...YEAH.
WHEW...!! THANK FREAKIN' GOD.
LET'S GO!!
WHAT'S UP?
SMELL THE PRIEST.
HUH?
SMELL HIM.

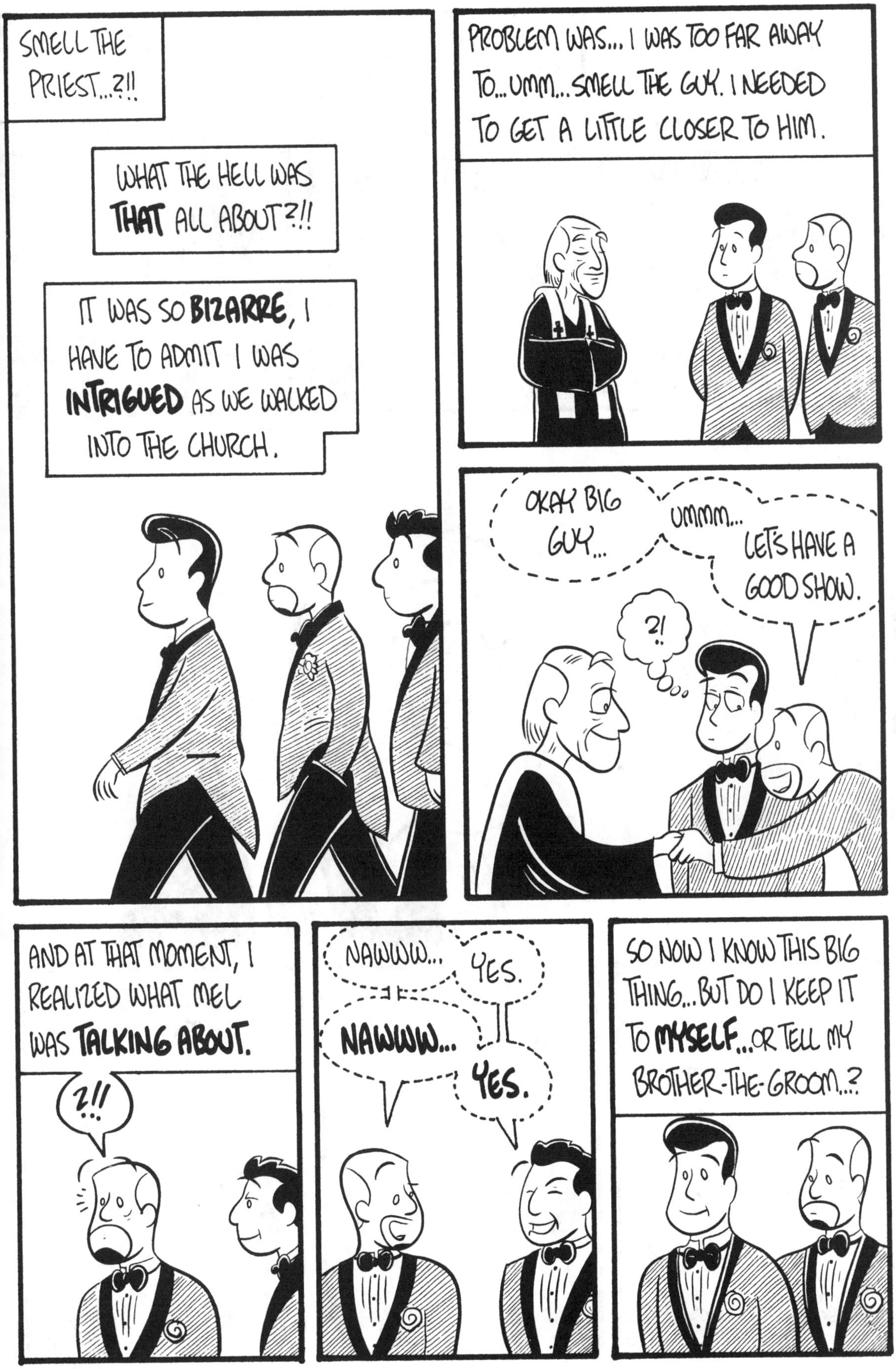
SMELL THE PRIEST...?!!
WHAT THE HELL WAS THAT ALL ABOUT?!!
IT WAS SO BIZARRE, I HAVE TO ADMIT I WAS INTRIGUED AS WE WALKED INTO THE CHURCH.
PROBLEM WAS... I WAS TOO FAR AWAY TO...UMM...SMELL THE GUY. I NEEDED TO GET A LITTLE CLOSER TO HIM.
OKAY BIG GUY...
UMMM... LET'S HAVE A GOOD SHOW.
?!
AND AT THAT MOMENT, I REALIZED WHAT MEL WAS TALKING ABOUT.
?!!
NAWWW...
YES.
NAWWW...
YES.
SO NOW I KNOW THIS BIG THING...BUT DO I KEEP IT TO MYSELF...OR TELL MY BROTHER-THE-GROOM..?

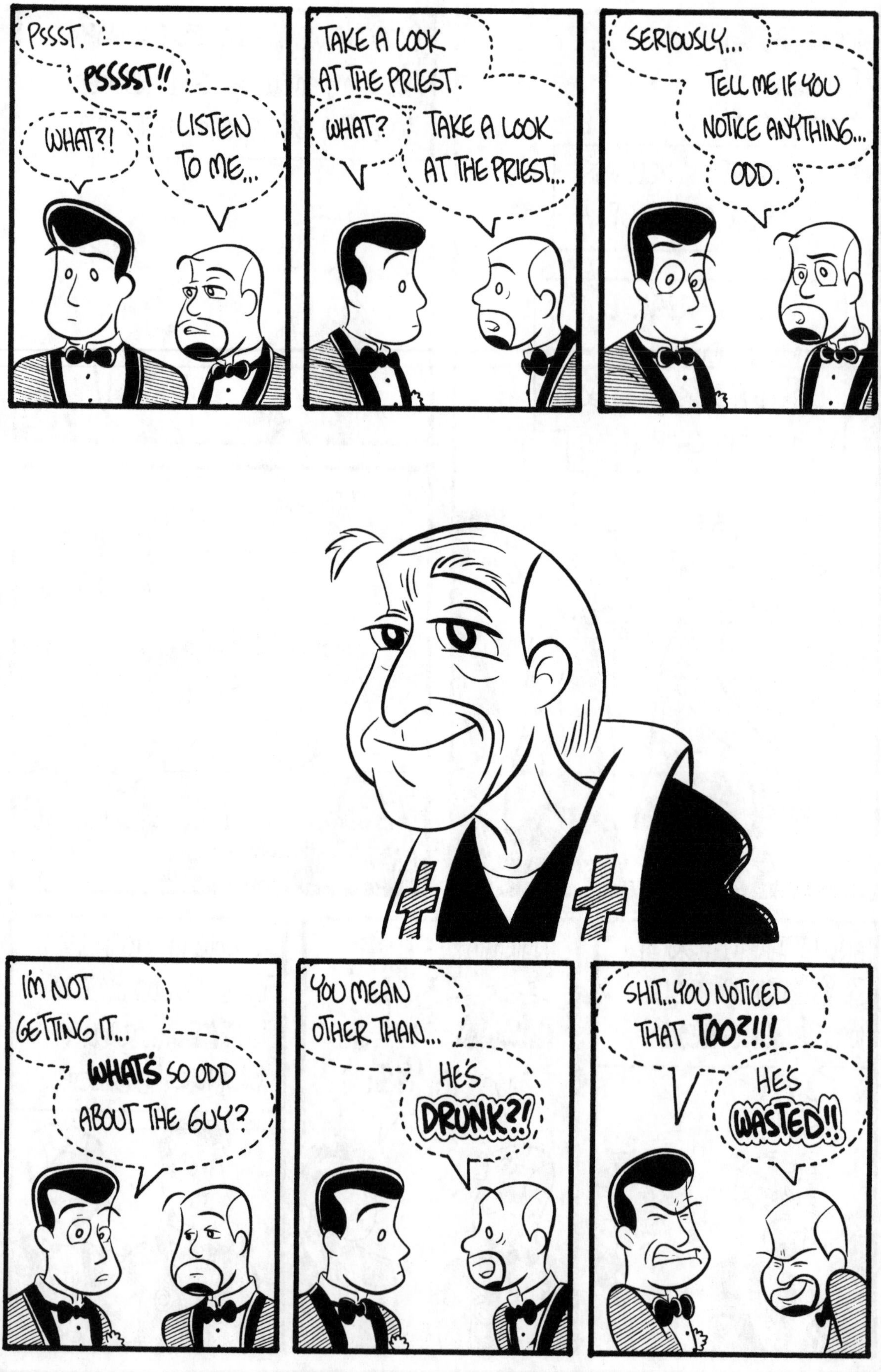
PSSST.
PSSSST!!
WHAT?!
LISTEN TO ME...
TAKE A LOOK AT THE PRIEST.
WHAT?
TAKE A LOOK AT THE PRIEST...
SERIOUSLY...
TELL ME IF YOU NOTICE ANYTHING... ODD.
I'M NOT GETTING IT...
WHAT'S SO ODD ABOUT THE GUY?
YOU MEAN OTHER THAN...
HE'S DRUNK?!
SHIT...YOU NOTICED THAT TOO?!!!
HE'S WASTED!!

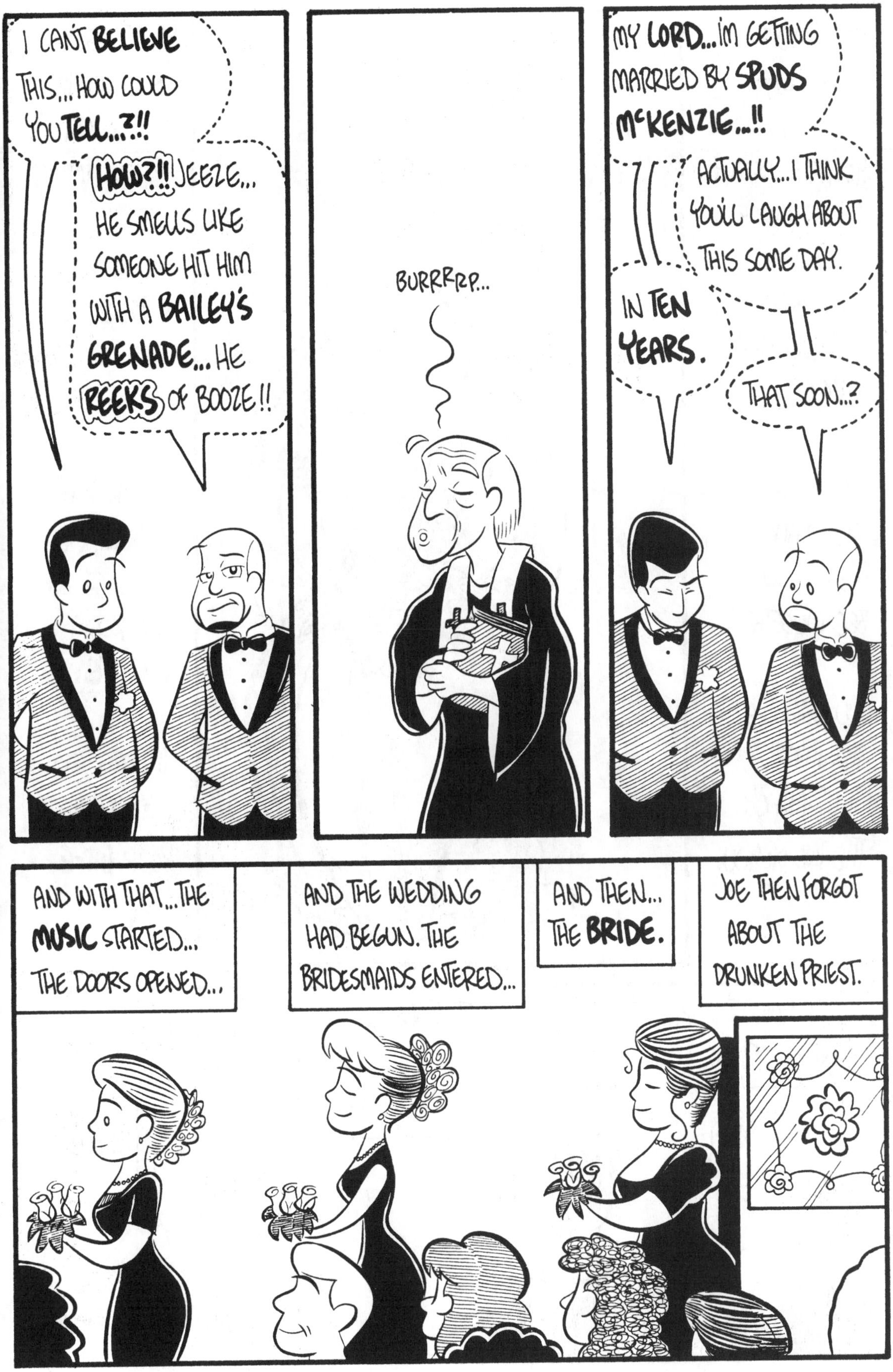
I CAN'T BELIEVE THIS... HOW COULD YOU TELL...?!!
HOW?!! JEEZE... HE SMELLS LIKE SOMEONE HIT HIM WITH A BAILEY'S GRENADE... HE REEKS OF BOOZE!!
BURRRRP...
MY LORD... I'M GETTING MARRIED BY SPUDS McKENZIE...!!
ACTUALLY... I THINK YOU'LL LAUGH ABOUT THIS SOME DAY.
IN TEN YEARS.
THAT SOON..?
AND WITH THAT... THE MUSIC STARTED... THE DOORS OPENED...
AND THE WEDDING HAD BEGUN. THE BRIDESMAIDS ENTERED...
AND THEN... THE BRIDE.
JOE THEN FORGOT ABOUT THE DRUNKEN PRIEST.

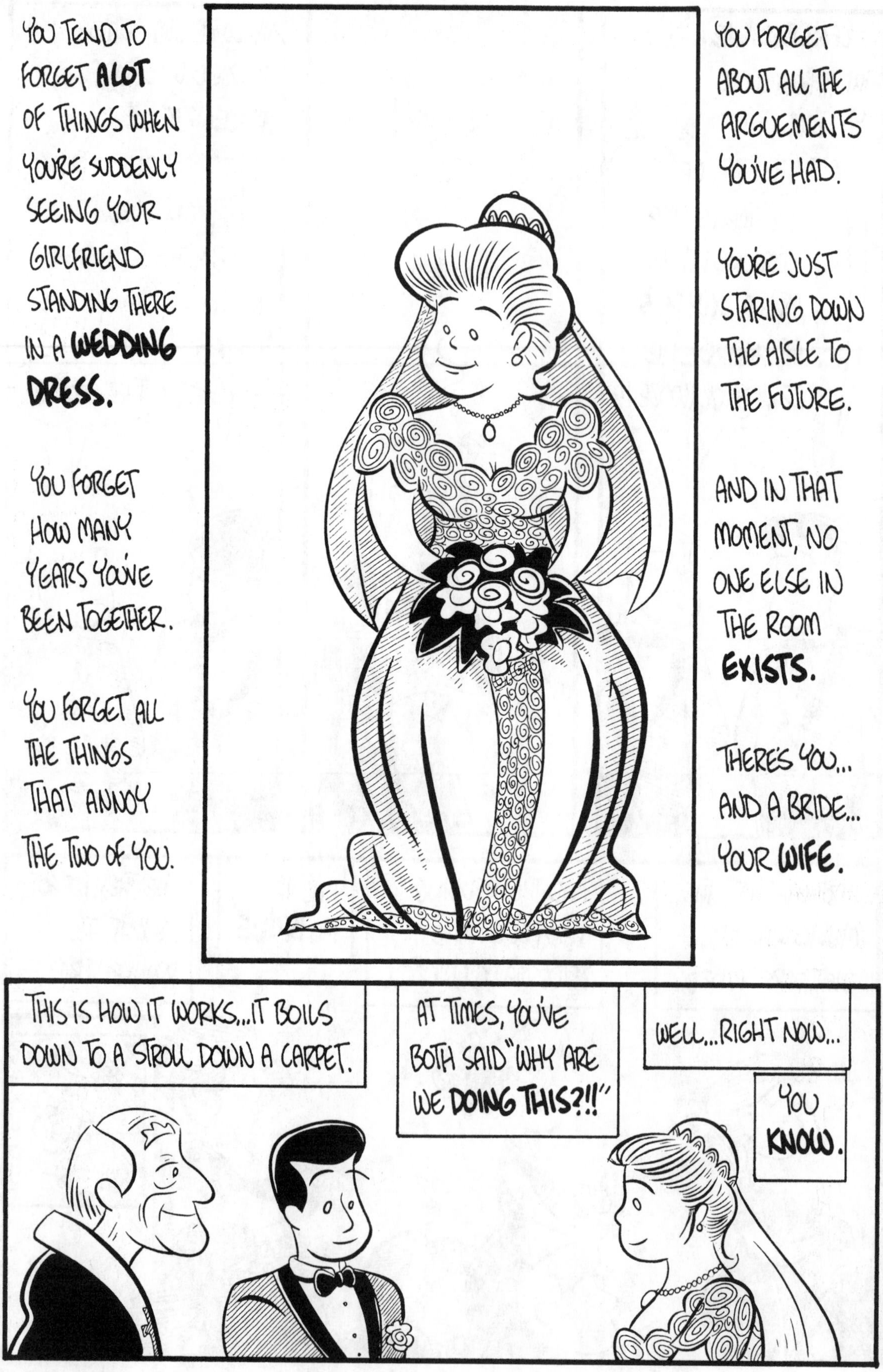
YOU TEND TO FORGET ALOT OF THINGS WHEN YOU'RE SUDDENLY SEEING YOUR GIRLFRIEND STANDING THERE IN A WEDDING DRESS.
YOU FORGET HOW MANY YEARS YOU'VE BEEN TOGETHER.
YOU FORGET ALL THE THINGS THAT ANNOY THE TWO OF YOU.
YOU FORGET ABOUT ALL THE ARGUEMENTS YOU'VE HAD.
YOU'RE JUST STARING DOWN THE AISLE TO THE FUTURE.
AND IN THAT MOMENT, NO ONE ELSE IN THE ROOM EXISTS.
THERE'S YOU... AND A BRIDE... YOUR WIFE.
THIS IS HOW IT WORKS...IT BOILS DOWN TO A STROLL DOWN A CARPET.
AT TIMES, YOU'VE BOTH SAID "WHY ARE WE DOING THIS?!!"
WELL...RIGHT NOW...
YOU KNOW.

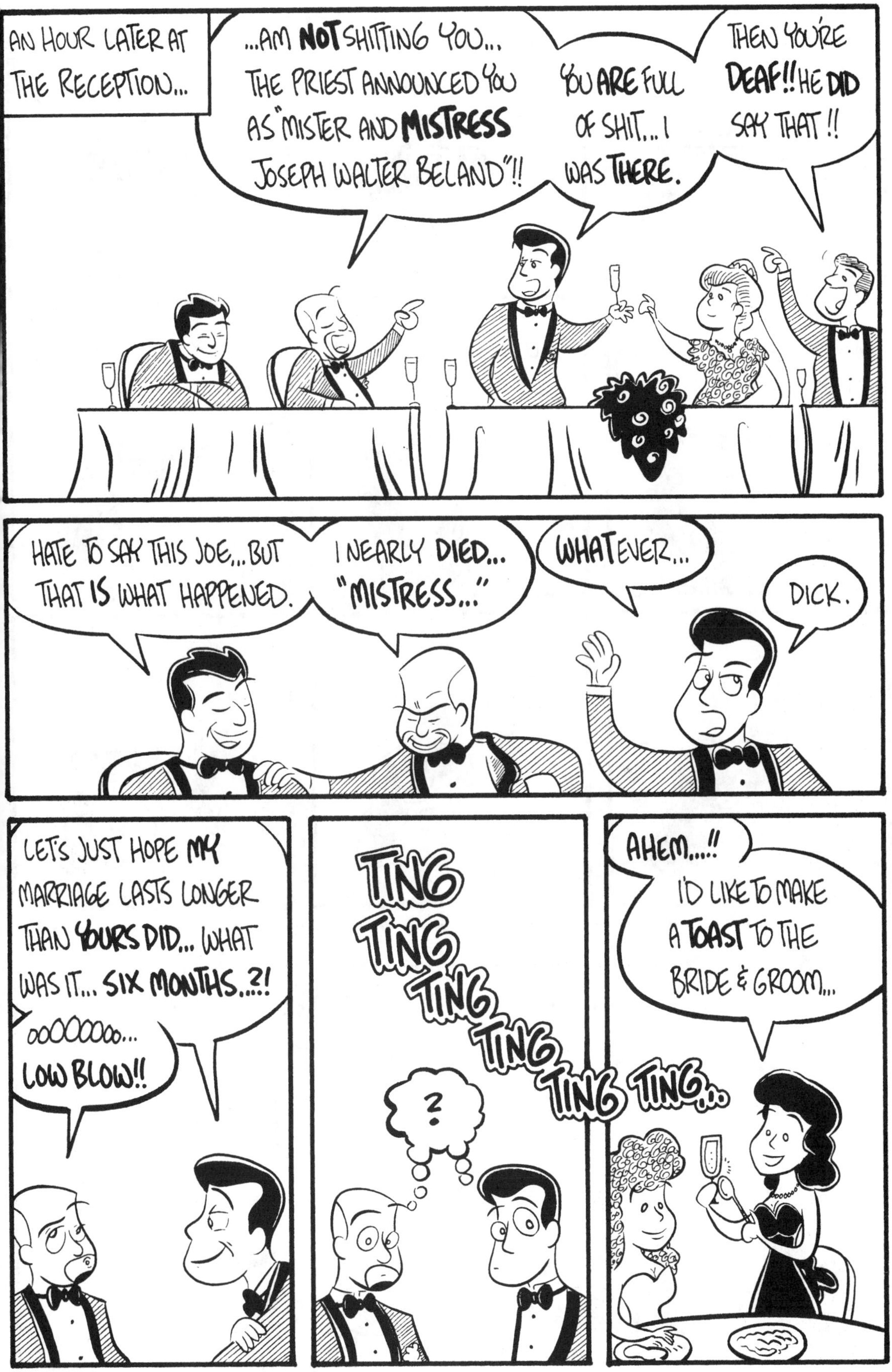
AN HOUR LATER AT THE RECEPTION...
...AM NOT SHITTING YOU... THE PRIEST ANNOUNCED YOU AS "MISTER AND MISTRESS JOSEPH WALTER BELAND"!!
YOU ARE FULL OF SHIT... I WAS THERE.
THEN YOU'RE DEAF!! HE DID SAY THAT !!
HATE TO SAY THIS JOE... BUT THAT IS WHAT HAPPENED.
I NEARLY DIED... "MISTRESS..."
WHATEVER...
DICK.
LET'S JUST HOPE MY MARRIAGE LASTS LONGER THAN YOURS DID... WHAT WAS IT... SIX MONTHS..?!
ooOOOOoo... LOW BLOW!!
TING TING TING TING TING TING...
?
AHEM...!!
I'D LIKE TO MAKE A TOAST TO THE BRIDE & GROOM...

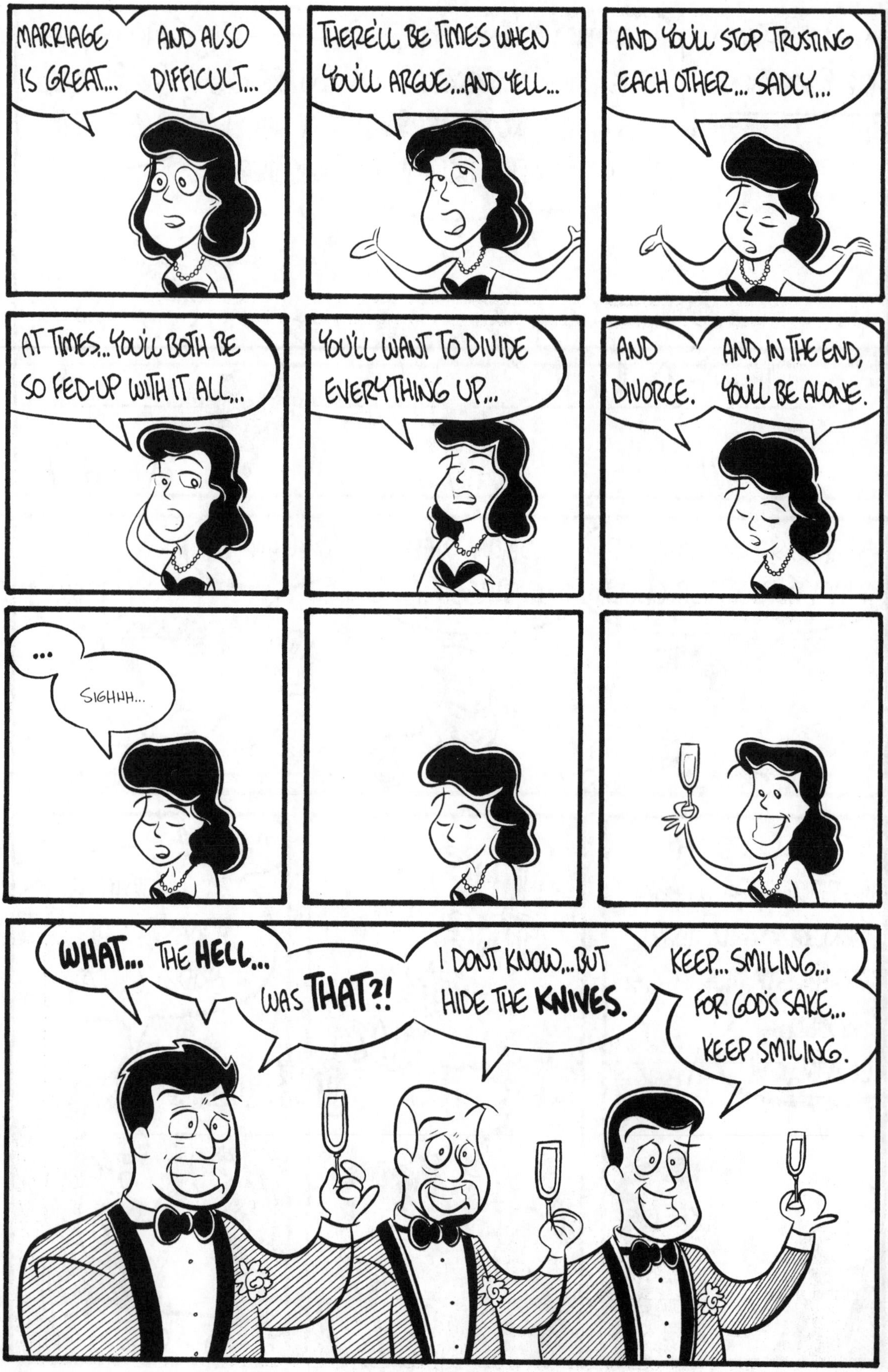

MARRIAGE IS GREAT...
AND ALSO DIFFICULT...
THERE'LL BE TIMES WHEN YOU'LL ARGUE...AND YELL...
AND YOU'LL STOP TRUSTING EACH OTHER... SADLY...
AT TIMES... YOU'LL BOTH BE SO FED-UP WITH IT ALL...
YOU'LL WANT TO DIVIDE EVERYTHING UP...
AND DIVORCE.
AND IN THE END, YOU'LL BE ALONE.
...
SIGHHH...
WHAT... THE HELL... WAS THAT?!
I DON'T KNOW...BUT HIDE THE KNIVES.
KEEP... SMILING... FOR GOD'S SAKE... KEEP SMILING.

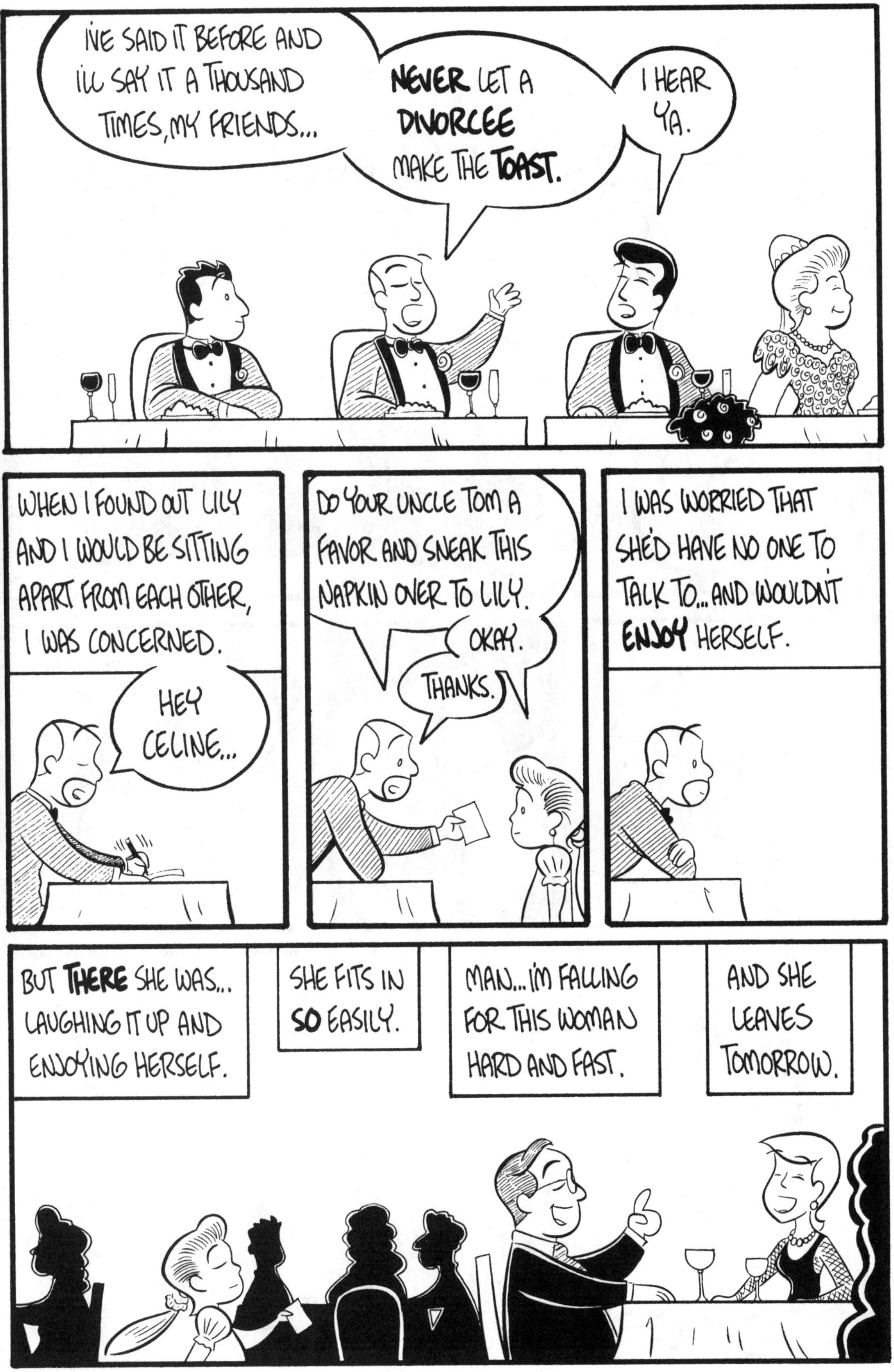
I'VE SAID IT BEFORE AND I'LL SAY IT A THOUSAND TIMES, MY FRIENDS...
NEVER LET A DIVORCEE MAKE THE TOAST.
I HEAR YA.
WHEN I FOUND OUT LILY AND I WOULD BE SITTING APART FROM EACH OTHER, I WAS CONCERNED.
HEY CELINE...
DO YOUR UNCLE TOM A FAVOR AND SNEAK THIS NAPKIN OVER TO LILY.
OKAY.
THANKS.
I WAS WORRIED THAT SHE'D HAVE NO ONE TO TALK TO... AND WOULDN'T ENJOY HERSELF.
BUT THERE SHE WAS... LAUGHING IT UP AND ENJOYING HERSELF.
SHE FITS IN SO EASILY.
MAN... I'M FALLING FOR THIS WOMAN HARD AND FAST.
AND SHE LEAVES TOMORROW.

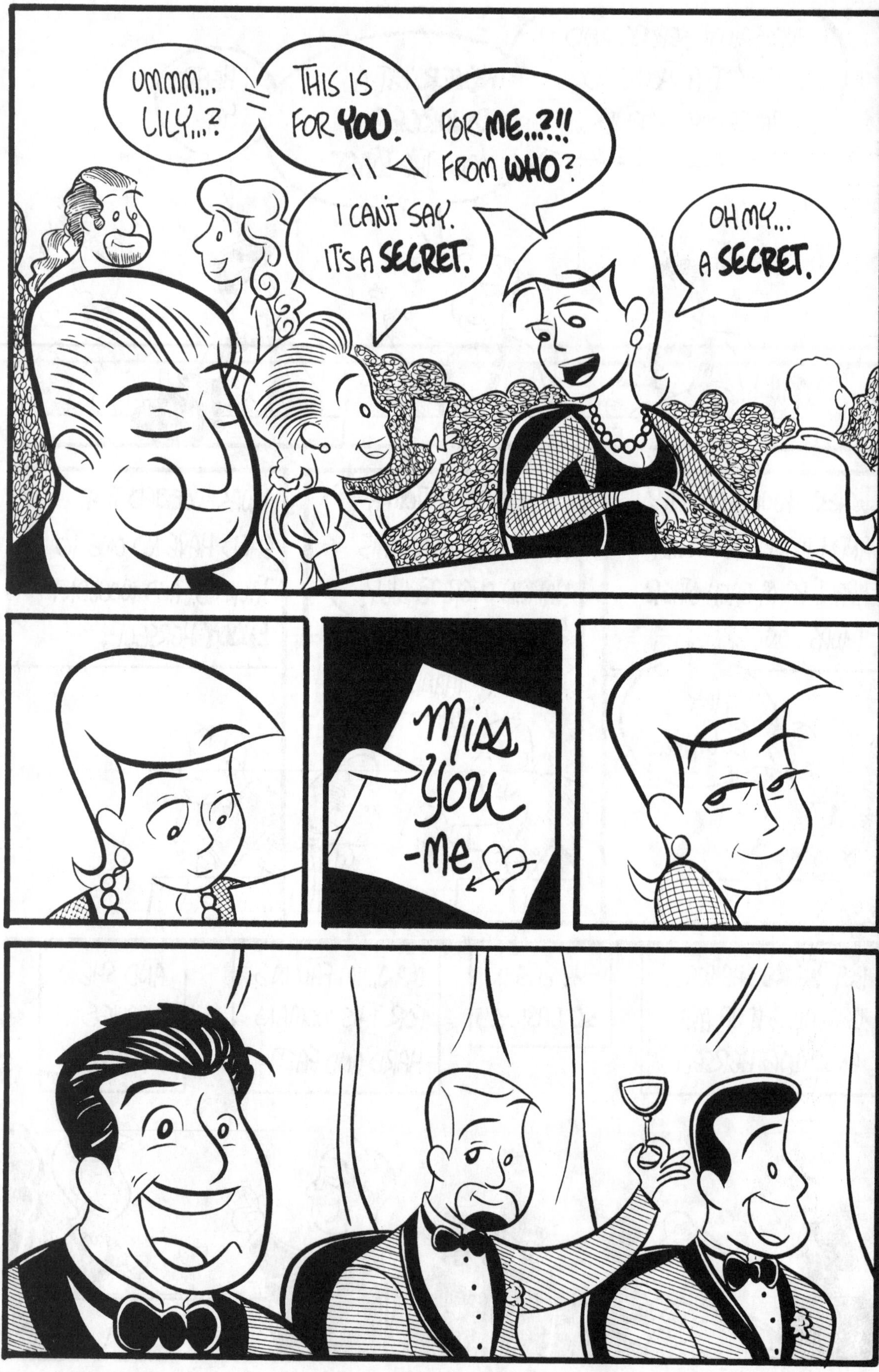
UMMM... LILY...?
THIS IS FOR YOU.
FOR ME...?!! FROM WHO?
I CAN'T SAY. IT'S A SECRET.
OH MY... A SECRET.
Miss You -Me

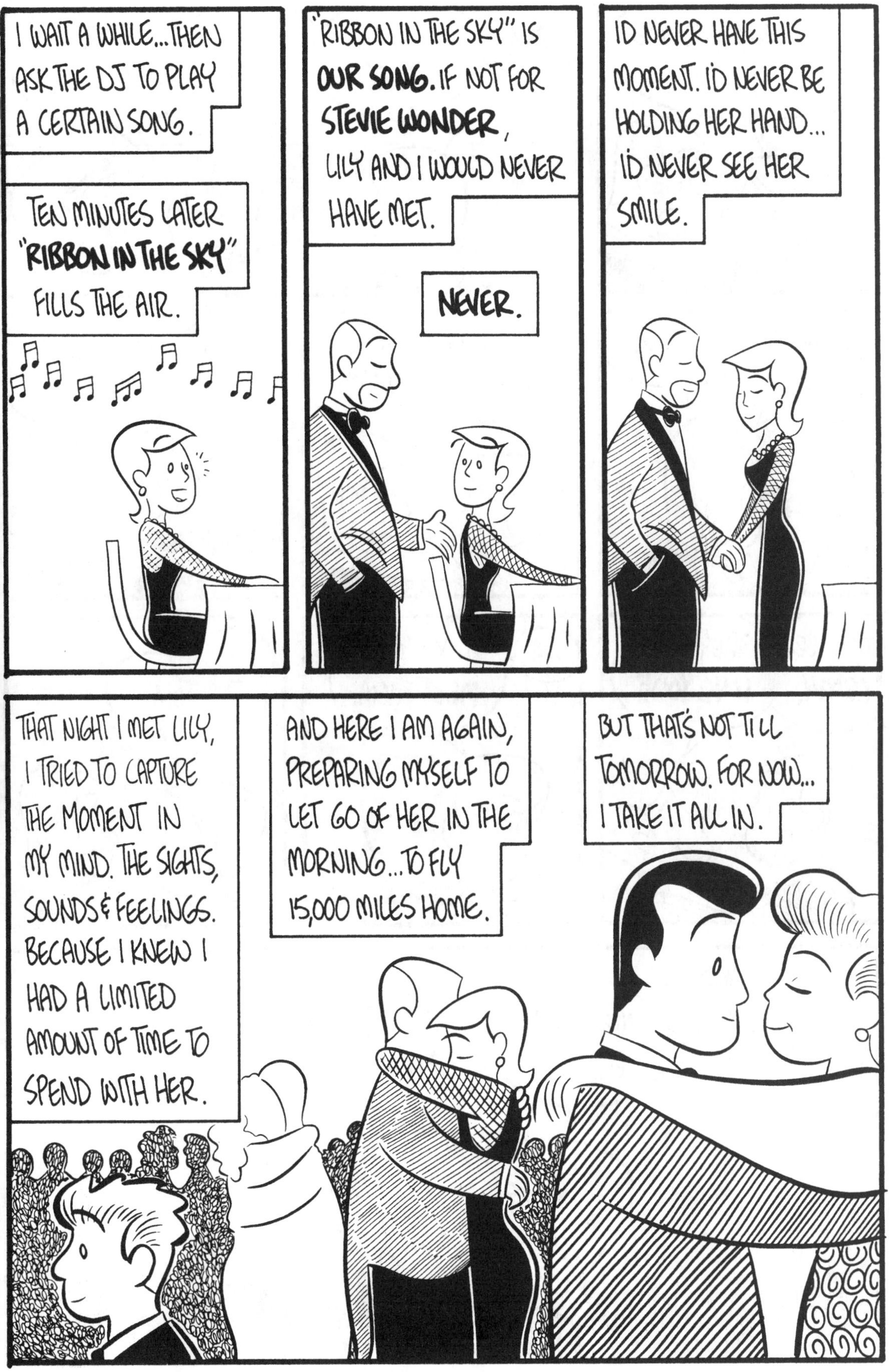

I WAIT A WHILE... THEN ASK THE DJ TO PLAY A CERTAIN SONG.
TEN MINUTES LATER "RIBBON IN THE SKY" FILLS THE AIR.
"RIBBON IN THE SKY" IS OUR SONG. IF NOT FOR STEVIE WONDER, LILY AND I WOULD NEVER HAVE MET.
NEVER.
I'D NEVER HAVE THIS MOMENT. I'D NEVER BE HOLDING HER HAND... I'D NEVER SEE HER SMILE.
THAT NIGHT I MET LILY, I TRIED TO CAPTURE THE MOMENT IN MY MIND. THE SIGHTS, SOUNDS & FEELINGS. BECAUSE I KNEW I HAD A LIMITED AMOUNT OF TIME TO SPEND WITH HER.
AND HERE I AM AGAIN, PREPARING MYSELF TO LET GO OF HER IN THE MORNING... TO FLY 15,000 MILES HOME.
BUT THAT'S NOT TILL TOMORROW. FOR NOW... I TAKE IT ALL IN.

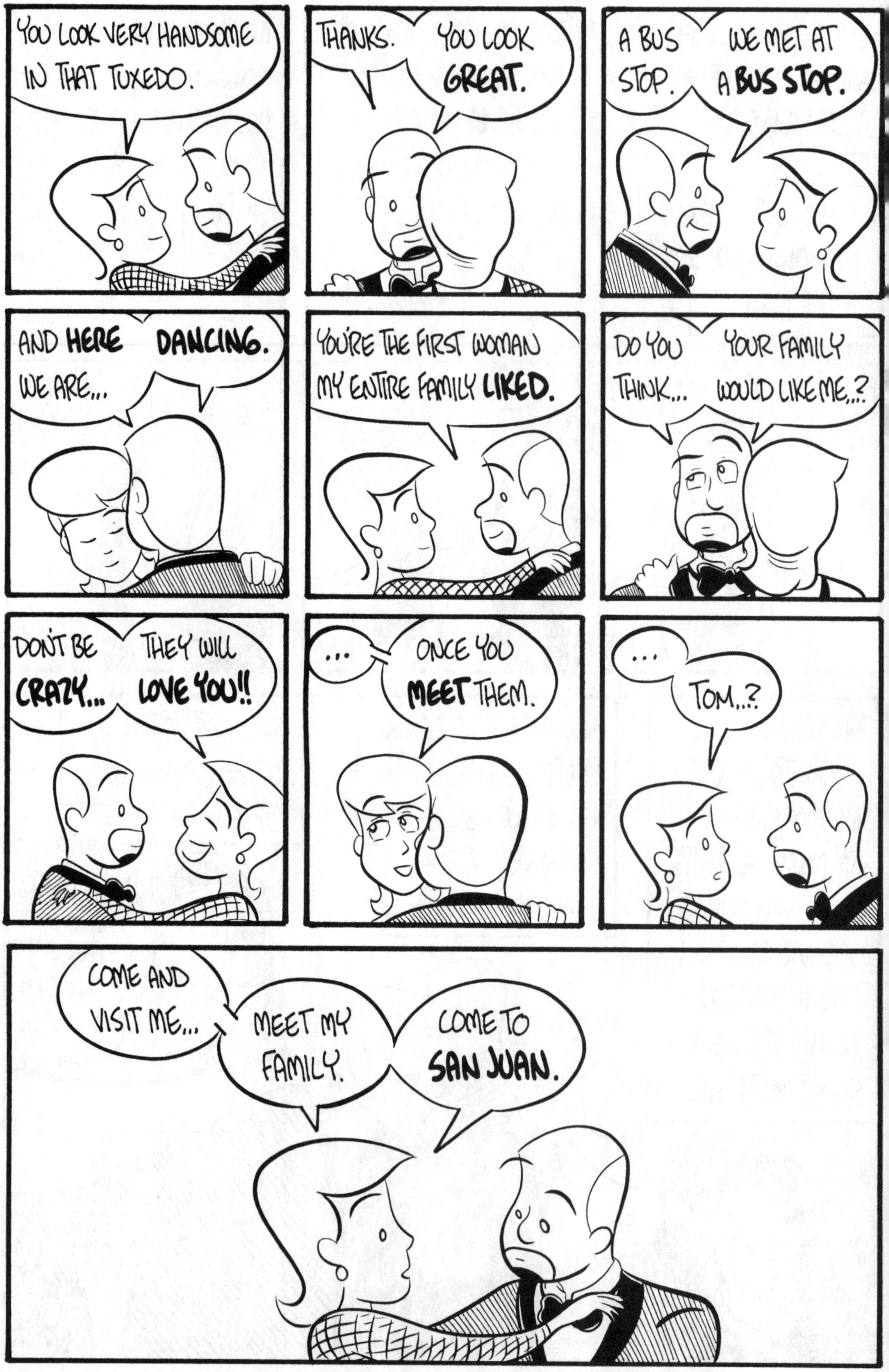
YOU LOOK VERY HANDSOME IN THAT TUXEDO.
THANKS.
YOU LOOK GREAT.
A BUS STOP.
WE MET AT A BUS STOP.
AND HERE WE ARE...
DANCING.
YOU'RE THE FIRST WOMAN MY ENTIRE FAMILY LIKED.
DO YOU THINK...
YOUR FAMILY WOULD LIKE ME..?
DON'T BE CRAZY...
THEY WILL LOVE YOU!!
...
ONCE YOU MEET THEM.
...
TOM..?
COME AND VISIT ME...
MEET MY FAMILY.
COME TO SAN JUAN.

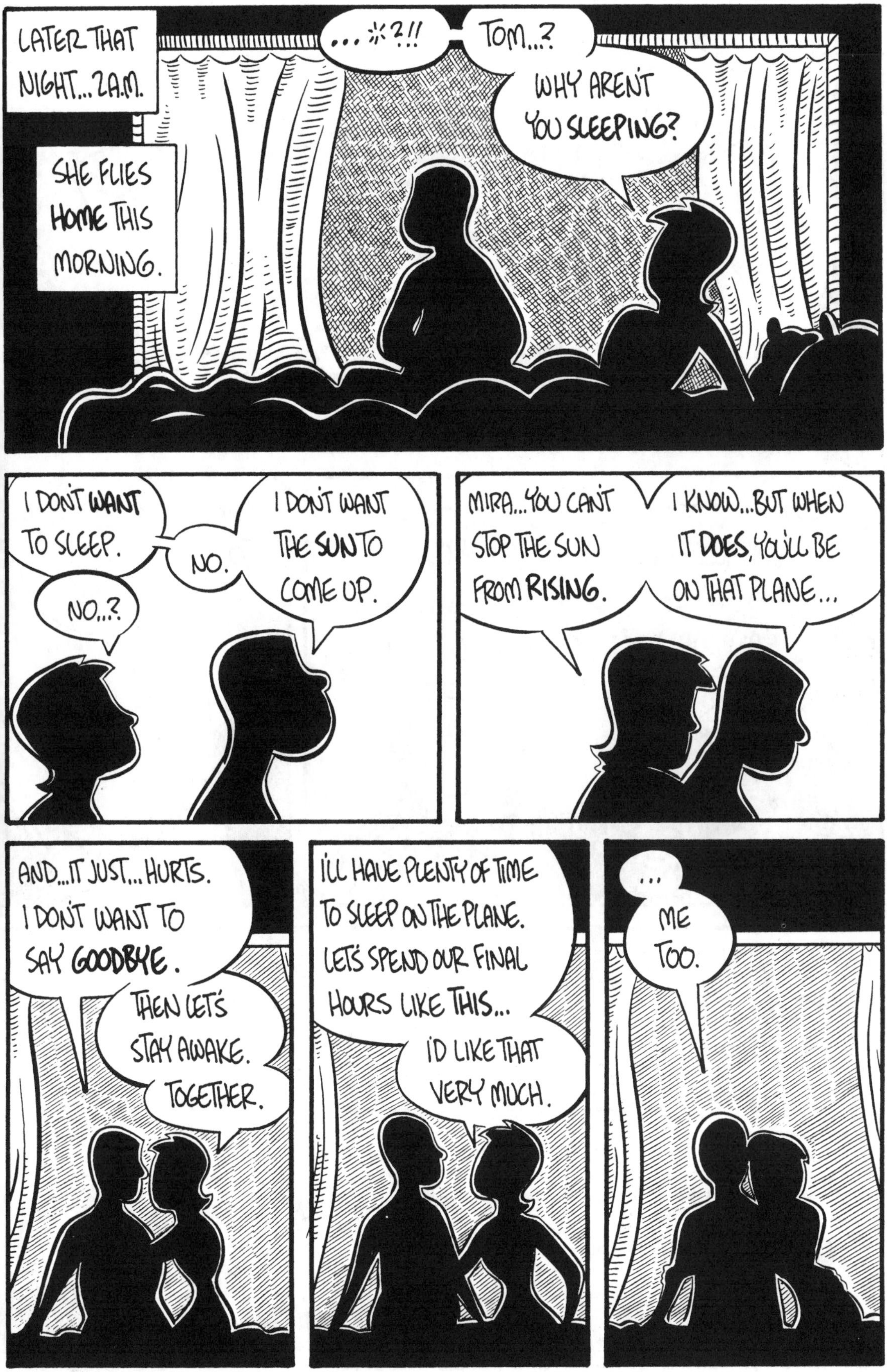

LATER THAT NIGHT... 2A.M.
SHE FLIES HOME THIS MORNING.
...*?!!
TOM...?
WHY AREN'T YOU SLEEPING?
I DON'T WANT TO SLEEP.
NO..?
NO.
I DON'T WANT THE SUN TO COME UP.
MIRA...YOU CAN'T STOP THE SUN FROM RISING.
I KNOW...BUT WHEN IT DOES, YOU'LL BE ON THAT PLANE...
AND...IT JUST...HURTS. I DON'T WANT TO SAY GOODBYE.
THEN LET'S STAY AWAKE. TOGETHER.
I'LL HAVE PLENTY OF TIME TO SLEEP ON THE PLANE. LET'S SPEND OUR FINAL HOURS LIKE THIS...
I'D LIKE THAT VERY MUCH.
...
ME TOO.

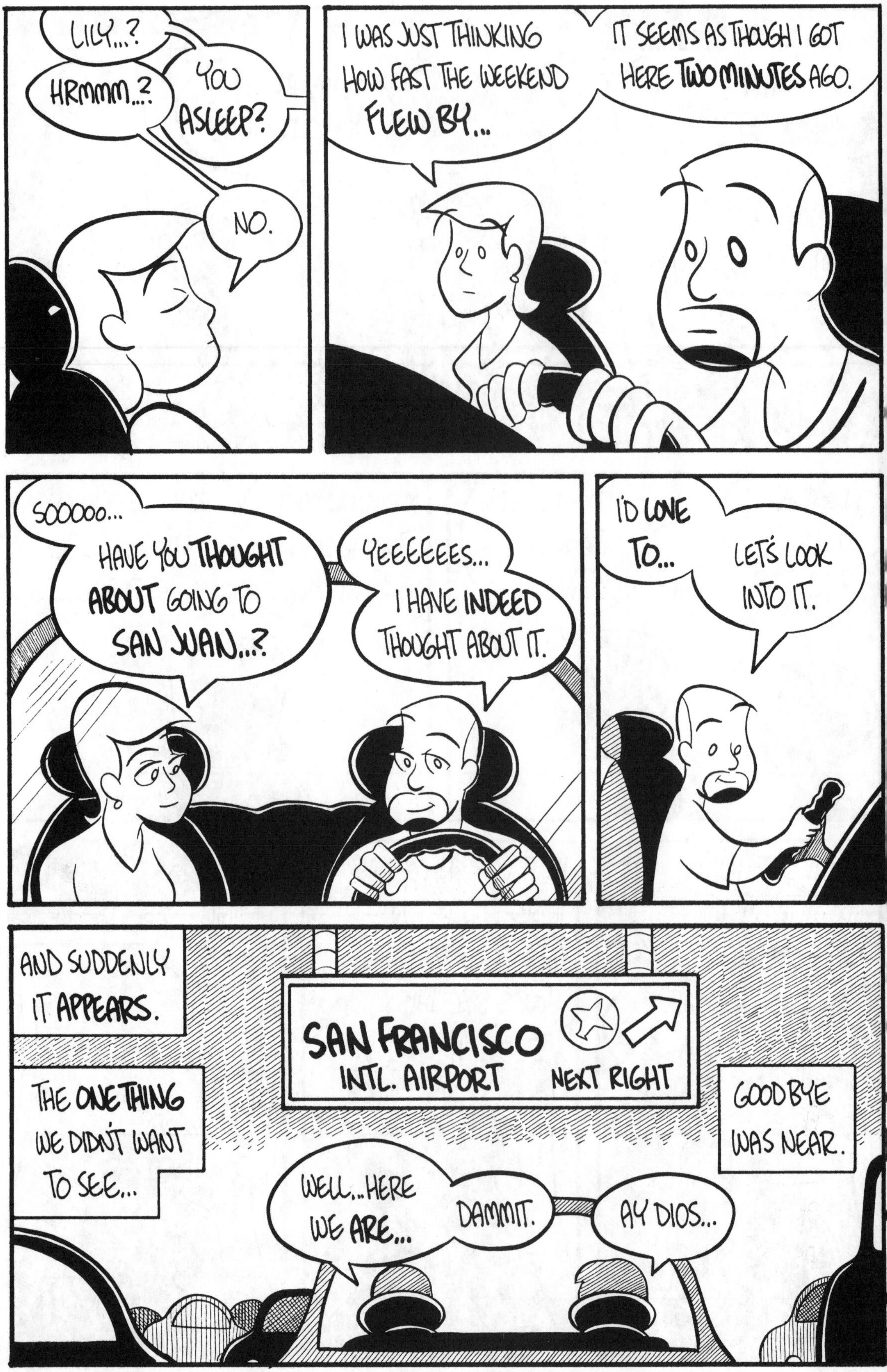
LILY...?
HRMMM...?
YOU ASLEEP?
NO.
I WAS JUST THINKING HOW FAST THE WEEKEND FLEW BY...
IT SEEMS AS THOUGH I GOT HERE TWO MINUTES AGO.
SOOOOO...
HAVE YOU THOUGHT ABOUT GOING TO SAN JUAN...?
YEEEEEES...
I HAVE INDEED THOUGHT ABOUT IT.
I'D LOVE TO...
LET'S LOOK INTO IT.
AND SUDDENLY IT APPEARS.
THE ONE THING WE DIDN'T WANT TO SEE...
SAN FRANCISCO
INTL. AIRPORT
NEXT RIGHT
GOODBYE WAS NEAR.
WELL...HERE WE ARE...
DAMMIT.
AY DIOS...

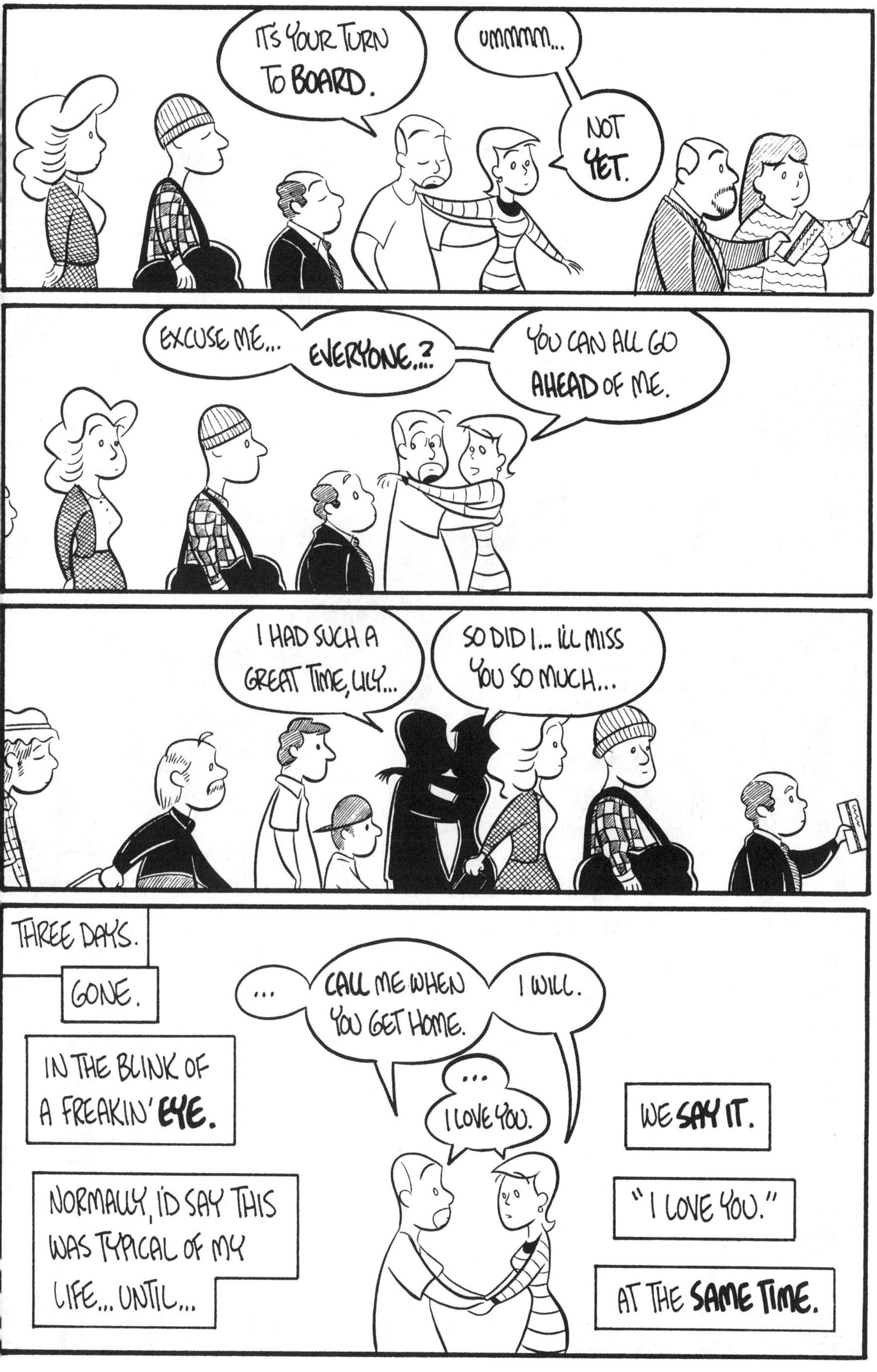
IT'S YOUR TURN TO BOARD.
UMMMM...
NOT YET.
EXCUSE ME...
EVERYONE...?
YOU CAN ALL GO AHEAD OF ME.
I HAD SUCH A GREAT TIME, LILY...
SO DID I... I'LL MISS YOU SO MUCH...
THREE DAYS.
GONE.
IN THE BLINK OF A FREAKIN' EYE.
NORMALLY, I'D SAY THIS WAS TYPICAL OF MY LIFE... UNTIL...
...
CALL ME WHEN YOU GET HOME.
I WILL.
...
I LOVE YOU.
WE SAY IT.
"I LOVE YOU."
AT THE SAME TIME.

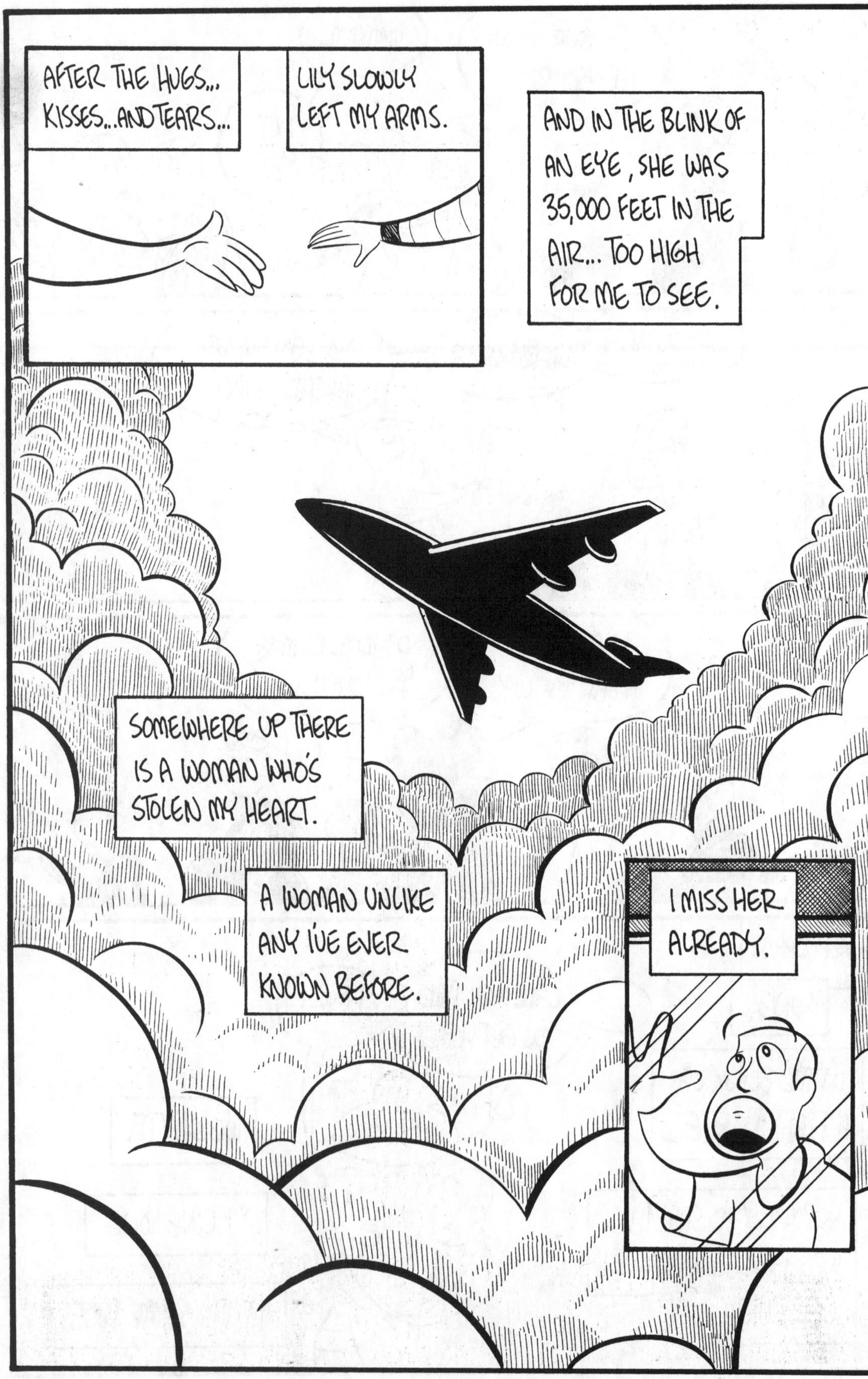
AFTER THE HUGS... KISSES...AND TEARS...
LILY SLOWLY LEFT MY ARMS.
AND IN THE BLINK OF AN EYE, SHE WAS 35,000 FEET IN THE AIR... TOO HIGH FOR ME TO SEE.
SOMEWHERE UP THERE IS A WOMAN WHO'S STOLEN MY HEART.
A WOMAN UNLIKE ANY I'VE EVER KNOWN BEFORE.
I MISS HER ALREADY.

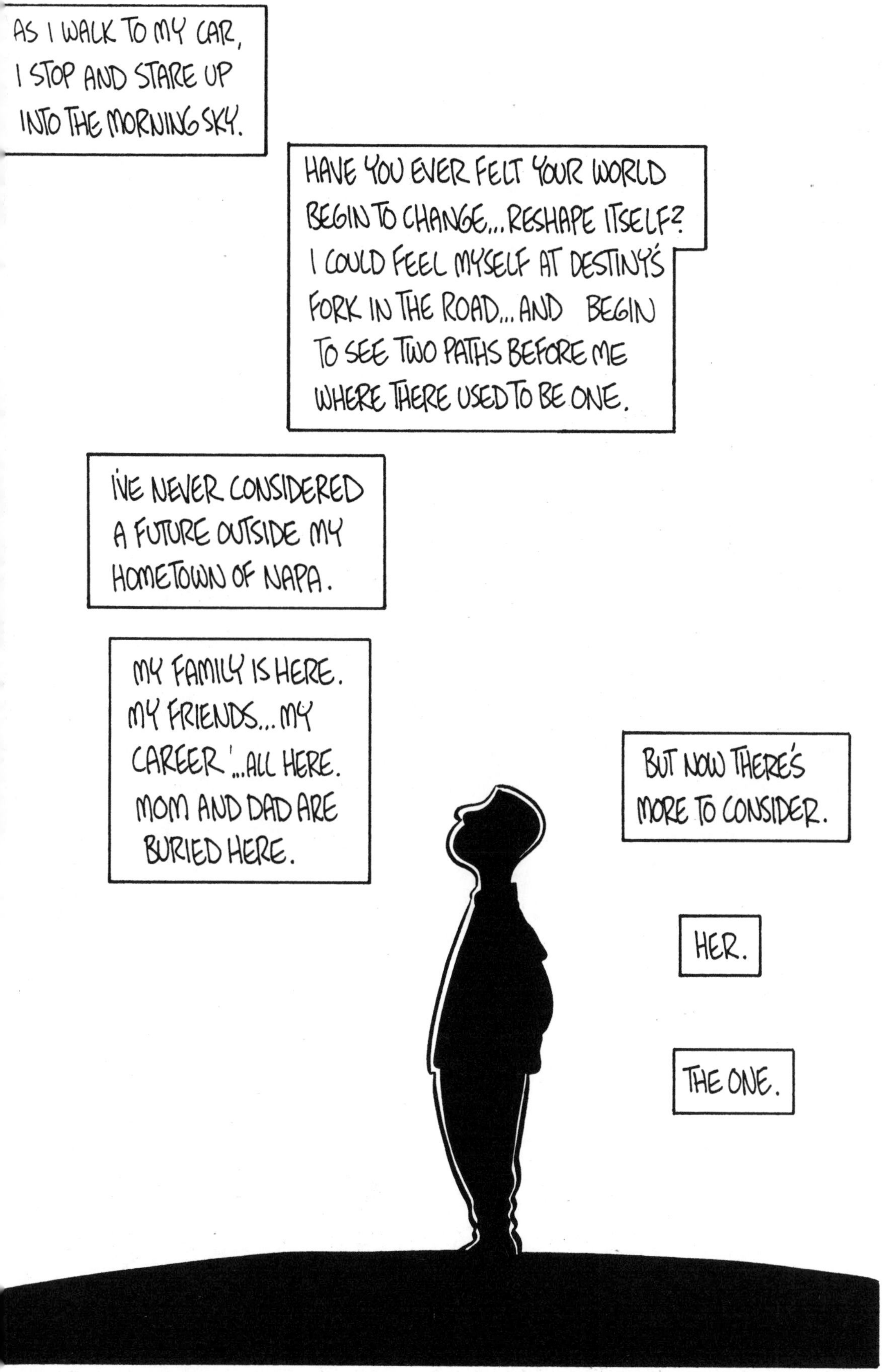
AS I WALK TO MY CAR, I STOP AND STARE UP INTO THE MORNING SKY.
HAVE YOU EVER FELT YOUR WORLD BEGIN TO CHANGE... RESHAPE ITSELF? I COULD FEEL MYSELF AT DESTINY'S FORK IN THE ROAD... AND BEGIN TO SEE TWO PATHS BEFORE ME WHERE THERE USED TO BE ONE.
I'VE NEVER CONSIDERED A FUTURE OUTSIDE MY HOMETOWN OF NAPA.
MY FAMILY IS HERE. MY FRIENDS... MY CAREER!...ALL HERE. MOM AND DAD ARE BURIED HERE.
BUT NOW THERE'S MORE TO CONSIDER.
HER.
THE ONE.

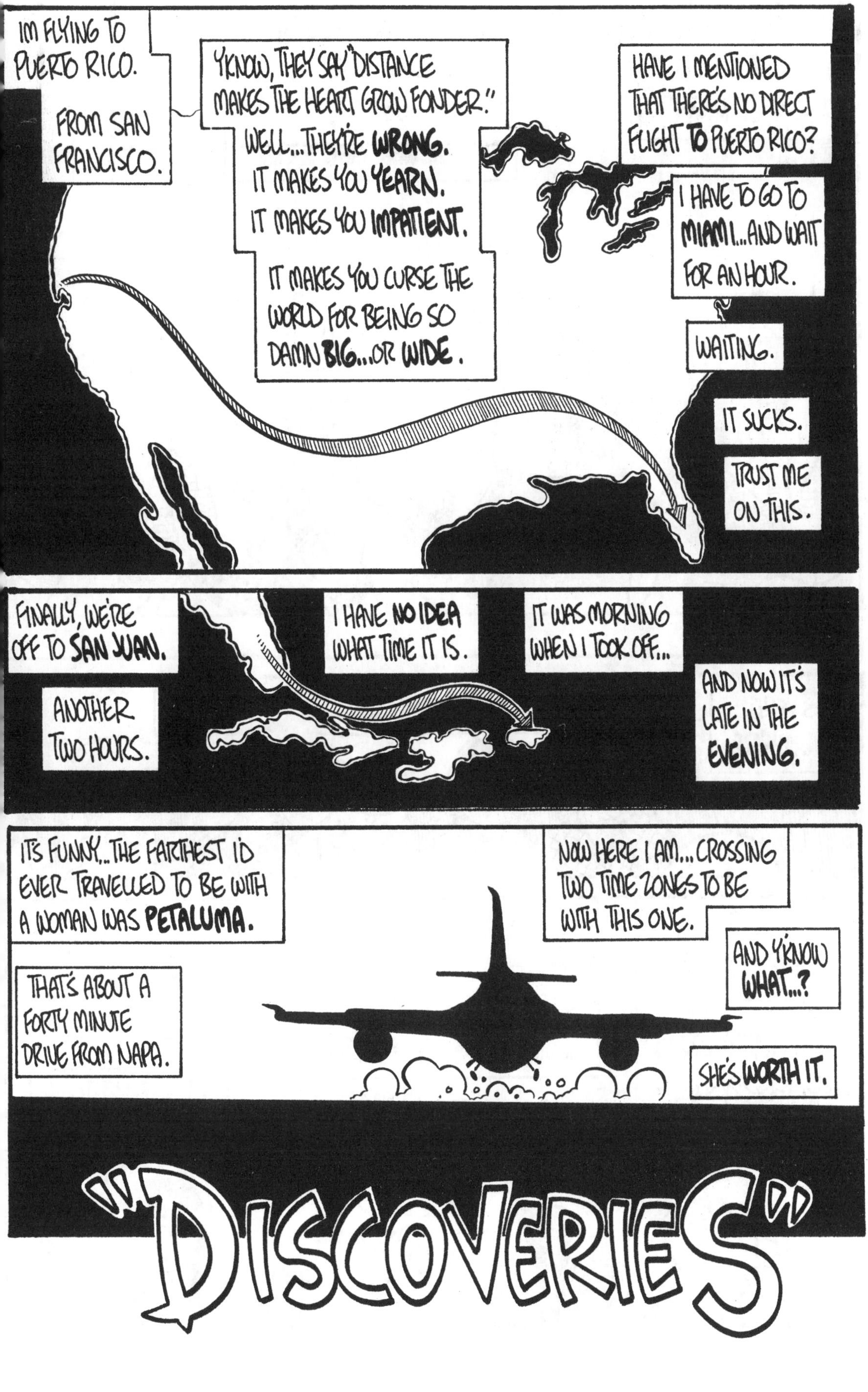
I'M FLYING TO PUERTO RICO.
FROM SAN FRANCISCO.
Y'KNOW, THEY SAY "DISTANCE MAKES THE HEART GROW FONDER."
WELL...THEY'RE WRONG. IT MAKES YOU YEARN. IT MAKES YOU IMPATIENT.
IT MAKES YOU CURSE THE WORLD FOR BEING SO DAMN BIG...OR WIDE.
HAVE I MENTIONED THAT THERE'S NO DIRECT FLIGHT TO PUERTO RICO?
I HAVE TO GO TO MIAMI...AND WAIT FOR AN HOUR.
WAITING.
IT SUCKS.
TRUST ME ON THIS.
FINALLY, WE'RE OFF TO SAN JUAN.
ANOTHER TWO HOURS.
I HAVE NO IDEA WHAT TIME IT IS.
IT WAS MORNING WHEN I TOOK OFF...
AND NOW IT'S LATE IN THE EVENING.
IT'S FUNNY...THE FARTHEST I'D EVER TRAVELLED TO BE WITH A WOMAN WAS PETALUMA.
THAT'S ABOUT A FORTY MINUTE DRIVE FROM NAPA.
NOW HERE I AM...CROSSING TWO TIME ZONES TO BE WITH THIS ONE.
AND Y'KNOW WHAT...?
SHE'S WORTH IT.
"DISCOVERIES"

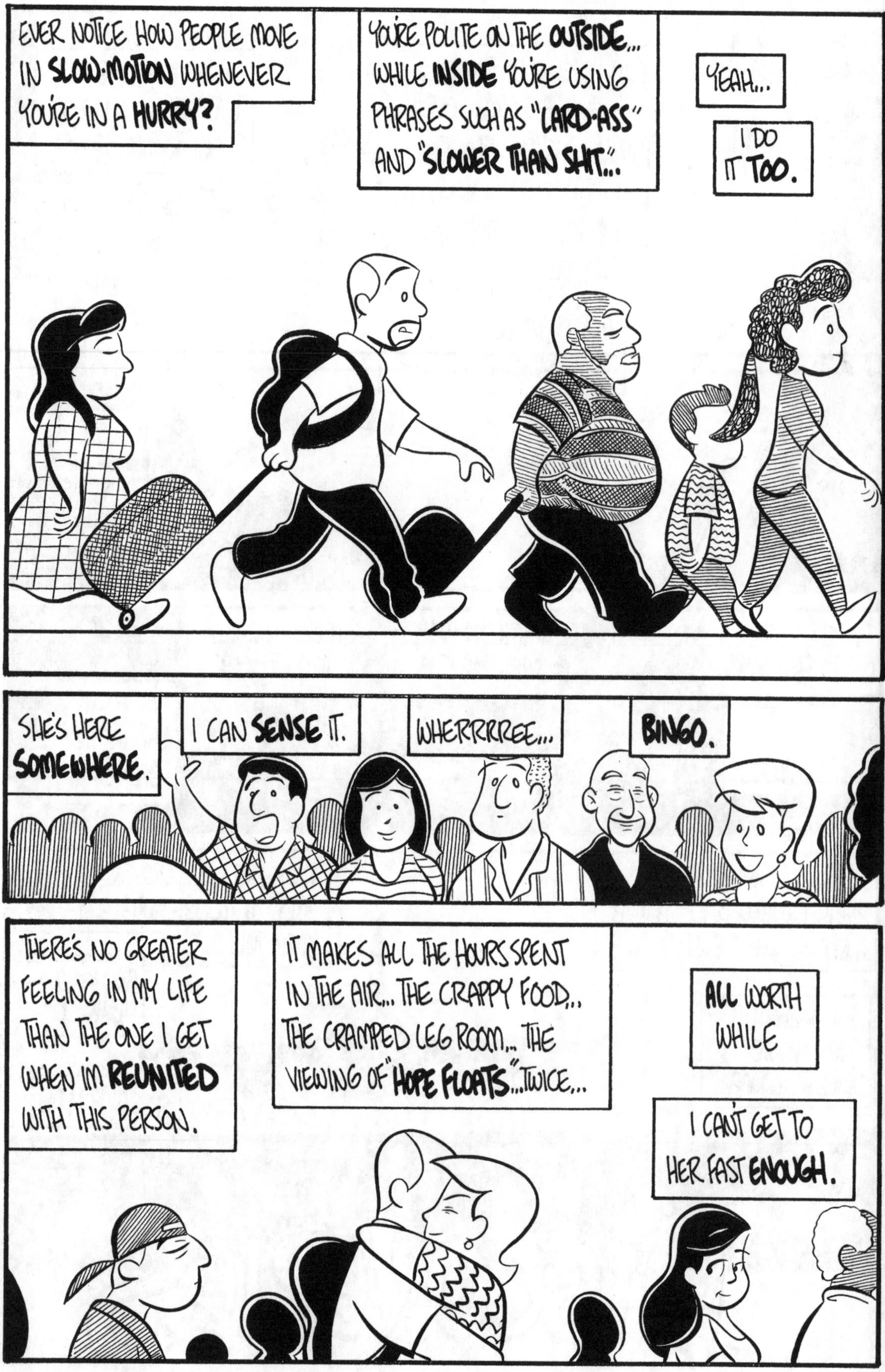

EVER NOTICE HOW PEOPLE MOVE IN SLOW-MOTION WHENEVER YOU'RE IN A HURRY?
YOU'RE POLITE ON THE OUTSIDE... WHILE INSIDE YOU'RE USING PHRASES SUCH AS "LARD-ASS" AND "SLOWER THAN SHIT"...
YEAH...
I DO IT TOO.
SHE'S HERE SOMEWHERE.
I CAN SENSE IT.
WHERRRREE...
BINGO.
THERE'S NO GREATER FEELING IN MY LIFE THAN THE ONE I GET WHEN I'M REUNITED WITH THIS PERSON.
IT MAKES ALL THE HOURS SPENT IN THE AIR... THE CRAPPY FOOD... THE CRAMPED LEG ROOM... THE VIEWING OF "HOPE FLOATS"...TWICE...
ALL WORTH WHILE
I CAN'T GET TO HER FAST ENOUGH.

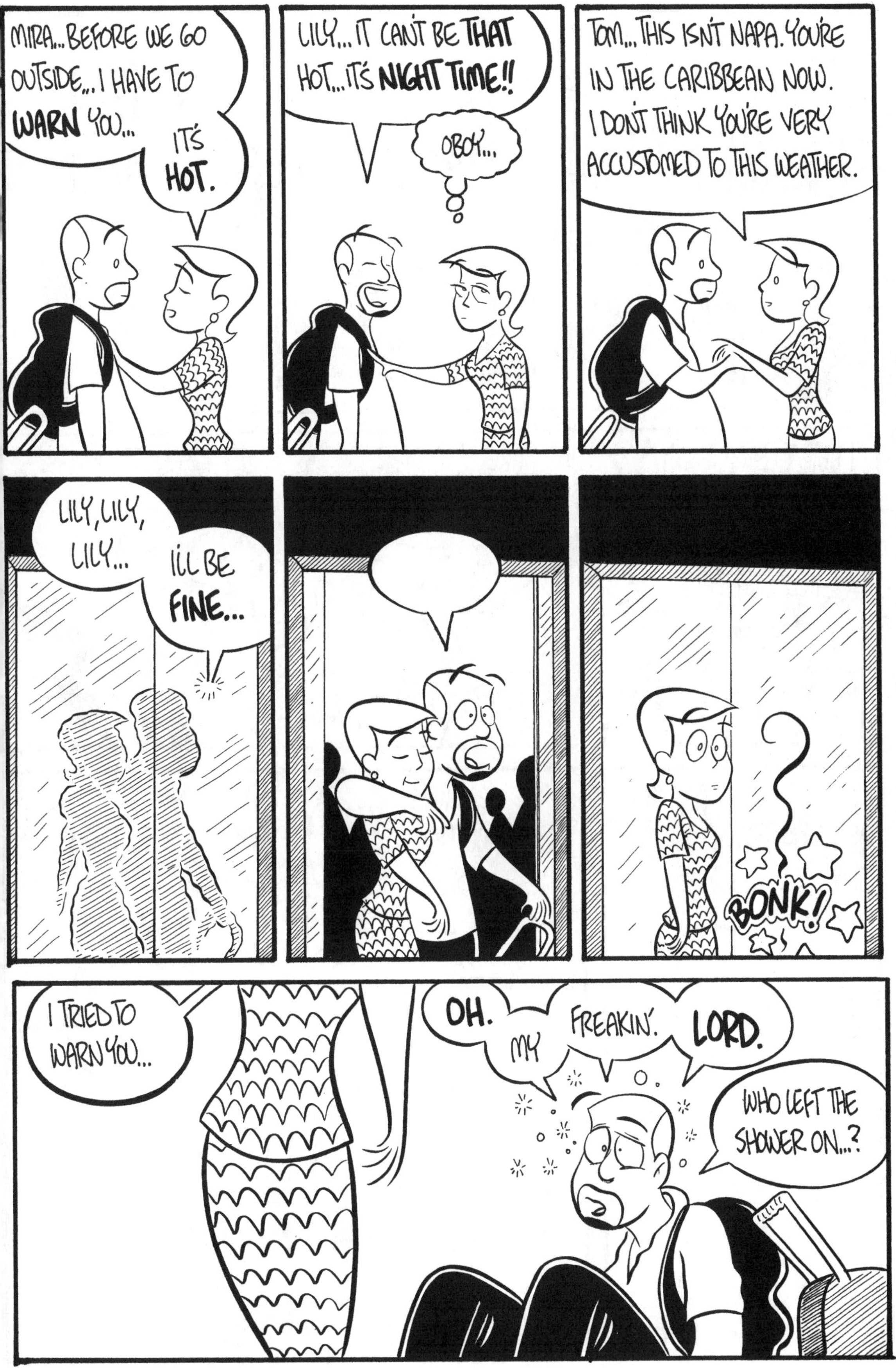
MIRA... BEFORE WE GO OUTSIDE... I HAVE TO WARN YOU...
IT'S HOT.
LILY... IT CAN'T BE THAT HOT... IT'S NIGHT TIME!!
OBOY...
TOM... THIS ISN'T NAPA. YOU'RE IN THE CARIBBEAN NOW. I DON'T THINK YOU'RE VERY ACCUSTOMED TO THIS WEATHER.
LILY, LILY, LILY...
I'LL BE FINE...
BONK!
I TRIED TO WARN YOU...
OH.
MY
FREAKIN'.
LORD.
WHO LEFT THE SHOWER ON...?

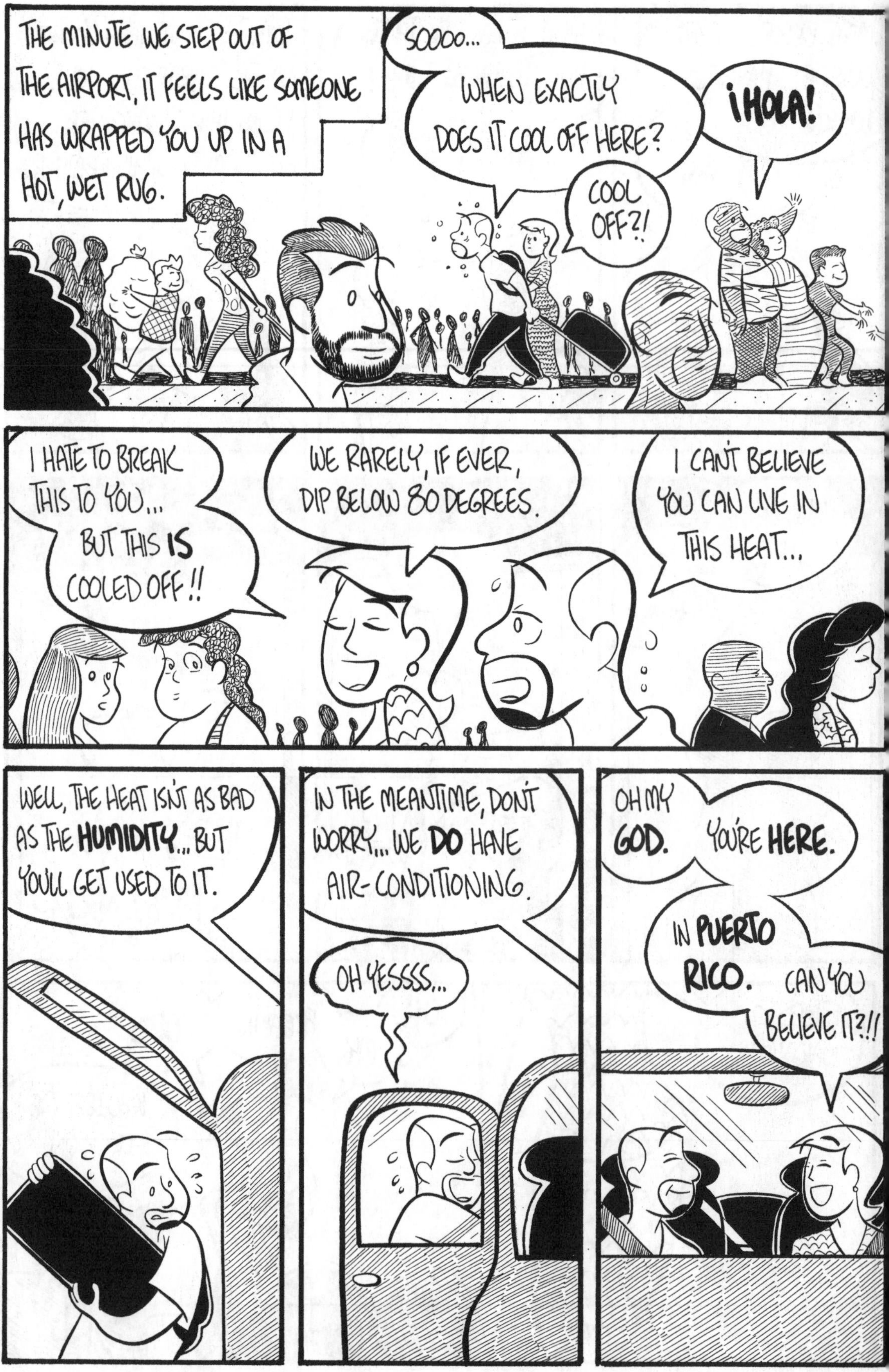

THE MINUTE WE STEP OUT OF THE AIRPORT, IT FEELS LIKE SOMEONE HAS WRAPPED YOU UP IN A HOT, WET RUG.
SOOOO...
WHEN EXACTLY DOES IT COOL OFF HERE?
COOL OFF?!
¡HOLA!
I HATE TO BREAK THIS TO YOU...
BUT THIS IS COOLED OFF!!
WE RARELY, IF EVER, DIP BELOW 80 DEGREES.
I CAN'T BELIEVE YOU CAN LIVE IN THIS HEAT...
WELL, THE HEAT ISN'T AS BAD AS THE HUMIDITY... BUT YOU'LL GET USED TO IT.
IN THE MEANTIME, DON'T WORRY... WE DO HAVE AIR-CONDITIONING.
OH YESSSS...
OH MY GOD.
YOU'RE HERE.
IN PUERTO RICO.
CAN YOU BELIEVE IT?!!

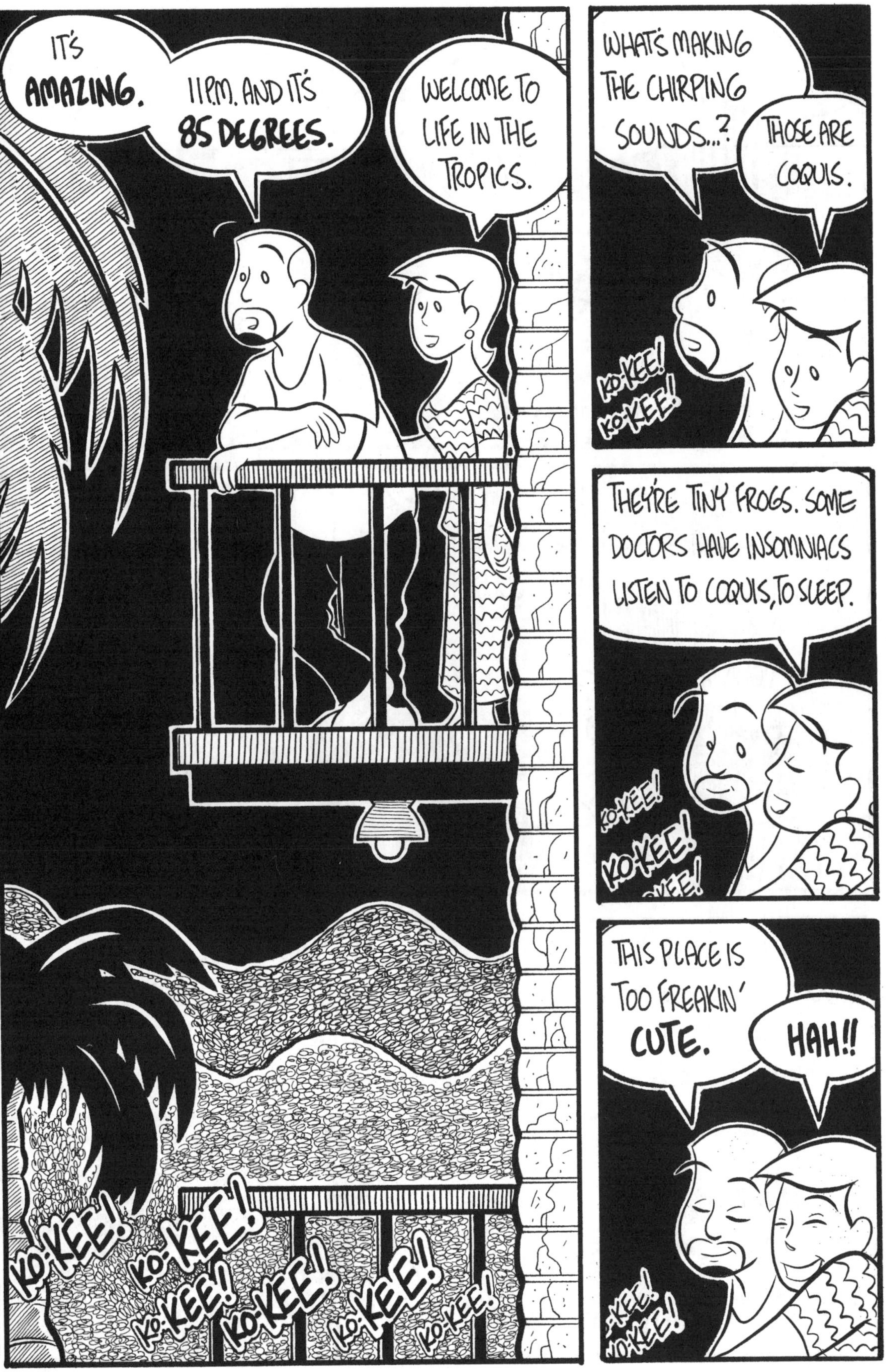

IT'S AMAZING.
11 P.M. AND IT'S 85 DEGREES.
WELCOME TO LIFE IN THE TROPICS.
KO-KEE! KO-KEE! KO-KEE! KO-KEE! KO-KEE! KO-KEE! KO-KEE!
WHAT'S MAKING THE CHIRPING SOUNDS...?
THOSE ARE COQUIS.
KO-KEE! KO-KEE!
THEY'RE TINY FROGS. SOME DOCTORS HAVE INSOMNIACS LISTEN TO COQUIS, TO SLEEP.
KO-KEE! KO-KEE!
THIS PLACE IS TOO FREAKIN' CUTE.
HAH!!

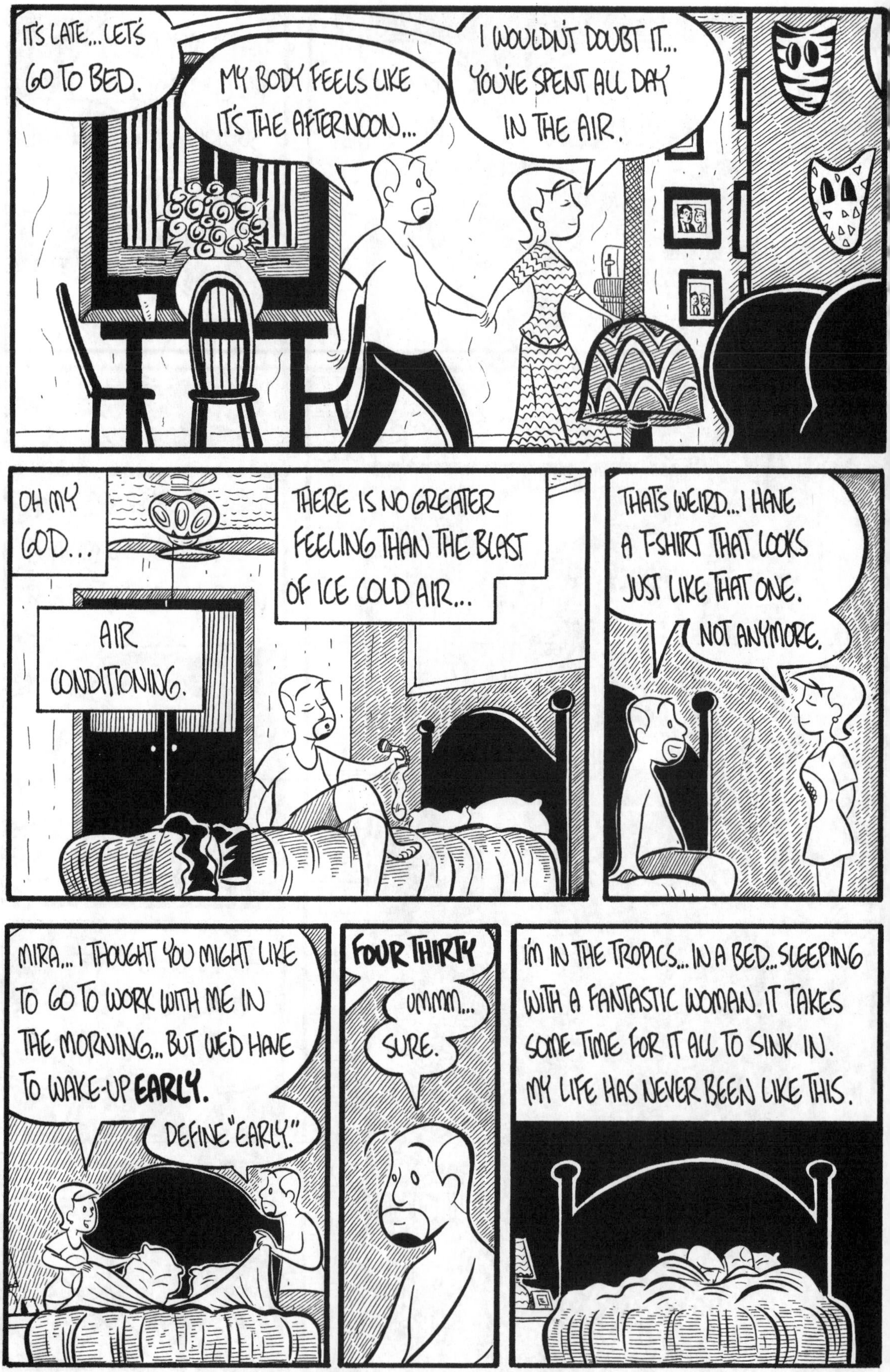
IT'S LATE... LET'S GO TO BED.
MY BODY FEELS LIKE IT'S THE AFTERNOON...
I WOULDN'T DOUBT IT... YOU'VE SPENT ALL DAY IN THE AIR.
OH MY GOD...
THERE IS NO GREATER FEELING THAN THE BLAST OF ICE COLD AIR...
AIR CONDITIONING.
THAT'S WEIRD... I HAVE A T-SHIRT THAT LOOKS JUST LIKE THAT ONE.
NOT ANYMORE.
MIRA... I THOUGHT YOU MIGHT LIKE TO GO TO WORK WITH ME IN THE MORNING... BUT WE'D HAVE TO WAKE-UP **EARLY.**
DEFINE "EARLY."
FOUR THIRTY
UMMM... SURE.
I'M IN THE TROPICS... IN A BED... SLEEPING WITH A FANTASTIC WOMAN. IT TAKES SOME TIME FOR IT ALL TO SINK IN. MY LIFE HAS NEVER BEEN LIKE THIS.

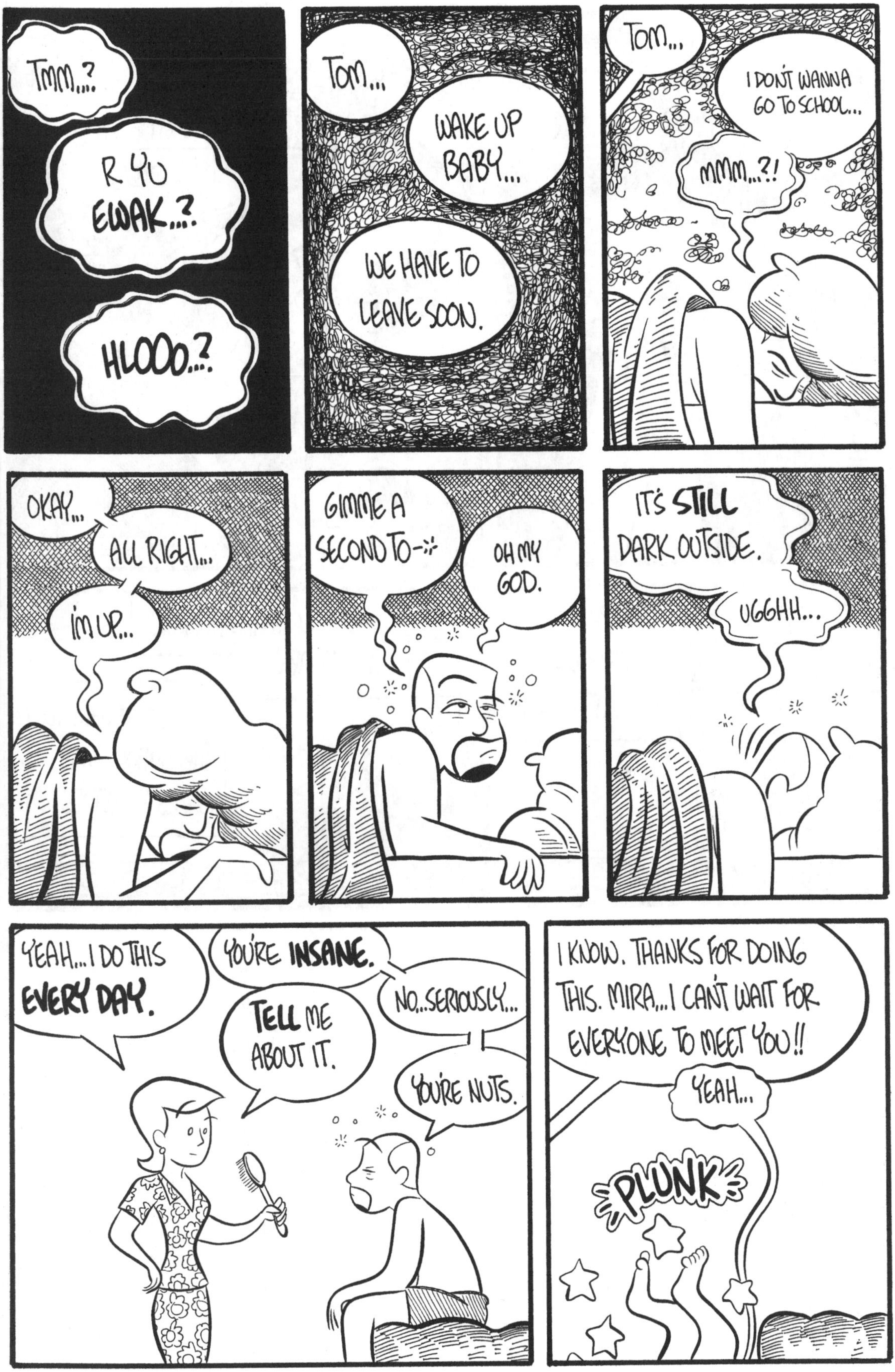
TMM...?
R YU EWAK...?
HLOOO...?
TOM...
WAKE UP BABY...
WE HAVE TO LEAVE SOON.
TOM...
I DON'T WANNA GO TO SCHOOL...
MMM...?!
OKAY...
ALL RIGHT...
I'M UP...
GIMME A SECOND TO-
OH MY GOD.
IT'S STILL DARK OUTSIDE.
UGGHH...
YEAH... I DO THIS EVERY DAY.
YOU'RE INSANE.
TELL ME ABOUT IT.
NO... SERIOUSLY...
YOU'RE NUTS.
I KNOW. THANKS FOR DOING THIS. MIRA... I CAN'T WAIT FOR EVERYONE TO MEET YOU!!
YEAH...
PLUNK

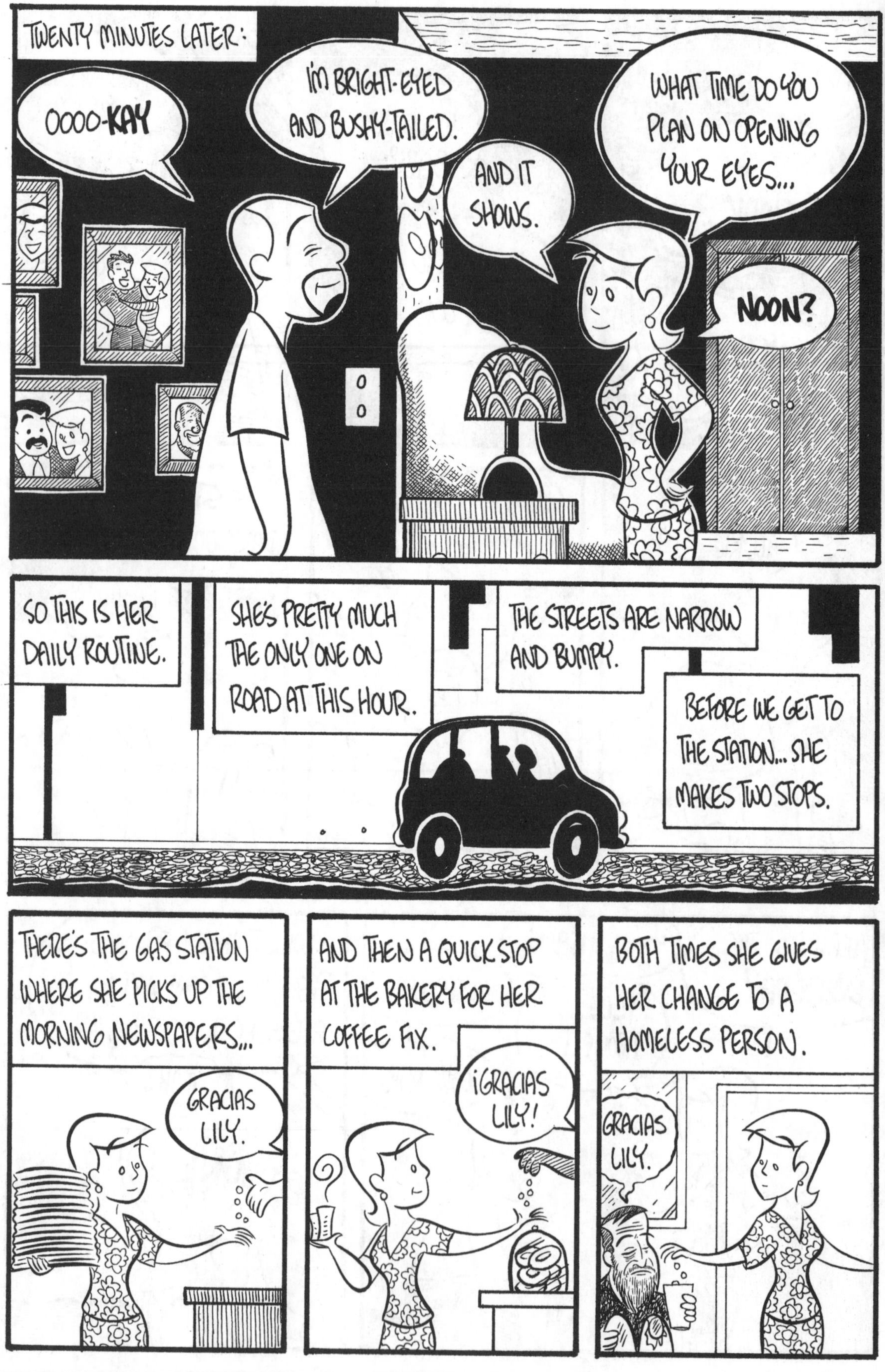
TWENTY MINUTES LATER:
OOOO-KAY
I'M BRIGHT-EYED AND BUSHY-TAILED.
AND IT SHOWS.
WHAT TIME DO YOU PLAN ON OPENING YOUR EYES...
NOON?
SO THIS IS HER DAILY ROUTINE.
SHE'S PRETTY MUCH THE ONLY ONE ON ROAD AT THIS HOUR.
THE STREETS ARE NARROW AND BUMPY.
BEFORE WE GET TO THE STATION... SHE MAKES TWO STOPS.
THERE'S THE GAS STATION WHERE SHE PICKS UP THE MORNING NEWSPAPERS...
GRACIAS LILY.
AND THEN A QUICK STOP AT THE BAKERY FOR HER COFFEE FIX.
¡GRACIAS LILY!
BOTH TIMES SHE GIVES HER CHANGE TO A HOMELESS PERSON.
GRACIAS LILY.

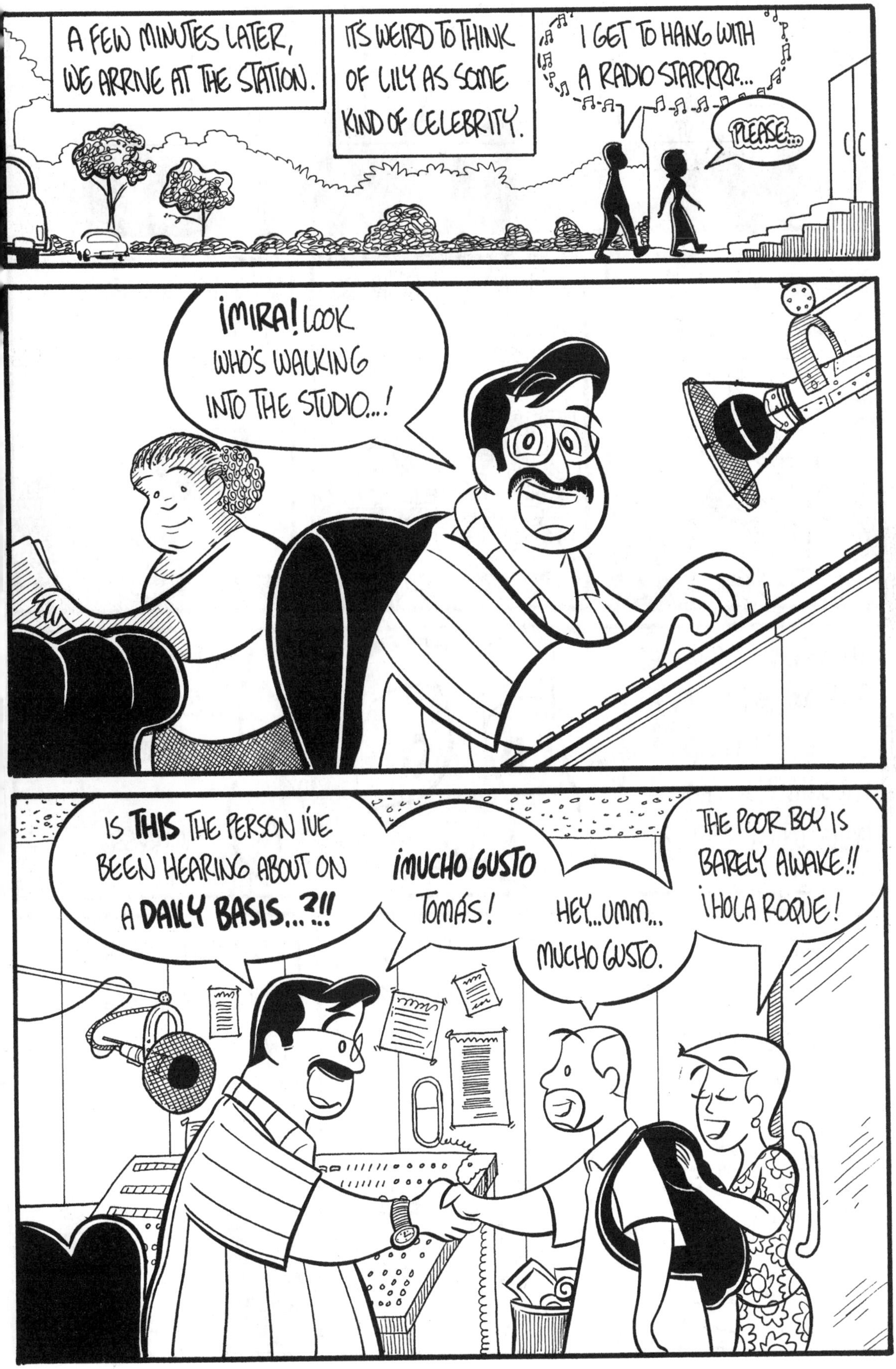
A FEW MINUTES LATER, WE ARRIVE AT THE STATION.
IT'S WEIRD TO THINK OF LILY AS SOME KIND OF CELEBRITY.
I GET TO HANG WITH A RADIO STARRRR...
PLEASE...
¡MIRA! LOOK WHO'S WALKING INTO THE STUDIO...!
IS THIS THE PERSON I'VE BEEN HEARING ABOUT ON A DAILY BASIS...?!!
¡MUCHO GUSTO TOMÁS!
HEY...UMM... MUCHO GUSTO.
THE POOR BOY IS BARELY AWAKE!! ¡HOLA ROQUE!

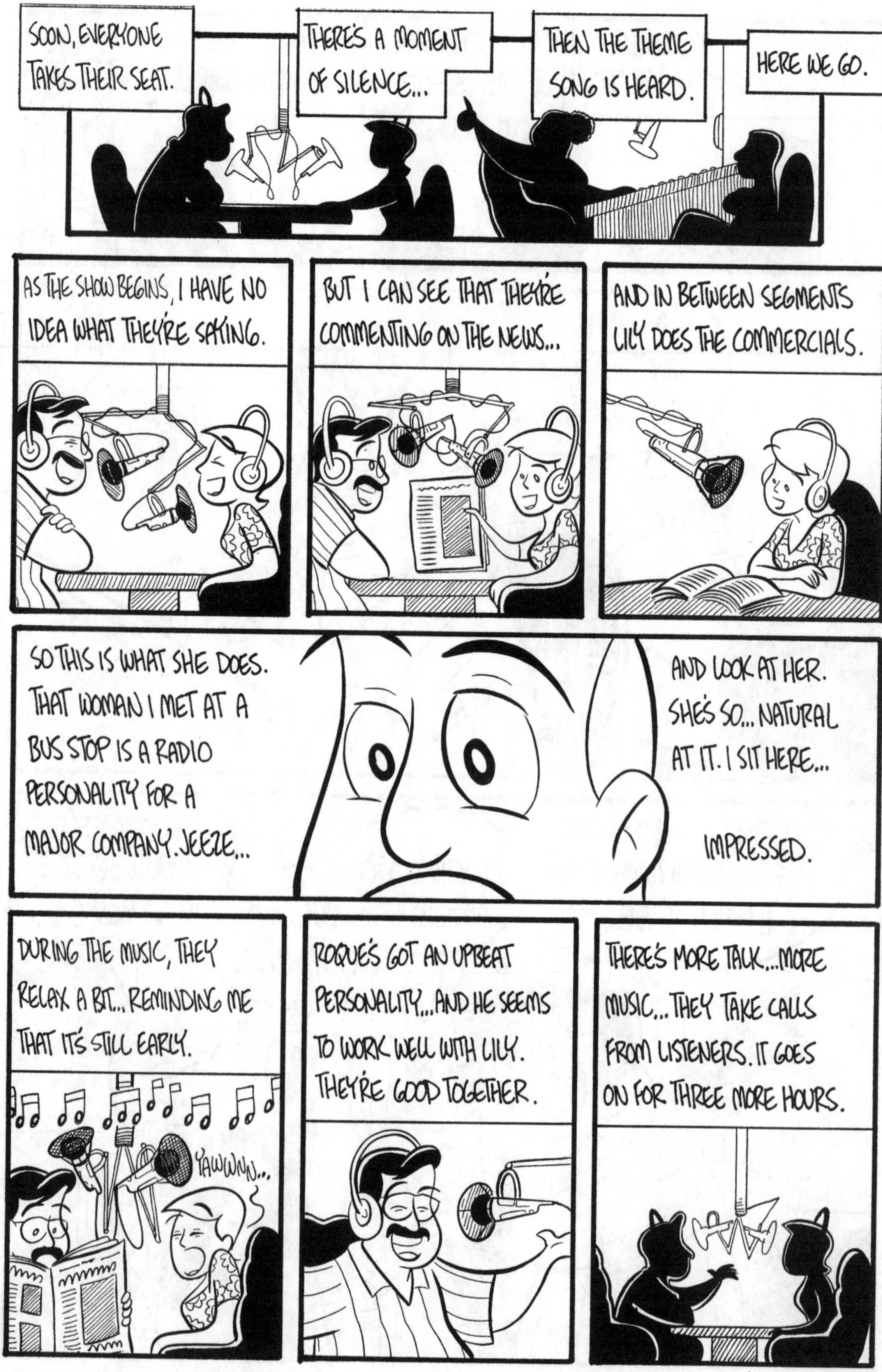
SOON, EVERYONE TAKES THEIR SEAT.
THERE'S A MOMENT OF SILENCE...
THEN THE THEME SONG IS HEARD.
HERE WE GO.
AS THE SHOW BEGINS, I HAVE NO IDEA WHAT THEY'RE SAYING.
BUT I CAN SEE THAT THEY'RE COMMENTING ON THE NEWS...
AND IN BETWEEN SEGMENTS LILY DOES THE COMMERCIALS.
SO THIS IS WHAT SHE DOES. THAT WOMAN I MET AT A BUS STOP IS A RADIO PERSONALITY FOR A MAJOR COMPANY. JEEZE...
AND LOOK AT HER. SHE'S SO... NATURAL AT IT. I SIT HERE...
IMPRESSED.
DURING THE MUSIC, THEY RELAX A BIT... REMINDING ME THAT IT'S STILL EARLY.
YAWWNN...
ROQUE'S GOT AN UPBEAT PERSONALITY... AND HE SEEMS TO WORK WELL WITH LILY. THEY'RE GOOD TOGETHER.
THERE'S MORE TALK... MORE MUSIC... THEY TAKE CALLS FROM LISTENERS. IT GOES ON FOR THREE MORE HOURS.

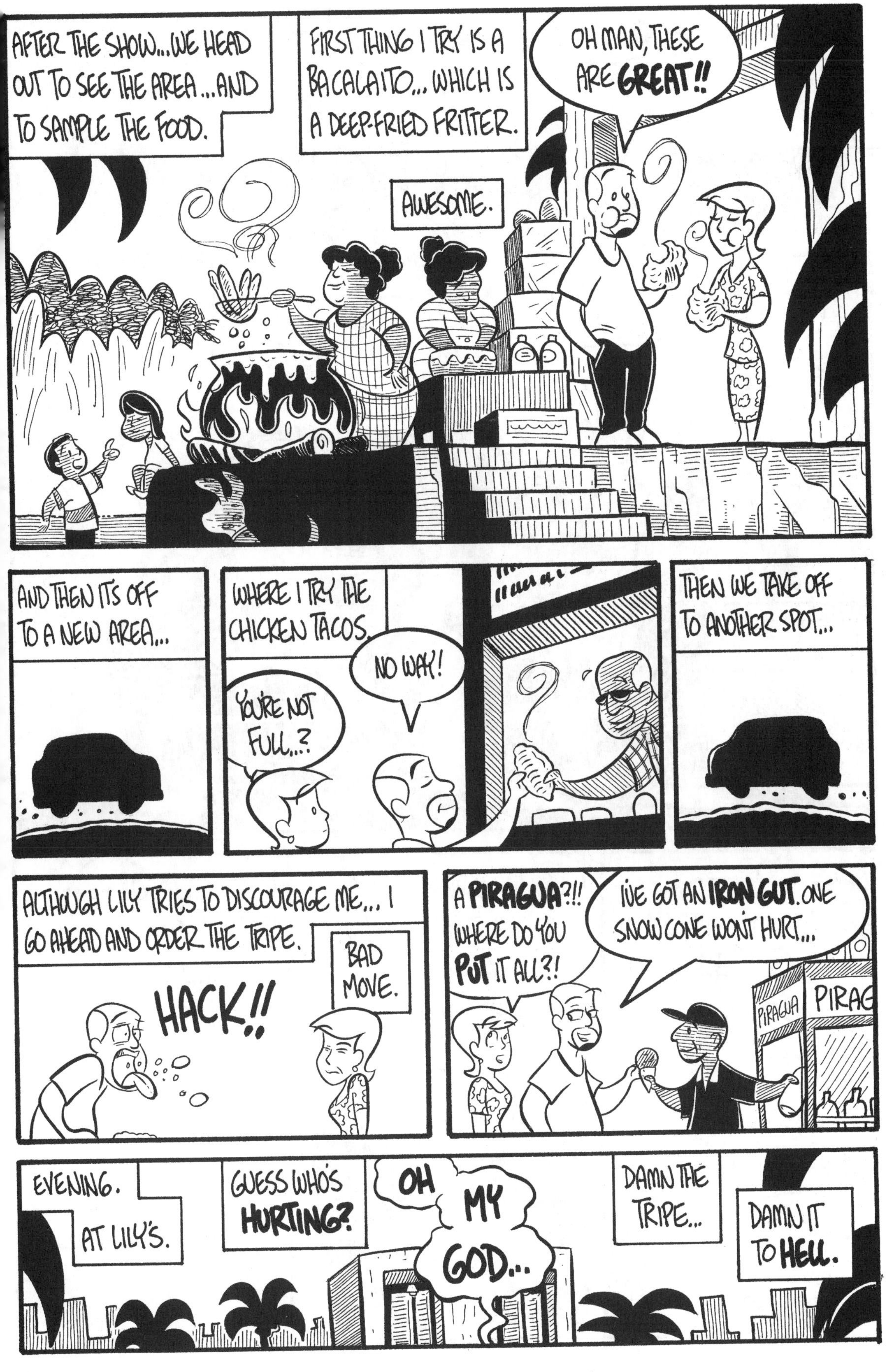
AFTER THE SHOW...WE HEAD OUT TO SEE THE AREA...AND TO SAMPLE THE FOOD.
FIRST THING I TRY IS A BACALAITO... WHICH IS A DEEP-FRIED FRITTER.
OH MAN, THESE ARE GREAT!!
AWESOME.
AND THEN ITS OFF TO A NEW AREA...
WHERE I TRY THE CHICKEN TACOS.
NO WAY!
YOU'RE NOT FULL...?
THEN WE TAKE OFF TO ANOTHER SPOT...
ALTHOUGH LILY TRIES TO DISCOURAGE ME... I GO AHEAD AND ORDER THE TRIPE.
BAD MOVE.
HACK!!
A PIRAGUA?!! WHERE DO YOU PUT IT ALL?!
I'VE GOT AN IRON GUT. ONE SNOW CONE WON'T HURT...
PIRAGUA
PIRAG
EVENING.
AT LILY'S.
GUESS WHO'S HURTING?
OH MY GOD...
DAMN THE TRIPE...
DAMN IT TO HELL.

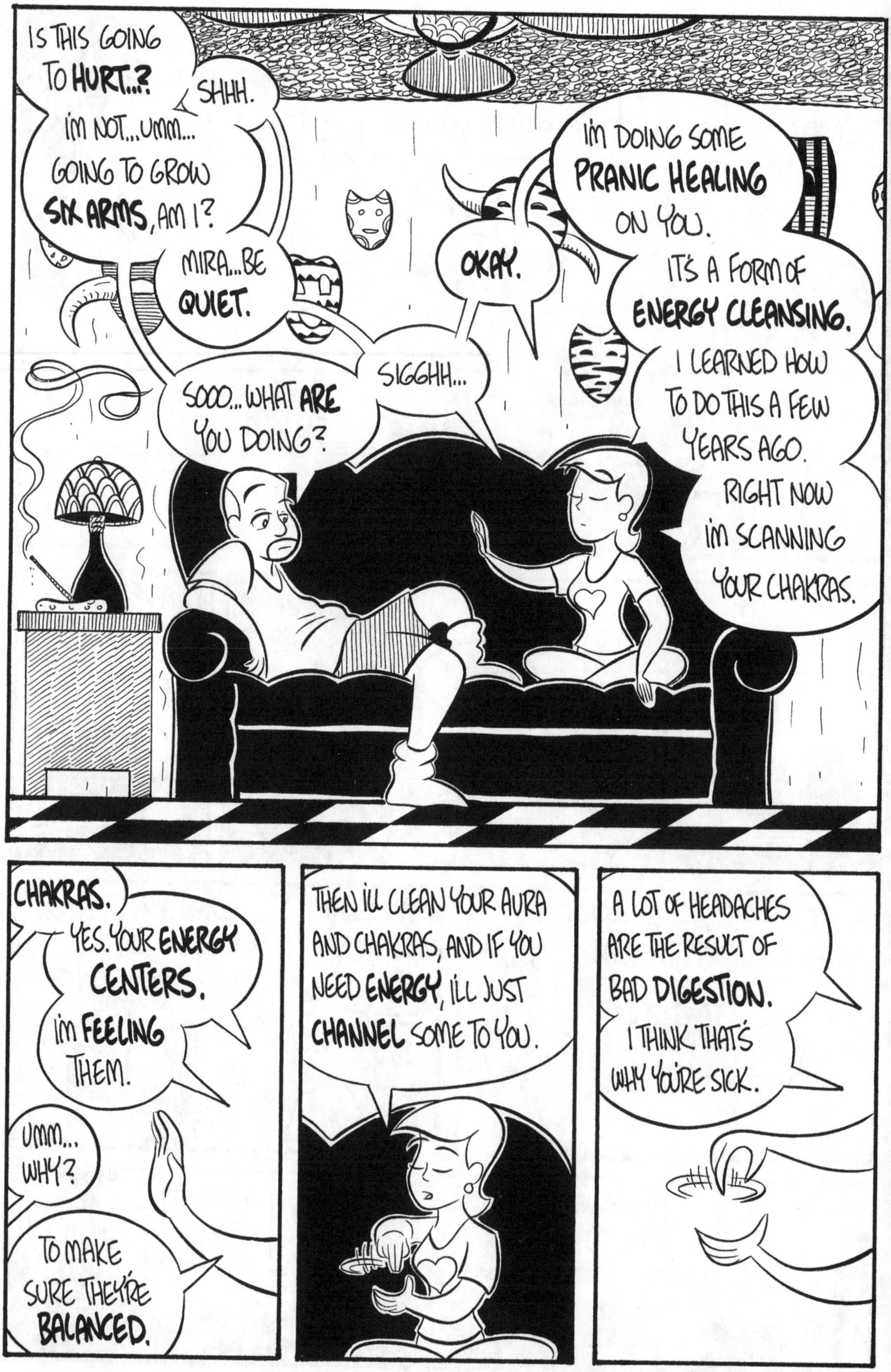
IS THIS GOING TO HURT...?
SHHH.
I'M NOT...UMM... GOING TO GROW SIX ARMS, AM I?
MIRA...BE QUIET.
SOOO... WHAT ARE YOU DOING?
SIGGHH...
OKAY.
I'M DOING SOME PRANIC HEALING ON YOU.
IT'S A FORM OF ENERGY CLEANSING.
I LEARNED HOW TO DO THIS A FEW YEARS AGO.
RIGHT NOW I'M SCANNING YOUR CHAKRAS.
CHAKRAS.
YES. YOUR ENERGY CENTERS.
I'M FEELING THEM.
UMM... WHY?
TO MAKE SURE THEY'RE BALANCED.
THEN I'LL CLEAN YOUR AURA AND CHAKRAS, AND IF YOU NEED ENERGY, I'LL JUST CHANNEL SOME TO YOU.
A LOT OF HEADACHES ARE THE RESULT OF BAD DIGESTION.
I THINK THAT'S WHY YOU'RE SICK.

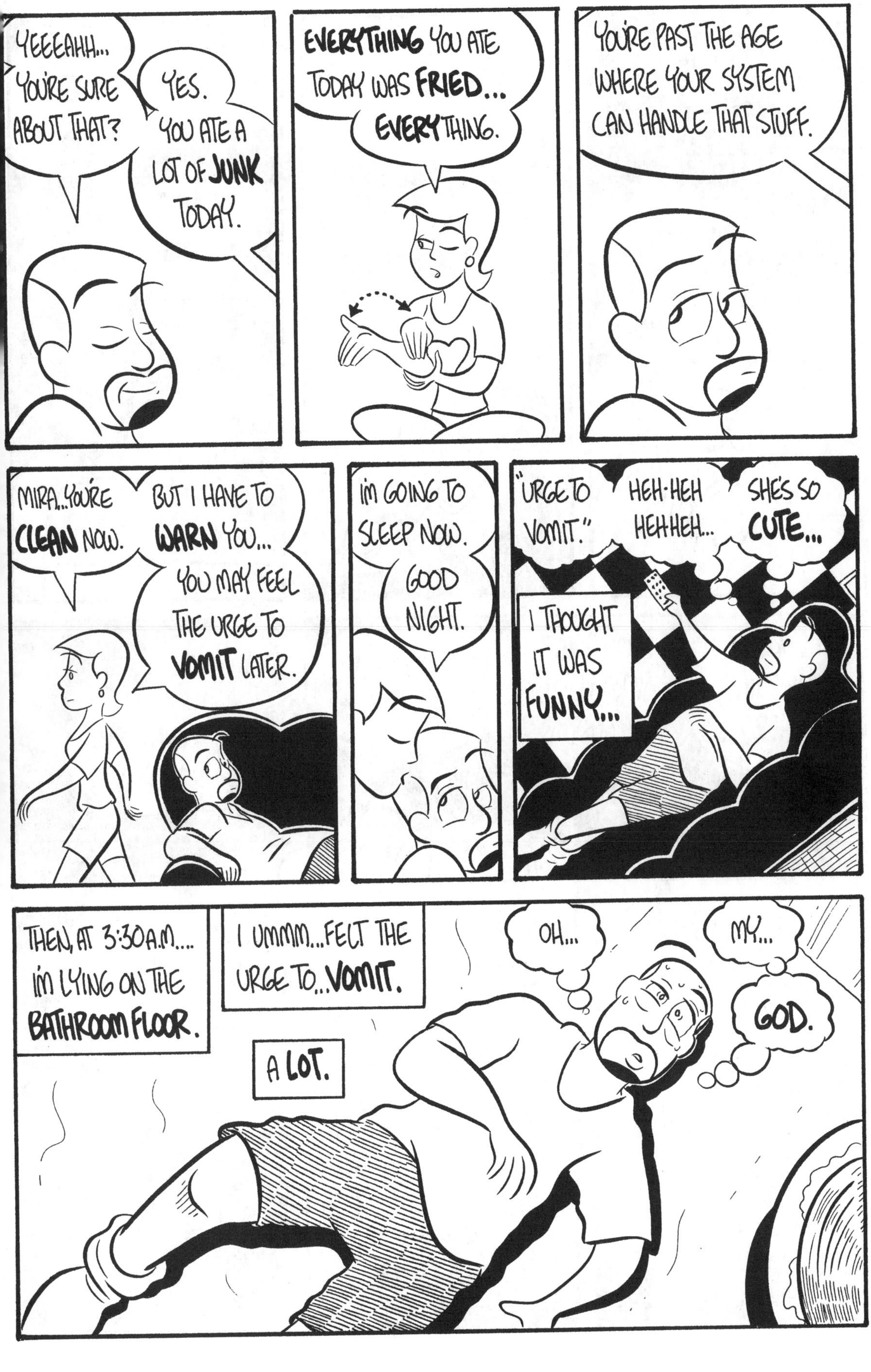
YEEEAHH... YOU'RE SURE ABOUT THAT?
YES. YOU ATE A LOT OF JUNK TODAY.
EVERYTHING YOU ATE TODAY WAS FRIED...
EVERYTHING.
YOU'RE PAST THE AGE WHERE YOUR SYSTEM CAN HANDLE THAT STUFF.
MIRA...YOU'RE CLEAN NOW.
BUT I HAVE TO WARN YOU...
YOU MAY FEEL THE URGE TO VOMIT LATER.
I'M GOING TO SLEEP NOW.
GOOD NIGHT.
"URGE TO VOMIT."
HEH-HEH HEH-HEH...
SHE'S SO CUTE...
I THOUGHT IT WAS FUNNY...
THEN, AT 3:30 A.M.... I'M LYING ON THE BATHROOM FLOOR.
I UMMM...FELT THE URGE TO...VOMIT.
A LOT.
OH...
MY...
GOD.

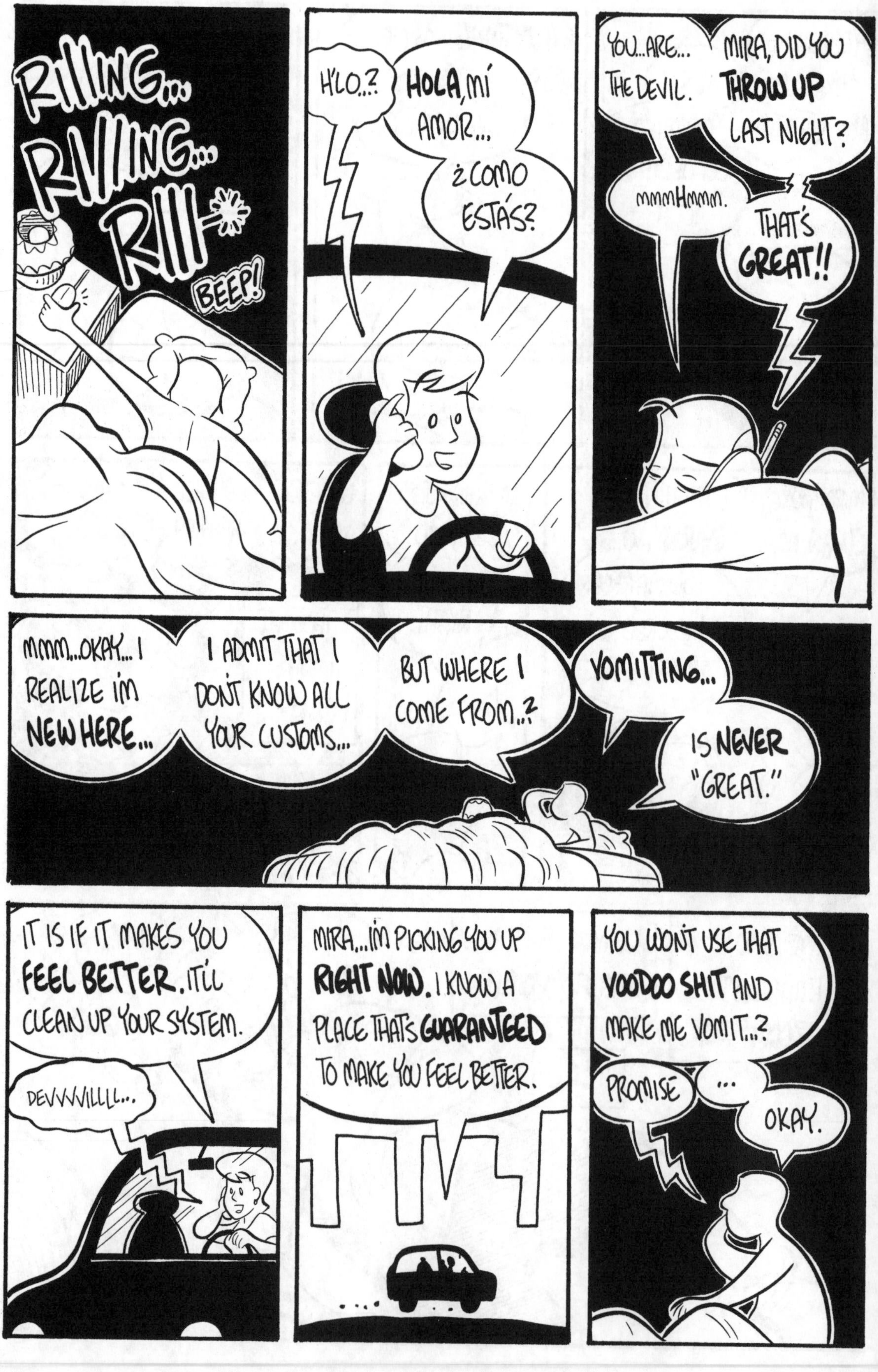
RIIIING... RIIIING... RIII
BEEP!
H'LO..?
HOLA, MÍ AMOR... ¿COMO ESTÁS?
YOU...ARE... THE DEVIL.
MIRA, DID YOU THROW UP LAST NIGHT?
MMMHMMM.
THAT'S GREAT!!
MMM...OKAY... I REALIZE I'M NEW HERE...
I ADMIT THAT I DON'T KNOW ALL YOUR CUSTOMS...
BUT WHERE I COME FROM..?
VOMITTING...
IS NEVER "GREAT."
IT IS IF IT MAKES YOU FEEL BETTER. IT'LL CLEAN UP YOUR SYSTEM.
DEVVVVILLLL...
MIRA...I'M PICKING YOU UP RIGHT NOW. I KNOW A PLACE THAT'S GUARANTEED TO MAKE YOU FEEL BETTER.
YOU WON'T USE THAT VOODOO SHIT AND MAKE ME VOMIT...?
PROMISE
...
OKAY.

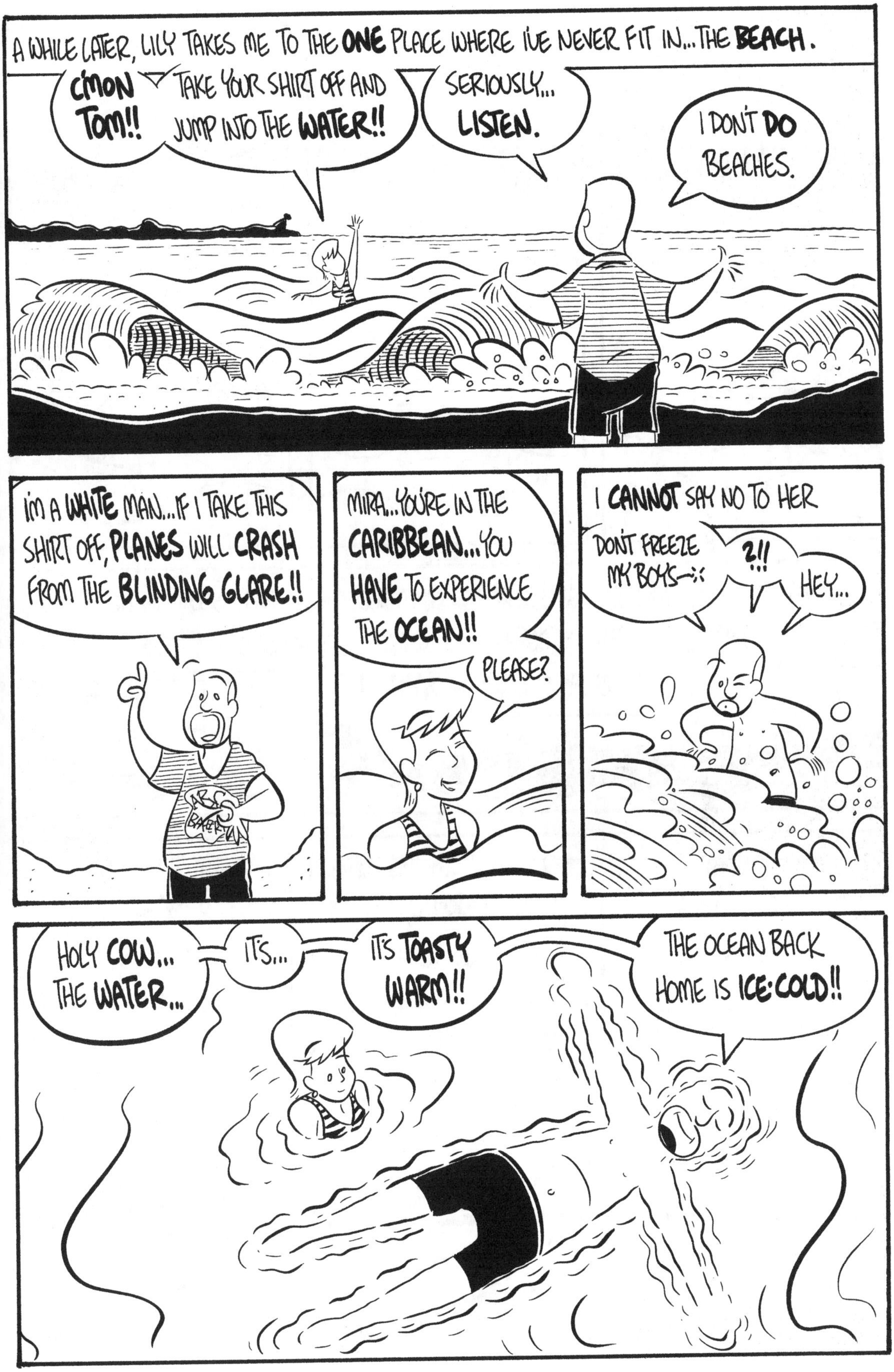
A WHILE LATER, LILY TAKES ME TO THE ONE PLACE WHERE I'VE NEVER FIT IN... THE BEACH.
C'MON TOM!!
TAKE YOUR SHIRT OFF AND JUMP INTO THE WATER!!
SERIOUSLY... LISTEN.
I DON'T DO BEACHES.
I'M A WHITE MAN... IF I TAKE THIS SHIRT OFF, PLANES WILL CRASH FROM THE BLINDING GLARE!!
MIRA... YOU'RE IN THE CARIBBEAN... YOU HAVE TO EXPERIENCE THE OCEAN!!
PLEASE?
I CANNOT SAY NO TO HER
DON'T FREEZE MY BOYS
?!!
HEY...
HOLY COW... THE WATER...
IT'S...
IT'S TOASTY WARM!!
THE OCEAN BACK HOME IS ICE-COLD!!

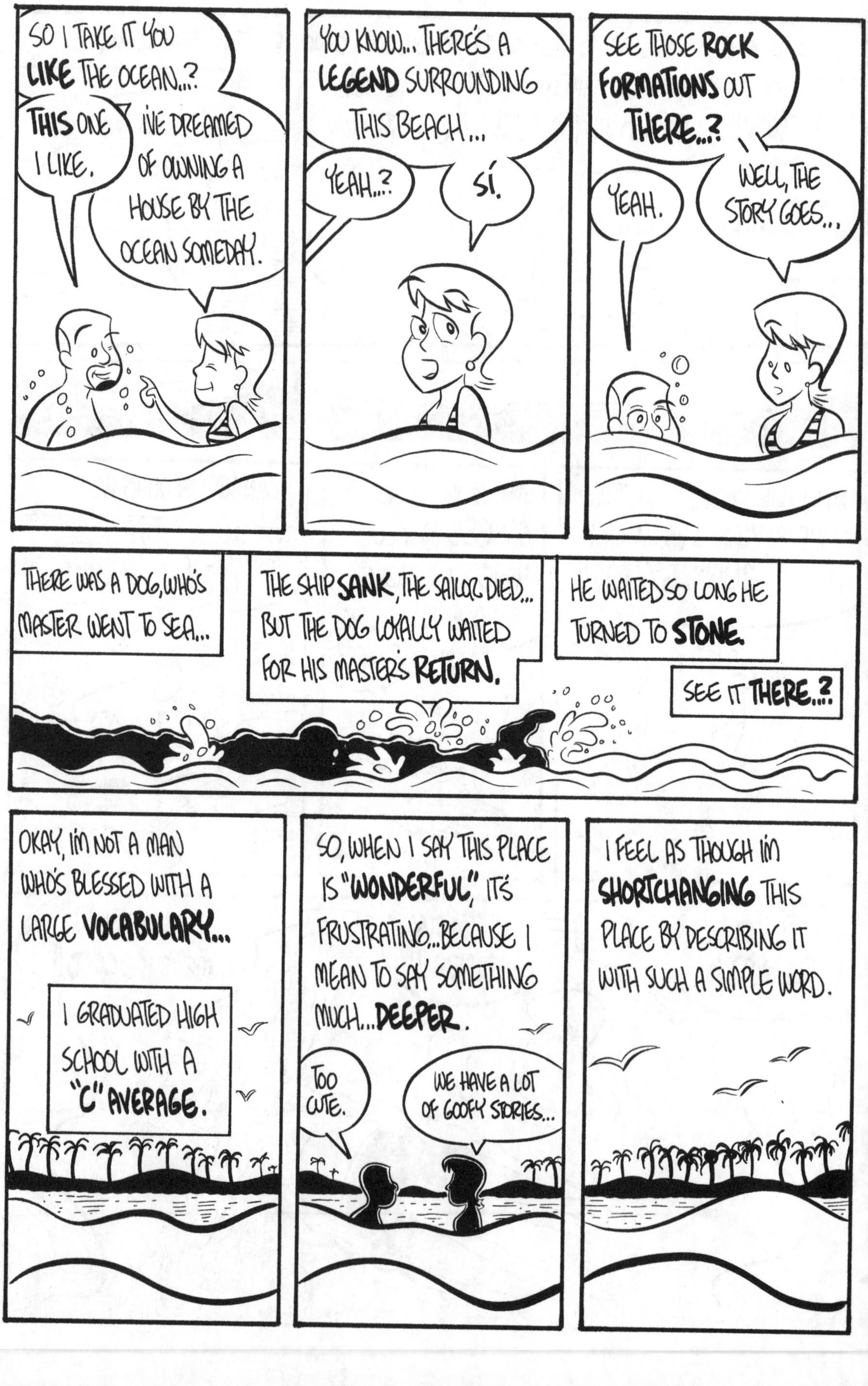

SO I TAKE IT YOU LIKE THE OCEAN...?
THIS ONE I LIKE.
I'VE DREAMED OF OWNING A HOUSE BY THE OCEAN SOMEDAY.
YOU KNOW... THERE'S A LEGEND SURROUNDING THIS BEACH...
YEAH...?
SÍ.
SEE THOSE ROCK FORMATIONS OUT THERE...?
YEAH.
WELL, THE STORY GOES...
THERE WAS A DOG, WHO'S MASTER WENT TO SEA...
THE SHIP SANK, THE SAILOR DIED... BUT THE DOG LOYALLY WAITED FOR HIS MASTER'S RETURN.
HE WAITED SO LONG HE TURNED TO STONE.
SEE IT THERE...?
OKAY, I'M NOT A MAN WHO'S BLESSED WITH A LARGE VOCABULARY...
I GRADUATED HIGH SCHOOL WITH A "C" AVERAGE.
SO, WHEN I SAY THIS PLACE IS "WONDERFUL," IT'S FRUSTRATING... BECAUSE I MEAN TO SAY SOMETHING MUCH... DEEPER.
TOO CUTE.
WE HAVE A LOT OF GOOFY STORIES...
I FEEL AS THOUGH I'M SHORTCHANGING THIS PLACE BY DESCRIBING IT WITH SUCH A SIMPLE WORD.

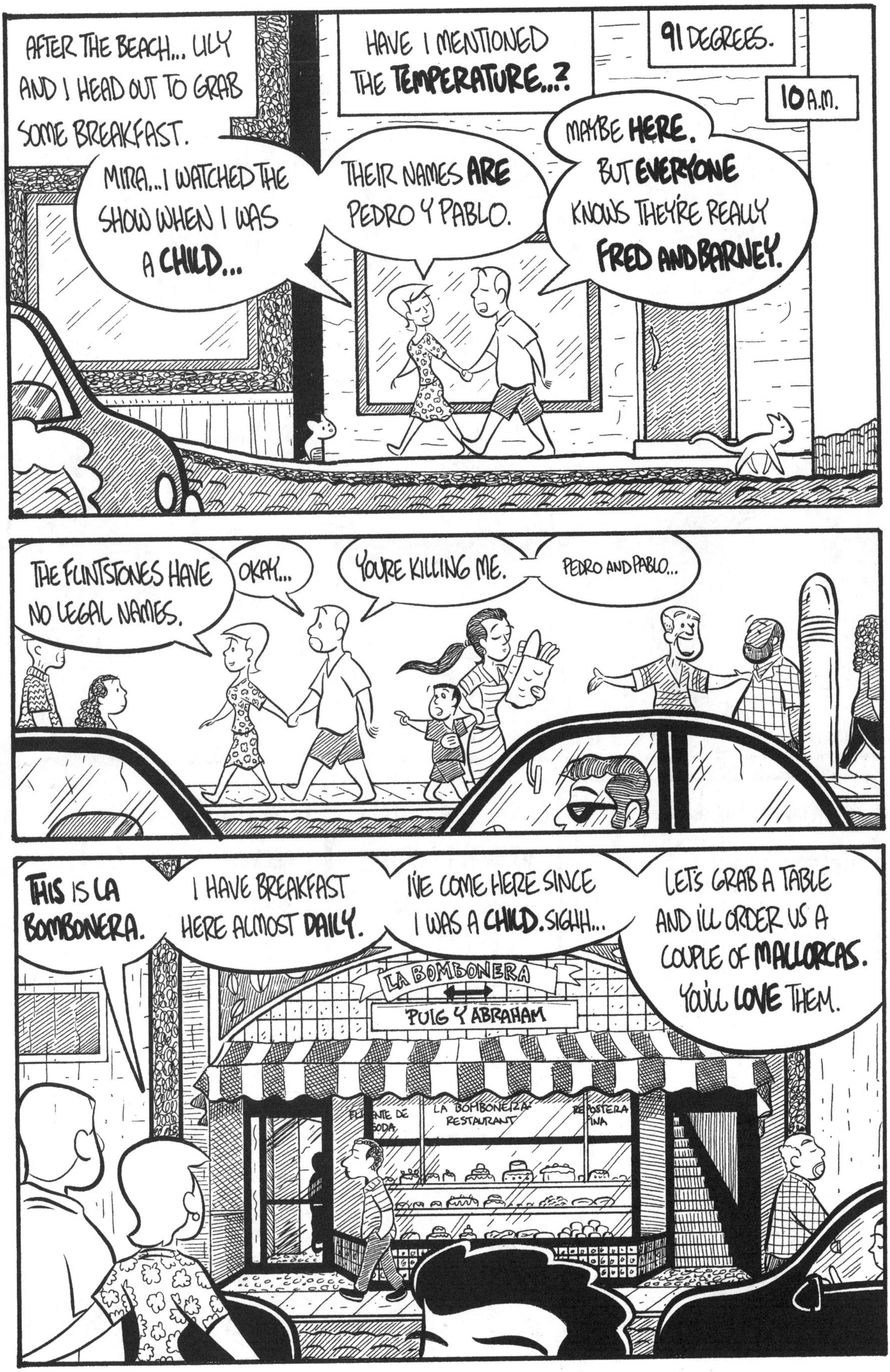
AFTER THE BEACH... LILY AND I HEAD OUT TO GRAB SOME BREAKFAST.
HAVE I MENTIONED THE TEMPERATURE...?
91 DEGREES.
10 A.M.
MIRA...I WATCHED THE SHOW WHEN I WAS A CHILD...
THEIR NAMES ARE PEDRO Y PABLO.
MAYBE HERE. BUT EVERYONE KNOWS THEY'RE REALLY FRED AND BARNEY.
THE FLINTSTONES HAVE NO LEGAL NAMES.
OKAY...
YOU'RE KILLING ME.
PEDRO AND PABLO...
THIS IS LA BOMBONERA.
I HAVE BREAKFAST HERE ALMOST DAILY.
I'VE COME HERE SINCE I WAS A CHILD. SIGHH...
LET'S GRAB A TABLE AND I'LL ORDER US A COUPLE OF MALLORCAS. YOU'LL LOVE THEM.
LA BOMBONERA
PUIG Y ABRAHAM
LA BOMBONERA RESTAURANT

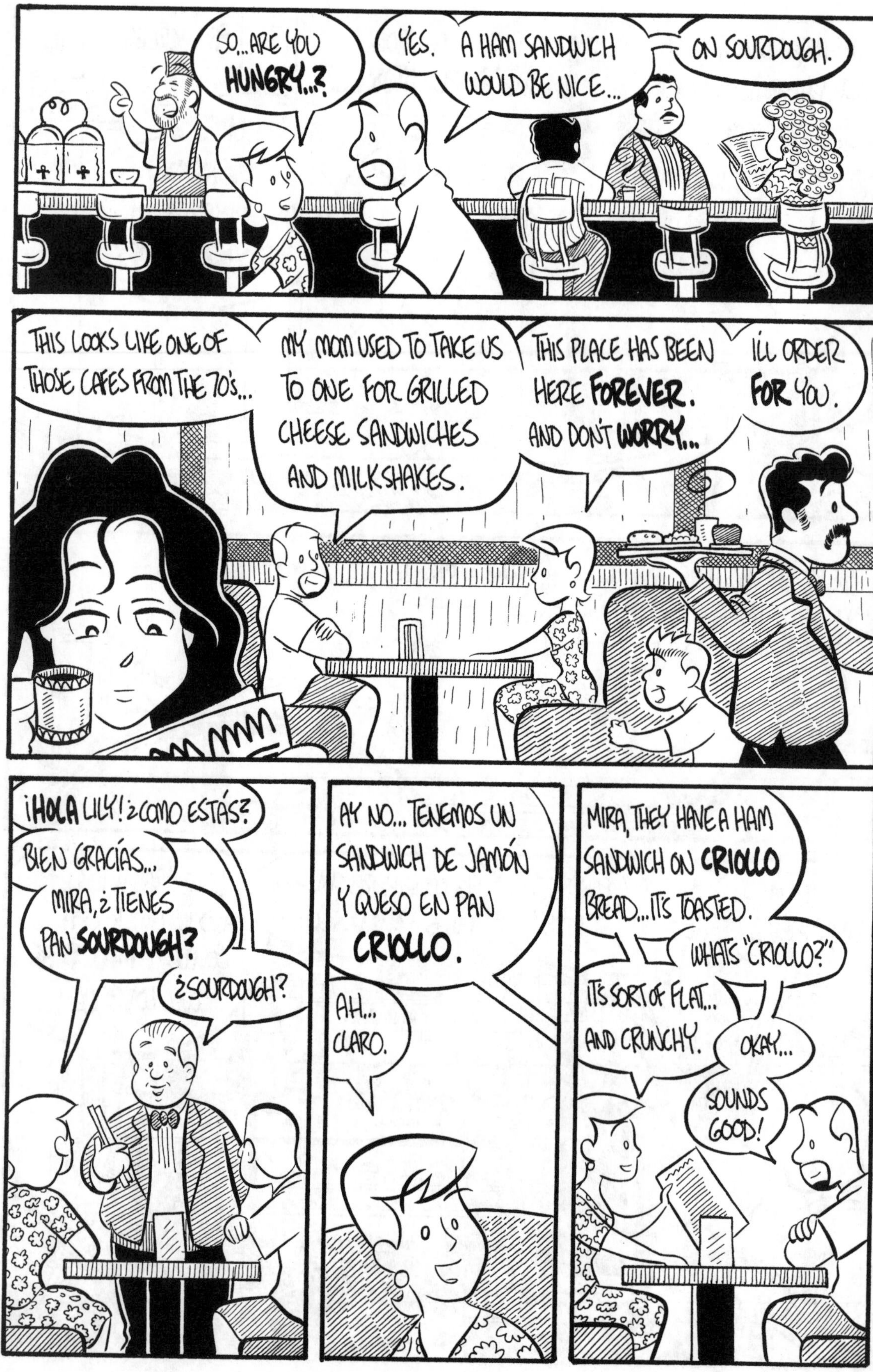

SO... ARE YOU HUNGRY...?
YES.
A HAM SANDWICH WOULD BE NICE...
ON SOURDOUGH.
THIS LOOKS LIKE ONE OF THOSE CAFES FROM THE 70's...
MY MOM USED TO TAKE US TO ONE FOR GRILLED CHEESE SANDWICHES AND MILKSHAKES.
THIS PLACE HAS BEEN HERE FOREVER. AND DON'T WORRY...
I'LL ORDER FOR YOU.
¡HOLA LILY! ¿COMO ESTÁS?
BIEN GRACÍAS...
MIRA, ¿TIENES PAN SOURDOUGH?
¿SOURDOUGH?
AY NO... TENEMOS UN SANDWICH DE JAMÓN Y QUESO EN PAN CRIOLLO.
AH... CLARO.
MIRA, THEY HAVE A HAM SANDWICH ON CRIOLLO BREAD... IT'S TOASTED.
WHAT'S "CRIOLLO?"
IT'S SORT OF FLAT... AND CRUNCHY.
OKAY...
SOUNDS GOOD!

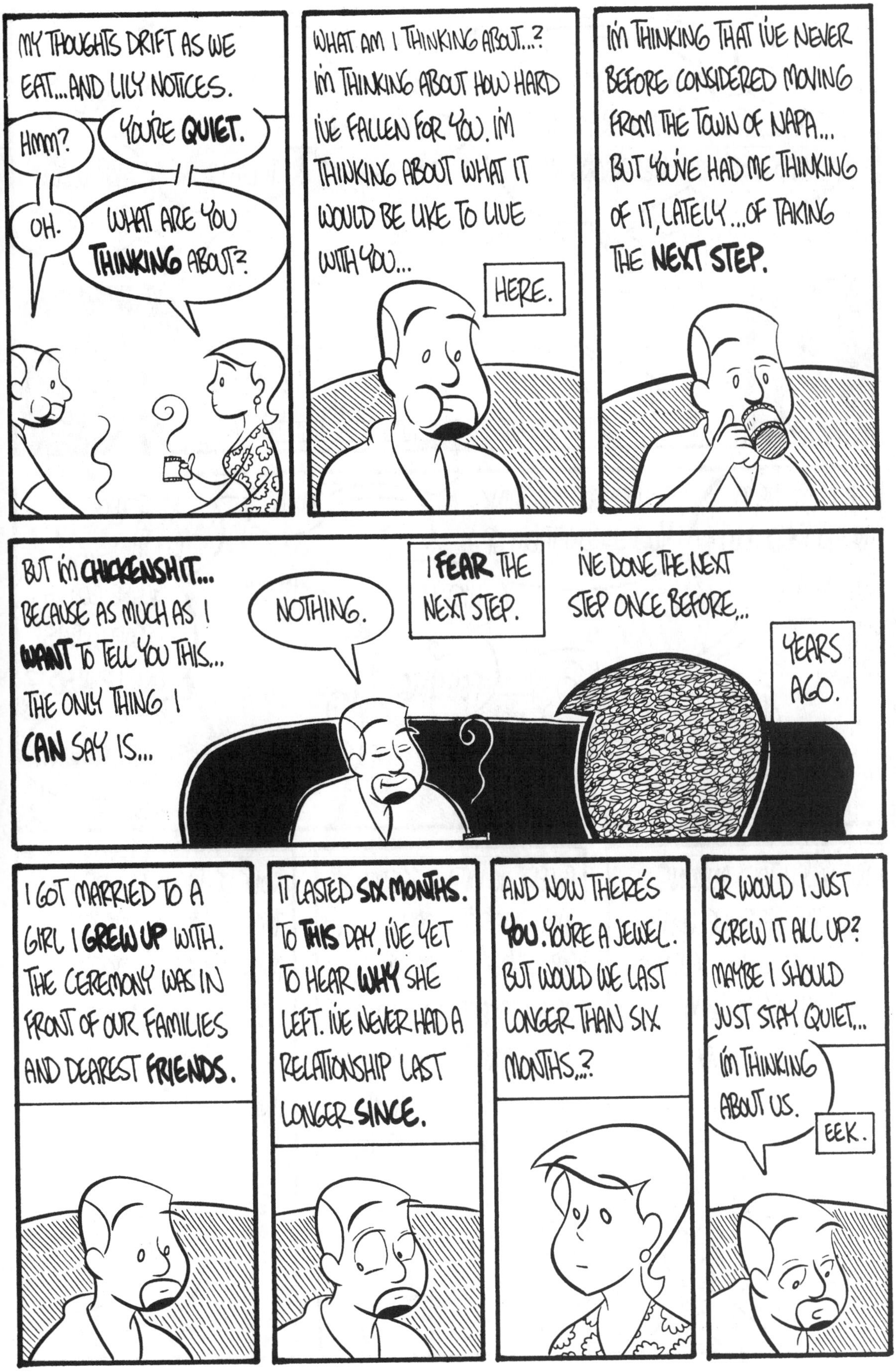
MY THOUGHTS DRIFT AS WE EAT... AND LILY NOTICES.
HMM?
YOU'RE QUIET.
OH.
WHAT ARE YOU THINKING ABOUT?
WHAT AM I THINKING ABOUT...? I'M THINKING ABOUT HOW HARD I'VE FALLEN FOR YOU. I'M THINKING ABOUT WHAT IT WOULD BE LIKE TO LIVE WITH YOU...
HERE.
I'M THINKING THAT I'VE NEVER BEFORE CONSIDERED MOVING FROM THE TOWN OF NAPA... BUT YOU'VE HAD ME THINKING OF IT, LATELY... OF TAKING THE NEXT STEP.
BUT I'M CHICKENSHIT... BECAUSE AS MUCH AS I WANT TO TELL YOU THIS... THE ONLY THING I CAN SAY IS...
NOTHING.
I FEAR THE NEXT STEP.
I'VE DONE THE NEXT STEP ONCE BEFORE...
YEARS AGO.
I GOT MARRIED TO A GIRL I GREW UP WITH. THE CEREMONY WAS IN FRONT OF OUR FAMILIES AND DEAREST FRIENDS.
IT LASTED SIX MONTHS. TO THIS DAY, I'VE YET TO HEAR WHY SHE LEFT. I'VE NEVER HAD A RELATIONSHIP LAST LONGER SINCE.
AND NOW THERE'S YOU. YOU'RE A JEWEL. BUT WOULD WE LAST LONGER THAN SIX MONTHS...?
OR WOULD I JUST SCREW IT ALL UP? MAYBE I SHOULD JUST STAY QUIET...
I'M THINKING ABOUT US.
EEK.

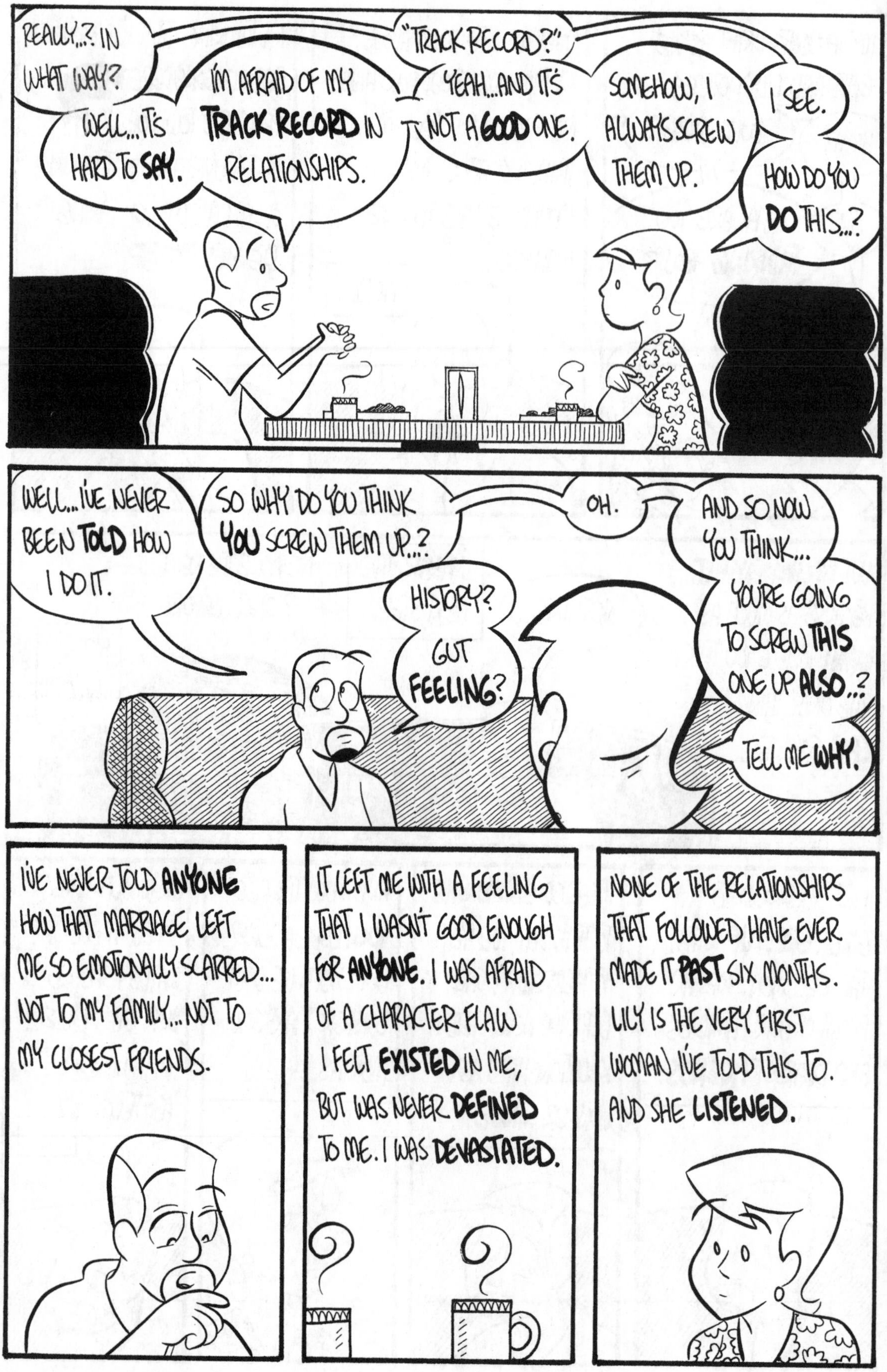

REALLY...? IN WHAT WAY?
WELL... IT'S HARD TO SAY.
I'M AFRAID OF MY TRACK RECORD IN RELATIONSHIPS.
"TRACK RECORD?"
YEAH... AND IT'S NOT A GOOD ONE.
SOMEHOW, I ALWAYS SCREW THEM UP.
I SEE.
HOW DO YOU DO THIS...?
WELL... I'VE NEVER BEEN TOLD HOW I DO IT.
SO WHY DO YOU THINK YOU SCREW THEM UP...?
OH.
HISTORY?
GUT FEELING?
AND SO NOW YOU THINK... YOU'RE GOING TO SCREW THIS ONE UP ALSO...?
TELL ME WHY.
I'VE NEVER TOLD ANYONE HOW THAT MARRIAGE LEFT ME SO EMOTIONALLY SCARRED... NOT TO MY FAMILY... NOT TO MY CLOSEST FRIENDS.
IT LEFT ME WITH A FEELING THAT I WASN'T GOOD ENOUGH FOR ANYONE. I WAS AFRAID OF A CHARACTER FLAW I FELT EXISTED IN ME, BUT WAS NEVER DEFINED TO ME. I WAS DEVASTATED.
NONE OF THE RELATIONSHIPS THAT FOLLOWED HAVE EVER MADE IT PAST SIX MONTHS. LILY IS THE VERY FIRST WOMAN I'VE TOLD THIS TO. AND SHE LISTENED.

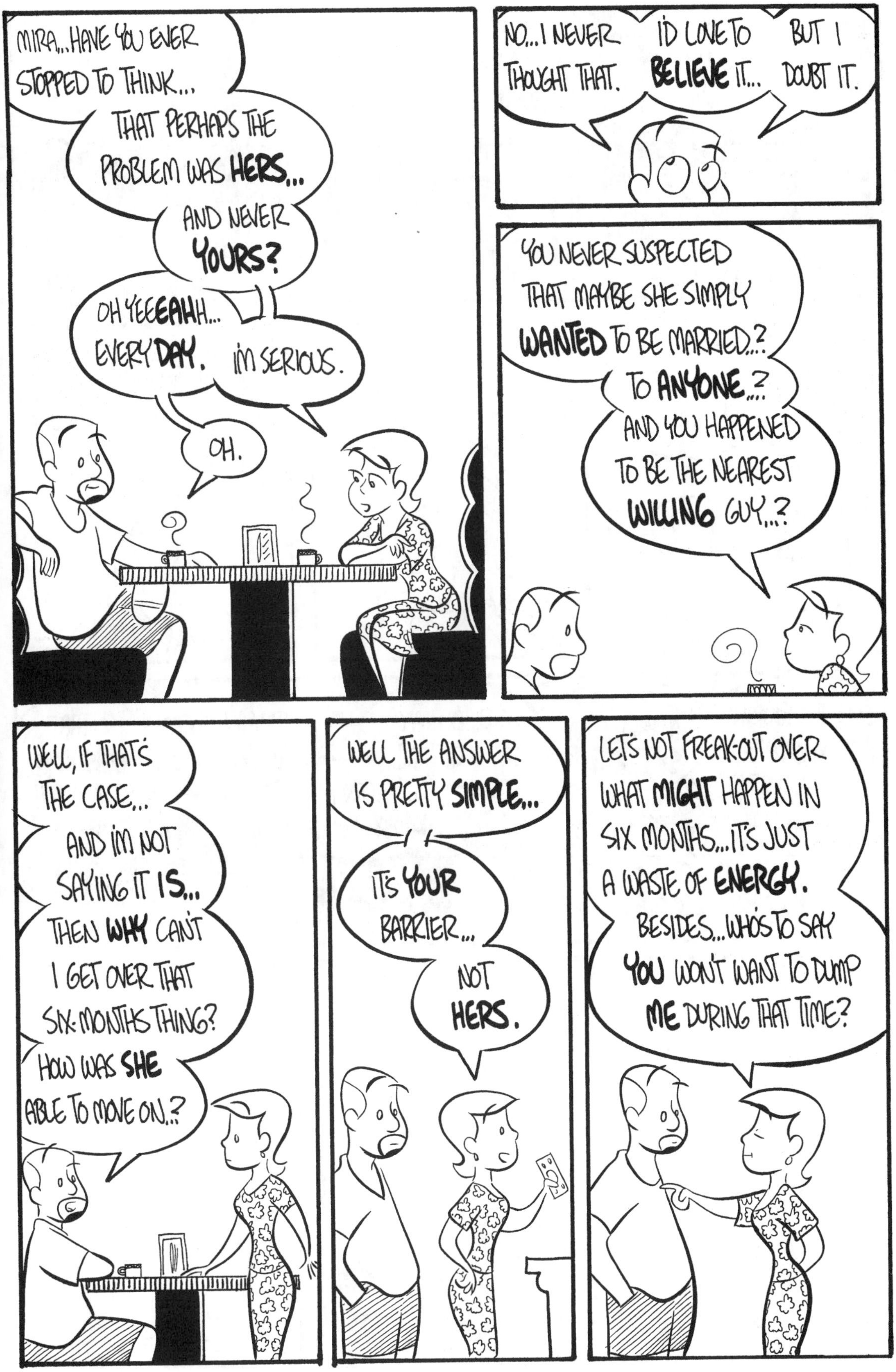
MIRA... HAVE YOU EVER STOPPED TO THINK...
THAT PERHAPS THE PROBLEM WAS **HERS...**
AND NEVER **YOURS?**
OH YEE**EAH**H... EVERY **DAY**.
I'M SERIOUS.
OH.
NO... I NEVER THOUGHT THAT.
I'D LOVE TO **BELIEVE** IT...
BUT I DOUBT IT.
YOU NEVER SUSPECTED THAT MAYBE SHE SIMPLY **WANTED** TO BE MARRIED...?
TO **ANYONE**...?
AND YOU HAPPENED TO BE THE NEAREST **WILLING** GUY...?
WELL, IF THAT'S THE CASE...
AND I'M NOT SAYING IT **IS...**
THEN **WHY** CAN'T I GET OVER THAT SIX-MONTHS THING?
HOW WAS **SHE** ABLE TO MOVE ON...?
WELL THE ANSWER IS PRETTY **SIMPLE...**
IT'S **YOUR** BARRIER...
NOT **HERS**.
LET'S NOT FREAK-OUT OVER WHAT **MIGHT** HAPPEN IN SIX MONTHS... IT'S JUST A WASTE OF **ENERGY**.
BESIDES... WHO'S TO SAY **YOU** WON'T WANT TO DUMP **ME** DURING THAT TIME?

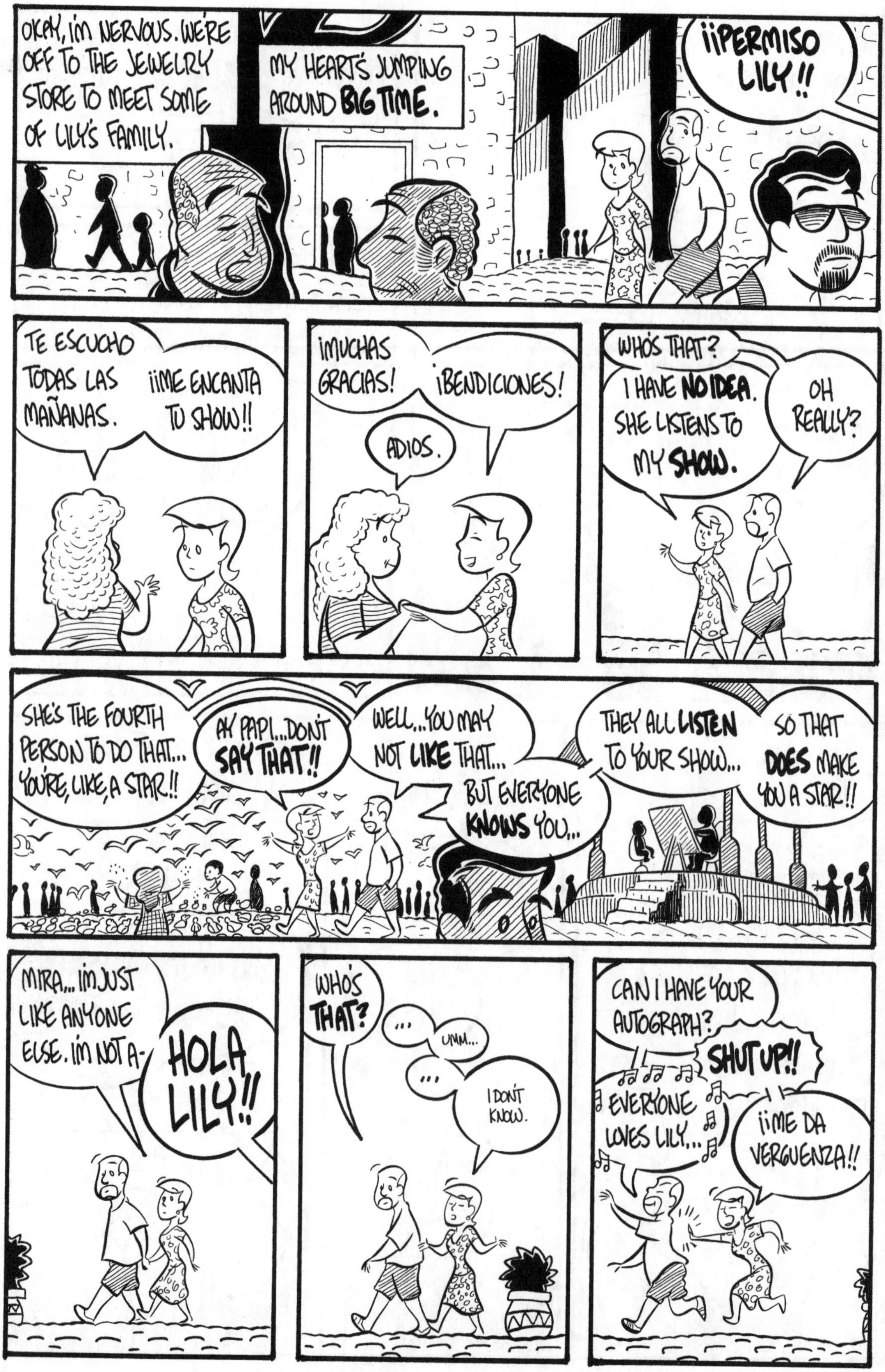
OKAY, I'M NERVOUS. WE'RE OFF TO THE JEWELRY STORE TO MEET SOME OF LILY'S FAMILY.
MY HEART'S JUMPING AROUND BIG TIME.
¡¡PERMISO LILY!!
TE ESCUCHO TODAS LAS MAÑANAS.
¡¡ME ENCANTA TU SHOW!!
¡MUCHAS GRACIAS!
¡BENDICIONES!
ADIOS.
WHO'S THAT?
I HAVE NO IDEA. SHE LISTENS TO MY SHOW.
OH REALLY?
SHE'S THE FOURTH PERSON TO DO THAT... YOU'RE, LIKE, A STAR!!
AY PAPI...DON'T SAY THAT!!
WELL...YOU MAY NOT LIKE THAT...
BUT EVERYONE KNOWS YOU...
THEY ALL LISTEN TO YOUR SHOW...
SO THAT DOES MAKE YOU A STAR!!
MIRA... I'M JUST LIKE ANYONE ELSE. I'M NOT A-
HOLA LILY!!
WHO'S THAT?
...
UMM...
...
I DON'T KNOW.
CAN I HAVE YOUR AUTOGRAPH?
SHUT UP!!
EVERYONE LOVES LILY...
¡¡ME DA VERGUENZA!!

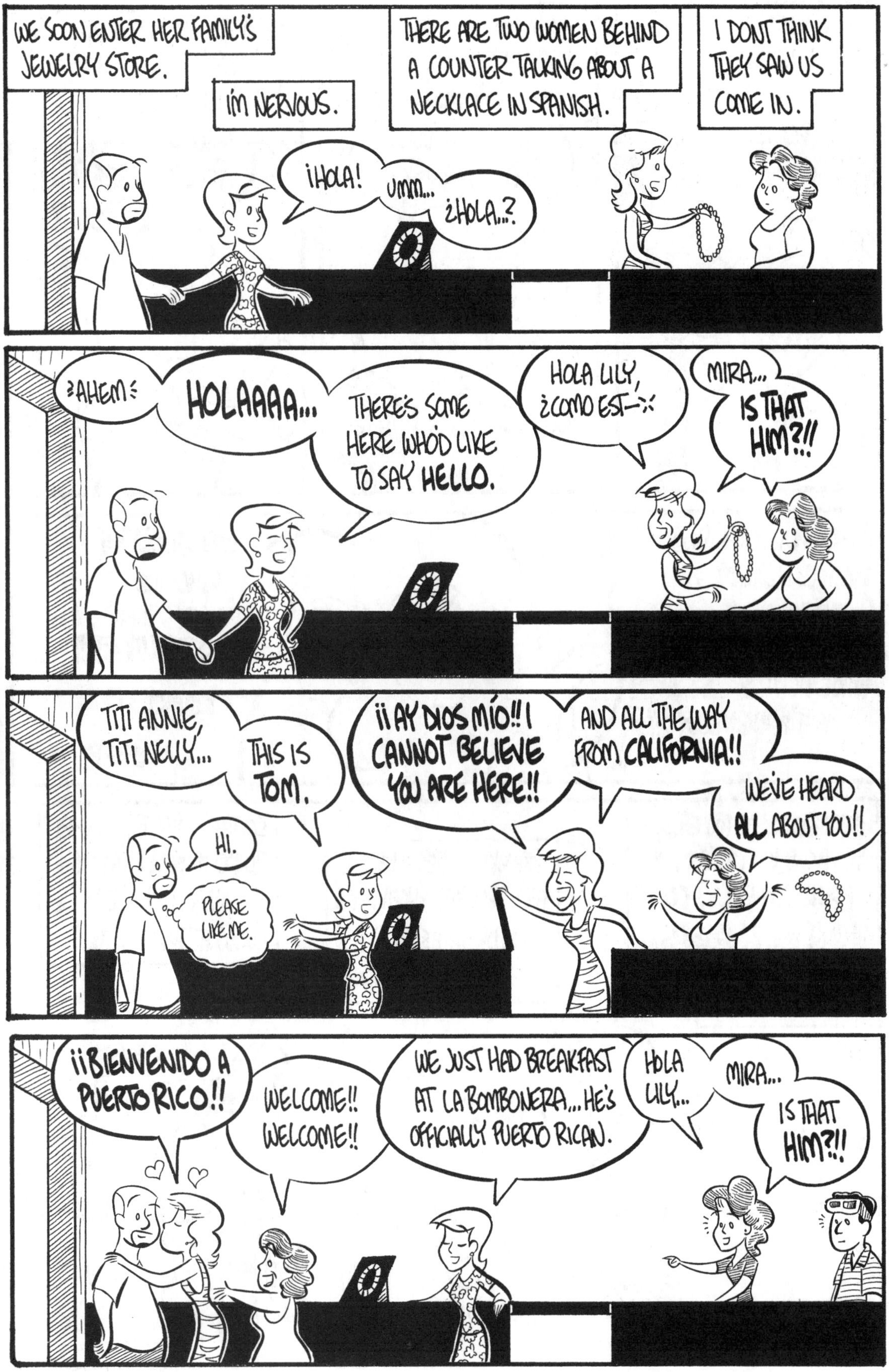
WE SOON ENTER HER FAMILY'S JEWELRY STORE.
I'M NERVOUS.
THERE ARE TWO WOMEN BEHIND A COUNTER TALKING ABOUT A NECKLACE IN SPANISH.
I DONT THINK THEY SAW US COME IN.
¡HOLA!
UMM... ¿HOLA..?
AHEM
HOLAAAA...
THERE'S SOME HERE WHO'D LIKE TO SAY HELLO.
HOLA LILY, ¿COMO EST—
MIRA... IS THAT HIM?!!
TITI ANNIE, TITI NELLY...
THIS IS TOM.
HI.
PLEASE LIKE ME.
¡¡AY DIOS MÍO!! I CANNOT BELIEVE YOU ARE HERE!!
AND ALL THE WAY FROM CALIFORNIA!!
WE'VE HEARD ALL ABOUT YOU!!
¡¡BIENVENIDO A PUERTO RICO!!
WELCOME!! WELCOME!!
WE JUST HAD BREAKFAST AT LA BOMBONERA... HE'S OFFICIALLY PUERTO RICAN.
HOLA LILY...
MIRA... IS THAT HIM?!!

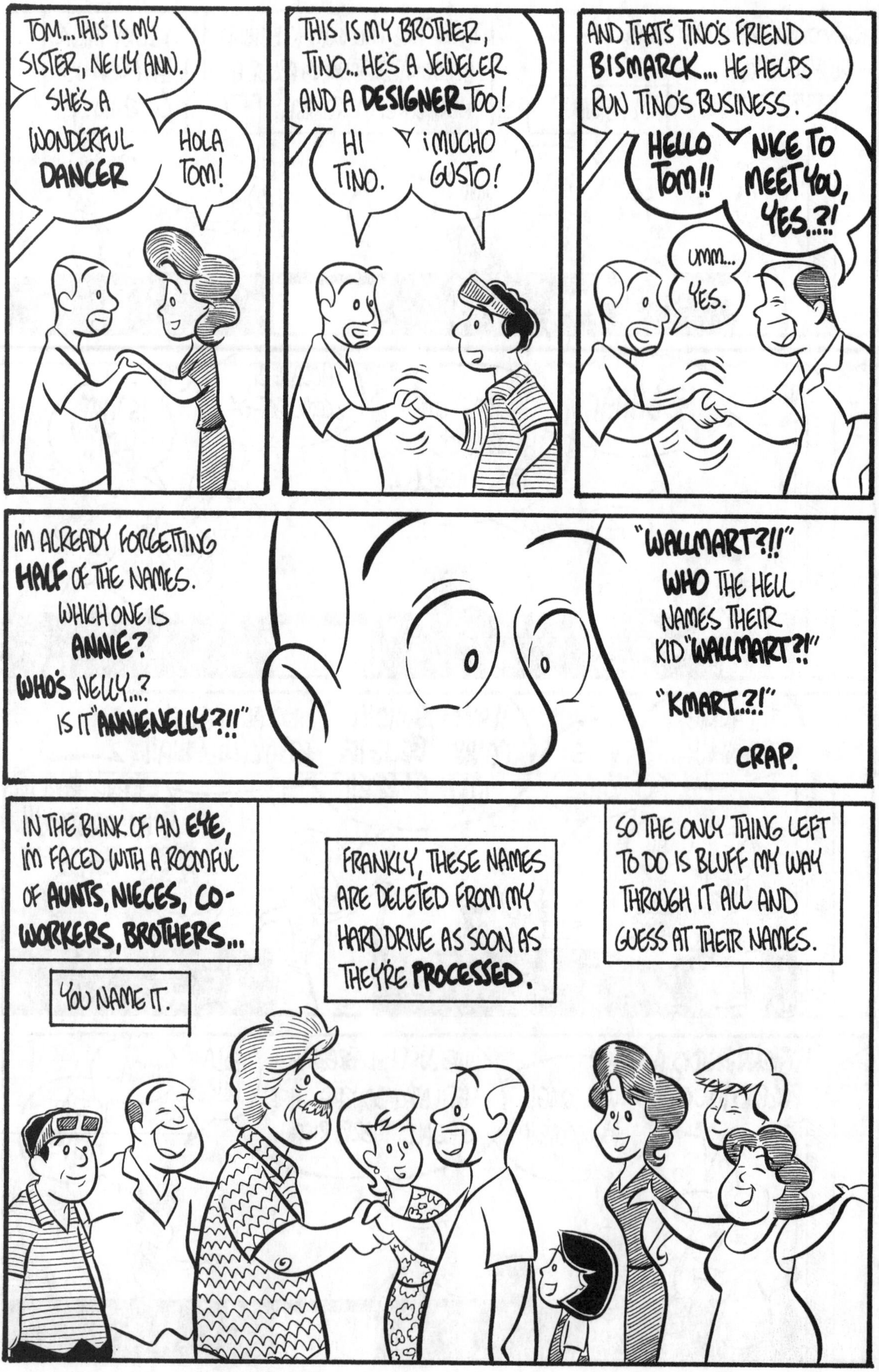

TOM... THIS IS MY SISTER, NELLY ANN.
SHE'S A WONDERFUL DANCER
HOLA TOM!
THIS IS MY BROTHER, TINO... HE'S A JEWELER AND A DESIGNER TOO!
HI TINO.
¡MUCHO GUSTO!
AND THAT'S TINO'S FRIEND BISMARCK... HE HELPS RUN TINO'S BUSINESS.
HELLO TOM!!
NICE TO MEET YOU, YES..?!
UMM... YES.
I'M ALREADY FORGETTING HALF OF THE NAMES.
WHICH ONE IS ANNIE?
WHO'S NELLY...?
IS IT "ANNIENELLY?!!"
"WALLMART?!!"
WHO THE HELL NAMES THEIR KID "WALLMART?!"
"KMART..?!"
CRAP.
IN THE BLINK OF AN EYE, I'M FACED WITH A ROOMFUL OF AUNTS, NIECES, CO-WORKERS, BROTHERS...
YOU NAME IT.
FRANKLY, THESE NAMES ARE DELETED FROM MY HARD DRIVE AS SOON AS THEY'RE PROCESSED.
SO THE ONLY THING LEFT TO DO IS BLUFF MY WAY THROUGH IT ALL AND GUESS AT THEIR NAMES.

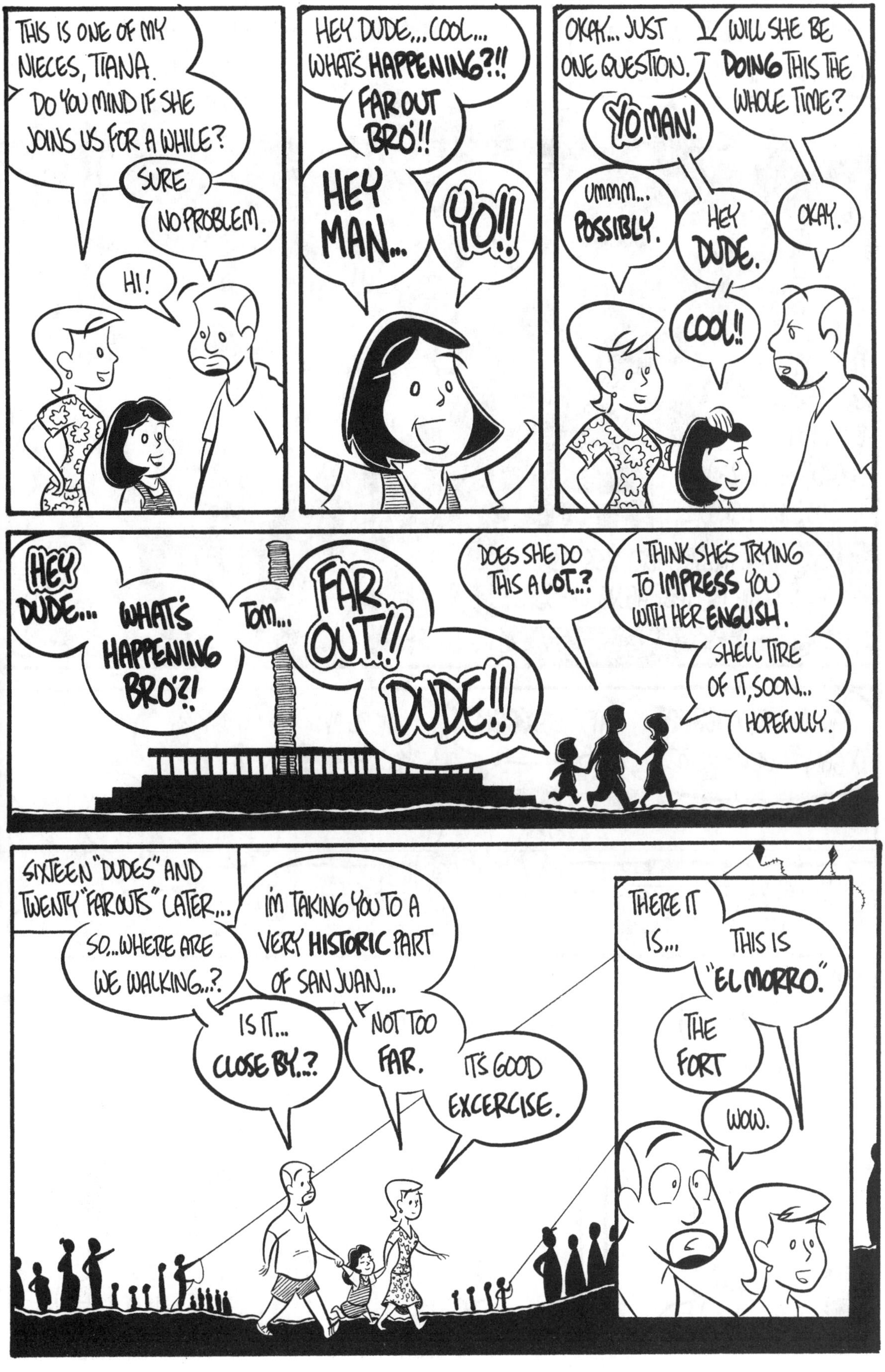

THIS IS ONE OF MY NIECES, TIANA. DO YOU MIND IF SHE JOINS US FOR A WHILE?
SURE NO PROBLEM.
HI!
HEY DUDE,... COOL... WHAT'S HAPPENING?!!
FAR OUT BRO'!!
HEY MAN...
YO!!
OKAY... JUST ONE QUESTION.
WILL SHE BE DOING THIS THE WHOLE TIME?
YO MAN!
UMMM... POSSIBLY.
HEY DUDE.
OKAY.
COOL!!
HEY DUDE...
WHAT'S HAPPENING BRO'?!
TOM...
FAR OUT!!
DUDE!!
DOES SHE DO THIS A LOT..?
I THINK SHE'S TRYING TO IMPRESS YOU WITH HER ENGLISH.
SHE'LL TIRE OF IT, SOON...
HOPEFULLY.
SIXTEEN "DUDES" AND TWENTY "FAR OUTS" LATER...
SO...WHERE ARE WE WALKING..?
I'M TAKING YOU TO A VERY HISTORIC PART OF SAN JUAN...
IS IT... CLOSE BY..?
NOT TOO FAR.
IT'S GOOD EXCERCISE.
THERE IT IS...
THIS IS "EL MORRO."
THE FORT
WOW.

THERE ARE MOMENTS WHERE YOU FACE HISTORY...AND IT STILLS YOU.

THIS IS ONE OF THEM.

SAN FELIPE DEL MORRO.

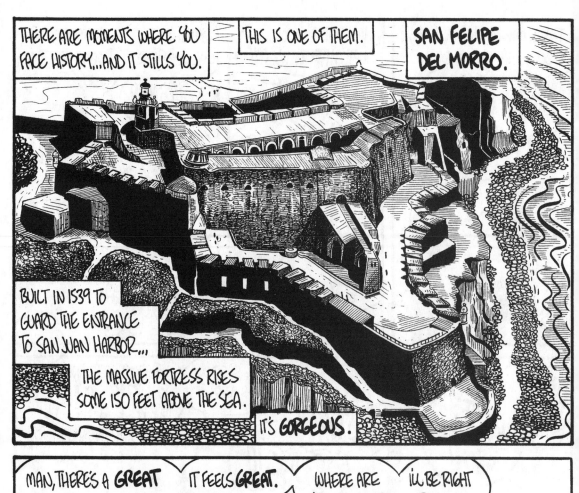

BUILT IN 1539 TO GUARD THE ENTRANCE TO SAN JUAN HARBOR...

THE MASSIVE FORTRESS RISES SOME 150 FEET ABOVE THE SEA.

IT'S GORGEOUS.

MAN, THERE'S A **GREAT** OCEAN BREEZE HERE.

IT FEELS **GREAT**.

WHERE ARE YOU **GOING?**

I'LL BE RIGHT BACK.

SHOULD WE GO **WITH** YOU OR STAY **HERE**...?

I'M GOING TO GET US SOMETHING TO **DRINK**. STAY THERE WITH **TIANA**...

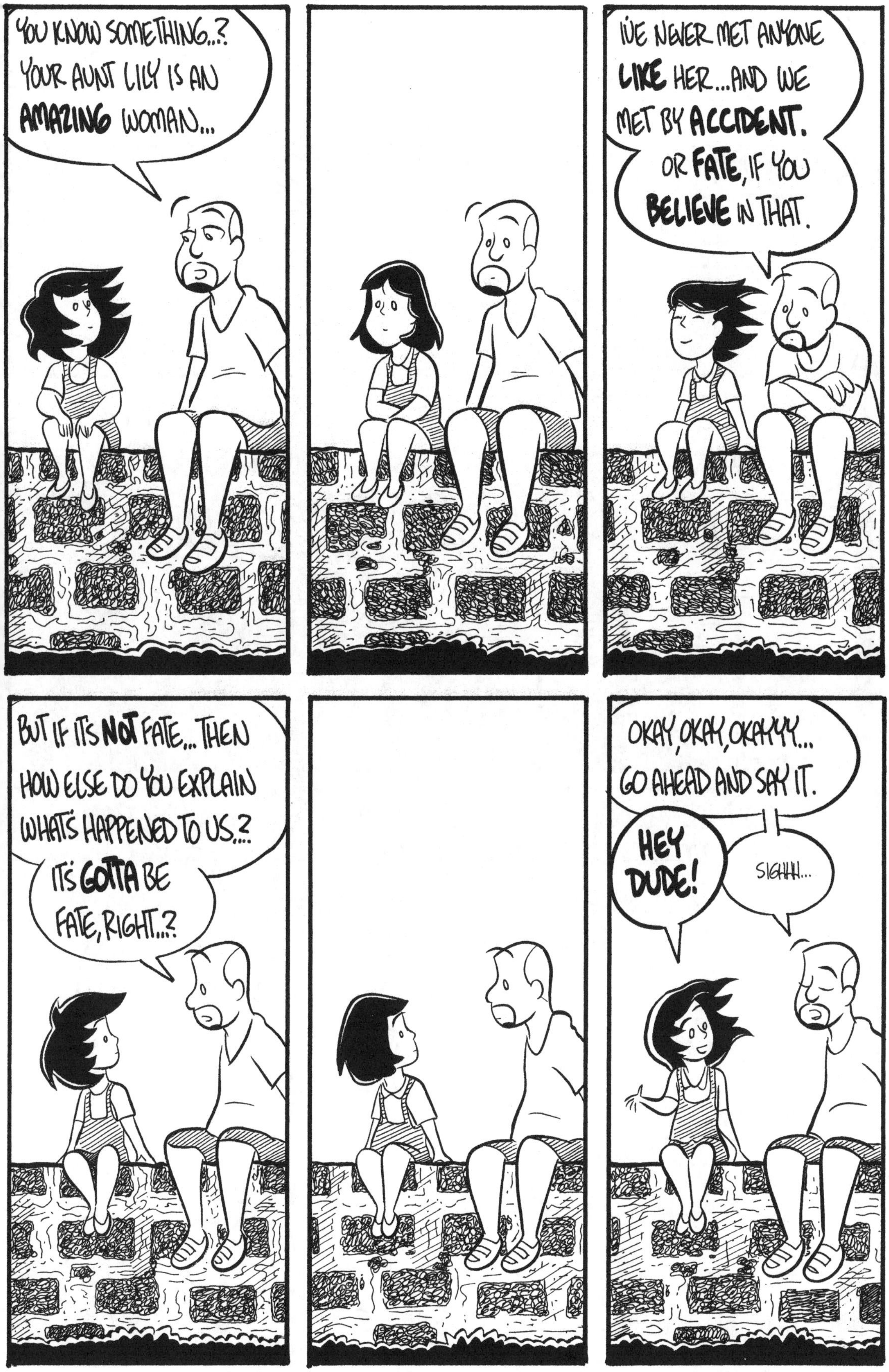
YOU KNOW SOMETHING..? YOUR AUNT LILY IS AN AMAZING WOMAN...
I'VE NEVER MET ANYONE LIKE HER...AND WE MET BY ACCIDENT.
OR FATE, IF YOU BELIEVE IN THAT.
BUT IF IT'S NOT FATE... THEN HOW ELSE DO YOU EXPLAIN WHAT'S HAPPENED TO US..?...
IT'S GOTTA BE FATE, RIGHT..?
OKAY, OKAY, OKAYYY... GO AHEAD AND SAY IT.
HEY DUDE!
SIGHHH...

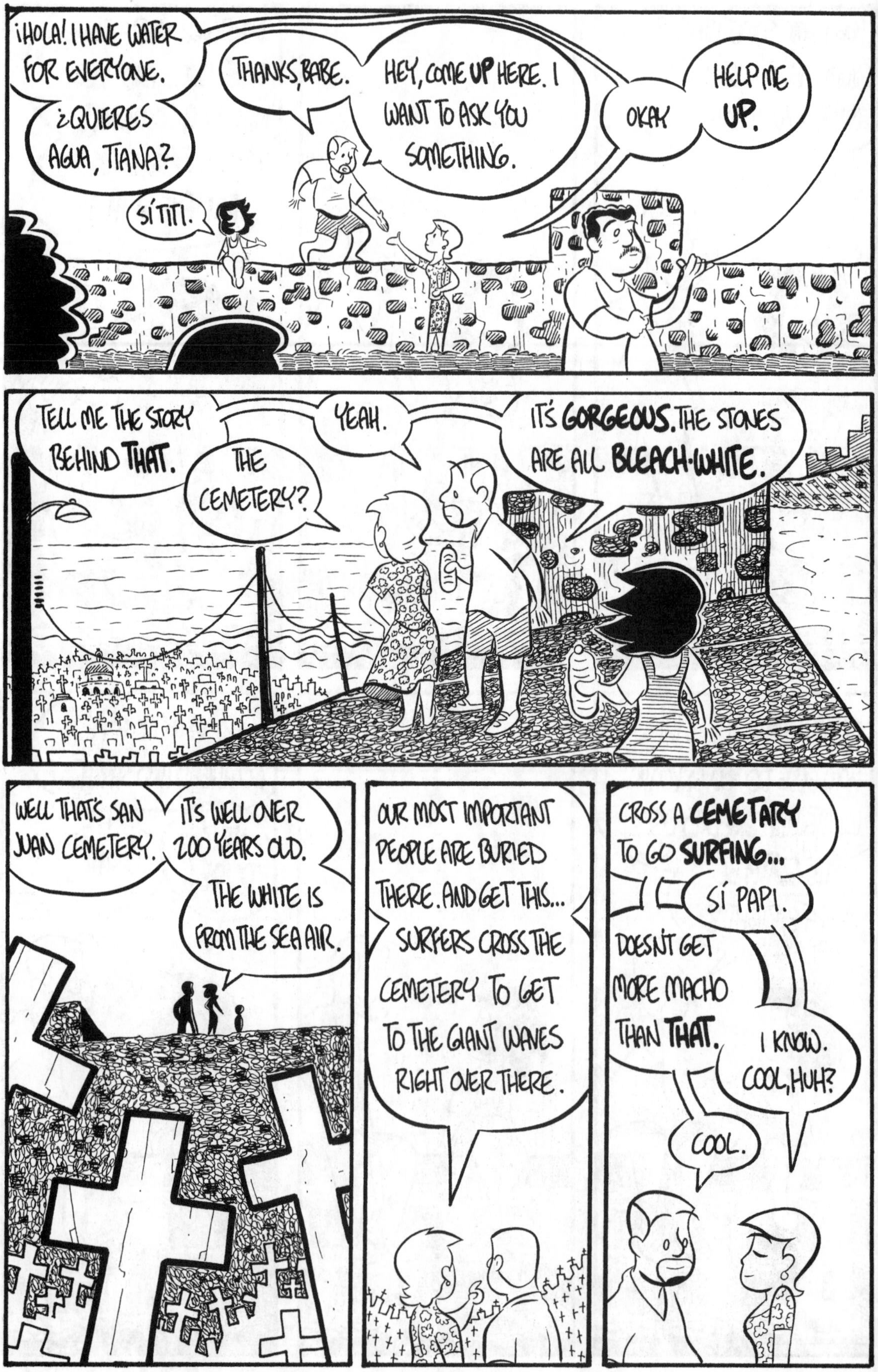
¡HOLA! I HAVE WATER FOR EVERYONE.
¿QUIERES AGUA, TIANA?
SÍ TITI.
THANKS, BABE.
HEY, COME UP HERE. I WANT TO ASK YOU SOMETHING.
OKAY
HELP ME UP.
TELL ME THE STORY BEHIND THAT.
THE CEMETERY?
YEAH.
IT'S GORGEOUS. THE STONES ARE ALL BLEACH-WHITE.
WELL THAT'S SAN JUAN CEMETERY.
IT'S WELL OVER 200 YEARS OLD.
THE WHITE IS FROM THE SEA AIR.
OUR MOST IMPORTANT PEOPLE ARE BURIED THERE. AND GET THIS...
SURFERS CROSS THE CEMETERY TO GET TO THE GIANT WAVES RIGHT OVER THERE.
CROSS A CEMETARY TO GO SURFING...
SÍ PAPI.
DOESN'T GET MORE MACHO THAN THAT.
I KNOW. COOL, HUH?
COOL.

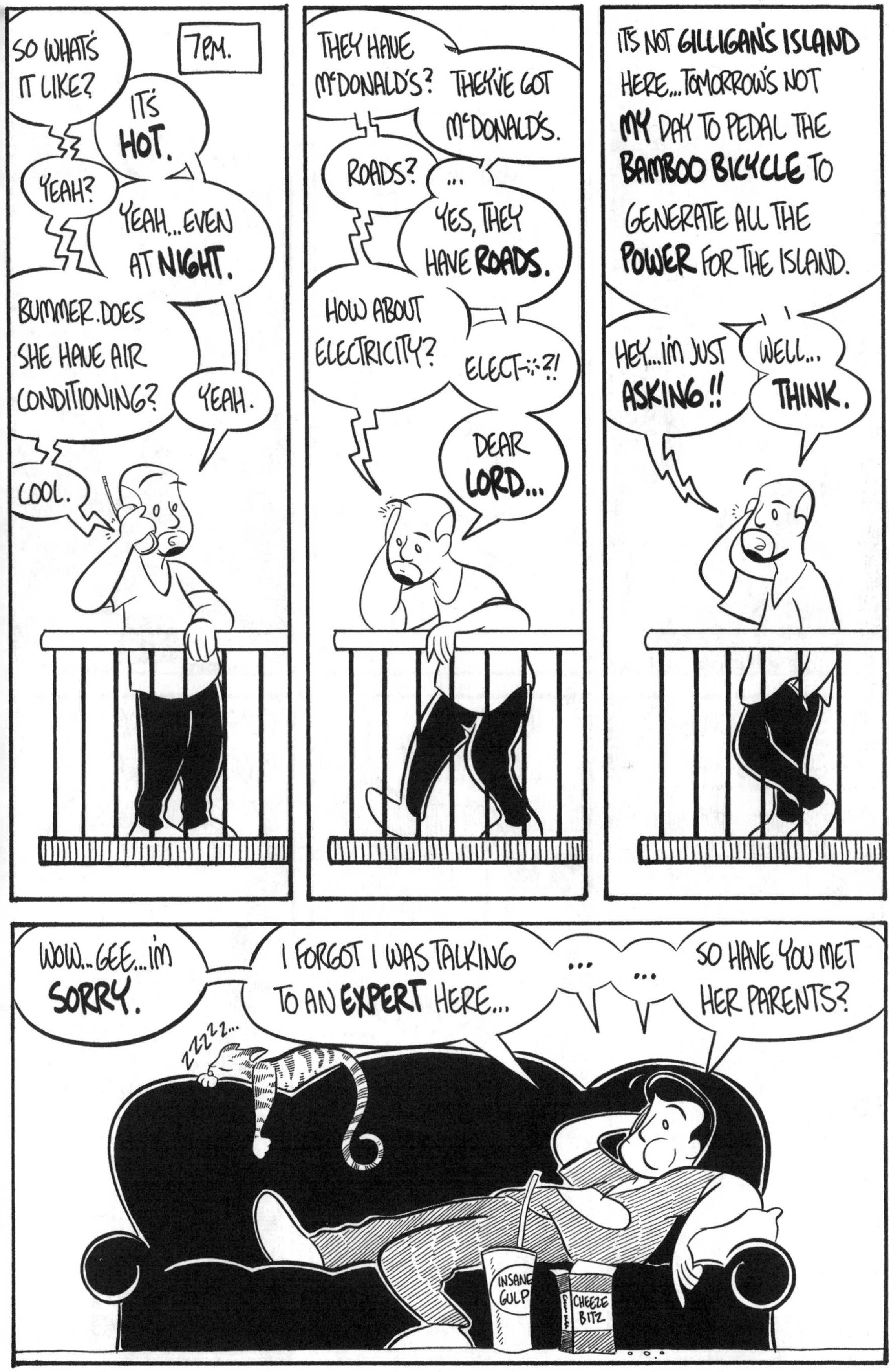
7P.M.
SO WHAT'S IT LIKE?
IT'S HOT.
YEAH?
YEAH...EVEN AT NIGHT.
BUMMER. DOES SHE HAVE AIR CONDITIONING?
YEAH.
COOL.
THEY HAVE McDONALD'S?
THEY'VE GOT McDONALD'S.
ROADS?
...
YES, THEY HAVE ROADS.
HOW ABOUT ELECTRICITY?
ELECT-?!
DEAR LORD...
IT'S NOT GILLIGAN'S ISLAND HERE... TOMORROW'S NOT MY DAY TO PEDAL THE BAMBOO BICYCLE TO GENERATE ALL THE POWER FOR THE ISLAND.
HEY... I'M JUST ASKING!!
WELL... THINK.
WOW... GEE... I'M SORRY.
I FORGOT I WAS TALKING TO AN EXPERT HERE...
...
...
SO HAVE YOU MET HER PARENTS?
ZZZZZ...
INSANE GULP
CHEEZE BITZ

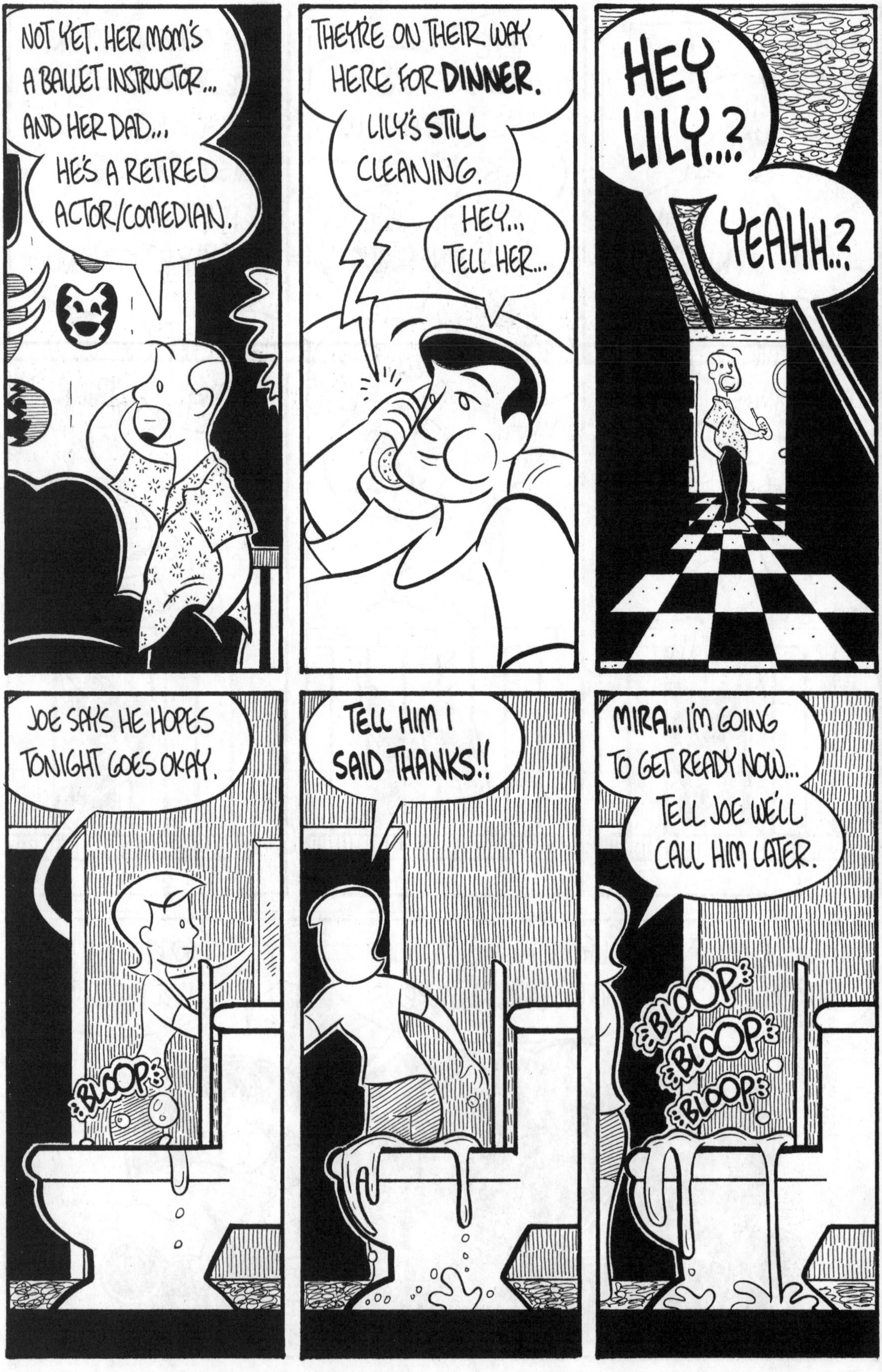
NOT YET. HER MOM'S A BALLET INSTRUCTOR...
AND HER DAD... HE'S A RETIRED ACTOR/COMEDIAN.
THEY'RE ON THEIR WAY HERE FOR DINNER.
LILY'S STILL CLEANING.
HEY... TELL HER...
HEY LILY...?
YEAHH..?
JOE SAYS HE HOPES TONIGHT GOES OKAY.
BLOOP
TELL HIM I SAID THANKS!!
MIRA... I'M GOING TO GET READY NOW...
TELL JOE WE'LL CALL HIM LATER.
BLOOP
BLOOP
BLOOP

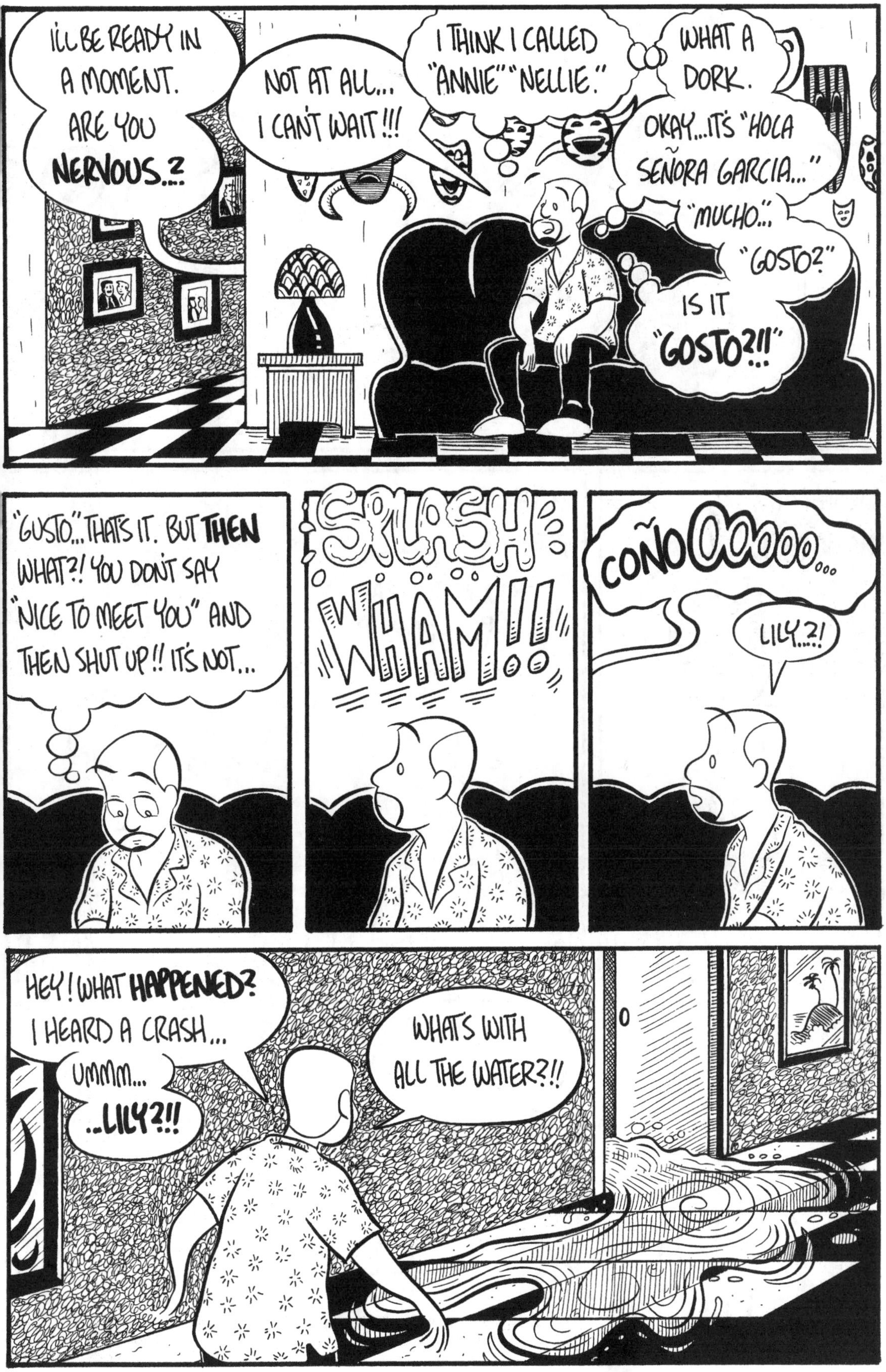
I'LL BE READY IN A MOMENT. ARE YOU NERVOUS..?
NOT AT ALL... I CAN'T WAIT!!!
I THINK I CALLED "ANNIE" "NELLIE."
WHAT A DORK.
OKAY...IT'S "HOLA SEÑORA GARCIA..."
"MUCHO..."
"GOSTO?"
IS IT "GOSTO?!!"
"GUSTO..." THAT'S IT. BUT THEN WHAT?! YOU DON'T SAY "NICE TO MEET YOU" AND THEN SHUT UP!! IT'S NOT...
SPLASH
WHAM!!
COÑOOOOOO...
LILY..?!
HEY! WHAT HAPPENED? I HEARD A CRASH...
UMMM...
..LILY?!!
WHAT'S WITH ALL THE WATER?!!

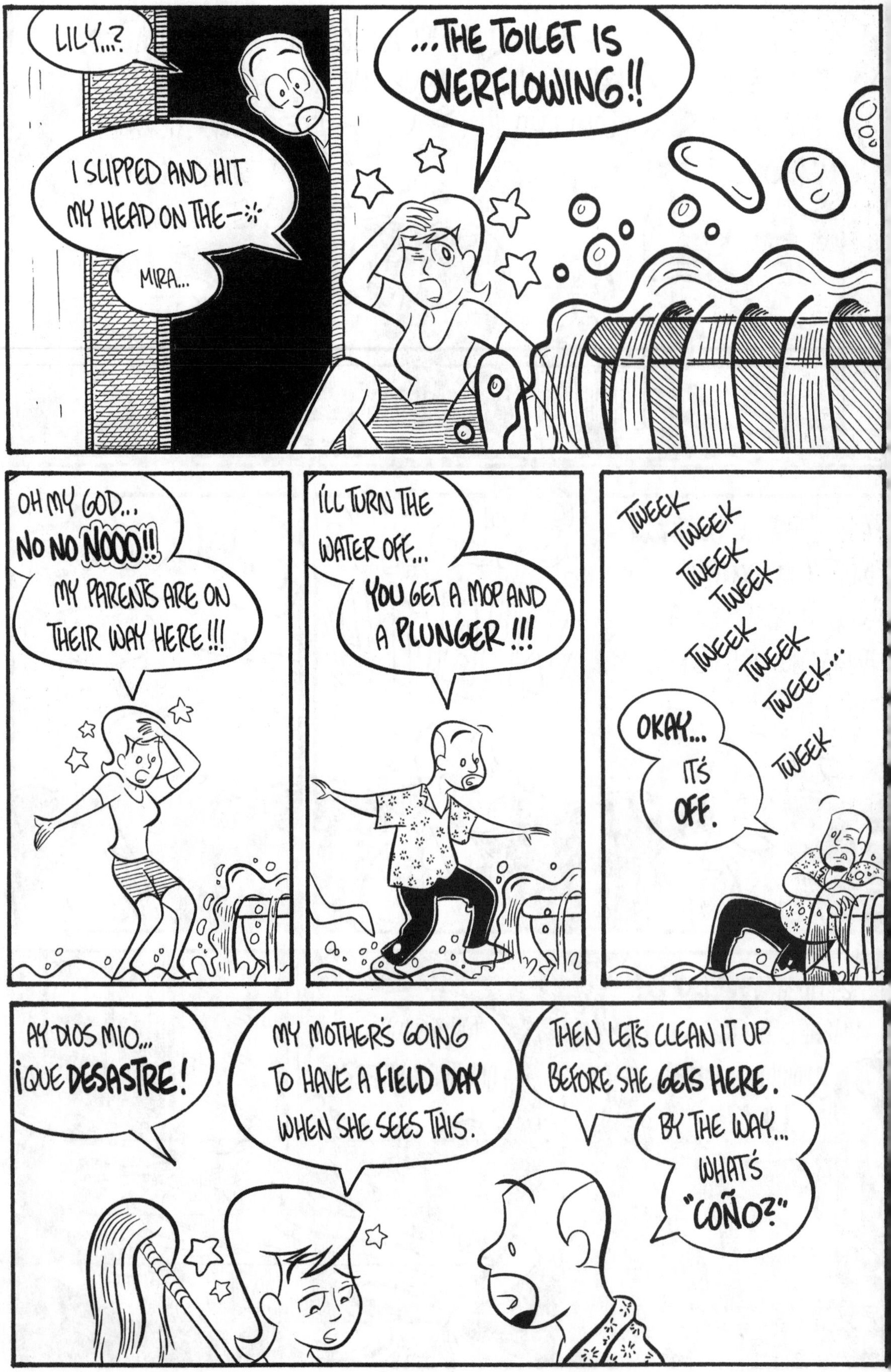
LILY...?
I SLIPPED AND HIT MY HEAD ON THE—
MIRA...
...THE TOILET IS OVERFLOWING!!
OH MY GOD... NO NO NOOO!!
MY PARENTS ARE ON THEIR WAY HERE!!!
I'LL TURN THE WATER OFF...
YOU GET A MOP AND A PLUNGER!!!
TWEEK TWEEK TWEEK TWEEK TWEEK TWEEK TWEEK... TWEEK
OKAY... IT'S OFF.
AY DIOS MIO... ¡QUE DESASTRE!
MY MOTHER'S GOING TO HAVE A FIELD DAY WHEN SHE SEES THIS.
THEN LET'S CLEAN IT UP BEFORE SHE GETS HERE.
BY THE WAY... WHAT'S "COÑO?"

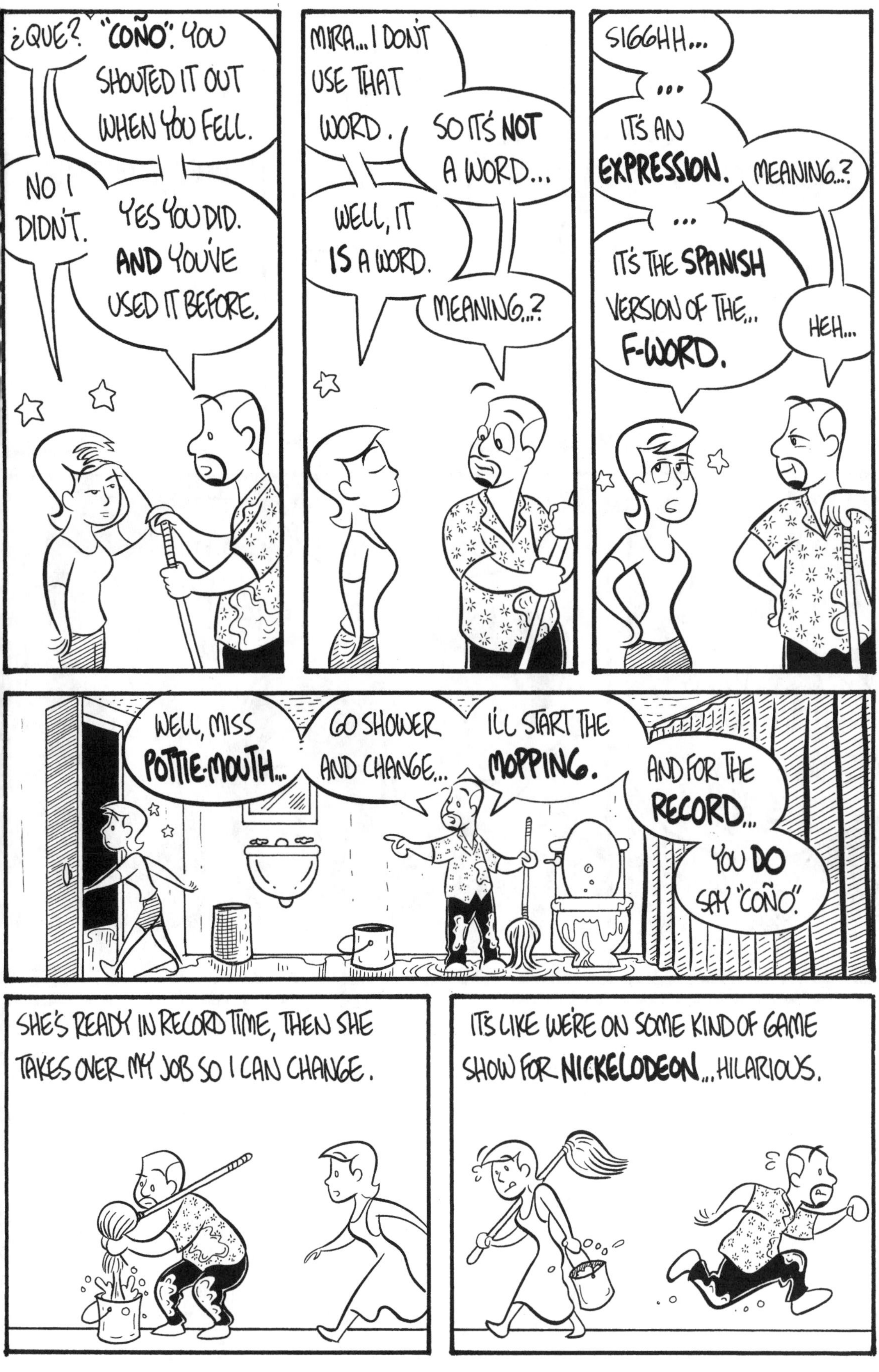
¿QUE?
"COÑO": YOU SHOUTED IT OUT WHEN YOU FELL.
NO I DIDN'T.
YES YOU DID. AND YOU'VE USED IT BEFORE.
MIRA... I DON'T USE THAT WORD.
SO IT'S NOT A WORD...
WELL, IT IS A WORD.
MEANING..?
SIGGHH...
...
IT'S AN EXPRESSION.
MEANING..?
...
IT'S THE SPANISH VERSION OF THE... F-WORD.
HEH...
WELL, MISS POTTIE-MOUTH...
GO SHOWER AND CHANGE...
I'LL START THE MOPPING.
AND FOR THE RECORD...
YOU DO SAY "COÑO."
SHE'S READY IN RECORD TIME, THEN SHE TAKES OVER MY JOB SO I CAN CHANGE.
IT'S LIKE WE'RE ON SOME KIND OF GAME SHOW FOR NICKELODEON... HILARIOUS.

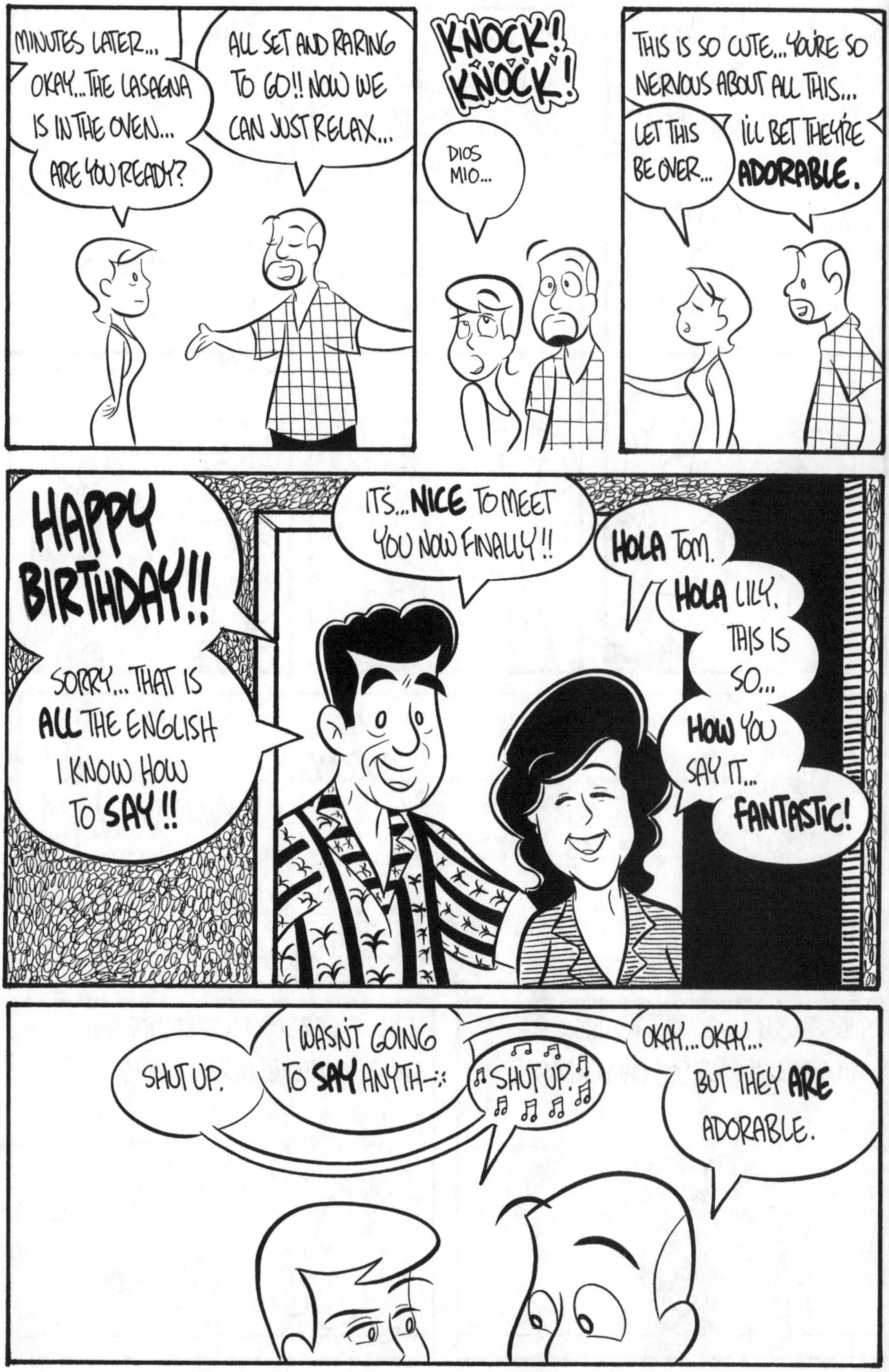
MINUTES LATER...
OKAY... THE LASAGNA IS IN THE OVEN... ARE YOU READY?
ALL SET AND RARING TO GO!! NOW WE CAN JUST RELAX...
KNOCK! KNOCK!
DIOS MIO...
THIS IS SO CUTE... YOU'RE SO NERVOUS ABOUT ALL THIS...
LET THIS BE OVER...
I'LL BET THEY'RE ADORABLE.
HAPPY BIRTHDAY!!
SORRY... THAT IS ALL THE ENGLISH I KNOW HOW TO SAY!!
IT'S... NICE TO MEET YOU NOW FINALLY!!
HOLA TOM.
HOLA LILY.
THIS IS SO...
HOW YOU SAY IT...
FANTASTIC!
SHUT UP.
I WASN'T GOING TO SAY ANYTH—
SHUT UP.
OKAY... OKAY... BUT THEY ARE ADORABLE.

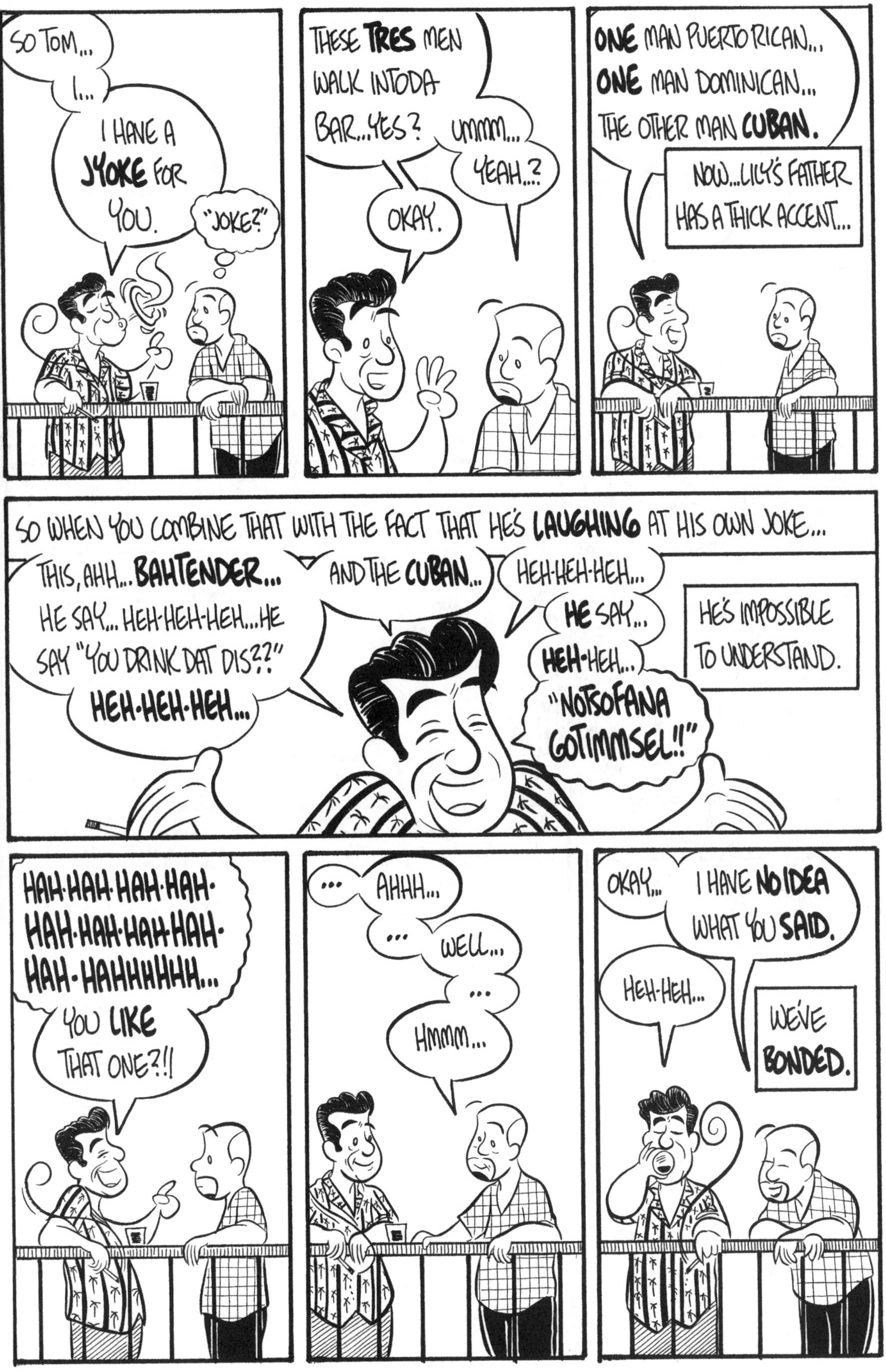
SO TOM...
I...
I HAVE A JYOKE FOR YOU.
"JOKE?"
THESE TRES MEN WALK INTODA BAR...YES?
UMMM...
YEAH...?
OKAY.
ONE MAN PUERTO RICAN... ONE MAN DOMINICAN... THE OTHER MAN CUBAN.
NOW...LILY'S FATHER HAS A THICK ACCENT...
SO WHEN YOU COMBINE THAT WITH THE FACT THAT HE'S LAUGHING AT HIS OWN JOKE...
THIS, AHH... BAHTENDER... HE SAY... HEH-HEH-HEH...HE SAY "YOU DRINK DAT DIS??"
HEH-HEH-HEH...
AND THE CUBAN...
HEH-HEH-HEH...
HE SAY...
HEH-HEH...
"NOTSOFANA GOTIMMSEL!!"
HE'S IMPOSSIBLE TO UNDERSTAND.
HAH-HAH-HAH-HAH-HAH-HAH-HAH-HAH-HAH-HAHHHHHH...
YOU LIKE THAT ONE?!!
...
AHHH...
...
WELL...
...
HMMM...
OKAY...
I HAVE NO IDEA WHAT YOU SAID.
HEH-HEH...
WE'VE BONDED.

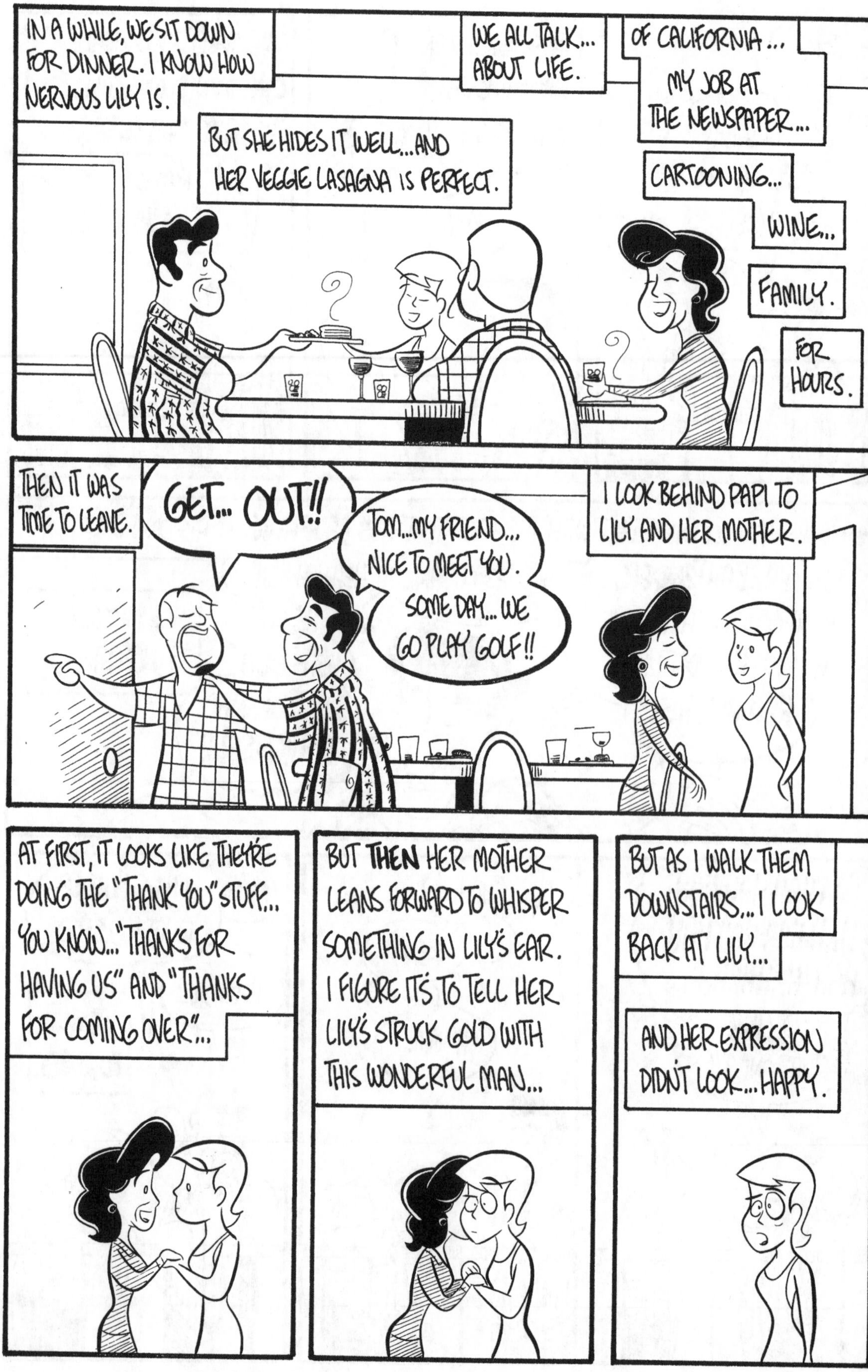

IN A WHILE, WE SIT DOWN FOR DINNER. I KNOW HOW NERVOUS LILY IS.
BUT SHE HIDES IT WELL...AND HER VEGGIE LASAGNA IS PERFECT.
WE ALL TALK... ABOUT LIFE.
OF CALIFORNIA...
MY JOB AT THE NEWSPAPER...
CARTOONING...
WINE...
FAMILY.
FOR HOURS.
THEN IT WAS TIME TO LEAVE.
GET... OUT!!
TOM...MY FRIEND... NICE TO MEET YOU. SOME DAY... WE GO PLAY GOLF!!
I LOOK BEHIND PAPI TO LILY AND HER MOTHER.
AT FIRST, IT LOOKS LIKE THEY'RE DOING THE "THANK YOU" STUFF... YOU KNOW... "THANKS FOR HAVING US" AND "THANKS FOR COMING OVER"...
BUT **THEN** HER MOTHER LEANS FORWARD TO WHISPER SOMETHING IN LILY'S EAR. I FIGURE IT'S TO TELL HER LILY'S STRUCK GOLD WITH THIS WONDERFUL MAN...
BUT AS I WALK THEM DOWNSTAIRS... I LOOK BACK AT LILY...
AND HER EXPRESSION DIDN'T LOOK...HAPPY.

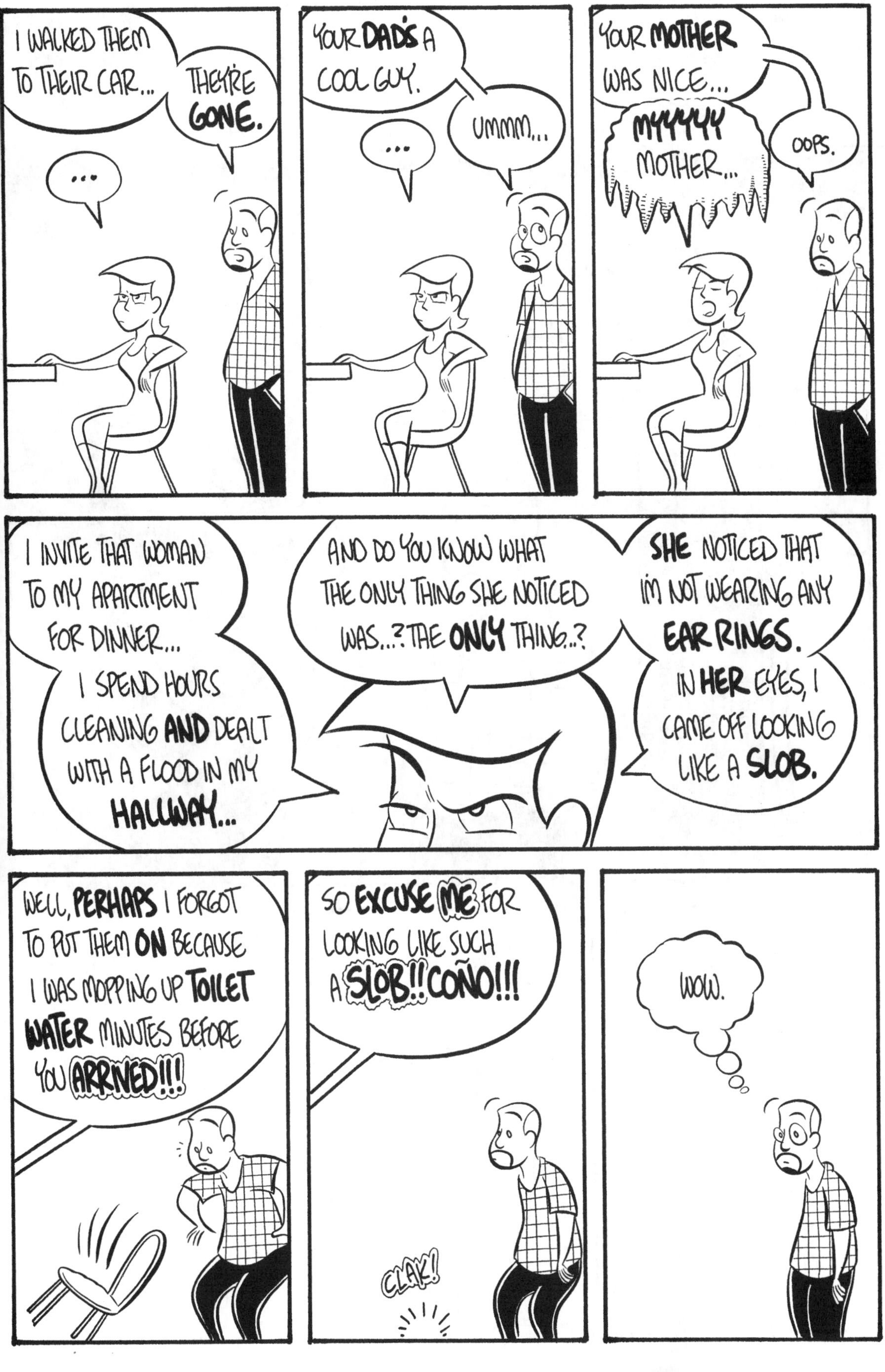
I WALKED THEM TO THEIR CAR...
THEY'RE GONE.
...
YOUR DAD'S A COOL GUY.
...
UMMM...
YOUR MOTHER WAS NICE...
MYYYYY MOTHER...
OOPS.
I INVITE THAT WOMAN TO MY APARTMENT FOR DINNER...
I SPEND HOURS CLEANING AND DEALT WITH A FLOOD IN MY HALLWAY...
AND DO YOU KNOW WHAT THE ONLY THING SHE NOTICED WAS...? THE ONLY THING..?
SHE NOTICED THAT I'M NOT WEARING ANY EAR RINGS.
IN HER EYES, I CAME OFF LOOKING LIKE A SLOB.
WELL, PERHAPS I FORGOT TO PUT THEM ON BECAUSE I WAS MOPPING UP TOILET WATER MINUTES BEFORE YOU ARRIVED!!!
SO EXCUSE ME FOR LOOKING LIKE SUCH A SLOB!! COÑO!!!
CLAK!
WOW.

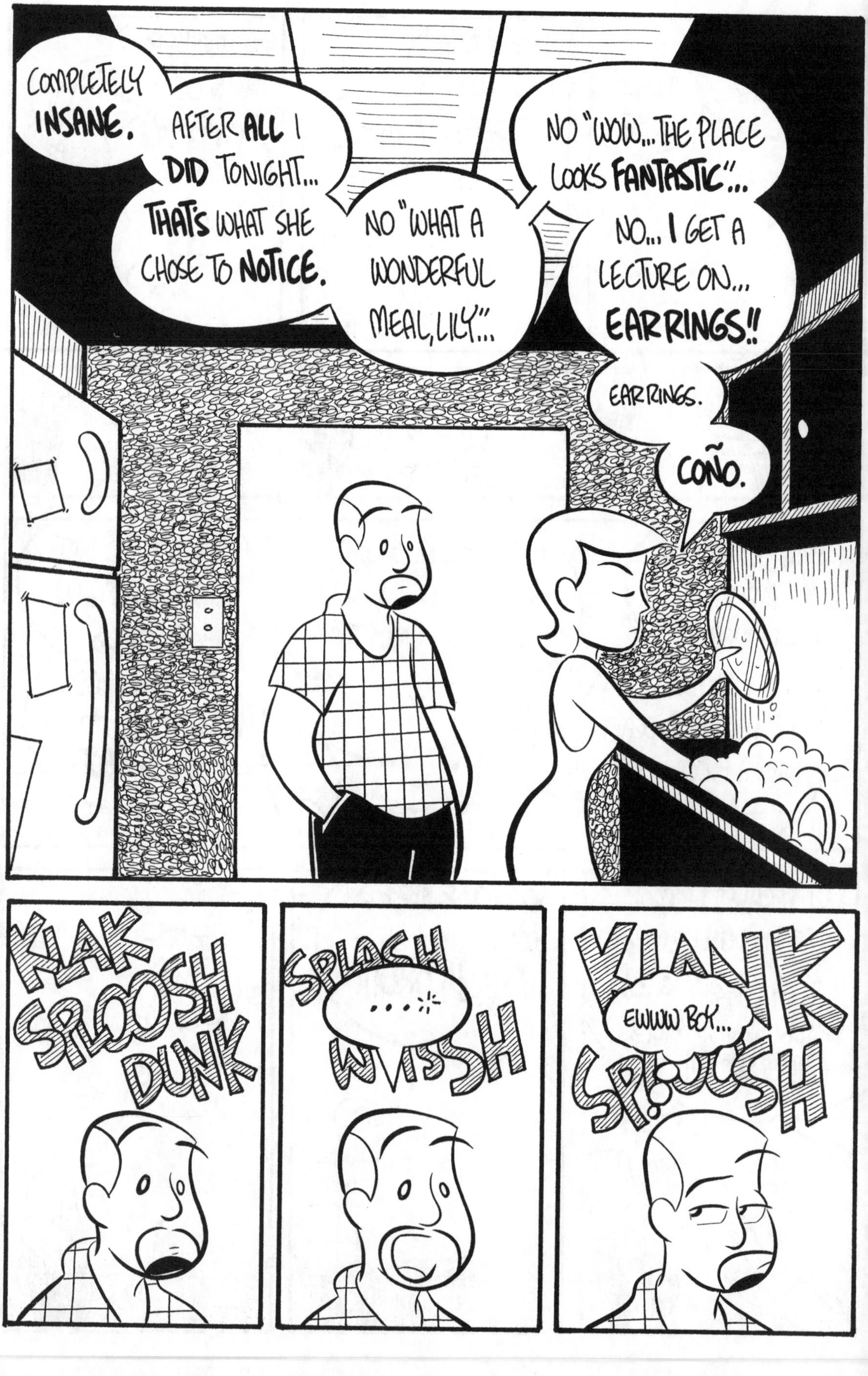
COMPLETELY INSANE.
AFTER ALL I DID TONIGHT... THAT'S WHAT SHE CHOSE TO NOTICE.
NO "WHAT A WONDERFUL MEAL, LILY"...
NO "WOW... THE PLACE LOOKS FANTASTIC"...
NO... I GET A LECTURE ON... EARRINGS!!
EARRINGS.
COÑO.
KLAK
SPLOOSH
DUNK
SPLOSH
...
WHISSH
EWWW BOY...
KLANK
SPLOOSH

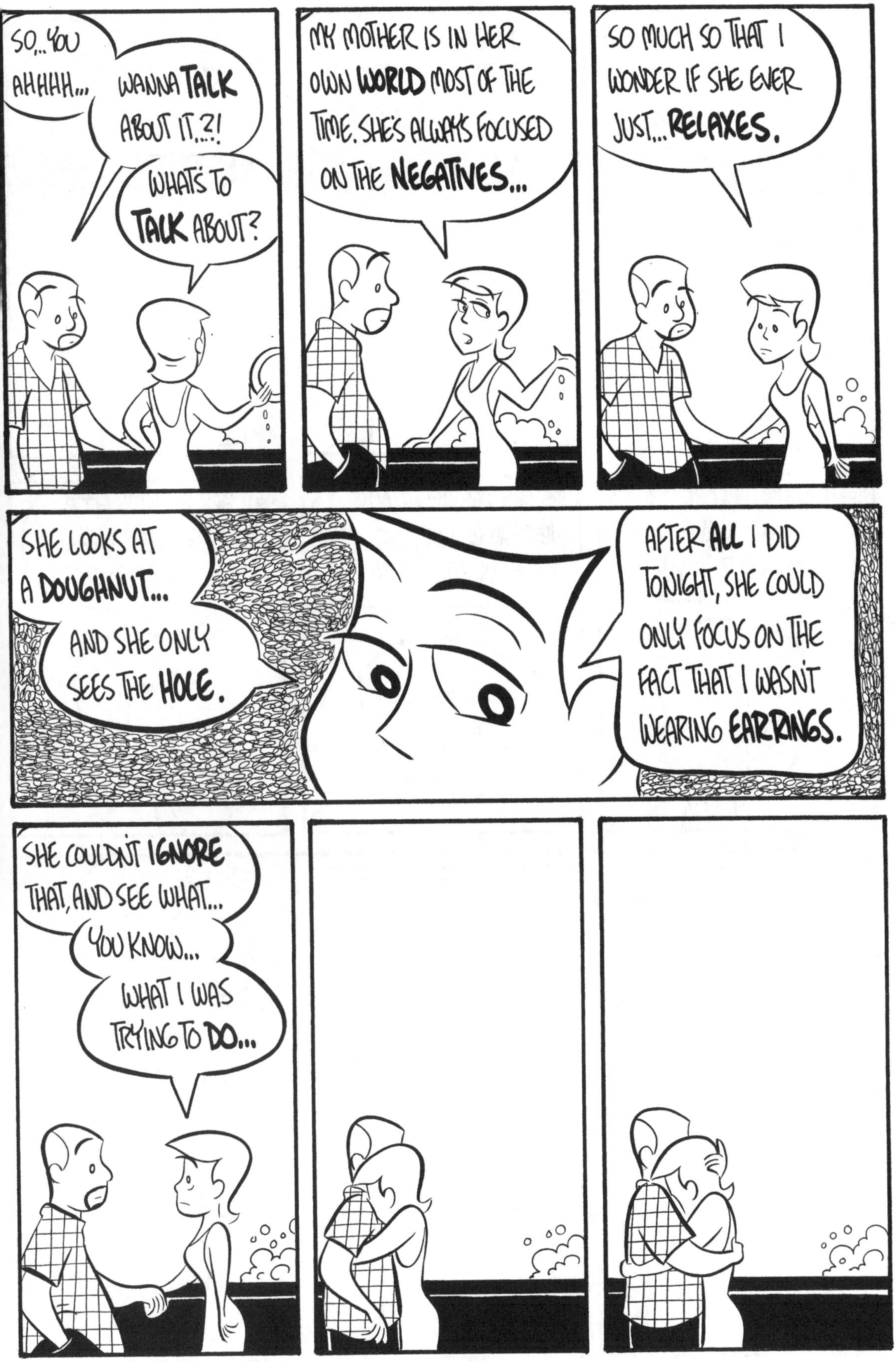
SO... YOU AHHHH...
WANNA TALK ABOUT IT...?!
WHAT'S TO TALK ABOUT?
MY MOTHER IS IN HER OWN WORLD MOST OF THE TIME. SHE'S ALWAYS FOCUSED ON THE NEGATIVES...
SO MUCH SO THAT I WONDER IF SHE EVER JUST... RELAXES.
SHE LOOKS AT A DOUGHNUT...
AND SHE ONLY SEES THE HOLE.
AFTER ALL I DID TONIGHT, SHE COULD ONLY FOCUS ON THE FACT THAT I WASN'T WEARING EARRINGS.
SHE COULDN'T IGNORE THAT, AND SEE WHAT...
YOU KNOW...
WHAT I WAS TRYING TO DO...

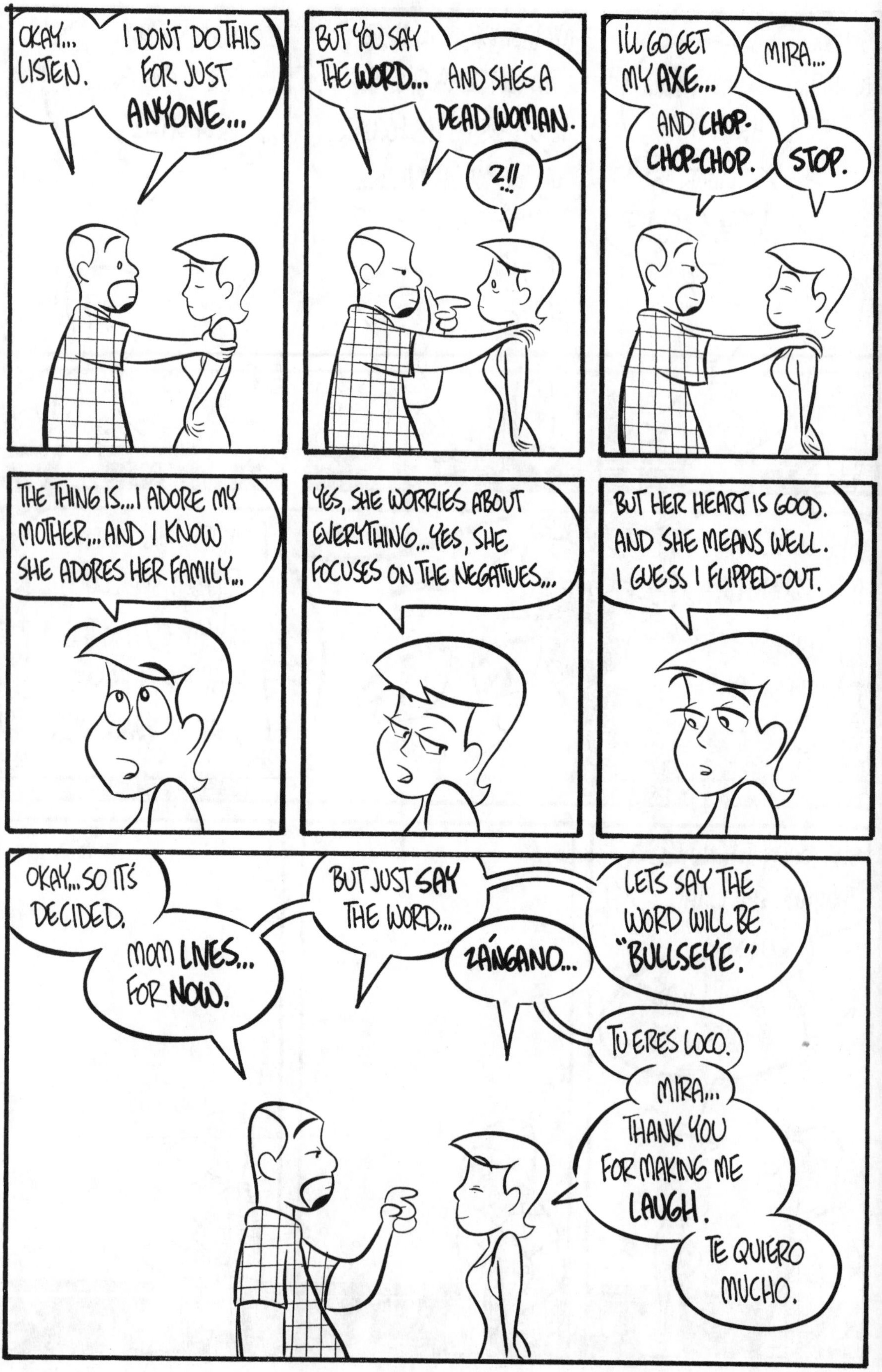
OKAY... LISTEN.
I DON'T DO THIS FOR JUST ANYONE...
BUT YOU SAY THE WORD...
AND SHE'S A DEAD WOMAN.
?!!
I'LL GO GET MY AXE...
AND CHOP-CHOP-CHOP.
MIRA...
STOP.
THE THING IS...I ADORE MY MOTHER...AND I KNOW SHE ADORES HER FAMILY...
YES, SHE WORRIES ABOUT EVERYTHING...YES, SHE FOCUSES ON THE NEGATIVES...
BUT HER HEART IS GOOD. AND SHE MEANS WELL. I GUESS I FLIPPED-OUT.
OKAY...SO IT'S DECIDED.
MOM LIVES... FOR NOW.
BUT JUST SAY THE WORD...
LET'S SAY THE WORD WILL BE "BULLSEYE."
ZÁNGANO...
TU ERES LOCO.
MIRA...
THANK YOU FOR MAKING ME LAUGH.
TE QUIERO MUCHO.

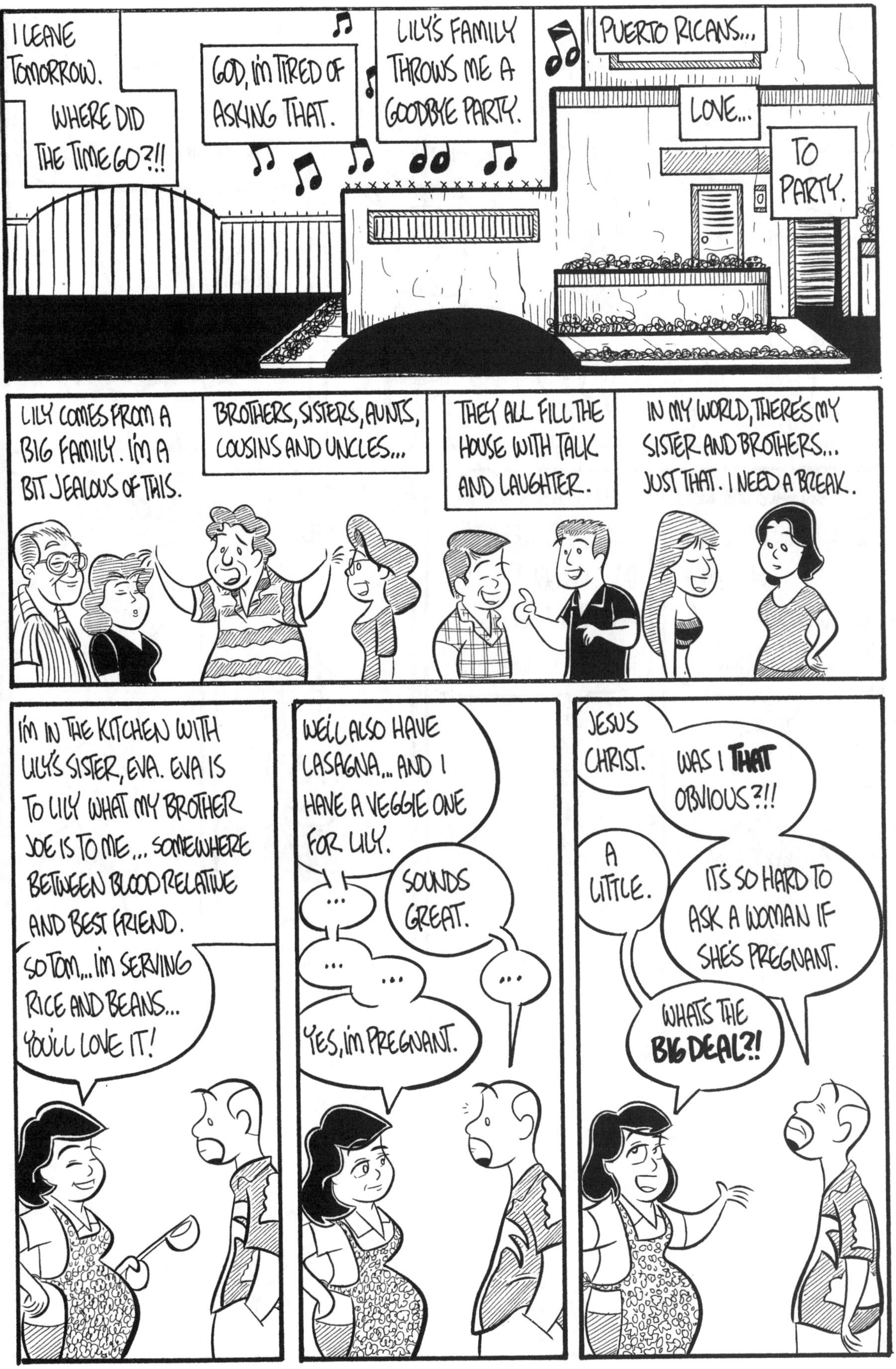
I LEAVE TOMORROW.
WHERE DID THE TIME GO?!!
GOD, I'M TIRED OF ASKING THAT.
LILY'S FAMILY THROWS ME A GOODBYE PARTY.
PUERTO RICANS...
LOVE...
TO PARTY.
LILY COMES FROM A BIG FAMILY. I'M A BIT JEALOUS OF THIS.
BROTHERS, SISTERS, AUNTS, COUSINS AND UNCLES...
THEY ALL FILL THE HOUSE WITH TALK AND LAUGHTER.
IN MY WORLD, THERE'S MY SISTER AND BROTHERS... JUST THAT. I NEED A BREAK.
I'M IN THE KITCHEN WITH LILY'S SISTER, EVA. EVA IS TO LILY WHAT MY BROTHER JOE IS TO ME... SOMEWHERE BETWEEN BLOOD RELATIVE AND BEST FRIEND.
SO TOM... I'M SERVING RICE AND BEANS... YOU'LL LOVE IT!
WE'LL ALSO HAVE LASAGNA... AND I HAVE A VEGGIE ONE FOR LILY.
SOUNDS GREAT.
...
...
...
...
YES, I'M PREGNANT.
JESUS CHRIST.
WAS I **THAT** OBVIOUS?!!
A LITTLE.
IT'S SO HARD TO ASK A WOMAN IF SHE'S PREGNANT.
WHAT'S THE **BIG DEAL?!**

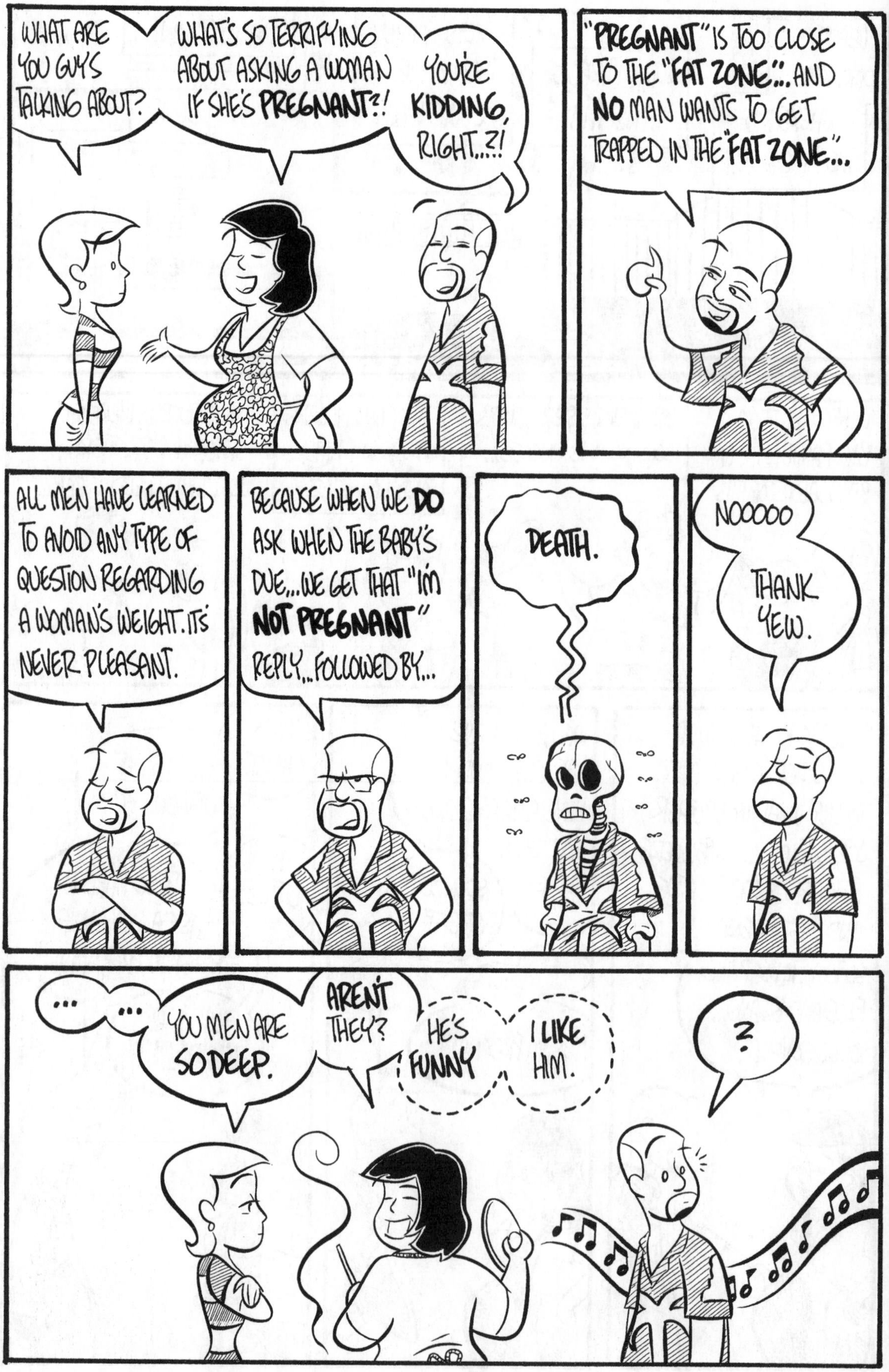

WHAT ARE YOU GUY'S TALKING ABOUT?
WHAT'S SO TERRIFYING ABOUT ASKING A WOMAN IF SHE'S PREGNANT?!
YOU'RE KIDDING, RIGHT...?!
"PREGNANT" IS TOO CLOSE TO THE "FAT ZONE"... AND NO MAN WANTS TO GET TRAPPED IN THE "FAT ZONE"...
ALL MEN HAVE LEARNED TO AVOID ANY TYPE OF QUESTION REGARDING A WOMAN'S WEIGHT. IT'S NEVER PLEASANT.
BECAUSE WHEN WE DO ASK WHEN THE BABY'S DUE,... WE GET THAT "I'M NOT PREGNANT" REPLY,... FOLLOWED BY...
DEATH.
NOOOOO
THANK YEW.
...
...
YOU MEN ARE SO DEEP.
AREN'T THEY?
HE'S FUNNY
I LIKE HIM.
?

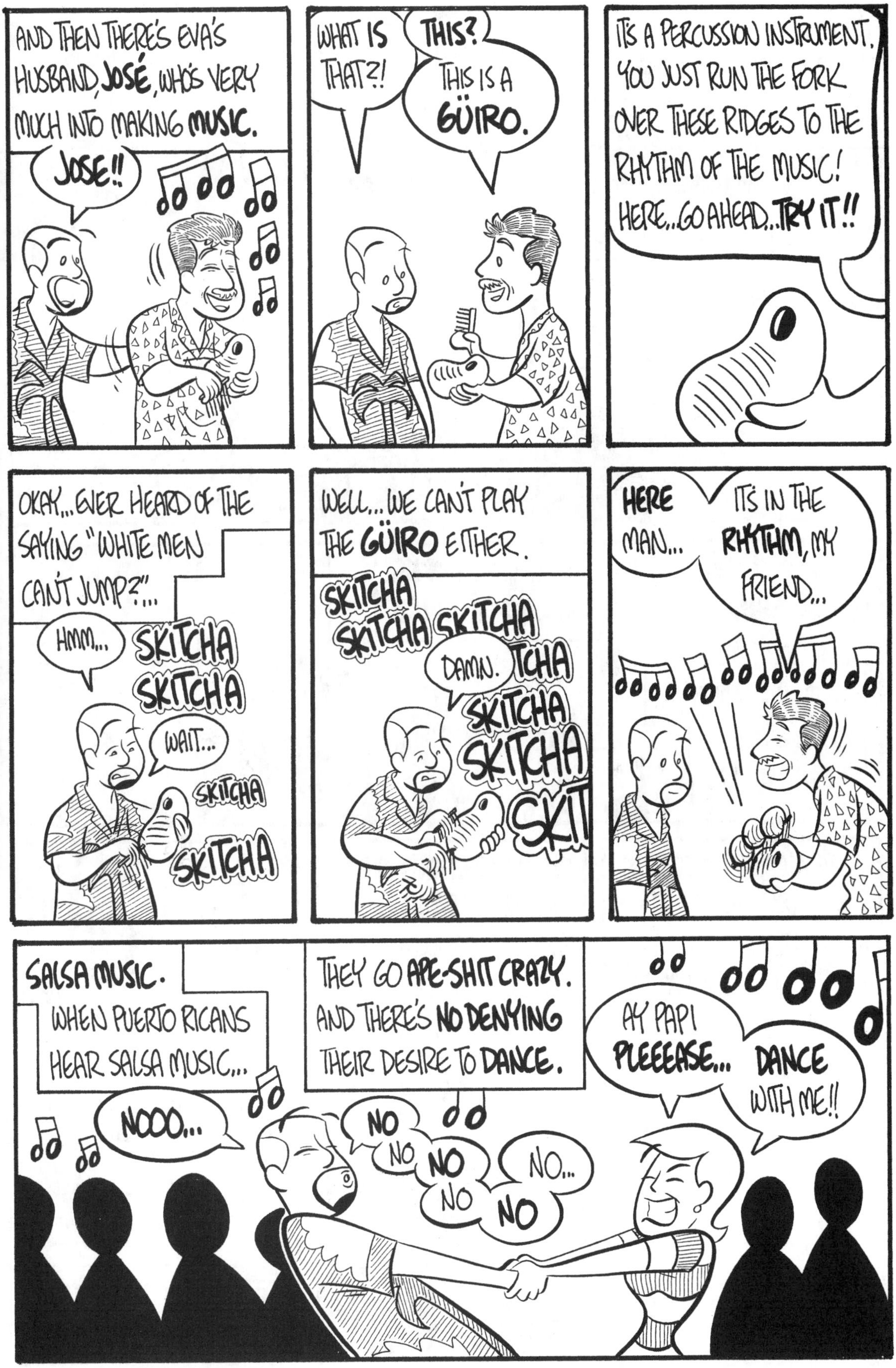
AND THEN THERE'S EVA'S HUSBAND, JOSÉ, WHO'S VERY MUCH INTO MAKING MUSIC.
JOSE!!
WHAT IS THAT?!
THIS?
THIS IS A GÜIRO.
IT'S A PERCUSSION INSTRUMENT. YOU JUST RUN THE FORK OVER THESE RIDGES TO THE RHYTHM OF THE MUSIC! HERE...GO AHEAD...TRY IT!!
OKAY,...EVER HEARD OF THE SAYING "WHITE MEN CAN'T JUMP?"...
HMM...
SKITCHA
SKITCHA
WAIT...
SKITCHA
SKITCHA
WELL...WE CAN'T PLAY THE GÜIRO EITHER.
SKITCHA
SKITCHA SKITCHA
DAMN.
TCHA
SKITCHA
SKITCHA
SKIT
HERE MAN...
IT'S IN THE RHYTHM, MY FRIEND...
SALSA MUSIC.
WHEN PUERTO RICANS HEAR SALSA MUSIC...
THEY GO APE-SHIT CRAZY. AND THERE'S NO DENYING THEIR DESIRE TO DANCE.
NOOO...
NO
NO
NO
NO
NO
NO...
AY PAPI PLEEEASE...
DANCE WITH ME!!

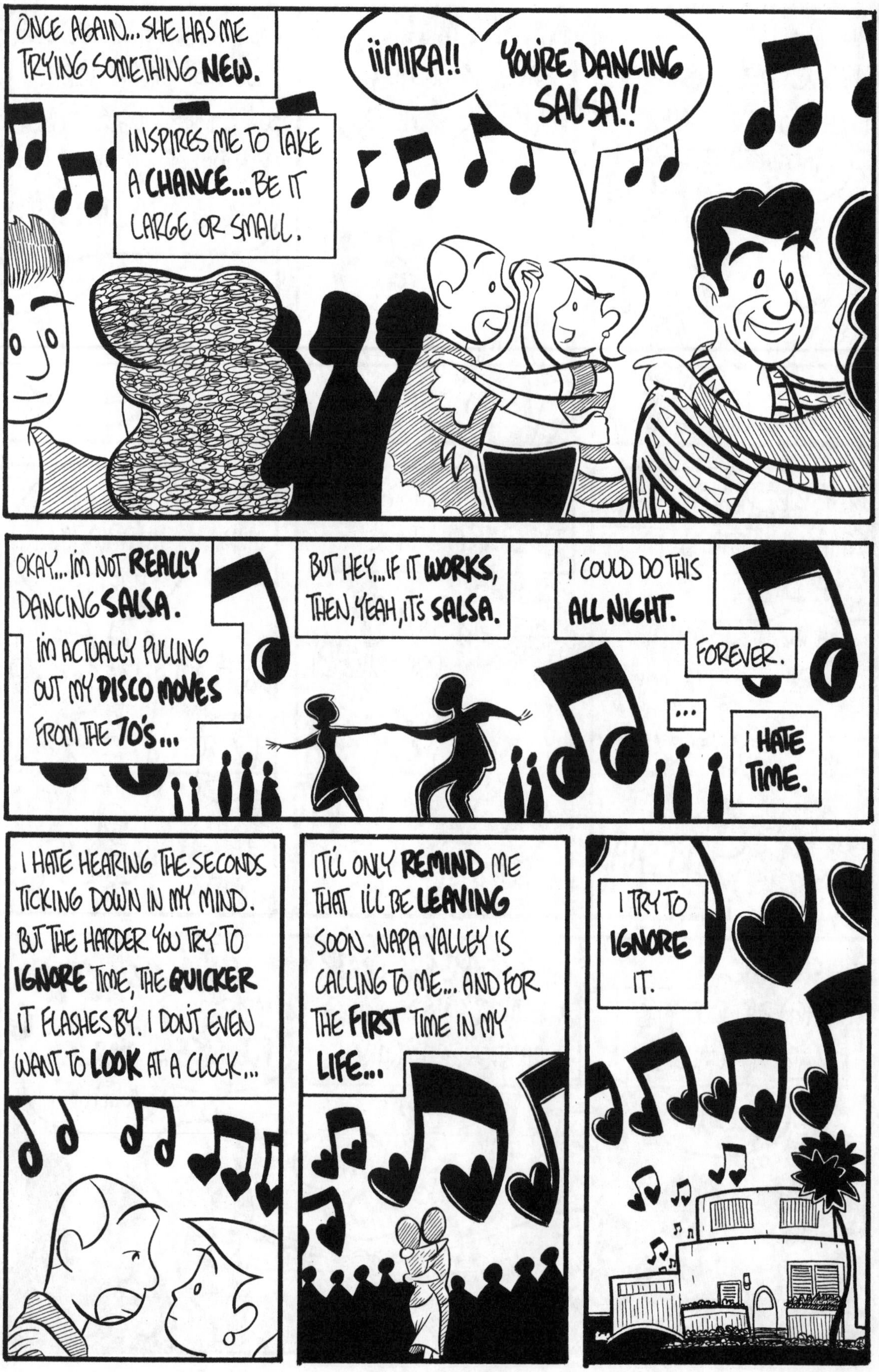
ONCE AGAIN... SHE HAS ME TRYING SOMETHING NEW.
INSPIRES ME TO TAKE A CHANCE... BE IT LARGE OR SMALL.
¡¡MIRA!!
YOU'RE DANCING SALSA!!
OKAY... I'M NOT REALLY DANCING SALSA.
I'M ACTUALLY PULLING OUT MY DISCO MOVES FROM THE 70'S...
BUT HEY... IF IT WORKS, THEN, YEAH, IT'S SALSA.
I COULD DO THIS ALL NIGHT.
FOREVER.
...
I HATE TIME.
I HATE HEARING THE SECONDS TICKING DOWN IN MY MIND. BUT THE HARDER YOU TRY TO IGNORE TIME, THE QUICKER IT FLASHES BY. I DON'T EVEN WANT TO LOOK AT A CLOCK...
IT'LL ONLY REMIND ME THAT I'LL BE LEAVING SOON. NAPA VALLEY IS CALLING TO ME... AND FOR THE FIRST TIME IN MY LIFE...
I TRY TO IGNORE IT.

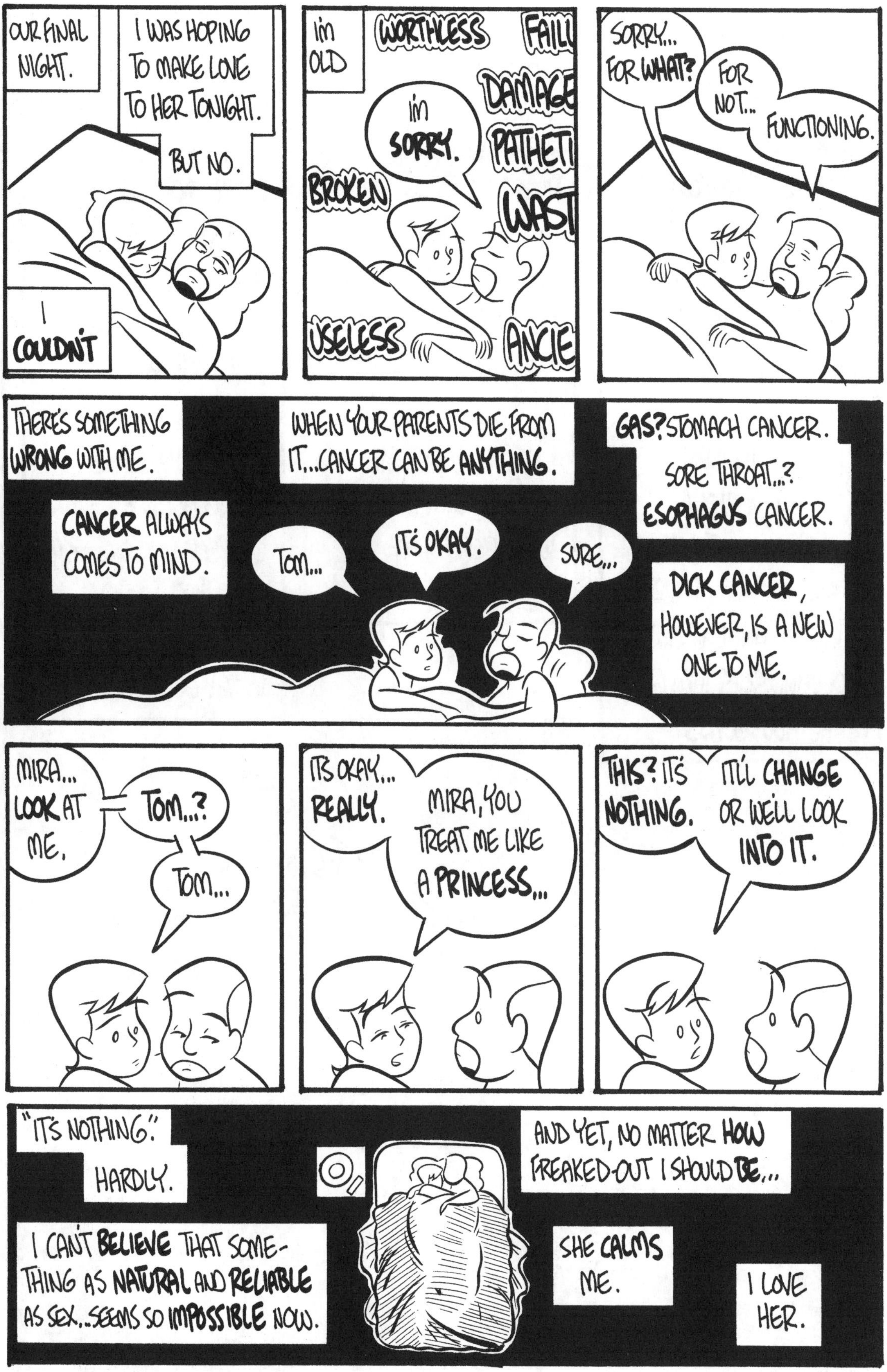

OUR FINAL NIGHT.
I WAS HOPING TO MAKE LOVE TO HER TONIGHT.
BUT NO.
I COULDN'T
I'M OLD
WORTHLESS
FAILU
DAMAGE
PATHETI
I'M SORRY.
BROKEN
WAST
USELESS
ANCIE
SORRY... FOR WHAT?
FOR NOT... FUNCTIONING.
THERE'S SOMETHING WRONG WITH ME.
WHEN YOUR PARENTS DIE FROM IT... CANCER CAN BE ANYTHING.
GAS? STOMACH CANCER.
SORE THROAT...? ESOPHAGUS CANCER.
CANCER ALWAYS COMES TO MIND.
TOM...
IT'S OKAY.
SURE...
DICK CANCER, HOWEVER, IS A NEW ONE TO ME.
MIRA... LOOK AT ME.
TOM...?
TOM...
IT'S OKAY... REALLY.
MIRA, YOU TREAT ME LIKE A PRINCESS...
THIS? IT'S NOTHING.
IT'LL CHANGE OR WE'LL LOOK INTO IT.
"IT'S NOTHING."
HARDLY.
AND YET, NO MATTER HOW FREAKED-OUT I SHOULD BE...
I CAN'T BELIEVE THAT SOMETHING AS NATURAL AND RELIABLE AS SEX... SEEMS SO IMPOSSIBLE NOW.
SHE CALMS ME.
I LOVE HER.

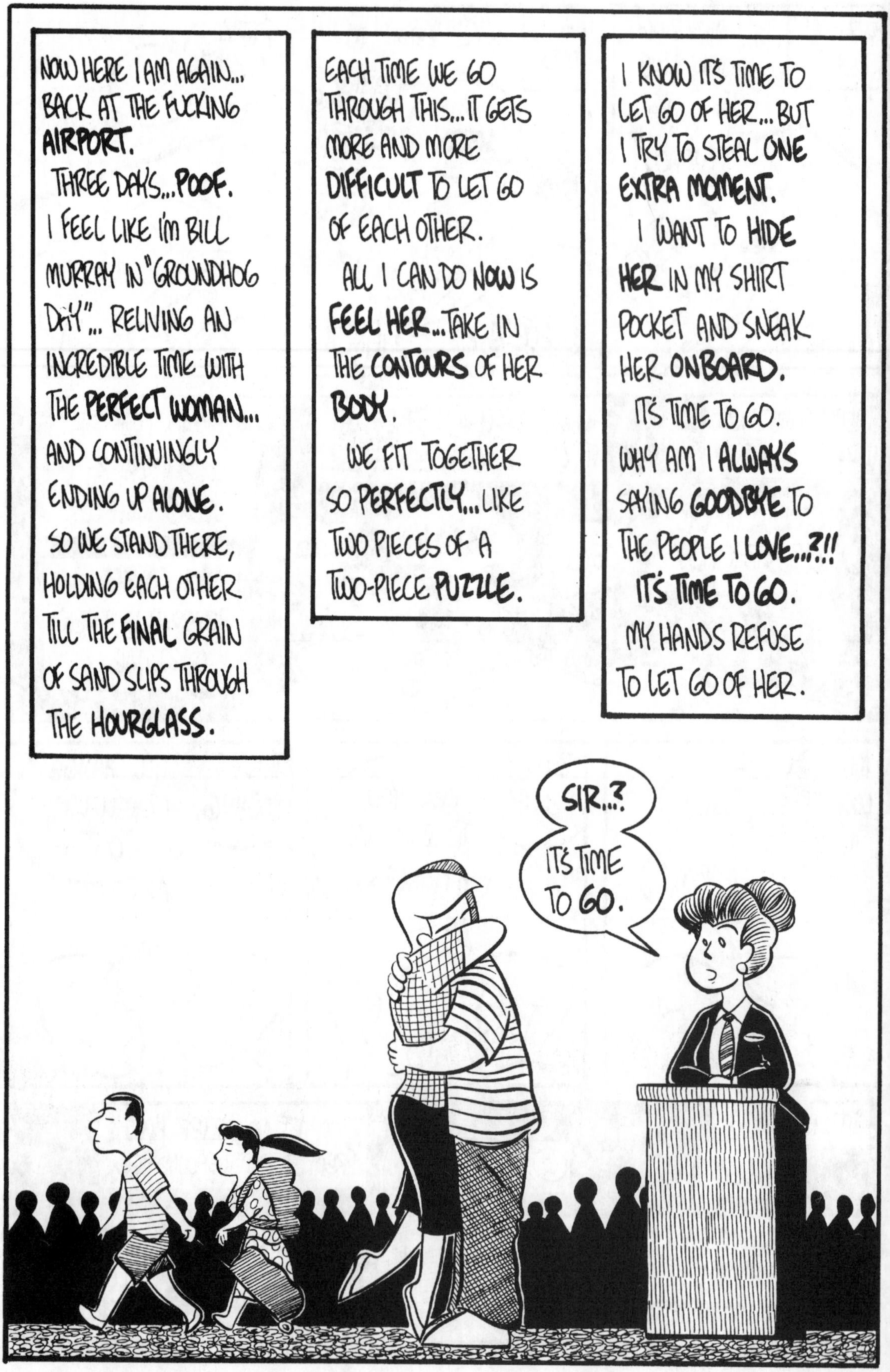
NOW HERE I AM AGAIN... BACK AT THE FUCKING AIRPORT.
THREE DAYS...POOF.
I FEEL LIKE I'M BILL MURRAY IN "GROUNDHOG DAY"... RELIVING AN INCREDIBLE TIME WITH THE PERFECT WOMAN... AND CONTINUINGLY ENDING UP ALONE.
SO WE STAND THERE, HOLDING EACH OTHER TILL THE FINAL GRAIN OF SAND SLIPS THROUGH THE HOURGLASS.
EACH TIME WE GO THROUGH THIS... IT GETS MORE AND MORE DIFFICULT TO LET GO OF EACH OTHER.
ALL I CAN DO NOW IS FEEL HER...TAKE IN THE CONTOURS OF HER BODY.
WE FIT TOGETHER SO PERFECTLY...LIKE TWO PIECES OF A TWO-PIECE PUZZLE.
I KNOW IT'S TIME TO LET GO OF HER... BUT I TRY TO STEAL ONE EXTRA MOMENT.
I WANT TO HIDE HER IN MY SHIRT POCKET AND SNEAK HER ONBOARD.
IT'S TIME TO GO.
WHY AM I ALWAYS SAYING GOODBYE TO THE PEOPLE I LOVE...?!!
IT'S TIME TO GO.
MY HANDS REFUSE TO LET GO OF HER.
SIR...?
IT'S TIME TO GO.

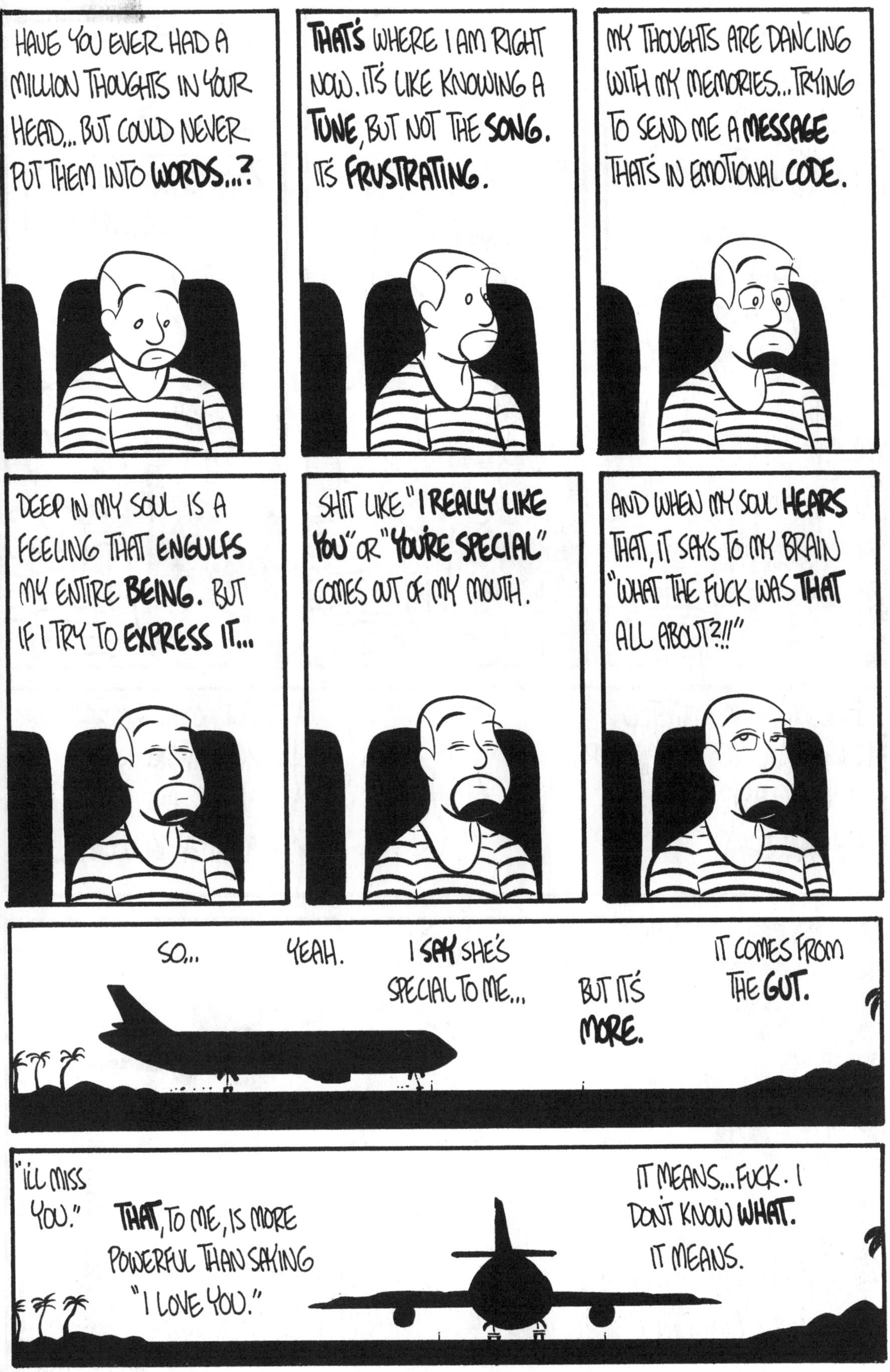
HAVE YOU EVER HAD A MILLION THOUGHTS IN YOUR HEAD... BUT COULD NEVER PUT THEM INTO WORDS...?
THAT'S WHERE I AM RIGHT NOW. IT'S LIKE KNOWING A TUNE, BUT NOT THE SONG. IT'S FRUSTRATING.
MY THOUGHTS ARE DANCING WITH MY MEMORIES... TRYING TO SEND ME A MESSAGE THAT'S IN EMOTIONAL CODE.
DEEP IN MY SOUL IS A FEELING THAT ENGULFS MY ENTIRE BEING. BUT IF I TRY TO EXPRESS IT...
SHIT LIKE "I REALLY LIKE YOU" OR "YOU'RE SPECIAL" COMES OUT OF MY MOUTH.
AND WHEN MY SOUL HEARS THAT, IT SAYS TO MY BRAIN "WHAT THE FUCK WAS THAT ALL ABOUT?!!"
SO...
YEAH.
I SAY SHE'S SPECIAL TO ME...
BUT IT'S MORE.
IT COMES FROM THE GUT.
"I'LL MISS YOU."
THAT, TO ME, IS MORE POWERFUL THAN SAYING "I LOVE YOU."
IT MEANS... FUCK. I DON'T KNOW WHAT. IT MEANS.

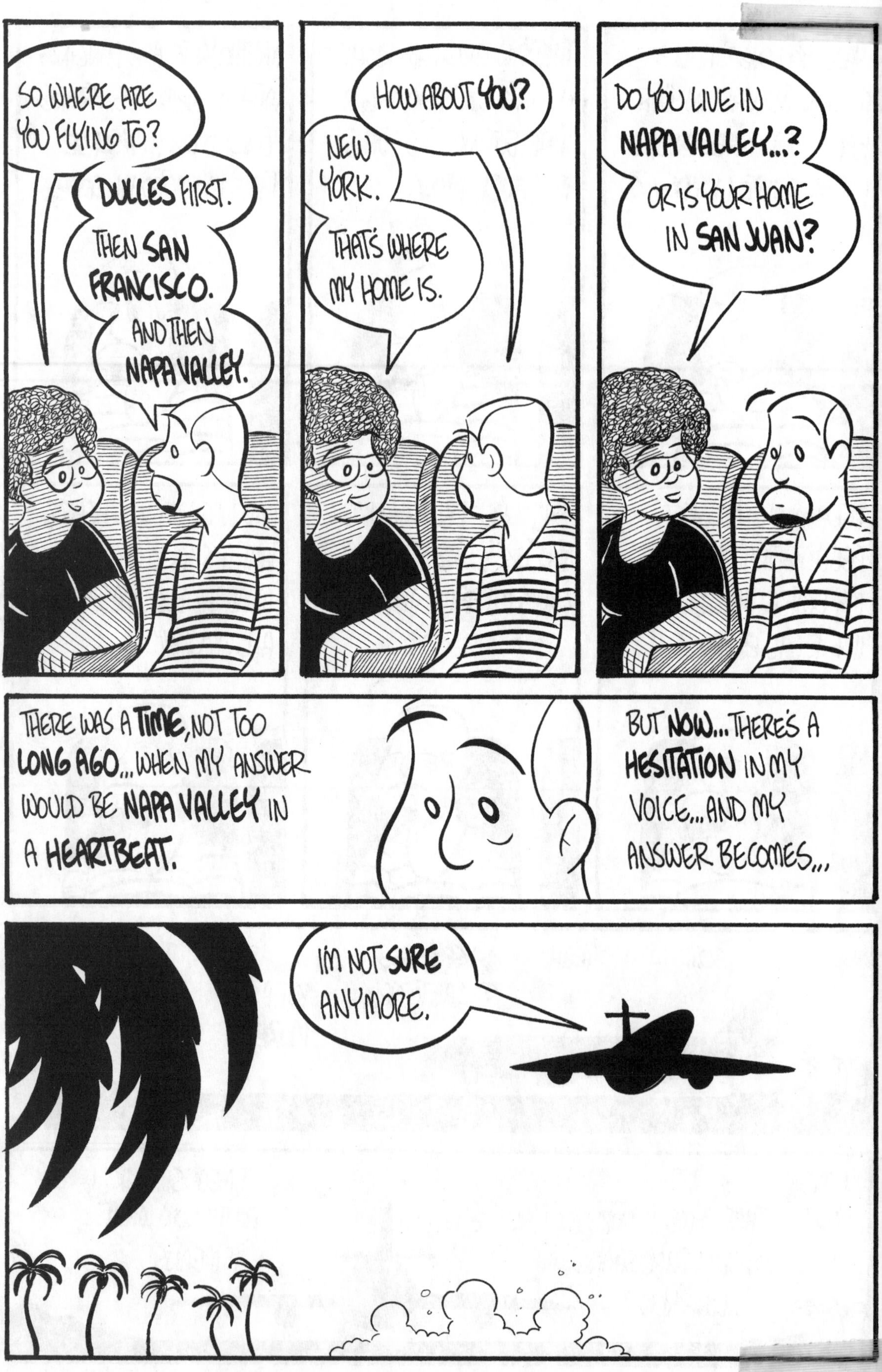

SO WHERE ARE YOU FLYING TO?
DULLES FIRST.
THEN SAN FRANCISCO.
AND THEN NAPA VALLEY.
HOW ABOUT YOU?
NEW YORK.
THAT'S WHERE MY HOME IS.
DO YOU LIVE IN NAPA VALLEY...?
OR IS YOUR HOME IN SAN JUAN?
THERE WAS A TIME, NOT TOO LONG AGO... WHEN MY ANSWER WOULD BE NAPA VALLEY IN A HEARTBEAT.
BUT NOW... THERE'S A HESITATION IN MY VOICE... AND MY ANSWER BECOMES...
I'M NOT SURE ANYMORE.